ADVANCED CLINICAL SKILLS AND PHYSICAL DIAGNOSIS

Second Edition

ADVANCED CLINICAL SKILLS AND PHYSICAL DIAGNOSIS

Second Edition

DALE BERG, MD

Director of Education, Jefferson Clinical Skills Center
Course Director, Advanced Physical Diagnosis,
Jefferson Medical College and Harvard Medical School
Associate Professor of Medicine
Jefferson Medical College
Philadelphia, Pennsylvania

Blackwell
Publishing

MT

© 2004 by Dale Berg, MD

Blackwell Publishing, Inc., 350 Main Street, Malden, Massachusetts 02148-5018, USA
Blackwell Publishing Ltd, 9600 Garsington Road, Oxford OX4 2DQ, UK
Blackwell Publishing Asia Pty Ltd, 550 Swanston Street, Carlton, Victoria 3053, Australia

04 05 06 07 5 4 3 2 1

ISBN: 1-4051-0433-3

Library of Congress Cataloging-in-Publication Data

Berg, Dale.
    Advanced clinical skills and physical diagnosis / Dale Berg.— 2nd ed.
        p. ; cm.
    Includes bibliographical references and index.
    ISBN 1-4051-0433-3 (pbk.)
    1. Diagnosis—Handbooks, manuals, etc.   2. Physical diagnosis—Handbooks, manuals, etc.
    [DNLM: 1. Diagnosis, Differential—Handbooks.   2. Diagnosis, Differential—Problems and Exercises.   3. Physical Examination—methods—Handbooks.   4. Physical Examination—methods—Problems and Exercises.   5. Clinical Competence—Handbooks.   6. Clinical Competence—Problems and Exercises. WB 39 B493a 2004]   I. Title.
    RC71.B475 2004
    616.07′5—dc22

                                                        2004000128

A catalogue record for this title is available from the British Library

Acquisitions: Beverly Copland
Development: Selene Steneck
Production: Jennifer Kowalewski
Cover and Interior design: Mary McKeon
Typesetter: SNP Best-set Typesetter Ltd., Hong Kong
Printed and bound by Sheridan Books in Ann Arbor, MI

For further information on Blackwell Publishing, visit our website:
www.blackwellpublishing.com

Notice: The indications and dosages of all drugs in this book have been recommended in the medical literature and conform to the practices of the general community. The medications described do not necessarily have specific approval by the Food and Drug Administration for use in the diseases and dosages for which they are recommended. The package insert for each drug should be consulted for use and dosage as approved by the FDA. Because standards for usage change, it is advisable to keep abreast of revised recommendations, particularly those concerning new drugs.

2/17/05

To Stephanie, Sara, Brian, Michael, and Christopher

Brief Contents

Contents

"Learn to see, learn to hear, learn to feel, learn to smell, and know that by practice alone you can become expert. Medicine is learned by the bedside and not in the classroom."

Sir William Osler

The accurate and deft use of physical diagnostic skills is integral to the provision of quality, efficient, and cost-effective health care. Physical examination techniques and outcomes, when performed and interpreted with scientific rigor and integrated with the patient's history, produce the fundamental data on which the evaluative and management schemes are based.

Over the past several years, curricula have been introduced, including one (Advanced Physical Diagnosis) by our group, with the objectives of reinforcing basic physical diagnostic skills and training nascent and evolving caregivers in more advanced skills of physical diagnosis. Although there are many solid textbooks on physical diagnosis, few, if any, complement and support the development of such curricula or assist a student of medicine in expanding his or her diagnostic acumen in this field, so central to being a physician. This work is a response to that need.

This book has been designed to be problem-based and outcome-oriented. Each chapter has been organized into three sections: **Basic Examination**, **Advanced Examination**, and **Diagnosis**.

In the design of the first two sections, basic and advanced techniques are described in basic medical language. The first section of each chapter describes specific procedures and techniques useful in the **basic** examination of the anatomic site covered in the chapter. All clinicians should know and be adept at these basic examinations. Each procedure is described in a succinct, step-by-step fashion and is followed by a specific set of outcomes. The outcomes are defined as a specific result detected by the examiner; that is, what is felt, heard, or seen by the examiner and then what these outcomes mean diagnostically. These outcomes may direct the examiner to perform other, more advanced procedures. The second section presents a set of **advanced** techniques organized in an "Approach to . . ." fashion. These techniques are the next steps after the basic examination is performed on the site. Based on what the examiner observes, as in the basic examination, these techniques are followed by different outcome scenarios that are then translated into specific diagnoses.

In the **diagnoses** section each diagnosis is explained in further detail. In each of these is a brief description of the mechanism of development or pathophysiology, symptoms and signs with previously discussed physical examination techniques, evaluation, treatment, and sometimes referral. The manifestations are correlated and cross-referenced with the examination sections of the chapter. This allows the clinician to rapidly "read up" on the tentative diagnosis divined by using the basic and advanced diagnostic techniques.

An example of this is medial knee pain in Chapter 12. The technique to define the site is explained in the Basic Examination (p. 248). The reader can then jump to the heading "Approach to patient with medial knee pain" in the Advanced Examination section (p. 253) to perform specific tests. If the outcome shows medial joint line tenderness posterior with a valgus stress test, an MCL sprain is the likely diagnosis. An explanation of MCL sprain is then provided in the Diagnosis section (p. 264).

The new edition is richly illustrated with updated photographs of classic findings and visual images of specific steps in a variety of procedures. There is also an emphasis on the musculoskeletal examination—specifically for sports-related injuries—and the new techniques available to the clinician.

This book is a tool to further challenge work in this field, to further define physical diagnosis in scientific and historical terms, to re-emphasize these fundamental skills in curricula, and to challenge students of medicine of all ages to become masters of these skills.

Dale Berg

CONTRIBUTORS

Katherine Worzala, MD, MPH
Director, Jefferson Clinical Skills Center
Assistant Professor of Medicine
Jefferson Medical College
Philadelphia, Pennsylvania

Robert Pachner, MD
Clinical Assistant Professor
Department Family Medicine
University of Wisconsin Medical School
Milwaukee, Wisconsin

CHAPTER 1
Vital Signs

Measure temperature: auricular or oral probe

PROCEDURE: Measure the temperature with the auricular or oral/sublingual probe.

OUTCOME: If the temperature is 98.2 to 98.8°F: ◆ **normal**
If 99.0 to 100.5°F: ◆ **low-grade fever**
If >100.5°F: ◆ **fever**
If <98.0°F:
◆ **hypothermia**
◆ **cerumen impaction**

Measure temperature: rectal probe

PROCEDURE: Measure the temperature using the rectal probe.

OUTCOME: If the temperature is 99.2 to 99.8°F: ◆ **normal**
If 100.0 to 101.5°F: ◆ **low-grade fever**
If >101.5°F: ◆ **fever**
If <99.0°F: ◆ **hypothermia**

Measure blood pressure: sphygmomanometer

PROCEDURE: With the patient sitting or supine, place the sphygmomanometer around the arm, 1 cm proximal to the antecubital fossa. Palpate the radial artery, and inflate the cuff to a pressure above which the pulse is absent. Place the diaphragm of the stethoscope over the antecubital fossa and auscult while slowly deflating the cuff at a rate of 2 mm Hg/sec; listen for and note the level of pressure that marks the appearance and disappearance of staccato sounds (Korotkoff sounds).

Caveat: For large arms use a large blood pressure cuff.
For small arms use a small blood pressure cuff.

OUTCOME: The onset of sounds is the systolic blood pressure. The disappearance of sounds is the diastolic blood pressure.
If <120/80: ◆ **normal**
If 120–129/81–85: ◆ **prehypertension**
If 130/86: ◆ **early hypertension**
If 140/90: ◆ **hypertension**

Measure pulse rate and rhythm

PROCEDURE: Using the tips of digits 2 and 3, palpate the pulse in the radial, carotid, or femoral sites, noting the rate in beats/min (bpm) and the rhythm.

OUTCOME: If the rate is 60 to 99 bpm: ◆ **normal**
If >100 bpm: ◆ **tachycardia**
If <60 bpm: ◆ **bradycardia**
If the rhythm is irregularly irregular: ◆ **atrial fibrillation**
If the rhythm has a regular pattern: ◆ **normal**

Inspect respiratory pattern

PROCEDURE: With the patient breathing at baseline, count the breaths and inspect the respiratory pattern for a period of at least 30 seconds (Fig 1-1).

OUTCOME: If 10 to 14 bpm: ◆**normal**
If >16 bpm: ◆ **hyperpnea**
If regular pattern: ◆ **normal**
If there are deep, rapid respirations (Kussmaul's sign; see Fig 1-1B): ◆ **severe metabolic acidosis**
If irregular periods of apnea, alternating with periods of 4 to 5 breaths of identical depth (Biot's sign; see Fig 1-1C):
◆ **elevated intracranial pressure**

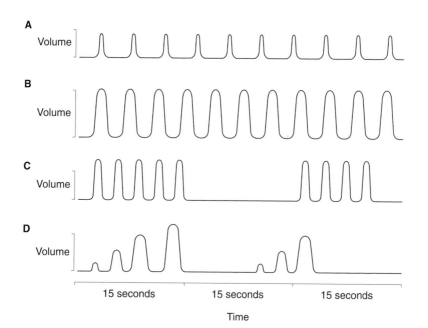

Figure 1-1 Breathing patterns. A. Normal. B. Kussmaul's. C. Biot's. D. Cheyne-Stokes.

If there is a cyclic breathing pattern of apnea followed by breaths of progressively increasing respiratory rate and depth (Cheyne-Stokes sign; see Fig 1-1D):
- ◆ **severe cerebral hypoxemia**
- ◆ **severe forward heart failure (see Chapter 4, p. 92).**

Measure weight

PROCEDURE: Weigh patient; compare with prior weight preferably.

OUTCOME: If weight has increased in setting of edema: ◆ **volume overload**
If weight has decreased in setting of dizziness on arising and tachycardia: ◆ **volume depletion**
If >10% over ideal body weight for height: ◆ **obese**
If >20% over ideal body weight for height: ◆ **morbidly obese**

Advanced Examination

APPROACH TO A PATIENT WITH A FEVER

Study fever curve

PROCEDURE: Take and record the patient's temperature every 6 to 8 hours. Study the data for any patterns.

OUTCOME: If the patient is febrile, with a variation of <1°:
◆ **continuous fever**
If febrile, with a variation of >2° over the course of each 24 hour period: ◆ **remittent fever**
If the patient has afebrile periods admixed with fever spikes:
◆ **intermittent fever**
If intermittent, such that there are several days of multiple fever spikes admixed with multiple days of being afebrile:
◆ **Pel-Ebstein fever**

APPROACH TO A PATIENT WITH ELEVATED BLOOD PRESSURE

Perform Osler's maneuver

PROCEDURE: With the patient supine:
1. Measure the patient's blood pressure using the standard technique (see p. 1).
2. Reinflate the sphygmomanometer to a level slightly above the systolic blood pressure (SBP) while palpating the radial pulse and artery.

OUTCOME: If the pulse and artery are no longer palpable at a level at or above the SBP: ◆ **normal**
If pulse is no longer palpable but the artery remains palpable (Osler's positive):
◆ **pseudohypertension of severe peripheral arteriosclerosis**

Measure blood pressure in both arms

PROCEDURE: Measure the blood pressure in the right upper extremity, left upper extremity, and left lower extremity. Note any differences.

OUTCOME: If the difference between SBPs is <10 mm Hg: ◆ **normal**
If the right arm SBP is >20 mm Hg higher than the left arm:
◆ **consider coarctation of the aorta (see Chapter 4, p. 92)**

Calculate pulse pressure

PROCEDURE: Measure the SBP and the diastolic blood pressure. Calculate the difference to get the pulse pressure.

OUTCOME: If the pulse pressure is 25% to 50% of the SBP: ◆ **normal**

If >50% of the SBP:
- ◆ aortic insufficiency (see Chapter 4, p. 90):
- ◆ high output states (e.g., hyperthyroidism)

If <25% of the SBP:
- ◆ pericardial effusion with tamponade (see Chapter 4, p. 95)
- ◆ constrictive pericarditis (see Chapter 4, p. 92)

Keys to Recording Findings

VITAL SIGNS

"VSS"

Blood pressure (BP)*

   Left arm ____mmHg

                  supine   standing

                  ○— ____mmHg   ____mmHg

                  ○— ____BPM   ____BPM

   Right arm ____mmHg

                  supine   standing

                  ○— ____mmHg   ____mmHg

                  ○— ____BPM   ____BPM

Heart rate (HR) ____BPM

Rhythm   Regular ❑

              Irregular Regular ❑

              Irregular Irregular ❑

Respiratory rate (RR) ____ BPM

Temperature ____°F

                ____°C

Weight   ____kg

           ____lbs

           Weight from past ____ Date ____

Pulse oximeter ____%

*Note:

Orthostatic parameters if volume depletion is
potentially present

Atrial fibrillation

The abnormal, random, noneffective twitching of atria due to atrial enlargement, ischemia, or hyperthyroidism. Symptoms include lightheadedness, palpitations, dyspnea, and chest pain; signs include irregularly irregular rhythm and a heart rate between 40 and 200 bpm; S_3 is the only possible gallop. Evaluation and treatment include an electrocardiogram, an echocardiogram, obtaining a thyroid-stimulating hormone, and referral to a cardiologist for ventricular rate control, cardioversion, and anticoagulation.

Bradycardia

Heart rate <60 bpm. The etiology may be physiologic in highly trained athletes; other etiologies include beta-blocker use, use of digoxin, sick sinus syndrome, or ischemic heart disease.

Continuous fever: See Fever.

Fever

Elevated body temperature. Low-grade fever is due to viral infections, whereas higher fevers may be due to bacterial or other etiologies. The three overall pattern types are **continuous**, which has little variation; **remittent**, which has variation but never returns to being afebrile, for example, the quotidian fever of *Plasmodium virax*; and **intermittent**, in which there are afebrile periods, for example, the tertian or quartan patterns of the *Plasmodium* species.

Hypertension

The abnormal elevation of systolic and/or diastolic blood pressure due to primary (idiopathic) or secondary (renal arterial stenosis, Cushing's syndrome, pheochromocytoma, coarctation of the aorta) etiologies. The condition is asymptomatic early in course. Later in course, signs and symptoms are related to target organ damage and underlying etiology as follows: retinal damage—flame hemorrhages, hard exudates, papilledema; heart failure—crackles, gallop, S_4 or S_3, laterally displaced point of maximal impulse; accelerated atherosclerotic disease—bruits; and aortic aneurysm—pulsatile abdominal mass. Concurrent signs of underlying etiology are **renal arterial stenosis**—abdominal bruit; Cushing's syndrome—moon facies, striae, and obesity; and coarctation—disparity between right and left BP. In elderly patients with isolated SBP elevation, Osler's maneuver should be performed to rule out a falsely elevated SBP (**pseudohypertension**). Evaluation and treatment include looking for baseline target organ damage, modifying concurrent risk factors for accelerated atherosclerosis, and administering agents to lower BP to normal.

Pel-Ebstein fever

A fever pattern due to a malignant lymphoproliferative disorder (e.g., Hodgkin's disease). Symptoms and signs include night sweats, unintentional weight loss, and nontender rubbery lymph node enlargement in one or more lymph node groups; advanced signs include splenomegaly, hepatomegaly, and pallor to mucous membranes and nail beds from associated anemia. Evaluation and treatment include referral to an oncologist for bone marrow and/or lymph node biopsy and for treatment.

Pseudohypertension: See Hypertension.

Severe metabolic acidosis

Due to any intrinsic anion-producing pathologic process, the most common being diabetic ketoacidosis (DKA). Symptoms and signs include decreased level of consciousness (even to coma), ketone odor on breath, and Kussmaul's pattern (see Fig 1-1B) of respirations. Evaluation should proceed with arterial blood gas and basic chemistry; if the anion gap is indeed increased, the obtaining of serum ketone, lactate, ethylene glycol, methanol, and salicylic acid levels is important. Treatment is with admission, fluid repletion, and management of the underlying disorder (e.g., insulin for DKA).

Tachycardia

Heart rate >100 bpm. The etiology may be physiologic and occur during exercise; other etiologies include volume depletion, hyperthyroidism, fever, anemia, and anxiety. Treatment is directed toward the underlying etiology.

CHAPTER 2

Head, Ears, Nose, and Throat (HENT)

Inspect auricles

PROCEDURE: Visually inspect and palpate each auricle.

OUTCOME: If there is a nontender papule on the superior edge of the helix:
◆ **Darwin's tubercle (normal variant)**
If there are one or more mildly tender firm papules on the edges of the helix and antihelix: ◆ **tophi of gout**
If the entire auricle is diffusely tender, swollen, and erythematous: ◆ **otitis externa maligna (Plate 1)**
If painless thickening and loss of all auricular structures:
◆ **cauliflower ear of old severe trauma**

Direct otoscopic examination: external ear canal

PROCEDURE: Grasp the superior aspect of the auricle and gently pull it posteriorly and superiorly. Gently insert the otoscope into the canal (Fig 2-1). Visually inspect the external ear canal itself; repeat in the contralateral ear.

OUTCOME: If the canal is diffusely edematous and erythematous:
◆ **otitis externa**
If there are firm nodules contiguous with bone covered with normal skin: ◆ **exostosis**
If waxy, brownish material is present in the canal:
◆ **cerumen impaction**

Direct otoscopic examination: tympanic membrane

PROCEDURE: Grasp the superior aspect of the auricle and gently pull it posteriorly and superiorly. Gently insert the otoscope into the canal (see Fig 2-1) and visually inspect the tympanic membrane (TM). Repeat in the contralateral ear.
If the TM is pale, gray, and translucent: ◆ **normal (Plate 2)**
If the umbo (tip of malleus) and the manubrium (handle of the malleus) are clearly demonstrated as evaginations through the TM: ◆ **normal (Plate 2)**
If there is a reflective, triangular "cone of light" with the apex at the umbo and the base pointing anterior and inferior:
◆ **normal (Plate 2)**

9

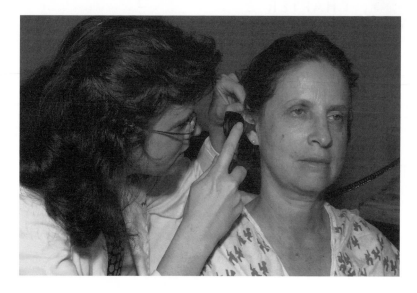

Figure 2-1 Otoscopy procedure. The otoscope is gently inserted into the auditory canal while the examiner gently pulls upward and slightly backward on the auricle.

If diffuse circumferential erythema on the TM:
 ◆ **otitis media (OM) (Plate 4)**
If the TM is retracted and yellow, with the malleus prominent and white, bubbles are present behind and there is a loss of the cone of light: ◆ **serous OM (Plate 3)**
If a diffusely red TM, with concurrent dilation of the peripheral vessels on the TM: ◆ **purulent OM (early)**
If a loss of the markings of the manubrium, umbo, and cone of light, with bulging: ◆ **purulent OM (Plate 4)**
If there are one or more vesicles filled with clear or bloody fluid, with adjacent petechiae at each vesicle base:
 ◆ **bullous myringitis**
If there is a plastic or metallic orifice in the inferior aspect of the TM, usually immediately inferior to the tip of the umbo:
 ◆ **tympanoplasty tube**
If there is a hole on the periphery (pars tensa) of the TM, often draining pus or blood: ◆ **perforated TM**
If yellow-white keratin-like papular lesion in an area adjacent to a posterosuperior TM perforation: ◆ **cholesteatoma**
If there is blood behind the TM (hemotympanum):
 ◆ **basilar skull fracture**

Palpate and inspect external nose

PROCEDURE: Visually inspect and palpate the bony and cartilage structures of the external nose.

OUTCOME: If the skin of the nose is thickened, indurated, nontender, and erythematous, with telangiectasiae: ◆ **rhinophyma**

If ecchymosis around both eyes and across the upper bridge of the nose (raccoon eyes; Fig 2-2): ◆ **basilar skull fracture**

If nasal bone step-off, with ecchymosis at the bridge of the nose:
◆ **nasal fracture**

Visually inspect oropharynx

PROCEDURE: Instruct the patient to open mouth as wide as possible and make the sound, "Ahhhhh." With a light source, visually inspect the oral, gingival, and pharyngeal mucosa.

OUTCOME: If there are multiple white patches/plaques on the mucosa, each with an erythematous base (Fig 2-3): ◆ **thrush (candidiasis)**

If there is a collection of white macules with red centers on the lateral oral mucosa opposite the premolars, that is, adjacent to Stensen's duct (Koplik's spots):
◆ **rubeola (see Chapter 14, p. 332)**

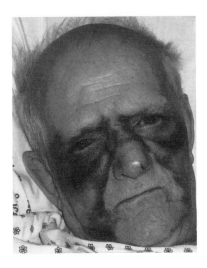

Figure 2-2 Raccoon eyes. Marked periorbital ecchymosis and antecedent facial trauma correlated with a basilar skull fracture.

Figure 2-3 Thrush. Chunky, white collections of material on mucous membranes and the surface of the tongue; quite characteristic of *Candida* infection.

If there is a symmetric distribution of lacy, reticulated, white lesions (Wickstram's sign):
> ◆ **lichen planus (see Chapter 14, p. 327)**

If there are multiple pigmented macules:
> ◆ **Peutz-Jeghers syndrome**

If one or more firm nodules are contiguous with bone on the lingual surface of the mandible: ◆ **torus mandibularis**

If there are multiple erosions and ulcerations:
> ◆ **autoimmune disorders (e.g., pemphigus, systemic lupus erythematosus)**
> ◆ **aphthous ulcers**
> ◆ **gingivostomatitis** (e.g., herpangia)

If there are multiple painful vesicles on the mucosa:
> ◆ **gingivostomatitis**

If there is a painless white or erythematous indurated ulcer on the mucosa: ◆ **squamous cell carcinoma**

Palpate and inspect gingiva

PROCEDURE: Using a light source and dental mirror, visually inspect and, using a gloved finger, palpate the patient's gums

OUTCOME: If there are red, swollen gingivae adjacent to the tooth margins (Fig 2-4), with swollen interdental papillae: ◆ **gingivitis vulgaris**
If the gingiva has receded, giving the appearance of longer teeth (see Fig 2-4): ◆ **gingivitis vulgaris with periodontitis**
If there is diffuse symmetric thickening to cover tooth crowns:
> ◆ **gingival enlargement**

If there is a pigmented macule adjacent to teeth with silver amalgam inlay(s): ◆ **amalgam tattoo**
If an orifice of a tract in the gingiva at the base of a carious tooth:
> ◆ **sinus tract from a periapical abscess**

Visually inspect teeth

PROCEDURE: Instruct the patient to open mouth. Visually inspect each tooth.

OUTCOME: If there is a large destroyed area in a tooth: ◆ **caries**
If black-yellow discoloration of the root is present adjacent to receded gingiva (Fig 2-4): ◆ **root caries**
If one or more teeth are diffusely worn down and shorter, with a rim of white enamel surrounding the central yellowish core (Fig 2-5): ◆ **attrition**
If there is notching of one or more of the teeth on the biting surface: ◆ **abrasions**
If there are multiple sites of rough yellow discoloration on the biting surfaces: ◆ **erosions**
If there is diffuse brown staining to the teeth: ◆ **nicotine stains**
If whitish material on the teeth is present adjacent to the gingiva:
> ◆ **tartar (calculus)**

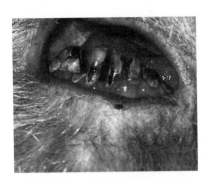

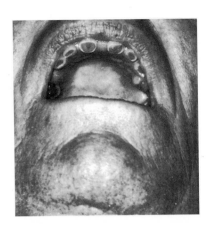

Figure 2-4 Severe gingivitis with root caries. Patient with halitosis, gingival recession, loosening and loss of teeth, purulent material at the interface between the teeth and the gingiva, and marked caries of the roots.

Figure 2-5 Tooth attrition. Diffuse advanced attrition of the teeth in this 78-year-old man.

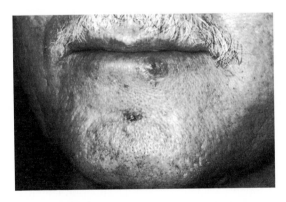

Figure 2-6 Herpes labialis. Painful cluster of vesicles that involves the lip and the skin outside the vermilion border.

Palpate and visually inspect lips

PROCEDURE: Visually inspect and, using gloved hands, palpate the lips of the patient.

OUTCOME: If there is a painless, indurated, ulcerating papule or plaque on the lip mucosa (usually lower lip):
♦ **squamous cell carcinoma**
If tender cluster of vesicles with small ulcers (Fig 2-6):
♦ **herpes labialis**

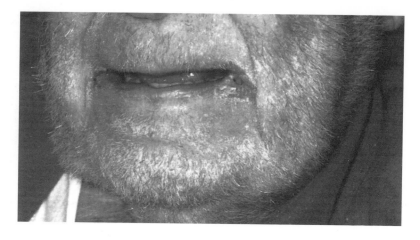

Figure 2-7 Angular chelosis (perlèche). Fissures and erythema on the angles of the mouth, most often due to an edentulous state or ill-fitting dentures. *Candida* usually is present in the sites.

If there are painful fissures perpendicular to the vermilion border of the lip (usually lower lip): ◆ **cheilitis**

If there is painful cracking, reddening, and crusting of the corners of the mouth (Fig 2-7): ◆ **angular cheilosis (perlèche)**

If itchy, diffuse, nonpitting swelling of the deep structure of the lips (Fig 2-8): ◆ **angioedema (see Chapter 14, p. 322)**

If there are multiple pigmented macules on the lips and oral mucosa: ◆ **Peutz-Jeghers syndrome**

Palpate and visually inspect tongue

PROCEDURE: Instruct the patient to open the mouth and maximally protrude the tongue. Visually inspect the superior, lateral, and sublingual areas of the mucosa and papillae of the tongue. With a gloved hand, palpate the surfaces of the tongue.

OUTCOME: If the tongue appears diffusely enlarged and thick, with multiple bite marks on the sides: ◆ **macroglossia**

If there are white patches/plaques with red bases on the tongue (see Fig 2-3): ◆ **thrush**

If multiple white, warty, painless plaques, each with hair-like projections from the surface: ◆ **hairy leukoplakia**

If smooth, red, shiny surface and a loss of all papillae except circumvallate (Fig 2-9): ◆ **atrophic glossitis**

If there are smooth, red, glossy patches, each with a white rim (Fig 2-10): ◆ **geographic tongue**

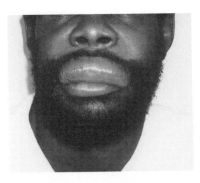

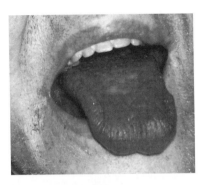

Figure 2-8 Angioedema. The upper lip here is markedly swollen and pruritic; concern of upper airway obstruction with stridor must be high in such a patient.

Figure 2-9 Atrophic glossitis. Loss of all filiform and fungiform papillae on the tongue surface with a resultant smooth, glossy appearance. Often due to deficiency of B_{12} or folate.

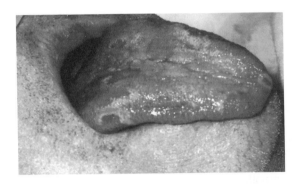

Figure 2-10 Geographic tongue. Benign, idiopathic, self-limited process in which there are red patches of denuded papilla, each with a rim of white; the process migrates over time.

If there are multiple pigmented macules on the tongue:
  ◆ **Peutz-Jeghers syndrome**
If multiple red-purple macules are present on the mucosa (Plate 5):
  ◆ **Rendu-Osler-Weber syndrome (see Chapter 14, p. 331)**
If purple papular soft venous structures are present on the ventral surface of the anterior two-thirds of the tongue (Fig 2-11):
  ◆ **sublingual varices**

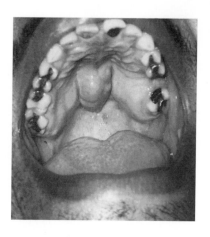

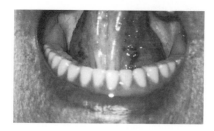

Figure 2-11 Sublingual varicosities. These may be normal but can be associated with chronic elevation of central venous pressures and thus correlated with an elevated jugular venous pressure.

Figure 2-12 Torus palatinus. Benign, nontender bony structure, covered with normal oral mucosa.

If there is an indurated, painless ulcer, especially on the lateral or ventral aspect: ◆ **squamous cell carcinoma**

If there are 8 to 10 papules on the posterior dorsum, arranged in a semicircle: ◆ **circumvallate papillae (normal)**

Palpate and visually inspect soft and hard palates

PROCEDURE: Instruct the patient to open the mouth. Visually inspect the hard and soft palate. With a gloved hand, palpate any lesions.

OUTCOME: If white patches/plaques are present: ◆ **thrush**

If there is an indurated, painless exophytic ulcer:

◆ **squamous cell carcinoma**

If there are multiple superficial, painful erosions of various sizes and shapes: ◆ **aphthous stomatitis**

If there is a nontender, smooth, firm nodule in the midline, covered with normal mucosa (Fig 2-12): ◆ **torus palatinus**

Palpate and visually inspect posterior pharynx

PROCEDURE: Instruct the patient to open the mouth, actively protrude the tongue, and make the sound "Ahhhh." With a light source, directly inspect the structures of the oropharynx.

OUTCOME: If diffuse swelling and lengthening of the uvula: ◆ **pharyngitis**

If diffuse erythema on the posterior pharynx:

◆ **pharyngitis, nonexudative**

If diffuse erythema with exudate covering the posterior pharynx (Fig 2-13): ◆ **pharyngitis, exudative**

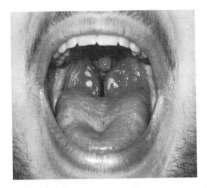

Figure 2-13 Exudative pharyngitis. Note the significant tonsillar swelling and moderate exudates that are present in the posterior pharynx. The patient had pharyngeal culture-positive beta-hemolytic *Streptococcus* infection.

If there is a red, fluctuant nodule adjacent to the tonsil: ◆ **quinsy**
If there is an indurated, painless, ulcerating plaque present:
    ◆ **squamous cell carcinoma**
If multiple ulcers, erosions, and vesicles are present:
    ◆ **herpangina of Coxsackie A gingivostomatitis**

Advanced Examination

APPROACH TO A PATIENT WITH BUMPS ON, OR PAINFUL, AURICLES

Inspect auricles: See under Basic Examination.

APPROACH TO A PATIENT WITH EXTERNAL CANAL PROBLEMS

Direct otoscopic examination: external ear canal: See under Basic Examination.

APPROACH TO A PATIENT WITH EARACHE AND/OR TYMPANIC MEMBRANE FINDINGS

Direct otoscopic examination: tympanic membrane: As in Basic Examination.

Palpate and inspect external nose: As in Basic Examination.

Palpate and visually inspect posterior pharynx: As in Basic Examination.

Palpate postauricular space
PROCEDURE: Directly palpate the crescent-shaped depression approximately 1 cm posterior to the external auditory canal on the affected side; repeat on the contralateral side for control.
OUTCOME: If there is no tenderness over the site: ◆ **no mastoiditis**
If tenderness over the site: ◆ **mastoiditis**

Otoscopic examination while patient blows nose
PROCEDURE: Perform an otoscopic examination while instructing the patient to pinch and blow nose.
OUTCOME: If fluid/pus presents in the external canal: ◆ **perforated TM**
If no fluid presents in the external canal:
◆ **probably no TM perforation**

APPROACH TO A PATIENT WITH A NOSE COMPLAINT

Palpate and inspect external nose: As in Basic Examination.

Inspect internal nasal structures and mucosa with speculum
PROCEDURE: With the patient sitting leaning forward, neck slightly extended with head in a "sniffing" position; if possible examiner gently presses on tip of nose; insert a nasal speculum into each naris. The light source must be either a headlight or a head

mirror. The patient should blow his or her nose before the visual inspection.

OUTCOME: If there is a serous discharge:
   ◆ **rhinitis, atopic**
   ◆ **rhinitis, viral**
   ◆ **basilar skull fracture**
If purulent discharge: ◆ **sinusitis**
If bloody discharge with swelling of the bridge: ◆ **nasal fracture**
If erythematous purple papule/nodule in the septum, visualized from either side: ◆ **septal hematoma**
If there is a hole in the septum: ◆ **septal perforation**
If the septum is laterally displaced: ◆ **deviated septum**
If one or more fleshy, pink, pedunculated lesions are present:
   ◆ **nasal polyps**

APPROACH TO A PATIENT WITH NECK LUMPS AND BUMPS

Inspect and palpate anterior neck masses
PROCEDURE: Palpate the anterior neck—the space between the sternocleido-mastoids—for masses or nodules; define location, size, mobility.

OUTCOME: If the cricoid cartilage cannot be palpated:
   ◆ **unable to assess thyroid; it is retrosternal**
If midline mass is nontender, smooth, diffuse, and adjacent to the cricoid cartilage (Fig 2-14): ◆ **diffuse goiter**
If midline mass is nontender, with multiple nodules within its substance adjacent to the cricoid cartilage: ◆ **multinodular goiter**
If tender edema in the midline submandibular area and anterior neck: ◆ **Ludwig's angina**
If an arc-shaped scar is in lower neck past thyroidectomy scar:
   ◆ **consistent with hypothyroidism**

Inspect and palpate lateral neck masses
PROCEDURE: Palpate the lateral neck (lateral to the sternocleidomastoid muscles) for masses or nodules; define location, size, and mobility.

OUTCOME: If there are unilateral or bilateral masses in the areas immediately anterior and inferior to the tragus and auricles (Fig 2-15):
   ◆ **parotid gland enlargement**
If one or more nodules or masses are present in the lateral neck:
   ◆ **lymph node enlargement**

Palpate enlarged lymph nodes
PROCEDURE: Palpate and describe the size, firmness, and location of any suspected lymph nodes.

OUTCOME: If there are bilaterally enlarged posterior cervical lymph nodes:
   ◆ **rubella (see also Chapter 14, p. 332)**

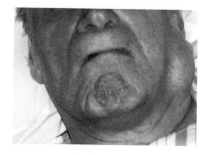

Figure 2-14 Goiter. This is a large goiter associated with severe long-standing iodide deficiency.

Figure 2-15 Parotid gland enlargement. Here the mass is unilateral, nontender, and quite firm. In this patient it was the result of a pleomorphic adenoma.

If there is an indurated, fixed, left supraclavicular node (Trossier's/Virchow's node):
> ◆ **metastatic visceral adenocarcinoma**

If the lymph nodes are rock hard and fixed to underlying tissue:
> ◆ **metastatic lymph node carcinoma**

If rubbery, matted, and nontender: ◆ **lymphoma**

If mobile, tender, and of new onset:
> ◆ **reactive lymphadenitis (infection)**

Palpate Virchow's node after Valsalva maneuver

PROCEDURE: Instruct the patient to rotate the head to the right actively and concurrently perform a Valsalva maneuver for 5 to 10 seconds. Palpate the left supraclavicular area during this procedure.

OUTCOME: If there is no mass or nodule palpable: ◆ **normal**
If a nodule is palpable:
> ◆ **enlarged Virchow's node, that is, Trossier's node**

APPROACH TO A PATIENT WITH SUSPECTED HYPERTHYROIDISM

Inspect and palpate anterior neck: See under Approach to a patient with neck lumps and bumps (see p. 19).

Visually inspect actively extended digits

PROCEDURE: Instruct the patient to extend both upper extremities actively so that the forearms are pronated and the digits are extended. Visually inspect the nail plates and the digits.

OUTCOME: If a fine tremor is present bilaterally (Marie's sign):
◆ **hyperthyroidism**
If onycholysis (separation of the distal nail plate from the nail bed—Plummer's sign): ◆ **hyperthyroidism**

Inspect eyelid location

PROCEDURE: With the patient in anatomic position and gazing anteriorly, visually inspect the anterior surface and adjacent structures of the patient's eyes.

OUTCOME: If the upper eyelid covers the upper limbus: ◆ **normal**
If the upper eyelid is superior to the limbus so that a crescent of white is demonstrable between the upper lid and limbus (Darymple's sign; Fig 2-16): ◆ **hyperthyroidism**

Inspect eyelid location during active, downward gaze

PROCEDURE: Instruct the patient to gaze downward, keeping the head steady. Visually inspect the activity of the upper eyelid.

OUTCOME: If the upper eyelids lag, and so a crescent of white develops between the upper eyelid and the limbus (von Graefe's sign):
◆ **hyperthyroidism**
If there is no such lag/movement: ◆ **normal**

Assess strength (power) of proximal muscle

PROCEDURE: Instruct the patient to lie in a supine position. Assess the patient's proximal muscle strength (see Chapter 7, p. 138).

OUTCOME: If there is proximal muscle weakness (1-4/5 power; Plummer's sign): ◆ **hyperthyroidism**
If strength is 5/5: ◆ **normal**

Auscult over apex

PROCEDURE: Instruct the patient to lie in a supine, left lateral decubital position. Auscult with the diaphragm over the apex.

Figure 2-16 Darymple's sign. Note the presence, at baseline, of sclera between the upper eyelid and the upper limbus; very indicative of hyperthyroidism.

OUTCOME: If a scratchy, midsystolic murmur is present (Mean-Lerman scratch): ◆ **hyperthyroidism**
If no such sound: ◆ **normal**

Auscult over closed eyes
PROCEDURE: Instruct the patient to close both eyes. Place the bell of the stethoscope over the upper eyelid of the closed eye and auscult; repeat in the contralateral eye.

OUTCOME: If there is a bruit over one or both eyes (Riesman's sign):
◆ **hyperthyroidism**
If no bruit: ◆ **normal**

Auscult over thyroid
PROCEDURE: Place the bell of the stethoscope over the goiter and auscult.

OUTCOME: If there is a bruit diffusely over the gland: ◆ **Graves' disease**
If no bruit: ◆ **normal**

Locate anterior eye relative to bony rim
PROCEDURE: Using direct light, visualize from the side of the anterior surface of the cornea relative to the supraorbital and infraorbital bony rims.

OUTCOME: If the corneal surface extends anterior to the level of the bony orbital rim:
◆ **exophthalmus of Graves' disease (see Goiter, p. 33)**
If corneal surface deep to or at the level of the bony orbital rim:
◆ **normal**

Visually inspect skin of anterior legs
PROCEDURE: Visually inspect and palpate the skin of the anterior aspects of the legs.

OUTCOME: If there are hyperpigmented and/or erythematous plaques:
◆ **pretibial myxedema**
If no plaques: ◆ **normal**

APPROACH TO A PATIENT WITH SUSPECTED HYPOTHYROIDISM

Inspect and palpate anterior neck: See under Approach to a patient with neck lumps and bumps (see p. 19).

Visually inspect eyebrows and hair
PROCEDURE: Visually inspect the eyebrows.

OUTCOME: If there is loss of the lateral eyebrows (Queen Anne's sign):
◆ **hypothyroidism**
If the eyebrows are full: ◆ **normal**
If there is patchy alopecia: ◆ **hypothyroidism**

Measure reflexes

PROCEDURE: Perform the Achilles and wrist extensor reflexes bilaterally. Visually inspect the duration of the contraction and relaxation phases.

OUTCOME: If there are equal relaxation and contraction phases: ◆ **normal**
If the relaxation phase is delayed and slow: ◆ **hypothyroidism**

Vital signs—specifically pulse

PROCEDURE: Measure pulse.

OUTCOME: If 60 to 99 bpm: ◆ **normal**
If <60 bpm: ◆ **consistent with hypothyroidism**

APPROACH TO A PATIENT WITH ORAL CAVITY BUMPS AND LESIONS

Visually inspect oropharynx: As in Basic Examination.

Note distribution of vesicles

PROCEDURE: Visually inspect the oral mucosa, the lips, the skin adjacent to the lips, and the skin of the palms and soles for vesicles.

OUTCOME: If the vesicles are limited to one side of the face, involving the skin or mucosa of one dermatome (V3, V2, or cranial nerve VII):
◆ **herpes zoster**
If vesicles are bilateral and involve the mucosa and the skin around the lips (i.e., crosses the vermilion border):
◆ **herpes simplex (primary)**
If there is a solitary cluster of vesicles on one lip, outside the vermilion border (see Fig 2-6):
◆ **herpes simplex (recurrent)**
If the vesicles are bilateral but limited to the mucosa and do not cross the vermilion border: ◆ **Coxsackie A**
If there are vesicles on one hand and one or both feet, along with oral vesicles: ◆ **hand-foot-and-mouth disease of Coxsackie A**

APPROACH TO A PATIENT WITH GINGIVAL LESIONS

Palpate and inspect gingiva: As in Basic Examination.

Inspect thickened gingiva

PROCEDURE: Visually inspect the surface of the thickened gingiva.

OUTCOME: If there is minimal bleeding: ◆ **phenytoin**
If diffuse bleeding: ◆ **gingivitis vulgaris**

Press gingiva with tongue depressor

PROCEDURE: Visually inspect and, with a sterile tongue depressor, press the gingiva adjacent to the tooth margins.

OUTCOME: If there is bleeding on palpation: ◆ **gingivitis vulgaris**
If purulent material is expressed from sulci:
◆ **severe purulent gingivitis**

APPROACH TO A PATIENT WITH TOOTH PROBLEMS

Palpate and inspect teeth: As in Basic Examination.

Percuss teeth

PROCEDURE: Using a dental instrument or tongue depressor, percuss the distal aspect of the affected tooth.

OUTCOME: If there is no tenderness: ◆ **normal**
If tenderness: ◆ **periapical abscess**

APPROACH TO A PATIENT WITH A SORE THROAT COMPLAINT

Visually inspect oropharynx: As in Basic Examination.

Visually inspect posterior pharynx: As in Basic Examination.

Palpate lymph nodes

PROCEDURE: Palpate nodes throughout node-bearing areas of the body; pay attention to cervical, axillary, and inguinal nodes.

OUTCOME: If there are tender jugulodigastric nodes:
◆ **streptococcus, beta-hemolytic**
If diffuse lymph node enlargement:
◆ **Infectious mononucleosis [Epstein-Barr virus (EBV), cytomegalovirus, human immunodeficiency virus (HIV)]**

APPROACH TO A PATIENT WITH A HEADACHE

Palpate and percuss over sinuses and face

PROCEDURE: Palpate and gently percuss over the bony structures and overlying skin of the face, starting with the asymptomatic side on the frontal area, the maxillary area, and finally the mandibular area; repeat on the symptomatic side.

OUTCOME: If there is tenderness to palpation/percussion over the maxillary sinus: ◆ **maxillary sinusitis**
If tenderness to palpation/percussion over the frontal sinus:
◆ **frontal sinusitis**
If severe tenderness in an ipsilateral, unilateral V2/V3 distribution when percussing over the lateral maxillary/mandibular face, especially at certain trigger points:
◆ **trigeminal neuralgia (tic douloureux)**
If tenderness overlying the maxillary or mandibular teeth:
◆ **dental caries**
If tenderness in the temporal artery:
◆ **temporal arteritis (see Chapter 3, p. 68)**

If tenderness over the temporomandibular joint:
- **temporomandibular joint dysfunction**

Transilluminate frontal sinuses
PROCEDURE: With the patient in a darkened room, place a small, bright light source in the medial aspect of the supraorbital notch on the affected side. Visually observe any transilluminability (i.e., pinkish hue) present in the frontal area. Repeat this on the contralateral side for comparison.

OUTCOME: If there is transilluminated light similar to the asymptomatic side: **normal**
If unilateral decreased transillumination:
- **ipsilateral frontal sinusitis**

Transilluminate maxillary sinuses: light source inferior orbital rim
PROCEDURE: With the patient gazing anteriorly with the mouth open, in a darkened room, place a small, bright light source over the midpoint of the inferior orbital rim. Visually observe any transilluminability (i.e., pinkish hue) in the hard palate. Repeat on the contralateral side for comparison.

OUTCOME: If there is no transilluminated light in either side:
- **bilateral maxillary sinusitis**
If unilateral decreased transillumination:
- **ipsilateral maxillary sinusitis**
If bilateral transillumination of equal intensity: **normal**

Auscult over temporomandibular joint
PROCEDURE: Place the bell of the stethoscope over the temporomandibular joint immediately anterior to the tragus and auscult as the patient opens and closes the mouth. Repeat on the contralateral side.

OUTCOME: If there are clicks/pops/crepitus:
- **temporomandibular joint dysfunction**
If no clicks: **normal**

Inspect oral mucosa and gingiva
PROCEDURE: Using a light source and a dental mirror, visually inspect patient's teeth and gums. Using a gloved hand, palpate the patient's teeth and gums.

OUTCOME: If there is an orifice in the gingiva at the base of a carious tooth:
- **periapical abscess**
If there is a large destroyed area in a tooth: **dental caries**

Inspect and percuss teeth: See under Approach to a patient with tooth problems.

Palpate occipital and neck muscles

PROCEDURE: Palpate the occipital areas of the head and the neck musculature.

OUTCOME: If there is tenderness in the occipital areas and/or trapezius muscles: ◆ **tension headache**
If no tenderness: ◆ **normal**

Assess visual acuity: As in Chapter 3, Basic Examination.

Direct otoscopic examination: tympanic membrane: As in Basic Examination.

Brudzinski's sign

PROCEDURE: With the patient supine, passively flex the neck. Observe the hips for any involuntary movement while the neck is flexed.

OUTCOME: If there is involuntary flexion at the hips (Brudzinski's sign):
◆ **acute meningitis**
If no involuntary flexion: ◆ **normal**

Kernig's sign

PROCEDURE: With the patient supine, passively flex the lower extremity at the hip. Once the hip is maximally flexed, passively extend the leg at the knee. Observe any involuntary activity at the neck.

OUTCOME: If there is involuntary flexion of the neck (Kernig's sign):
◆ **acute meningitis**
If no involuntary flexion: ◆ **normal**

APPROACH TO A PATIENT WITH RECENT HEAD TRAUMA

Inspect mastoid areas

PROCEDURE: Visual inspection of the mastoid areas.

OUTCOME: If there are unilateral or bilateral ecchymoses in the mastoid area (Battle's sign): ◆ **basilar skull fracture**
If no ecchymoses: ◆ **normal or <48 hours after trauma**

Visually inspect face

PROCEDURE: Visually inspect the face.

OUTCOME: If bilateral periorbital ecchymoses (raccoon eyes) are present (see Fig 2-2): ◆ **basilar skull fracture**
If no ecchymoses: ◆ **normal**

Palpate bones of face and skull

PROCEDURE: Palpate over the skull and facial bones.

OUTCOME: If there are any areas of skull depression:
◆ **depressed skull fracture**

If palpable, "step-offs" in the facial bones (e.g., the zygomatic arch, the orbital rim): ◆ **facial fractures**

Direct otoscopic examination: tympanic membrane
PROCEDURE: As in Basic Examination and Figure 2-1.

OUTCOME: If there is blood behind the tympanic membrane (hemotympanum): ◆ **basilar skull fracture**
If no blood present: ◆ **normal**

Test corneal reflex
PROCEDURE: Open the eye of the comatose patient and touch the cornea with a sterile cotton-tipped swab. Note the reaction of both eyes.

OUTCOME: If blink occurs bilaterally:
◆ **midbrain-level coma (midbrain is functioning), cranial nerves V1 and VII intact**
If no blink occurs: ◆ **brainstem-level coma**

Test doll's reflex (Bielschowsky's sign)
PROCEDURE: With the patient supine, open the eyes bilaterally and then passively rotate the patient's head to the left and then to the right, repeating the rotation as necessary. Observe the movements of the eyes. The C-spine must be cleared for fractures radiographically before examination.

OUTCOME: If the eyes conjugately track to the same point while the head is rotated (i.e., the eyes remain as if gazing straight ahead even though the head is moved):
◆ **midbrain level (midbrain is functioning)**
If the eyes move with the head when laterally rotated (as though the eyes were painted on the face of a doll): ◆ **brainstem level**

Observe posture
PROCEDURE: With the patient supine and at baseline, observe the posturing of the patient's extremities.

OUTCOME: If the upper extremities are flexed and supinated, the lower extremities extended:
◆ **decorticate posturing of high midbrain-level coma**
If the head, both upper extremities, and both lower extremities are maximally extended:
◆ **decerebrate posturing of brainstem-level coma**

Shine light into pupil
PROCEDURE: Shine a light into the pupil (see Fig 3-2, p. 45).

OUTCOME: If there is direct and consensual miosis:
◆ **midbrain level (midbrain is functioning)**
If no change to light: ◆ **pontine-level coma**
If the pupils are mydriatic and immobile:
◆ **medullary-level coma (or death)**

Keys to Recording Findings

ENT

"Unremarkable"

A. Auricles/external canal

Note sites of pain, swelling, nodules or papules; note sites of swelling, discharge, cerumen

A.

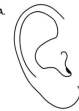

B. Tympanic membrane

Note the light reflex—cone shaped versus diffuse versus absent; note if bulging versus retracted; note color: white versus red; note any vesicles, papules or perforations

B.

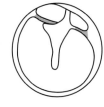

C. Nose/nares

Note position of the septum—midline versus deviated; note any polyps, note sites of mucosal thickening, nodules or perforation in nasal septum; note any discharge—clear, white, yellow, green or red

C.

D. Oropharynx and tongue

Note sites of nodules, vesicles, ulcers, erosions, plaques, papules; note color of these entities: white, red; note posterior pharynx: erythema, swelling, exudates, nodules, vesicles; note the tongue papilla: present versus atrophic; note presence, distribution and color (white, black) of any tongue coating.

D.

E. Teeth and gingival surface

Note any caries, tooth fracture, attrition; note the gingiva for any recession, swelling, papules, vesicles, erosions, or ulcers.

    M = Molars

    P = Premolars

    C = Canines

    I = Incisors

E.

Maxillary

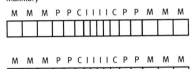

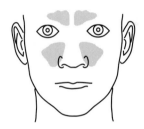

Mandibular

F. Anterior face/sinuses

Note sites of tenderness to percussion frontal and maxillary sinuses; note sites to decreased transillumination frontal and maxillary sinuses; note any lymph node enlargement in anterior neck.

F.

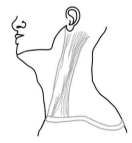

G. Lateral face/neck

Note sites of tenderness, nodules or masses in parotid gland; note any lymph node enlargement in lateral neck.

G.

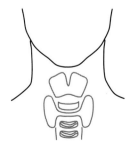

H. Thyroid

Note enlargement (goiter) or decreased size of thyroid; note sites of any nodules, masses, bruits or scars.

H.

Diagnoses

Abrasion: See Loss of tooth substance.

Acute meningitis

Inflammation of meninges, often due to infections with bacterial agents, for example, *Neisseria meningitidis, Streptococcus pneumoniae, Haemophilus influenzae*, or a virus. Symptoms include bilateral occipital headache with modest neck stiffness and pain; signs include decreased level of consciousness or delirium, nuchal rigidity, Kernig's sign, and Brudzinski's sign. Evaluation and treatment include lumbar puncture and administration of broad-spectrum parenteral antibiotics, for example, third-generation cephalosporin.

Amalgam tattoo

Accidental exposure of the mucosa to amalgam during dental restoration work. Asymptomatic; signs include blackish-gray macules in the mucosa adjacent to the area of tooth restoration. Evaluation and treatment involve clinical recognition and patient reassurance.

Angular cheilosis (perlèche)

Candidal infection involving the angles of the mouth due to edentulous or ill-fitting dentures; deficiency of vitamin B_{12}, folate, or iron may contribute. Symptoms and signs include erythematous, crusting fissures on the angles of the mouth (see Fig 2-7) and concurrent oral thrush or atrophic glossitis. Evaluation and treatment include elevation of serum B_{12} and folate levels, serum iron studies, and referral to a dentist as appropriate.

Aphthous stomatitis/ulcers (canker sores)

Prevalent process probably due to an autoimmune (either cell-mediated or humoral) process. Symptoms and signs include one or more painful, round ulcers on the oral or tongue mucosa. Ulcers are 5 to 10 mm in diameter and may appear in clusters. Evaluation and treatment are symptomatic (e.g., chlorhexidine mouthwash).

Atrophic glossitis

Deficiency of one or more of the water-soluble B vitamins—B_1 (niacin), B_2 (riboflavin), folate, or B_{12}. Symptoms include a burning sensation and dysgeusia; signs include loss of the filiform and then the fungiform papillae with resultant slick, smooth, atrophic appearance (see Fig 2-9). Evaluation and treatment include replenishing the B-complex vitamins.

Attrition: See Loss of tooth substance.

Basilar skull fracture

Due to trauma to the head. Symptoms and signs include a significant decrease in level of consciousness, as well as anisocoria, clear serous rhinorrhea, bilateral periorbital ecchymoses (see Fig 2-2), hemotympanum, and, after 48 hours, Battle's sign. The extraocular muscles should be assessed and the facial bones palpated, in order to rule out **facial fractures**. Evaluation includes facial and skull cervical plain films and a computed tomographic (CT) scan without contrast of the head and base of skull. Treatment is with advanced trauma life support (ATLS) protocol and urgent/emergent referral to a neurosurgeon.

Bullous myringitis

Due to an infection with *Mycoplasma pneumoniae* or a virus, specifically Epstein-Barr virus (EBV). Symptoms include mild decreased auditory acuity and modest otalgia; signs include a tympanic membrane (TM) with one or more vesicles with petechia. Concurrent dry cough and crackles indicate mycoplasma infection. Evaluation and treatment include initiation of systemic antibiotics, specifically an erythromycin-based regimen.

Caries/periapical abscess

Breakdown of the enamel by bacteria located adjacent to the gingivae. Symptoms include tooth pain and sensitivity to temperature extremes or to chewing; signs include tenderness to tooth percussion, breakage of the tooth, concurrent swelling of the gingivae at base, a sinus tract draining foul-smelling material, and severe tenderness, which indicate the development of a periapical abscess. Evaluation and treatment include analgesia, antibiotics for a periapical abscess, and referral to a dentist.

Cauliflower ear

Due to past recurrent trauma, usually from wrestling or boxing. Symptoms and signs include painless deformity of the auricle, with a loss of structures, but no change in auricular size. Prevention is the only treatment.

Cerumen

Due to a waxy substance in the external canal. Symptoms and signs include a sensation of fullness in the ear, decreased auditory acuity, and the brown waxy substance. Concurrent external otitis is common. Treatment is by gentle irrigation with warm water to remove the wax.

Chelitis

Accelerated tissue degeneration due to chronic ultraviolet (UV) light exposure; marked increased risk in squamous cell carcinoma. Symptoms and signs include painful fissures perpendicular to the vermilion border of the lip and concurrent hyperpigmented areas and erosions (lower lip more commonly involved). Evaluation and treatment include prevention, that is, applying sunscreen and lip balm, thus limiting UV light exposure, and referral to an ear-nose-throat (ENT) specialist.

Cholesteatoma

Nonmalignant expanding cyst lined with stratified squamous epithelium adjacent to the TM. Symptoms include fullness in the ear and decreased auditory acuity; signs include a peripheral yellow-white papule on the TM that may appear to be invading adjacent tissue, along with concurrent posterior–superior perforation. Refer the patient to an ENT surgeon for resection.

Coma

Profound decrease in level of consciousness due to toxic agents, metabolic processes, head trauma, infection, or intracranial events. Symptoms and signs include an unarousable patient and no voluntary movement. Other signs are dependent on the etiology: for narcotic overdose, miosis; for uncal herniation, anisocoria; for trauma, ecchymosis; meningitis, Kernig's sign, and fever; and for encephalopathy, asterixis. Further signs are dependent on the level of decreased consciousness: decorticate posturing, spontaneous respirations, doll's eyes (gaze ahead) in midbrain level, decerebrate posturing, loss of spontaneous respirations, and doll's eyes (gaze with head) in brainstem level. Within the brainstem-level classification, pupil responses further define specific sublevels: **Pontine level** is indicated by nonreactive pupils at midpoint and **medullary level** by dilated, nonreactive pupils. Treatment is directed toward the underlying etiology.

Coxsackie A: See Gingivostomatitis.

Deviated nasal septum

Due to a displaced nasal fracture. Symptoms include a history of recurrent sinusitis and rhinitis and decreased airflow in the nares; signs include deviation of the septum from the midline plane and obstruction to airflow through the nares. Refer the patient to an ENT surgeon for correction.

Erosion: See Loss of tooth substance.

Exostosis

Benign, exuberant bony growths in the external ear canal. Symptoms and signs include one or more nontender, asymptomatic, bilateral bony prominences in the external ear canals; may obscure the TM. Evaluation and treatment are clinical recognition only; no intervention is indicated.

Facial fracture: See Basilar skull fracture and Nasal fracture.

Geographic tongue

Benign, idiopathic, self-limited desquamation of the superficial mucosa of the dorsal and lateral tongue. Symptoms include burning or dysgeusia, or both; signs include red patches of desquamation of the superficial mucosa and of the filiform papillae; areas migrate over time. These red areas are surrounded by rims of white (see Fig 2-10). Evaluation and treatment include clinical recognition and support.

Gingival enlargement
Due to severe gingivitis vulgaris, use of cyclosporin A or **phenytoin**, or invasion by M5 (monocytic) acute myelocytic leukemia (AML). Symptoms include various amounts of pain and gingival bleeding; signs are increased size of interdental papillae (mild) or gingiva covering the crowns of teeth (severe). Evaluation and treatment include clinical recognition, prevention via flossing and improved oral hygiene, and, if suspicion for leukemia, a peripheral complete blood count.

Gingivitis vulgaris (periodonitis)
Prevalent process (most common reason for tooth loss in the United States today) due to bacterial plaques and calculus that develop at or beneath the gum line. Symptoms include pain and gingival bleeding; signs include gingival swelling (see Fig 2-4), increased depth of the gingival sulci, gingival erythema with bleeding, swelling of the papillae, **tartar,** and calculus at the gum line. Advanced form shows tooth roots, as well as caries and purulent material adjacent to the gum line. Individual teeth may be lost. Evaluation and treatment include the use of chlorhexidine mouthwash and prevention by using a soft-bristled brush and flossing daily. The patient should be referred to a dentist.

Gingivostomatitis
Primary or recurrent viral infection of the gingival and oral mucosa due to herpes simplex, herpes zoster, and Coxsackie A. General symptoms and signs include painful ulcers with antecedent vesicles. Symptoms and signs for specific etiologies are as follows:

> Painful vesicles, pustules, and ulcers on the oral mucosa and perioral skin, bilaterally in **primary herpes simplex**
>
> Painful vesicles and ulcers on the oral mucosa and posterior pharynx (herpangina), bilaterally; does not cross vermilion border and may involve skin of palms and soles in **primary Coxsackie A**
>
> Vesicles on the vermilion border and skin of the lip (see Fig 2-6); rarely affects the mucosa in **recurrent herpes simplex**
>
> Painful vesicles in V2, V3, or cranial nerve VII dermatome, unilaterally in **herpes zoster**

Treat with chlorhexidine mouthwash and, in herpes infection, systemic acyclovir.

Goiter
Diffuse enlargement of the thyroid gland due to Hashimoto's disease, endemic goiter (see Fig 2-14), or Graves' disease, or nodular enlargement due

to multinodular goiter or Plummer's disease. General symptoms and signs include a diffuse or nodular enlargement and, if very large, positive Pemberton's sign. For specific conditions, symptoms and signs are as follows:

> **Hypothyroidism:** Symptoms—cold, malaise, constipation; signs—hypothermia, bradycardia, thickened doughy skin, alopecia, loss of lateral eyebrow hair (Queen Anne's sign), slowed relaxation phase of deep tendon reflexes, coarse hair
>
> **Hyperthyroidism:** Symptoms—hyperdefecation, weight loss, warmth, palpitations, anxiety; signs—alopecia, brisk reflexes, thin hair, fine tremor, lid lag, von Graefe's and Dalrymple's sign (see Fig 2-16)
>
> **Graves' disease:** Hyperthyroidism, bruit over gland, exophthalmos, pretibial myxedema

Evaluation is with thyroid function tests. Treatment is specific to underlying cause: for endemic goiter, iodide replacement; hypothyroidism, levothyroxine; Graves' disease, thyroid ablation, and referral to an endocrinologist.

Graves' disease: See Goiter.

Hairy leukoplakia
Due to EBV infection of the papillae of the tongue, in cell-mediated immunocompromise, for example, acquired immunodeficiency syndrome (AIDS). Symptoms and signs include clusters of distinct, white, shaggy (hairy) lesions on the dorsum of the tongue. They do not coalesce but do resist scraping with a tongue blade. The underlying immunosuppression should be treated; chlorhexidine mouthwash may be of benefit.

Head trauma: See Coma and Basilar skull fracture.

Herpes simplex, primary/recurrent (herpes labialis):
See Gingivostomatitis.

Herpes zoster: See Gingivostomatitis.

Hyperthyroidism: See Goiter.

Hypothyroidism: See Goiter.

Infectious mononucleosis: See Pharyngitis, exudative.

Loss of tooth substance
Independent of caries and trauma; this includes **abrasion** due to localized grinding on toothpicks or pipes, **attrition** due to diffuse wearing of teeth (e.g., decades of mastication), and **erosion** due to diffuse wearing of teeth by chemicals (e.g., carbonated beverages or from bulimia). Symptoms include diffuse pain and sensitivity to temperature extremes. Signs include notches

on the occlusal surfaces for **abrasion**; for **attrition**, diffusely worn-down tooth edges (see Fig 2-5); and for **erosion**, diffuse yellow discoloration (loss of enamel) on lingual surfaces. Concurrent caries are not uncommon. Evaluation and treatment includes clinical recognition and referral to a dentist.

Ludwig's angina: See Pharyngitis, exudative.

Lymph node enlargement

Most commonly due to **reactive lymphadenitis** caused by local or systemic infection; other etiologies include **metastatic neoplasia,** for example, carcinoma or primary **lymphoma.** Symptoms and signs are specific to the etiology: tender, enlarged mobile nodes in reactive lymphadenitis; rock-hard, fixed nontender nodes in metastatic carcinoma; nontender, rubbery, matted-together nodes with "B" symptoms of night sweats, weight loss, and fever (Pel-Ebstein's fever) in lymphoma. Treat the underlying etiology. If suspicion of neoplasia is moderate to high, refer the patient to a surgeon for biopsy.

Lymphoma: See Lymph node enlargement.

Macroglossia

Diffuse infiltration of the tongue due to **amyloidosis, hypothyroidism**, or **acromegaly**. Symptoms include biting of the sides and tip of the tongue; signs include an enlarged tongue that may even appear smooth. Symptoms and signs for specific etiologies: recurrent diarrhea, hepatomegaly, right heart failure, ecchymosis, and purpura in amyloidosis; goiter, cold, alopecia, decreased deep tendon reflexes, delayed relaxation phase of reflexes in hypothyroidism; increased size of hands and feet, increased space between teeth with coarsening of the facial features in acromegaly. Evaluation and treatment depend on the etiology: **amyloidosis**, biopsy of skin; **hypothyroidism,** check a plasma thyroid-stimulating hormone (TSH); and **acromegaly**, referral to an endocrinologist.

Mastoiditis: See Purulent otitis media.

Metastatic disease: See Lymph node enlargement.

Mumps

Inflammation of the parotid glands due to infection with paramyxovirus. Symptoms include bilateral pain in the jaw and fever, with pain increasing after eating something sour; signs include loss of the angle of the jaw (see Fig 2-15), a displacement of the pinna up and outward, and erythema at Stensen's duct. Evaluation and treatment include support with fluids, rest, and acetaminophen.

Nasal fracture

Due to direct trauma. Symptoms and signs include acute tenderness, swelling, anterior epistaxis, and bilateral periorbital ecchymoses (see Fig 2-2). Concurrent septal hematoma and septal deviation are not uncommon. Evaluation includes radiography. The extraocular muscles should be assessed (see Fig 7-6) and the facial bones palpated, in order to assess for **facial fractures**. Treatment includes systemic antibiotics (as this is an open fracture) and referral to an ENT surgeon within 4 to 5 days.

Nasal polyps

Due to chronic severe atopic rhinitis, foreign body (e.g., nasal ring) or aspirin hypersensitivity; polyps are exuberant inflammatory tissue covered with mucosa. Symptoms include severe atopic rhinitis, unilateral or bilateral nasal airflow obstruction, a feeling of fullness in the nares; signs include a boggy, grape-like mass in one or both nares at the middle or lower turbinates or nasal septum. Treat with nasal steroids and refer the patient to an allergist or ENT surgeon.

Otitis externa

Superficial infection of the external auditory canal with *Staphylococcus aureus* and *Streptococcus* species (spp). Risk factors include cerumen impaction, trauma to the canal with cleaning, and swimming in lake water. Symptoms include a unilateral earache; signs include swelling, crusting, and edema in the canal that prevent visualization of the TM, as well as some purulent discharge. Evaluation and treatment include cleansing the canal of cerumen and applying topical otic agents; no referrals are necessary.

Otitis externa maligna

Due to *Pseudomonas aeruginosa* infection of the auricle; increased risk in immunosuppressed patients, especially those with uncontrolled diabetes mellitus or those taking high-dose steroids. Symptoms and signs include an acute painful auricle with diffuse swelling and tenderness (Plate 1); concurrent fever is common. Evaluation and treatment include broad-spectrum antibiotics and admission, as well as referral to an ENT and an infectious diseases consultant.

Perforation of the tympanic membrane

Due to acute otitis media or baro/noise/direct trauma to the TM. Symptoms include acute onset of discharge and decreased auditory acuity; pain acutely decreases if the TM perforates due to otitis media and markedly increases or is precipitated by a trauma-related condition. Signs include purulent or bloody discharge in the canal. The perforation has rough edges and purulent discharge from the perforation, located on the periphery of the TM in otitis media; the perforation has smooth edges and bloody discharge from the perforation, located in the center of the TM in trauma-related cases. Evaluation and treatment include antibiotics, proscription of fluid into the auditory canal, effective analgesia, and nonemergent referral to an ENT specialist.

Periapical abscess: See Caries.

Peutz-Jeghers syndrome

Autosomal dominant process of pigmented hamartomas in the gastrointestinal tract, with slight increase in the risk of gastrointestinal malignant neoplasia. Symptoms and signs include multiple pigmented macules on the lips, buccal mucosa, fingers, palms, soles, and rectum. Evaluation and treatment include obtaining a family history and referring the patient to a gastroenterologist for annual colonoscopy.

Pharyngitis, exudative

Infection of the pharyngeal mucosa and adjacent lymphoid tissue with **beta-hemolytic streptococci** or **a virus, usually EBV, to form an infectious mononucleosis**. Symptoms include acute onset of sore throat, fevers, and no rhinorrhea or cough; signs include diffuse erythema with exudate of the tonsils and posterior pharynx (see Fig 2-13). In streptococcal pharyngitis, the jugulodigastric nodes are enlarged. In EBV, diffuse lymphadenopathy is present. Complications include a fluctuant nodule adjacent to the tonsils, that is, peritonsillar abscess **(quinsy)** or submental swelling with stridor due to spread into the deep cervical structures **(Ludwig's angina)**. Evaluation and treatment are based on suspicion of streptococcus: if high, treat with penicillin or erythromycin; if intermediate, obtain rapid screen or culture for basis of treatment. For quinsy or Ludwig's angina, initiate antibiotics and proceed with emergent referral with an ENT surgeon.

Pharyngitis, nonexudative

Infection of the pharyngeal mucosa, usually with a ribonucleic acid (RNA)-based virus (e.g., rhinovirus). Symptoms include subacute onset of sore throat, low-grade fevers, rhinorrhea, cough, and myalgias; signs include diffuse erythema of the tonsils and posterior pharynx without exudate, shotty cervical lymph node enlargement, and nasal congestion. Evaluation and treatment consist of symptomatic relief.

Purulent otitis media

Bacterial infection of the middle ear with *Streptococcus* spp, *H. influenzae*, or *Branhamella catarrhalis*. Symptoms include a unilateral decrease in auditory acuity, modest to severe otalgia, and, rarely, otorrhea; antecedent rhinorrhea and scratchy sore throat may also be present. Signs include TM erythema and bulging, with a loss of bony landmarks, and marked decrease in the cone of light reflex (Plate 4). **Mastoiditis**, infectious inflammation of the mastoid immediately posterior to the auricle, may be a sequela in some cases. A **tympanoplasty tube** may be present if there was a prior infection requiring drainage. Evaluation and treatment include systemic antibiotics; if recurrent, referral to an ENT specialist may be indicated.

Quinsy: See Pharyngitis, exudative.

Rhinitis, atopic
Prevalent condition (15% in the United States), due to allergen–immunoglobulin E (IgE)/histamine-mediated mechanism; allergens include pollens, molds, dusts, hair, or danders. Symptoms include seasonal sneezing, itchy eyes, and serous rhinorrhea; signs include bilateral nasal congestion and rhinorrhea and bilateral serous conjunctivitis. The condition recurs on a seasonal basis. Evaluation and treatment include avoidance, antihistamines, nasal steroids, nasal antihistamines, and referral to an allergist.

Rhinitis, viral
Due to enterovirus, coronavirus, or rhinovirus and spread by direct contact of infected mucus to membranes. Self-limited complete resolution occurs in 2 to 5 days. Symptoms include bilateral rhinorrhea, sore throat, sneezing, nonproductive cough, mild bilateral watery eyes, and a "popping" sensation in the ears; signs include serous otitis media (Plate 3), low-grade fever, erythema of the posterior pharynx without exudate, and shotty cervical node enlargement. Evaluation and treatment include symptomatic relief via judicious use of decongestants, acetaminophen, and cough suppressants.

Rhinophyma
Hypertrophy of the sebaceous glands in nasal skin. Symptoms and signs include symmetric nasal skin hypertrophy; a bulbous, erythematous nose; and bilateral, as well as concurrent, rosacea. The patient should be referred to a dermatologist.

Serous otitis media
Middle ear inflammation due to an atopic or a viral condition; common and self-limited. Symptoms include mild decreased auditory acuity and a "popping" sensation with mild earache, as well as concurrent nasal congestion, frontal headaches, and nonproductive cough; signs include TM retraction with a yellow hue to the TM and air bubbles behind and decreased cone of light reaction (Plate 3). Evaluation and treatment include symptomatic relief with decongestants and acetaminophen.

Severe purulent gingivitis: See Gingivitis vulgaris.

Sinusitis
Due to a blockage in a sinus ostia, with stasis of material and bacterial infection (*S. pneumoniae*, *H. influenzae*, or *B. catarrhalis*). Symptoms include unilateral headache, fevers, cough, and halitosis. Signs for specific types are as follows: unilateral tenderness to palpation and percussion over the supraorbital area, green nasal discharge, lack of transilluminability in frontal sinusitis, unilateral tenderness over the maxillary sinus, green nasal discharge, and lack of transilluminability in maxillary sinusitis. Evaluation and treatment include systemic antibiotics and, if recurrent, CT scan of the sinuses and referral to an ENT specialist.

Sjögren's disease

Autoimmune destruction of the salivary glands associated with mixed connective tissue disease or rheumatoid arthritis. Symptoms include dry eyes (keratoconjunctivitis siccae), dry mouth, caries, and dysgeusia; signs include bilateral, nontender **parotid gland enlargement**, lacrimal gland enlargement, and positive Schirmer's sign. Evaluation and treatment include referral to an ophthalmologist and a rheumatology specialist; lubricating eye drops are also indicated.

Squamous cell carcinoma (lip)

Risks include exposure to UV light and use of smoking or chewing tobacco. Symptoms and signs include painless ulcer or exophytic lesion on the lip (lower lip more commonly involved). Cervical node enlargement indicates metastatic disease. The patient should be referred to an ENT specialist for excisional biopsy.

Squamous cell carcinoma (oral mucosa)

Risks include smoking or chewing tobacco and chronic ethanol ingestion. Symptoms and signs include a painless nonhealing, indurated ulcer on the oral mucosa; an exophytic component to the ulcer is common. Cervical node enlargement may indicate metastatic disease. The patient should be referred to an ENT specialist for excisional biopsy.

Squamous cell carcinoma (tongue)

Risks include smoking or chewing tobacco and chronic ethanol ingestion. Symptoms and signs include a painless, nonhealing, indurated ulcer on the lateral or ventral surface of the tongue; there may be an exophytic component. The patient should be referred to an ENT specialist for excisional biopsy.

Streptococcus, beta-hemolytic: See Pharyngitis, exudative.

Sublingual varices

Due to chronic increased central venous pressure or increasing age; prevalence is high in older individuals. The condition is asymptomatic. Signs include soft and symmetrically placed red-blue to purple venous structures on the ventral surface of the anterior two-thirds of the tongue (see Fig 2-11); concurrent increased jugular venous pressure, hepatomegaly (see Fig 6-6, p. 123), and peripheral edema may also be present in right heart failure. Evaluation and treatment include clinical recognition of varices and, if present, right heart failure.

Tartar (calculus): See Gingivitis vulgaris.

Temporomandibular joint dysfunction

Sprain or degeneration, or both, of the temporomandibular joint due to trauma, bruxism, or chewing of ice. Symptoms include jaw pain anterior to the tragus and popping at the joint with mastication; signs include popping revealed by auscultation of the joint and concurrent trismus or masseter muscle spasm. Evaluation and treatment include analgesia and referral to a dentist or oral surgeon.

Tension headache

Stress-related strain of the neck and head muscles. Symptoms include a generalized, bilateral frontal or occipital headache, or both (worse in the afternoons), as well as mild to moderate tenderness in the trapezius and occipital muscles. Treat with a nonsteroidal anti-inflammatory drug (NSAID) or acetaminophen.

Thrush

Infection of the oral, tongue, and pharyngeal mucosa with *Candida* spp, including *Candida albicans*, due to local or systemic immunosuppression (via, e.g., systemic steroids, chemotherapy, AIDS, or steroid inhalers). Symptoms and signs include white plaque-like areas with thickened curdle-like material on the tongue, posterior pharynx, gingiva, and oral mucosa (see Fig 2-3). The lesions bleed at the base when scraped. Evaluation includes microscopic analysis with potassium hydroxide; treatment is with topical clotrimazole or systemic fluconazole.

Tophi

Due to long-standing gout. Symptoms and signs include mildly tender papules on the edge of the helix and antihelix, as well as concurrent podagra, monarticular arthritis, and other tophi on elbows, hands, and knees. Treatment includes NSAIDs, colchicine, allopurinol, and, if indicated, referral to a rheumatologist.

Torus mandibularis

Benign bony exostosis on the mandible. Symptoms and signs include the presence of one or more painless sessile, nontender, firm, gingival-covered nodules on the lingual surface of the mandible, often bilaterally. Evaluation and treatment include clinical recognition and reassurance.

Torus palatinus

Benign exostosis of bone from the hard palate (see Fig 2-12). Symptoms and signs include a sessile, firm nodule in the midline of the hard palate, covered with normal mucosa. Evaluation and treatment include clinical recognition and reassurance.

Trigeminal neuralgia (tic douloureux)

Damage to one or more branches of the trigeminal nerve at or distal to the trigeminal ganglion due to neoplasia or viral infection. Symptoms include recurrent, lancinating, severe pain in the distribution of V1, V2, and/or V3 on one side of the face; signs include no facial weakness but severe pain and marked lacrimation on palpation or even light touch of trigger points of the face. Evaluation should proceed with magnetic resonance imaging (MRI) of the posterior fossa; treatment is with effective analgesia and referral to a neurology and pain clinic.

Tympanoplasty tube: See Purulent otitis media.

Virchow's/Trossier's node: See Lymph node enlargement.

CHAPTER 3
Eye

Basic Examination

Snellen chart: 20 feet

PROCEDURE: Instruct the patient to remove any eyeglasses and to move to a position 20 feet from a Snellen chart placed at eye level. Use either a Snellen chart with letters or, if the patient is illiterate or a non-English speaker, the Snellen chart with "E"s in various directions. Instruct the patient to cover one eye and read or state the direction of E. Repeat, covering the contralateral eye. Note the line in which the patient misses two or more letters:

1. The first number is the number of feet from the chart.
2. The second number is the line on the Snellen chart above the one in which the patient missed more than two letters.

OUTCOME: If 20/20: ◆ **normal acuity**
If 20/30 or greater: ◆ **abnormal acuity**
If 20/50: ◆ **prerequisite for automobile license in most states**
If 20/200 (i.e., cannot see the top line):
◆ **legally blind; perform Snellen at 15 and 10 feet**

Snellen chart: 15 and 10 feet

PROCEDURE: Instruct the patient to walk slowly toward the chart, stopping at 15 and 10 feet and keeping the contralateral eye covered at all times. Ask the patient to say when the letter becomes clear enough to see. Note the distance from the chart.

OUTCOME: If the patient can see the top line at 15 feet: ◆ **20/400**
If can see the top line at 10 feet: ◆ **20/800**
If cannot see the top line at 10 feet:
◆ **perform the finger-counting test**

Finger-counting test: 3 feet, 2 feet, and 1 foot

PROCEDURE: With adequate light and keeping the contralateral eye covered, put two or three fingers up 3 feet in front of the patient and instruct him or her to state the number of fingers held up. Repeat at 2 feet and at 1 foot from the patient's face.

OUTCOME: If the patient correctly counts fingers (CF) at 3 feet: ◆ **CF/3 feet**
If correctly counts fingers (CF) at 2 feet: ◆ **CF/2 feet**
If correctly counts fingers (CF) at 1 foot: ◆ **CF/1 foot**
If cannot see fingers at 1 foot: ◆ **perform hand movement test**

Hand movement test: 3 feet, 2 feet, and 1 foot

PROCEDURE: With adequate light and keeping the contralateral eye covered, move hand 3 feet in front of the patient and instruct him or her to state when the hand movement starts and stops. Repeat at 2 feet and at 1 foot from the patient's face.

OUTCOME: If the patient can see hand movement (HM) at 3 feet:
  ◆ **HM/3 feet**
If can see hand movement (HM) at 2 feet: ◆ **HM/2 feet**
If can see hand movement (HM) at 1 foot: ◆ **HM/1 foot**
If is unable to see hand movement at 1 foot:
  ◆ **perform light perception test**

Shine a light from 3 feet away to test light perception

PROCEDURE: With the lights dimmed, shine a light source from various positions from a distance of 3 feet. Ask the patient where the light source is located.

OUTCOME: If patient can state the location: ◆ **LP (light perception only)**
If no light is perceived: ◆ **NLP; totally blind**

Snellen chart: with eyeglasses on

PROCEDURE: Perform the Snellen chart test with the patient wearing eyeglasses.

OUTCOME: If 20/20 with eyeglasses: ◆ **refractory problem alone**
If there is only partial improvement:
  ◆ **refractory problem or concurrent nonrefractory problem**
If no improvement: ◆ **nonrefractory problem**

Snellen chart: through pinhole

PROCEDURE: Perform the Snellen chart with the patient looking through a piece of cardboard with a pinhole in it.

OUTCOME: If the patient's vision improves: ◆ **refractory problem**
If there is no vision improvement by looking through the pinhole: ◆ **nonrefractory problem**

Visually inspect pupils in darkened room

PROCEDURE: In a slightly darkened room, visually inspect the patient's pupils, noting their diameter and shape. Miosis = constriction; mydriasis = dilation

OUTCOME: If both pupils are 2 to 5 mm: ◆ **normal**
If both pupils are small, <2 mm: ◆ **miosis (e.g., from narcotics)**
If both pupils are large, >5 mm:
  ◆ **mydriasis** (e.g., due to flight-or fight reflex of catecholamines, severe brainstem damage, or death)
If there is a >0.4 mm difference in the diameters of the pupils:
  ◆ **anisocoria**

If unilateral miosis: ◆ **Horner's syndrome**
If unilateral mydriasis:
- ◆ **topical mydriatics to that eye**
- ◆ **acute angle glaucoma**
- ◆ **Argyll Robertson pupil**
- ◆ **monocular blindness**

If there are whitish areas in the lens (Fig 3-1): ◆ **cataract**

Shine light into pupils

PROCEDURE: With the patient gazing to the front in a dimly lit room, shine a light source from a distance of 30 to 40 cm directly into the pupil. Observe the response of the pupil (direct) and the contralateral pupil (consensual). After 5 seconds without light, repeat in the contralateral pupil. Miosis = constriction; mydriasis = dilation.

OUTCOME: If there is no direct constriction of one pupil but the other pupil constricts (consensual intact; Fig 3-2A):
- ◆ **topical mydriatics**
- ◆ **acute angle glaucoma**
- ◆ **Argyll Robertson pupil**

If neither pupil constricts (loss of direct and consensual; Fig 3-2B): ◆ **monocular blindness**

If there is no direct constriction in the pupil but direct constriction in the contralateral side (unilateral mydriasis; Fig 3-2C):
- ◆ **topical mydriatics**
- ◆ **acute angle glaucoma**
- ◆ **Argyll Robertson pupil**
- ◆ **monocular blindness involving that eye**

If neither pupil constricts when shining a light in either eye (Fig 3-2D):
- ◆ **death**
- ◆ **brainstem-level coma (see Chapter 2, p. 32)**
- ◆ **bilateral blindness**

Observe accommodation-constriction of pupils

PROCEDURE: With the patient gazing to the front in a dimly lit room, instruct him or her to focus directly on your finger placed at a midpoint

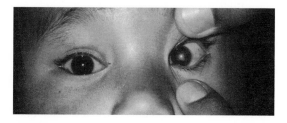

Figure 3-1 Cataract. This child has a dense cataract in the left eye (OS); visual acuity was 20/200 in OS.

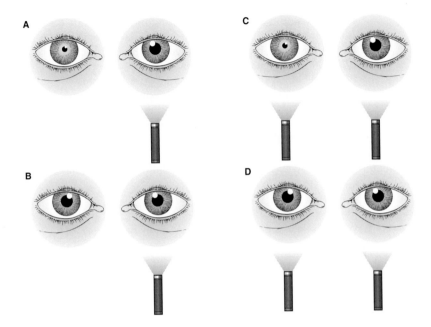

Figure 3-2 Direct and consensual constriction of pupils to light. *Step 1:* Shine a light source into the pupil in question. **A.** No direct constriction, consensual intact: topical mydriatics or Argyll Robertson pupil. **B.** No direct or consensual constriction: monocular blindness. *Step 2:* After no light for 5 seconds, shine the light into the contralateral pupil. **C.** No direct constriction, but direct constriction of the contralateral pupil: topical mydriatics, Argyll Robertson pupil, or monocular blindness. **D.** No direct constriction in either pupil: death or profound very low brainstem damage.

30 cm anterior to the eyes. Instruct the patient to follow the finger as it is slowly, but steadily, moved toward the nose. Observe the activity of the pupils in these converging eyes. (Recall constriction = miosis.)

OUTCOME: If the affected pupil constricts with convergence:
◆ **Argyll Robertson pupil**
If the affected pupil does not constrict with convergence:
◆ **another diagnosis**

Visually inspect anterior chamber, lens, and iris using slit lamp or direct light

PROCEDURE: Use direct light or the slit lamp to inspect the iris, lens, and anterior chamber visually.

OUTCOME: If there are pigmented clumps in both of the irises (Lisch sign):
◆ **neurofibromatosis**
If there is a pie-shaped area, contiguous with the pupil, across the entire iris: ◆ **iridectomy scar**

If solitary dot in the iris: ◆ **laser iridotomy scar (Plate 6B)**
If one or more pigmented lesions in the iris: ◆ **nevi/freckles**
If one or more pigmented lesions in iris with poikiloscoria
(Plate 7): ◆ **malignant melanoma of iris**
If there is blood in the anterior chamber: ◆ **hyphema**
If pus in the anterior chamber: ◆ **hypopyon**
If there are opacities in the lens (see Fig 3-1): ◆ **cataract**
If one or more opacities are in the corneum (Plate 6A):
◆ **corneal scarring**

Administer extraocular eye movements examination: See Chapter 7, as in Basic Examination (Fig 7-6, p. 146).

Test visual field by confrontation

PROCEDURE: With the patient sitting, place yourself opposite and at same level as the patient's gaze. You and the patient fix your gaze on each other's nose; the patient closes his or her right eye, and you close your left eye. Move an object from periphery inward from four different directions until both you and the patient can see the object. Repeat on the contralateral side. Note any discrepancy between the patient's perceptions and yours.

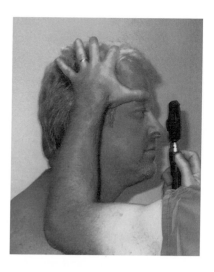

Figure 3-3 Position for ophthalmoscopy. Note position of hands and scope relative to the patient's eye; the examiner uses his or her left eye to examine the patient's left eye and his or her right eye to examine the patient's right eye. Start from a distance, find the white reflex, then look through the ophthalmoscope to see the red reflex and direct the scope toward that site, adjusting the lens so as to see the fundus itself clearly.

OUTCOME: If the patient can see in the horizontal plane 70 to 80 degrees from the center (total: 170 degrees): ◆ **normal**

If can see in the vertical plane 60 to 70 degrees from the center (total: 130 degrees): ◆ **normal**

If one entire eye has no vision: ◆ **monocular blindness**

If the blindness is in the same half of both visual fields:
◆ **homonymous hemianopsia**

If in the opposite halves of the visual fields:
◆ **heteronymous hemianopsia**

If in both temporal halves: ◆ **bitemporal hemianopsia**

If there is a loss of part of the field: ◆ **scotoma**

If a decrease in peripheral fields and increase in size of blind spot (Bjerrum's arcuate scotoma): ◆ **open angle glaucoma**

Perform direct fundoscopic examination

PROCEDURE: After dilating the pupil with one to two drops of 1% tropicamide solution, examine the retina using an ophthalmoscope (Fig 3-3), finding the optic cup and disc, then tracing one or two arteries/veins in each of the four quadrants. Note the color and contour of the retina and the size and shape of the vessels.

OUTCOME: If the disc has a cup-disc ratio of less than 1:3, paired vessels radiating from the disc, a normal-appearing macula, and no sites of bleeding: ◆ **normal (Plate 8)**

If any other findings:
◆ **abnormality may be present** (see Advanced Examination sections on the retina)

Advanced Examination

APPROACH TO A PATIENT WITH A RED EYE

Inspect conjunctivae; evert upper and lower eyelids

PROCEDURE: Have the patient gently close both eyes. Place the wooden end of a cotton swab longitudinally over the superior aspect of the upper eyelid. Gently press the swab deeply; concurrently, grasp the upper palpebral margin and evert the eyelid. Inspect the conjunctivae and the discharge using direct light or a slit lamp. Repeat, using the lower eyelid and then the contralateral eye.

OUTCOME: If there is stringy discharge with chemosis on the palpebral surfaces: ◆ **atopic conjunctivitis**

If serous discharge: ◆ **viral conjunctivitis**

If purulent discharge (Plate 9): ◆ **bacterial conjunctivitis**

If unilateral mydriasis until perilimbal flushing, and diffuse reddening of conjunctivae: ◆ **acute angle glaucoma (Plate 10)**

If an irregular, red, macular area in the palpebral or visceral conjunctivae: ◆ **subconjunctival hemorrhage (Plate 11)**

If marked thickening and redness of conjunctivae, appears to be "meaty": ◆ **chemosis**

Perform slit-lamp examination of cornea and anterior chamber

PROCEDURE: Perform a slit-lamp examination of the cornea and anterior chamber.

OUTCOME: If the cornea is transparent: ◆ **normal**

If the cornea is translucent:

    ◆ **corneal abrasion (Plate 12)**

    ◆ **acute keratitis (Plate 13)**

If generally transparent but has patches of translucency:

    ◆ **superficial punctate keratitis, actinic or chemical related**

If there is an opacity in the cornea (Plate 6A):

    ◆ **corneal ulcer**

    ◆ **keratitis scar (old)**

If one or more blood vessels in the cornea: ◆ **healed keratitis**

If there is an air-fluid level, with the fluid being yellow/white:

    ◆ **hypopyon**

If air-fluid level, with the fluid being red: ◆ **hyphema**

If there is a circumcorneal flush, limbic vessel dilation, and anterior chamber cloudiness: ◆ **anterior uveitis**

Perform fluorescein staining with cobalt blue light source

PROCEDURE: Apply 1 to 2 drops of fluorescein dye to the affected eye. With a cobalt blue light source, observe the cornea using the slit lamp.

OUTCOME: If there is a patch of green: ◆ **corneal abrasion (Plate 12)**
If linear pattern of green:
  ◆ **corneal abrasion due to foreign body or eyelash**
If dendritic pattern of green: ◆ **herpes keratitis**
If ring (annular) pattern of green:
  ◆ **corneal abrasion or ulceration due to contact lens**
If punctate pattern of green:
  ◆ **superficial punctate keratitis/actinic keratitis**
If there is no green staining: ◆ **normal**

Palpate preauricular lymph nodes

PROCEDURE: Palpate the area immediately anterior to the tragus, feeling for the preauricular node.

OUTCOME: If the preauricular node is palpable: ◆ **viral conjunctivitis**
If the preauricular node is not palpable: ◆ **another etiology**

Perform Schirmer's test

PROCEDURE: Instruct the patient to open the eye. Evert the lower eyelid slightly and place a strip of folded filter paper on the inside surface of the lateral lower lid for 5 minutes.

OUTCOME: If there is >5 mm of wetness: ◆ **normal**
If <5 mm of wetness:
  ◆ **keratoconjunctivitis sicca (Sjögren's disease)**

Transilluminate anterior chamber

PROCEDURE: Shine a light into the anterior chamber of the unaffected eye, from the lateral canthus and directed nasally. The light source may be a penlight, an ophthalmoscope, or preferably a slit lamp. Attempt to transilluminate the entire anterior chamber from this site. Note the presence of any shadows.

OUTCOME: If the anterior chamber is transilluminable (no shadows):
  ◆ **normal**
If there is a crescent-shaped shadow on the nasal side of the anterior chamber (crescent sign): ◆ **acute angle glaucoma**

APPROACH TO A PATIENT WITH SCLERAL/CORNEAL FINDINGS

Visually inspect sclerae

PROCEDURE: Visually inspect the sclerae using either direct light.

OUTCOME: If there is a fan-shaped, triangular, vascularized, cream-colored papule in the visceral conjunctiva medial to the pupil (Fig 3-4):
  ◆ **pterygium**
If a yellow papule of fat in the visceral conjunctiva medial or lateral to the pupil: ◆ **pinguecula**
If diffuse yellow discoloration to the sclerae and conjunctivae (Plate 14): ◆ **icterus**

Figure 3-4 Pterygium. Batwing-shaped area of connective tissue on medial aspect of both sclerae; may cause mischief by growing over the sclera.

If a cream-colored ring around the limbus in both eyes:
 ◆ **arcus senilis**

APPROACH TO A PATIENT WITH SUSPECTED CATARACT

Test visual acuity: As in Basic Examination (Snellen chart).

Visually inspect pupils in darkened room: As in Basic Examination.

Use slit-lamp examination to describe cataract

PROCEDURE: Using a slit lamp, image the lens and attempt to demonstrate the location of the cataract.

OUTCOME: If the opacity is in the center: ◆ **nuclear cataract**
If opacity has a wheel-spokes pattern: ◆ **cortical cataract**
If opacity is in the central posterior lens, immediately deep to the lenticular capsule: ◆ **posterior subcapsular cataract**

APPROACH TO A PATIENT WITH POTENTIAL CHRONIC OPEN ANGLE GLAUCOMA

Perform direct fundoscopic examination

PROCEDURE: As in Basic Examination (see Fig 3-3).

OUTCOME: If there is an increased cup-disc ratio—the cup is >60% the size of the disc: ◆ **open angle glaucoma, suspect**
If the cup is deep: ◆ **open angle glaucoma, suspect**
If there is a nasal shift of the vessels (i.e., a paucity of vessels on the temporal side): ◆ **open angle glaucoma, high suspect**
If diffuse decrease in the number of vessels at the margins:
 ◆ **open angle glaucoma, high suspect**

Visual field assessment-as in basic examination

APPROACH TO A PATIENT WITH SUSPECTED PAPILLEDEMA

Perform direct fundoscopic examination

PROCEDURE: As in Basic Examination (see Fig 3-3).

OUTCOME: If there is an absence in spontaneous pulsations in veins:
   ◆ **papilledema**
If the disc margins are blurred:
   ◆ **papilledema (Plates 15 and 16)**
If there is a star-shaped macula (macular star): ◆ **papilledema**
If there are flame hemorrhages, as well as soft exudates in the area around the disc (see Plates 15 and 16): ◆ **papilledema**

APPROACH TO A PATIENT WITH YELLOW/WHITE BLOTCHES ON THE RETINA

Perform direct fundoscopic examination

PROCEDURE: As in Basic Examination (see Fig 3-3).

OUTCOME: If there are clusters of tiny, discrete, yellow-white spots:
   ◆ **drusen**
If one or more fluffy, nonglistening, pale white spots with fuzzy borders are present not adjacent to any vessels, up to or greater than a disc-diameter size (Plate 17): ◆ **soft exudates**
If there are clusters of yellow spots that have discrete borders and a shiny, waxy appearance (Plate 18): ◆ **hard exudates**
If pigmented soft exudates are grouped around the disc:
   ◆ **chorioretinitis: tuberculosis**
If there is one large, white soft exudate that is not near disc, along with smaller satellite lesions:
   ◆ **chorioretinitis: toxoplasmosis**
If there are multiple, large, yellow, soft exudates, sometimes referred to as resembling a "cheese pizza":
   ◆ **chorioretinitis: cytomegalovirus (CMV)**
   ◆ **chorioretinitis: histoplasmosis**

APPROACH TO A PATIENT WITH BLACK OR PIGMENTED BLOTCHES ON THE RETINA

Perform direct fundoscopic examination

PROCEDURE: As in Basic Examination (see Fig 3-3).

OUTCOME: If there are irregularly shaped, deeply pigmented lesions:
   ◆ **healed chorioretinitis**
If multiple uniform black spots on the periphery:
   ◆ **photocoagulation sites for diabetic retinopathy**
If multiple punctate black spots: ◆ **choroidal hemorrhages**
If there is one irregularly shaped black spot:
   ◆ **malignant melanoma**

If the macula has one or more rings of pigment within it:
- ◆ **bull's-eye maculopathy**

APPROACH TO A PATIENT WITH RED BLOTCHES ON THE RETINA

Perform direct fundoscopic examination

PROCEDURE: As in Basic Examination (see Fig 3-3).

OUTCOME: If one or more small (about same size as vessel diameter), round, red dots, that is, bulges with distinct margins, are present, each adjacent to an artery (Plate 18):
- ◆ **microaneurysms of diabetes mellitus**

If one or more cylindrical red spots, up to one-half disc diameter in size: ◆ **blot hemorrhages of:**
- ◆ **hypertension**
- ◆ **systemic lupus erythematosus (SLE)**

If there are flame-shaped red spots: ◆ **flame hemorrhages of:**
- ◆ **severe hypertension (Plate 17)**
- ◆ **intracranial bleeds**
- ◆ **papilledema (Plate 16)**
- ◆ **central retinal vein occlusion (Plate 19)**

If there is one white-centered red macule:
- ◆ **Roth's spots (Litten's spots) of endocarditis**
- ◆ **Roth's spots of leukemia**

If presence of brown-reddish substance interfering with fundoscopic examination (Plate 20): ◆ **vitreous hemorrhage**

If the macula alone is red, relative to the rest of the retina (Plate 21): ◆ **cherry-red macula of retinal arterial occlusion**

If the entire retina is pale, compared to the other retina (Plate 21):
- ◆ **central retinal artery occlusion**

APPROACH TO A PATIENT WITH DIABETES AND/OR HYPERTENSION OR VESSEL CHANGES

Perform direct fundoscopic examination

PROCEDURE: As in Basic Examination (see Fig 3-3).

OUTCOME: If the arteries are <50% of the size of the accompanying vein:
- ◆ **hypertensive changes, Keith-Wagner-Barker (KWB) type I**

If there is nicking (space between artery and vein) at crossover sites: ◆ **hypertensive changes (KWB type II)**

If there are flame or blot hemorrhages (see Plates 16 and 17):
- ◆ **hypertensive changes (KWB type III)**

If there is papilledema (Plate 16):
- ◆ **hypertensive changes (KWB type IV)**

If the arteries have light reflexes in their longitudinal aspects (Plate 17): ◆ **copper or silver wiring of hypertension**
If there are discrete yellow spots with shiny, waxy appearances (Plate 18): ◆ **hard exudates**
If one or more small, round, red dots with distinct margins are present, each adjacent to an artery (Plate 18):
  ◆ **microaneurysms of diabetes mellitus**
If one or more fluffy, nonglistening, pale white spots with fuzzy borders, up to one disc diameter in size:
  ◆ **soft exudates of microinfarctions of diabetes mellitus**
If one or more small tortuous vessels adjacent to the soft exudates: ◆ **neovascularization of diabetes mellitus**
If one or more streaks in the retina with increased color, a change in retina contour, and a loss of the normal pattern of disc, veins, and arteries, especially in the upper temporal retina:
  ◆ **retinal detachment**
If one or more areas of ill-defined redness (Plate 20):
  ◆ **vitreous hemorrhage**
If one or more glistening, yellow, fixed spots in the retinal arteries: ◆ **Hollenhorst plaques (cholesterol plaques)**

APPROACH TO A PATIENT WITH PERIORBITAL STRUCTURE ABNORMALITIES

Inspect periorbital tissues with eyes open in neutral position

PROCEDURE: With the patient gazing anteriorly, visually inspect the orbits and tissues adjacent to the eyes.

OUTCOME: If erythema and inflammation with scales of the eyelid margins are present (Plate 22): ◆ **blepharitis**
If there is a tender pustule on the eyelid margin edge (Plate 22):
  ◆ **external hordeolum (sty)**
If tender pustule deep to the eyelid margin:
  ◆ **internal hordeolum**
If nontender papule deep to the eyelid margin (Fig 3-5):
  ◆ **chalazion**
If there are irregularly bordered yellow papules/plaques on the medial aspect of the upper and lower eyelids (Fig 3-6):
  ◆ **xanthelasma (see Chapter 14, p. 336)**
If the upper eyelid edge is >2 mm inferior to the upper corneal margin: ◆ **ptosis, including Horner's syndrome**
If upper eyelid is not touching the upper corneal margin:
  ◆ **lid lag of hyperthyroidism (see Chapter 2, p. 34)**
If diffuse erythema and swelling of the upper and lower eyelids are present without proptosis (Plate 23):
  ◆ **preseptal cellulitis**

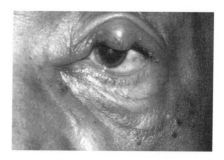

Figure 3-5 Chalazion. Nontender enlargement of one or more meibothian glands in the upper eyelid. Associated with seborrheic blepharitis and often has antecedent styes (external hordeolae) or internal hordeolum.

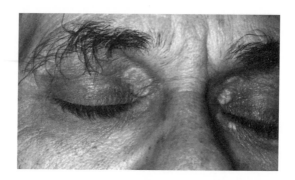

Figure 3-6 Xanthelasma. Creamy yellow plaques and patches in periorbital skin. Associated with severe hyperlipidemia, especially elevated triglycerides.

If diffuse erythema and swelling of the upper and lower eyelids with proptosis and decreased extraocular eye movements (EOM):
    ♦ **orbital cellulitis**

Inspect position of eyelids while closed

PROCEDURE: Visually inspect the position of the eyelids after instructing the patient to actively close the eyes.

OUTCOME: If the patient is unable to close eyelids fully:
    ♦ **peripheral cranial nerve (CN) VII palsy (see Chapter 7, p. 172)**
If able to close eyelids, but the eyelashes are turned inward:
    ♦ **entropion**
If able to close eyelids, but the eyelashes are turned outward (Plate 9): ♦ **ectropion**

APPROACH TO A PATIENT WITH STRABISMUS

Shine light into pupils from 3 feet

PROCEDURE: Instruct the patient to look at a penlight held at a distance of 3 feet. Visually observe the reflection of the light from the pupils.

OUTCOME: If the reflection is from the same part of the pupil: ◆ **normal**
If reflection is different, such that both pupils are deviated inward: ◆ **esotropia (cross-eyed)**
If reflection is different, such that both pupils are deviated outward: ◆ **exotropia (wall-eyed)**

Inspect eyes while they follow a moving object

PROCEDURE: In a room with neutral ambient light, instruct the patient to focus on one object, such as a finger. Visually inspect the position of the eyes.

OUTCOME: If an eye is medially displaced:
◆ **esotropia (cross-eyed, convergent strabismus)**
If laterally displaced:
◆ **exotropia (wall-eyed, divergent strabismus)**

Perform active range-of-motion exercise for eyes

PROCEDURE: With the patient gazing forward, instruct him or her to follow your finger in the six directions of medial, lateral, diagonal superotemporal, diagonal superonasal, diagonal inferonasal, and diagonal inferotemporal (see Fig 7-6, p. 146).

OUTCOME: If there is no eye movement except in the lateral and inferonasal directions: ◆ **CN III palsy**
If there is unilateral loss of ability to elevate and nasally move an eye: ◆ **inferior oblique palsy of a blowout fracture**
If loss of inferonasal movement:
◆ **CN IV palsy**
◆ **superior oblique defect**
If loss of lateral movement:
◆ **CN VI palsy**
◆ **lateral rectus defect**

Perform cover test of eyes

PROCEDURE: Instruct the patient to focus on one object (e.g., your finger). Immediately after the patient focuses on the object, place a cover over one of his or her eyes for several seconds, then remove it. Visually inspect the eye immediately after the removal of the cover for any movement. Repeat the test on the contralateral side.

OUTCOME: If there is no turning in or out of the eye: ◆ **normal**
If movement toward the nose: ◆ **exophoria (outward turning)**

If movement toward the temporal side:
  ◆ **esophoria (inward turning)**

APPROACH TO A PATIENT WITH ACUTE MONOCULAR BLINDNESS

Perform direct fundoscopic examination

PROCEDURE: See under Basic Examination.

OUTCOME: If the retina is diffusely pale, with decreased artery size and a cherry-red macula (Plate 21):
  ◆ **central retinal artery occlusion**
  ◆ **temporal arteritis**
If an overall increase in redness; dilated/enlarged retinal veins (>2 times the size of the corresponding artery); multiple splinter, blot, and flame hemorrhages; and soft exudates adjacent to the retinal veins, optic disc, and macula occur (Plate 19):
  ◆ **central retinal vein occlusion**
If streaks in the retina, increased color, a change in retina contour, and a loss of the normal pattern of disc, veins, and arteries, especially in the upper temporal retina:
  ◆ **retinal detachment**
If there is a large amount of a brown and reddish substance interfering with the retina examination (Plate 20):
  ◆ **vitreous hemorrhage**

Auscult carotid arteries

PROCEDURE: Use procedure described on page 84 (see Fig 4-7).

OUTCOME: If there is a bruit: ◆ **carotid atherosclerotic disease**
If no bruit: ◆ **normal**

Palpate temporal arteries

PROCEDURE: Palpate the ipsilateral temporal artery where it runs immediately anterior to the tragus. Examine superiorly from the tragus, feeling for tenderness or nodules.

OUTCOME: If there is tenderness or nodularity: ◆ **temporal arteritis**
If no tenderness or nodularity: ◆ **normal**

Keys to Recording Findings

EYES

"VF: OS 20/20, OD 20/20; EOMI, PERLA, Extraocular structures and fundi unremarkable, no visual field deficits"

A. Visual acuity, with and without eyeglasses

OS (oculus sinistra, left eye):

Without: 20/_____

With: 20/_____

OD (oculus dextra, right eye):

Without 20/_____

With: 20/_____

If worse than 20/800, report

CF (count fingers) from 3 feet, 2 feet, or 1 foot, or

HM (hand movement) from 3 feet, 2 feet or 1 foot, or

Light perceived versus no light perceived (NLP)

B. Pupils: PERRLA

Pupils equal round, reactive to light and accommodation. Note any anisocoria: > 0.4 mmHg difference in diameter; note pupil size use key to note size, mydriasis—dialation > 6mm; note miosis—constricted < 2 mm; note response of pupils to direct and consensual light; accommodation: pupils constrict with convergence.

C. Extraocular movements (EOMI)

Note any paralysis (tropia) or weakness (phoria) to eye movement; note any ptoptosis (exophthalamus). Recall the 3 "Rules of Eye Movement":

1. All recti muscles move eyeball out, except medial rectus

2. All oblique muscles move eyeball in and opposite of superior/inferior

3. Superior oblique 4, lateral rectus 6, all the rest 3

A. Visual Acuity (x = # on chart of highest line seen)

V_f OS   with glasses   20/x_____

without glasses 20/x_____

V_f OD   with glasses   20/x_____

without glasses 20/x_____

If > 20/800: CF at 3, 2, and 1 foot. _____

If > CF1: HM at 3, 2, and 1 foot. _____

If > HM1: LP or NLP. _____

B. PERRLA (Pupils equal round, reactive to light and accommodation)

Pupil size OS _____mm

OD _____mm

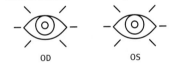

OD   OS

C. EOMI (Extraocular muscles intact)

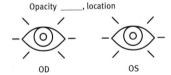

OD   OS

D. Lens Clear _____

Opacity _____, location

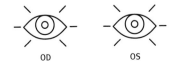

OD   OS

E. Conjunctival and Extraocular Structure

Normal _____

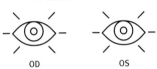

OD   OS

D. Lens

Clear versus opacity, note location of opacity if present

E. Periorbital structures

Note any redness, swelling; note discharge—watery, white, purulent, papules, nodules; note color changes—red, white, blue, yellow; note cornea: transparent, translucent or opaque

F. Fundi

Note size of cup and disc ratio, papilledema; note site of hemorrhages, microaneurysms, exudates—soft and hard, overall color of the fundi

G. Visual fields

Draw on any deficits on the fields

F. Fundi

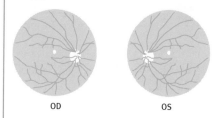

OD   OS

G. Visual Fields

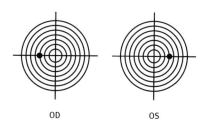

OD   OS

Each circle is 5° from central fixation point.

Acute keratitis: See Herpes simplex keratitis.

Anisocoria
Congenital or acquired difference in the size of pupils of >0.5 mm (see Fig 3-2). If the condition is acquired, head computed tomography (CT) should be performed to rule out acute intracranial pathology. Referral to an ophthalmologist and/or neurologist may be indicated.

Anterior uveitis
Due to infections, such as herpes, or to trauma-related or systemic disorders, such as rheumatoid arthritis and sarcoidosis. Symptoms include photophobia and epiphora (excessive tearing); signs include miosis, perilimbic conjunctival injection, and cloudiness (flare) in the anterior chamber due to cells; on slit-lamp examination precipitate and cells also may be present on the corneal endothelium. Complications include open angle glaucoma, posterior adhesions (synechiae), **band keratopathy**, and hypopyon. The patient should be referred to an ophthalmologist.

Arcus senilis
Normal with increasing age; in younger individuals **(arcus juvenilis)**, may be due to hyperlipidemia. An asymptomatic cream-colored ring of material appears around the cornea, separated from the limbus by a clear zone. Evaluation and treatment include clinical recognition and lipid panel.

Argyll Robertson pupil
Neurosyphilis-related damage to the Edinger-Westphal nucleus, associated with tabes dorsalis. Symptoms and signs include mydriatic pupil at the outset, no miosis with direct light or accommodation (see Fig 3-2C), and concurrent peripheral neuropathy in stocking-glove distribution (see Fig 7-4A). Evaluation includes serum VDRL (Venereal Disease Research Laboratory test for syphilis) and FTA-abs (fluorescent treponemal antibody absorption test) and cerebrospinal fluid (CSF) examination with VDRL. Treatment includes parenteral penicillin and referral to an infectious diseases specialist. This condition is exceedingly rare today.

Bitemporal hemianopsia: See Visual field cuts.

Blepharitis
Inflammation of the palpebral edge due to *Staphylococcus aureus* or, more commonly, seborrheic dermatitis. Symptoms include sensation of scratchiness and redness in the eyes; signs include erythema and scale formation on the eyelids (Plate 22); concurrent conjunctival injection is common. Evalua-

tion and treatment include gentle scrubbing of the eyelid margins with a moistened cotton-tipped applicator each morning. In severe cases application of topical antibiotic ointment to the eyelid margins may be needed.

Blot hemorrhages
Blot-shaped retinal hemorrhages smaller than flame hemorrhages, usually smaller than the diameter of retinal arteries; associated with hypertensive and diabetic retinopathy. See hypertensive changes/retinopathy.

Brown's syndrome: See Strabismus.

Bull's-eye maculopathy
Drug-related development of macular degeneration, usually due to hydroxychloroquine. Symptoms and signs include insidious onset of bilateral decreased visual acuity and a pattern of pigment likened to a bull's eye at the macule. Hydroxychloroquine should be discontinued and the patient referred to an ophthalmologist.

Carotid atherosclerotic disease: See Hollenhorst plaques and Chapter 4, p. 91 (Atherosclerosis).

Cataract
Risk factors are increasing age, chronic steroid use, Marfan's syndrome, congenital lues, and congenital toxoplasmosis. Symptoms and signs include decreased visual acuity and a cloudy lens (see Fig 3-1). The location of the cataract is either **nuclear, cortical, or posterior subcapsular**; there is concurrent superior lens subluxation in Marfan's syndrome. Evaluation and treatment include referral to an ophthalmologist for extraction when mature.

Central retinal artery occlusion
Due to an arterial thromboembolic event; risks include thrombus in the left heart, atrial fibrillation, left-sided endocarditis, atrial enlargement, and plaques in the carotid artery. Symptoms include acute onset of painless monocular blindness. Fundoscopic examination shows a **cherry-red macula**, an optic disc that is pale compared to surrounding retinal tissue, and diffusely narrowed arteries (Plate 21). Evaluation includes electrocardiogram (ECG) and echocardiogram. Treatment includes emergent referral to an ophthalmologist; anticoagulation with heparin must be strongly considered.

Central retinal vein occlusion
Due to long-standing, uncontrolled, severe systemic hypertension. Symptoms include acute painless monocular blindness. Fundoscopic examination shows the retina to be markedly edematous, with hemorrhages and dilated tortuous veins (i.e., "blood and thunder" appearance; see Plate 19); neovascularization of the iris may also develop. Control the hypertension and emergently refer the patient to an ophthalmologist.

Chalazion

Chronic inflammation of a meibomian gland, that is, a chronic internal hordeolum. The condition is characterized by an asymptomatic, indurated lesion deep from the palpebral margin (see Fig 3-5) and a past history of an internal hordeolum. The patient should be referred to an ophthalmologist.

Chemosis: See Conjunctivitis, atopic.

Cherry-red macula: See Central retinal artery occlusion.

Chorioretinitis: See Soft exudates.

Conjunctivitis, atopic

Histamine-mediated vasodilation of conjunctival vessels due to exposure to an allergen. Symptoms and signs include sensations of scratchiness and dryness in one or both eyes; no decrease in visual acuity; diffuse conjunctival injection and edema **(chemosis)**; no purulence; no anterior chamber findings or fluorescein uptake; and concurrent rhinorrhea and sneezing. Treat by avoidance (of allergen), nasal steroids, antihistamines, and topical naphazoline to the eyes.

Conjunctivitis, bacterial

Due to *Streptococcus pneumoniae*, *S. aureus*, *Haemophilus aegyptius*, *Moraxella* species (spp), or, rarely in the United States, *Chlamydia trachomatis* or *Neisseria gonorrhoeae*. Symptoms include mild decrease in visual acuity and mild discomfort; signs include acute onset of copious purulent discharge from both eyes (Plate 9). In trachoma, severe keratoconjunctivitis presents with papillae and follicles (white elevations) on the palpebral conjunctiva of the upper eyelid, with concurrent entropion and trichiasis. Evaluation and treatment include Gram's stain of purulent discharge and instillation of topical antibiotics; if trachoma or gonococcus is suspected, systemic antibiotics and referral to an ophthalmologist are necessary.

Conjunctivitis, viral

Due to a virus, usually an adenovirus; transmission is via direct contact with infected fluid. Symptoms and signs include unilateral or bilateral erythema of the conjunctivae, copious watery discharge, ipsilateral preauricular lymphadenopathy, decrease in visual acuity, and no conjunctival purulence. Fluorescein examination shows little to no uptake; if there is uptake it is superficial and punctate. Evaluation and management include topical vasoconstrictors, such as naphazoline (e.g., Naphcon A), and elective referral to an ophthalmologist.

Corneal abrasion

Scratch, contact lens, or foreign body–related erosion of the cornea. Symptoms include acute onset of unilateral eye discomfort and erythema; patient may relate a history of foreign body, mild decreased visual acuity, nonpurulent conjunctivitis, and normal anterior chamber. Fluorescein examination shows scratch or patch uptake in cobalt blue light (Plate 12). Evaluation and treatment include lavage; instillation of an antibiotic agent; systemic analgesia, for example, oral narcotic agent; and a patch to the affected eye; if there is no improvement in 24 hours, refer the patient to an ophthalmologist.

Corneal ulcer

Scratch, contact lens, or foreign body–related ulcer of the cornea. Symptoms include acute onset of unilateral eye pain and erythema; patient may relate a history of foreign body, decreased visual acuity, purulent conjunctivitis, **chemosis**, and a corneal opacity. Fluorescein examination shows scratch or patch uptake in cobalt blue light. On slit-lamp examination there may be concurrent anterior uveitis or **hypopyon**. Evaluation and treatment include instillation of an antibiotic agent and a cycloplegic agent and effective analgesia, as well as a patch to the affected eye and referral to an ophthalmologist.

Drusen

Focal thickening of Bruch's membrane; the condition increases with increasing age and is correlated with macular degeneration. Symptoms are minimal until advanced; signs include multiple small, uniformly shaped yellow blots on the retina and decreased central vision. Referral to an ophthalmologist is indicated for close follow-up.

Ectropion

Eversion of the eyelid due to scarring or Bell's palsy that may result in drying, thus increasing the risk of irritation and infection of the conjunctivae and cornea. Symptoms and signs include conjunctivitis (Plate 9) and a superficial punctate uptake on cornea with the fluorescein examination. Treatment includes lubricating eye drops, patch placement, and referral to an ophthalmologist.

Entropion

Inversion of the eyelid due to scarring, with concurrent trichiasis (i.e., inversion of the eyelashes) and irritation of the cornea. Symptoms and signs include conjunctivitis and linear uptake on cornea with the fluorescein examination. Treatment includes lubricating eye drops, patch placement, and referral to an ophthalmologist.

Esophoria/esotropia: See Strabismus.

Exophoria/exotropia: See Strabismus.

Flame hemorrhages

Retinal hemorrhages associated with hypertensive and diabetic retinopathy. Symptoms and signs include underlying hypertension or diabetes, or both;

variable degrees of visual acuity deficit; and flamed-shaped hemorrhages (Plates 16 and 17) (larger than blot hemorrhages). Evaluation and treatment include treating and controlling the underlying disease and referral to an ophthalmologist.

Glaucoma, acute angle

Congenital narrowing of the anterior chamber that, with acute mydriasis, leads to obstruction to flow of the aqueous humor and profoundly increases intraocular pressure. Symptoms and signs include a decrease in visual acuity, headache, red eye with mydriasis, a narrow angle in the anterior chamber, corneal edema (Plate 10), and a crescent shadow sign in the contralateral eye. Evaluation and treatment include acetazolamide and emergent referral to an ophthalmologist for laser iridotomy.

Glaucoma, open angle

Slow increase in intraocular pressure (IOP) due to obstruction to flow; risk factors are increasing age and anterior chamber trauma, especially a hyphema. Symptoms and signs include insidious visual loss (peripheral fields often affected more than central), scotomas, and a normal iridocorneal angle. Fundoscopy shows a deep, enlarged optic cup (>60% of the disc) and nasalization of the retinal vessels. Evaluation is with IOP measurement, obtaining formal sophisticated visual field assessment and optic nerve function testing. If IOP >20 mm Hg, refer the patient to an ophthalmologist for follow-up; if IOP >28 mm Hg, topical beta-blockers (e.g., timolol) are indicated.

Hard exudates

Leakage of fluid from retinal vessels into the retina due to hypertension or nonproliferative diabetic retinopathy. The condition is asymptomatic; signs include multiple small (usually a fraction of a disc diameter), yellow spots adjacent to the arterioles (Plate 18), with concurrent **microaneurysms** and flame hemorrhages. The patient should be referred to an ophthalmologist; treatment is specific to the underlying etiology.

Herpes simplex keratitis

Herpes simplex infection of the cornea. Symptoms and signs include unilateral decreased visual acuity, unilateral conjunctivitis, eyelid edema, a dendritic pattern of gray corneal ulcers (see Plate 13), and concurrent vesicular blepharitis. Fluorescein examination shows a dendritic pattern of ulcers in cobalt blue light. Evaluation and treatment include instillation of a cycloplegic agent (e.g., pilocarpine), systemic acyclovir therapy, and emergent referral to an ophthalmologist.

Herpes zoster keratitis

Herpes zoster infection of the cornea. Symptoms and signs include unilateral decreased visual acuity, unilateral keratitis and conjunctivitis, eyelid edema, and gray corneal pseudodendritic patches (see Plate 13), as well as a concurrent painful vesicular rash in the dermatone of V1. Fluorescein examination shows a pseudodendritic pattern in cobalt blue light. Evaluation and treatment include instillation of a cycloplegic agent (e.g., pilocarpine), systemic acyclovir therapy, and emergent referral to an ophthalmologist.

Heteronymous hemianopsia: See Visual field cuts.

Hollenhorst plaques
Cholesterol emboli in the vessels of the retina secondary to **carotid atherosclerotic disease**; highly correlated with cerebrovascular accidents (CVA) and retinal artery occlusion (Plate 21). Quite asymptomatic unless a concurrent cerebrovascular accident or retinal arterial occlusion is present; signs include the presence of yellow refractile dots in the retinal arterioles. Evaluation and treatment include assessment of the carotid arteries, ECG, echocardiogram, and referral to an internist.

Homonymous hemianopsia: See Visual field cuts.

Hordeolum
A small abscess in the upper or lower eyelid. **Internal hordeola** involve meibomian glands, deep from the palpebral margin; **external hordeola (sty)** involve the glands of Moll or Zeis, immediately adjacent to the palpebral margin. Symptoms and signs include a palpable, indurated area in the involved eyelid. Internal hordeola have a deep location (see Fig 3-5); external hordeola are located on the margin (Plate 22), with a central area of purulence and surrounding erythema. Concurrent conjunctivitis is common. Evaluation and treatment include warm compresses to the affected eye and topical antibiotics.

Hypertensive changes/retinopathy
Acquired changes in the vessels and background of the retina secondary to uncontrolled hypertension. Asymptomatic until advanced, signs include arteriovenous (AV) nicking, copper/silver wiring of retinal arterioles, flame and blot hemorrhages (Plate 17), and even papilledema (Plate 16). The KWB classification is correlated with the severity of the hypertension. Treatment is hypertension control.

Hyphema
Due to trauma to the eye (e.g., firecracker explosion near the eye), neovascularization of the iris, or malignant melanoma. Symptoms and signs include decrease in visual acuity and a blood level in the anterior chamber; open angle glaucoma is a late sequela. The patient should be emergently referred to an ophthalmologist.

Hypopyon
Due to corneal ulcer or anterior uveitis. Symptoms and signs include pain and pus level in the anterior chamber, as well as concurrent keratitis, corneal

ulcer, and anterior uveitis. The patient should be emergently referred to an ophthalmologist.

Icterus
Due to an elevated bilirubin (total bilirubin > 3 mg/dL) deposited in the conjunctivae. Symptoms and signs include a yellow discoloration of the conjunctivae overlying the sclera (Plate 14), in addition to the underlying etiology (see Liver Disease, p. 132). Treatment is directed toward the underlying hemolytic or hepatic disorder.

Inferior oblique palsy: See Strabismus.

Keratoconjunctivitis sicca (Sjögrens): See Sjögren's, p. 39.

Lateral rectus defect: See Strabismus.

Malignant melanoma
Primary is in the uvea, including the choroid and iris; quite rare. The condition is asymptomatic until late. Signs of a lesion in the choroid include an elevated, slate-gray lesion in the fundus with uneven pigment, as well as concurrent vitreous bleeding; signs include, if primary, in the iris, a raised, pigmented lesion with increased vessels (see Plate 7), as well as distortion of the pupil poikiloscoria and a hyphema. The patient should be referred to an ophthalmologist.

Microaneurysms
Microaneurysms are associated with hypertensive and nonproliferative diabetic retinopathy. Symptoms and signs include red bumps or bulges in the retinal arteries, often adjacent to branch points. Evaluation and treatment are referral to ophthalmology and control of the underlying condition.

Miosis
Constriction of the pupil(s). Bilateral miosis is secondary to the physiologic effect of light or due to narcotic use (see Fig 3-2); unilateral miosis (i.e., anisocoria) is secondary to Horner's syndrome. Symptoms and signs are referable to the underlying condition, for example, Horner's miosis, ptosis, and anhidrosis. Evaluate and treat the underlying disorder; for example, obtain a chest radiograph and assess neck structures.

Monocular blindness
Complete loss of vision in one eye. The most common etiologies are trauma, retinal detachment, hemorrhage into the vitreous (Plate 20), retinal vein thrombosis (Plate 19), central retinal artery thrombosis (Plate 21), acute angle glaucoma (Plate 10), and temporal arteritis. Symptoms and signs are referable to the underlying diagnosis. In all cases, emergent referral to an ophthalmologist is indicated.

Mydriasis

Dilation of the pupils. Bilateral mydriasis is secondary to catecholamines or medullary-level coma; unilateral mydriasis may be due to Argyll Robertson pupil (see Fig 3-2), **topical mydriatics**, acute angle glaucoma, or uncal herniation. Symptoms and signs are referable to the underlying diagnosis. Treatment is directed toward the underlying etiology, and referral to a neurologist is indicated.

Neovascularization: See Soft exudates.

Nevi/freckles (in iris)

Most commonly a normal variant but may be due to neurofibromatosis, Down syndrome, or malignant melanoma. Symptoms and signs include one or more pigmented or hypopigmented collections in the substance of the iris (may be bilateral); in **neurofibromatosis** (Lisch nodules), the collections are based on the circumference of the iris, with concurrent café au lait spots on the skin and neurofibromas; in Down syndrome, there are hypopigmented areas (Brushfield's spots) in the iris; in malignant melanoma, there are pigmented areas as well as a change in the shape of the iris (Plate 7) and hyphema. Evaluation and treatment include referral to an ophthalmologist.

Neurofibromatosis (Lisch nodules): See Nevi/freckles (in iris).

Orbital cellulitis

Due to contiguous spread of sinusitis, maxillary tooth infection, or facial infection with *Streptococcus*, anaerobes, or *Staphylococcus*. Symptoms and signs include swelling of the orbital tissue, exophthalmos, fever, **chemosis**, injection, and ophthalmoplegia; the eyelids often are swollen shut. Evaluation includes CT scan of the orbit; treatment is with parenteral antibiotics and referral to an infectious disease specialist.

Palsy of cranial nerve III, IV, or VI: See Strabismus.

Papilledema

The swelling/inflammation of the optic disc due to intracranial edema or optic neuritis. Head trauma, skull fractures, cerebral edema, hypertensive emergency, SLE, and multiple sclerosis are potential etiologies. Symptoms and signs are as demonstrated in Plates 15 and 16 and also are referable to the underlying etiology. Referral to an ophthalmologist is indicated as well as emergent head CT and adequate control of any underlying hypertension.

Photocoagulation: See Soft exudates.

Pinguecula

Benign collection of adipose tissue in the conjunctivae; risk factors include ultraviolet (UV) light exposure and increasing age. Asymptomatic; signs include one or more yellow papules medial or lateral to the cornea, often bilateral. Evaluation and treatment include recognition and reassurance.

Preseptal cellulitis

Infection of the structures anterior to the orbital septum with *Streptococcus* or *Staphylococcus*, due to a sty, cut, or insect bite. Symptoms and signs include swelling and tenderness with erythema in the affected eyelid (Plate 23), but no exophthalmos or ophthalmoplegia. Evaluation and treatment include systemic, usually oral, antibiotics and local warm compresses.

Pterygium

Exuberant growth of connective tissue in the conjunctivae; risk factors include UV light exposure, chronic irritation, and increasing age. The condition is asymptomatic; signs include triangular yellow plaques in the area medial to the cornea (may be over the cornea; see Fig 3-4), often bilateral. If the condition is bothersome to the patient, he or she can be referred to an ophthalmologist.

Refractory problems

Due to changes in eyeball length or lens refractive capacity. Specific conditions are as follows:

> **Myopia:** "Nearsighted"; unable to see at a distance, eyeball is long, image is in front of the retina
>
> **Hyperopia:** "Farsighted"; unable to see near, eyeball is short, image is behind the retina
>
> **Astigmatism:** Asymmetric defect in the cornea or lens
>
> **Presbyopia:** Age-related myopia

Symptoms and signs include headaches in the afternoon, blurred vision, and decreased night vision. The retina is normal. The Snellen chart result is 20/40 or greater in myopia. Refer the patient to an ophthalmologist or optometrist for spectacles or contact lenses.

Retinal detachment

Separation of the neurosensory retina from the retinal pigmented epithelium; risks include myopic thinning of the peripheral retina, trauma, or diabetes-related vitreous bleeds. Symptoms include painless monocular blindness, a "curtain" of floaters/flashes being drawn over the visual field from top to bottom. Fundoscopic examination shows a gray membrane floating in the vitreous, with or without hemorrhage, most commonly at the superior temporal retina. Evaluation and treatment include complete bed rest and referral to an ophthalmologist.

Roth's (Litten's) spots: See Soft exudates.

Scotoma: See Visual field cuts.

Soft exudates

Destruction of retinal tissue via infarctions due to diabetic retinopathy, or septic emboli from endocarditis, or **infectious chorioretinitis** (from CMV, histoplasma, or toxoplasma), or **autoimmune chorioretinitis** (from SLE). Symptoms include decreased vision with scotomas. Fundoscopy shows large (up to several disc diameters) pale to yellow areas (Plate 17), adjacent areas of increased pigment when healing, and adjacent **neovascularization** and bleeding in diabetic retinopathy. Several uniform circular black areas at the periphery of the fundus appearing concurrently are indicative of therapeutic laser **photocoagulation**. **Roth's spots** of endocarditis have a rim of red. The patient should be referred to an ophthalmologist; treatment is specific to the underlying etiology.

Strabismus

A weakness **(esophoria, exophoria)** or a paralysis **(esotropia, exotropia)** of one or more of the extraocular muscles, due to a congenital defect, an orbital fracture, or trauma-related **CN III, IV, or VI palsy**. Symptoms include headaches and double vision; signs include loss of one or more components of EOM (tropia) (see Fig 7-6) or a positive cover test (phoria). Refer the patient to an ophthalmologist.

Subconjunctival hemorrhage

Benign spontaneous bleeding in the visceral conjunctiva. Symptoms and signs include a painless red macule on the sclera of one eye and no change in visual acuity. Treatment is with reassurance.

Superficial punctate keratitis/actinic keratitis/chemical burns

Desiccation due to Bell's palsy, chemical exposure to acidic or basic substances, or actinic (UV) damage from welding, snow blindness, or looking at the sun during a total eclipse. Symptoms and signs include bilateral eye pain and photophobia, decreased visual acuity, nonpurulent conjunctivitis, and a normal anterior chamber. Fluorescein staining shows a superficial punctate pattern in cobalt blue light. Evaluation and treatment include lavage for a chemical burn, instillation of a cycloplegic agent and a patch to the affected eye(s), and referral to an ophthalmologist.

Superior oblique defect: See Strabismus.

Temporal arteritis

Granulomatous vasculitis of the middle-sized arteries, especially branches of the external carotid artery. Symptoms include unilateral headaches, jaw claudication on mastication, and monocular blindness; signs include tenderness to palpation over the ipsilateral temporal artery, proximal muscle weakness, and waddling gait. Evaluation includes erythrocyte sedimentation rate (ESR)—usually >100 minutes—and referral to an ENT specialist for temporal artery biopsy; treatment includes systemic steroids and referral to a rheumatologist.

Topical mydriatics: See Mydriasis.

Visual field cuts

Due to open angle glaucoma, optic nerve damage at the optic chiasm (sella turcica tumor), or CVA of the optic cortex. Symptoms and signs are specific to the underlying etiology: arcuate **scotoma** in open angle glaucoma, **bitemporal hemianopsia** (the most common **heteronymous hemianopsia**) in optic chiasm tumors, and **homonymous hemianopsia** or quadranopsia in contralateral optic tract or cortex lesions. Evaluation includes formal visual field mapping by an ophthalmologist, IOP measurement, and CT scan of the head. For any tumor, refer the patient to a neurosurgeon.

Vitreous hemorrhage

Due to either trauma, retinal detachment, or severe proliferative diabetic retinopathy. Symptoms and signs include a marked decrease in visual acuity; fundoscopic examination shows blood (Plate 20) often precluding complete imaging of the retina, and concurrent diabetic retinopathy or retinal detachment is common. Emergent referral to an ophthalmologist is indicated.

CHAPTER 4
Cardiology

Basic Examination

Palpate chest wall

PROCEDURE: With the patient in the left lateral decubital position (Fig 4-1), place your dominant hand on several sites in the left and then the right parasternal area. Palpate the chest wall with the palmar surface of the digits and palm of the hand.

OUTCOME: If there is palpable elevation of the chest wall with each systole in the left midclavicular line, in the fourth intercostal space, approximately the size of a quarter:
◆ **normal point of maximal impulse (PMI); apex**
If the PMI is inferior or lateral to the fourth space:
◆ **left ventricular enlargement**
If PMI is larger than a quarter (coin):
◆ **left ventricular enlargement**
If there is diffuse elevation on the left parasternal side with each systole; not contiguous with the PMI: ◆ **heave**
If diffuse elevation on the right parasternal side with each systole: ◆ **lift of right ventricular failure**
If a vibratory sensation is present:
◆ **thrill (i.e., 4/6, 5/6, or 6/6 murmur)**

Auscult chest; note and grade intensity of murmur

PROCEDURE: With the patient in a left lateral decubital position (see Fig 4-1), auscult the murmur using the diaphragm. Grade the intensity.

OUTCOME: If murmur is heard, but only after listening carefully for 10 seconds (softer than S_1 and S_2): ◆ **1/6**
If heard immediately after placing a stethoscope on the chest (same intensity as S_1 and S_2): ◆ **2/6**
If loud but without a thrill (louder than S_1 and S_2): ◆ **3/6**
If loud and with a thrill: ◆ **4/6**
If heard with the stethoscope placed at an angle on the chest, with a thrill: ◆ **5/6**
If heard without a stethoscope, with a thrill: ◆ **6/6**

Auscult murmur; note position in cycle and site where it is loudest

PROCEDURE: With patient in 20 degrees of left lateral decubital position (see Fig 4-1), auscult over the base and apex using the diaphragm. The patient should be breathing at baseline. The normal order of

Figure 4-1 Left lateral decubital position. Best position to hear and thus examine and feel the apex and S_1.

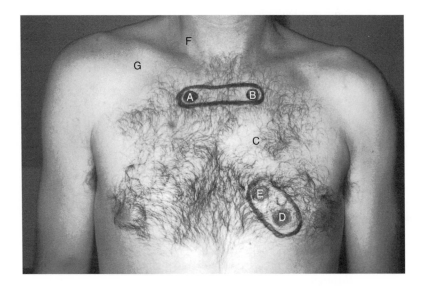

Figure 4-2 Base of heart. On right base is the A, aortic valve; on the left base is the B, pulmonic valve; C, left midsternal border site. Apex of heart: at the midclavicular line, fourth interspace is D, mitral valve, and E, tricuspid valve. F, right carotid area; G, right infraclavicular area.

valvular closure is MTAP: mitral, tricuspid, aortic, pulmonic (Fig 4-2).

OUTCOME: If there is a systolic murmur loudest at base (see Fig 4-2A,B):
- ◆ aortic stenosis (see Fig 4-2A)
- ◆ aortic sclerosis (see Fig 4-2A)

◆ idiopathic hypertrophic subaortic stenosis (IHSS), also known as *asymmetric septal hypertrophy* (ASH) or HOCUM (see Fig 4-2A)
◆ pulmonic stenosis (see Fig 4-2B)

If diastolic murmur loudest at base:
◆ aortic insufficiency (see Fig 4-2A)

If diastolic murmur loudest at apex:
◆ mitral stenosis (see Fig 4-2D)

If systolic murmur loudest at apex (see Fig 4-2D,E):
◆ mitral regurgitation (see Fig 4-2D)
◆ tricuspid regurgitation (see Fig 4-2E)
◆ mitral valve prolapse (MVP; see Fig 4-2D)

If diastolic sound at apex (see Fig 4-2D,E), not a murmur:
◆ S_3 gallop
◆ S_4 gallop
◆ opening snap (OS)

If systolic sound at apex (see Fig 4-2D,E), not a murmur:
◆ click of MVP

If systolic sound at base (see Fig 4-2A,B), not a murmur:
◆ split S_2

If sound of creaky leather, systole, and/or diastole:
◆ pericardial rub

Auscult for radiation

PROCEDURE: Using the diaphragm, auscult the carotids, left axilla, and left scapula. Note the site of radiation of the murmur from the location where it is loudest.

OUTCOME: If there is no radiation: ◆ nonspecific finding
If there is a systolic murmur from the base into the right neck and clavicle (see Fig 4-2F,G): ◆ aortic stenosis
If systolic murmur from apex into the axilla:
◆ mitral regurgitation
If systolic murmur from apex into the left paravertebral area (i.e., through to the back):
◆ mitral regurgitation
◆ ventricular septal defect (VSD)

Advanced Examination

APPROACH TO A PATIENT WITH A MURMUR OF EQUAL INTENSITY AT BASE AND APEX

Auscult base after premature ventricular complex

PROCEDURE: Auscult using the diaphragm over the base, listening for the murmur after a premature ventricular complex. (One obviously needs to have the patient on a cardiac monitor.)

OUTCOME: If the murmur increases in intensity after the extrasystole:
- ◆ **loudest at the base**

If remains the same intensity after the extrasystole:
- ◆ **loudest at the apex**

Auscult base before and during hand grip

PROCEDURE: With the patient supine and breathing at baseline, auscult over the base using the diaphragm, before and during hand grip. For hand grip, instruct the patient to forcibly make fists with both hands.

OUTCOME: If there is an increase in systolic murmur:
- ◆ **excludes a lesion at the base**

If a decrease in systolic murmur: ◆ **excludes a lesion at the apex**

Auscult base of heart with patient standing or sitting

PROCEDURE: Auscult with the diaphragm over the base of heart with the patient standing or sitting and leaning forward (Fig 4-3).

OUTCOME: If the sound or murmur is louder: ◆ **finding is from the base**

If the sound or murmur is same:
- ◆ **finding is probably from the apex**

APPROACH TO A PATIENT WITH A SYSTOLIC MURMUR LOUDEST AT BASE

Auscult second interspace

PROCEDURE: With the patient upright, slightly leaning forward and breathing at baseline, auscult over the base with the diaphragm. Pay attention to the specific site at which the murmur is loudest.

OUTCOME: If the murmur is loudest in the left second interspace (see Fig 4-2B): ◆ **pulmonic stenosis**

If loudest in the right second interspace (see Fig 4-2A):
- ◆ **aortic stenosis**
- ◆ **aortic sclerosis**

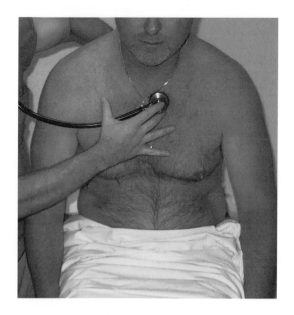

Figure 4-3 Site to auscult base with patient leaning forward. Note diaphragm of stethoscope placed over the right base, that is, the aortic valve. This position is best to listen for the second heart sound (S_2) and for any mischief at the base.

Determine any radiation of murmur into right infraclavicular area

PROCEDURE: With the patient upright, slightly leaning forward and breathing at baseline, auscult using the diaphragm over the right midinfra-clavicular area (see Fig 4-2G). Describe and detail any radiation of the murmur.

OUTCOME: If there is no radiation into the infraclavicular area:
   ◆ **aortic sclerosis**
   If radiation into the infraclavicular area: ◆ **aortic stenosis**

Determine any radiation of murmur into right carotid area

PROCEDURE: With the patient upright, slightly leaning forward and breathing at baseline, auscult using the diaphragm over the right carotid area (see Fig 4-2F).

OUTCOME: If there is no radiation of the murmur: ◆ **aortic sclerosis**
   If radiation of the murmur: ◆ **aortic stenosis**

Calculate pulse pressure

PROCEDURE: Measure the blood pressure by auscultation. Determine the pulse pressure—the difference between the systolic and diastolic blood pressures.

OUTCOME: If normal (40–60 mm Hg): ◆ **aortic sclerosis**
If narrow (<40 mm Hg): ◆ **aortic stenosis**

Auscult base, listening for splitting of second heart sound

PROCEDURE: With the patient upright, slightly leaning forward (see Fig 4-3) and breathing at baseline, auscult over the base using the diaphragm with patient in full expiration, then full inspiration. Pay attention to the second heart sound.

OUTCOME: If there is S_2 splitting in inspiration that resolves in expiration (physiologic splitting) (Fig 4-4A):
◆ **aortic sclerosis; this is also the normal finding**
If S_2 splitting in expiration that resolves in inspiration (paradoxical splitting; Fig 4-4B): ◆ **aortic stenosis**

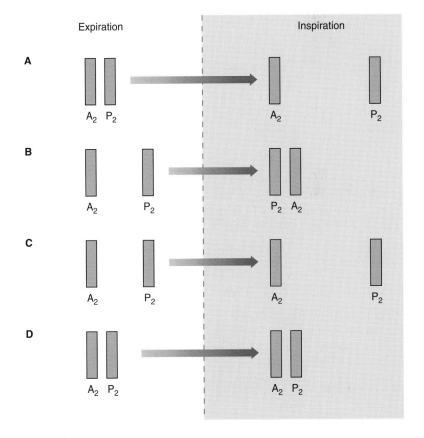

Figure 4-4 Splitting of the second heart sound. A. Physiologic. B. Paradoxical. C. Fixed and wide. D. Fixed and narrow.

Palpate carotid arteries

PROCEDURE: With the patient supine and breathing at baseline, gently palpate each of the carotid arteries; palpate deep to the sternocleidomastoid and feel pulse for 10 beats, then perform on other side. Use yourself for a control.

OUTCOME: If the carotid/arterial upstroke is brisk (Fig 4-5A):
- ◆ **aortic sclerosis**

If slow and low (pulsus parvus et tardus; Fig 4-5B):
- ◆ **aortic stenosis**

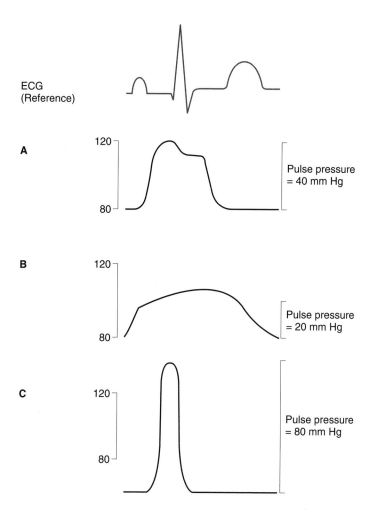

Figure 4-5 Pulse wave forms. A. Normal. B. Pulsus parvus et tardus. C. Corrigan's pulse. ECG, electrocardiogram.

Palpate for brachioradial delay

PROCEDURE: With the patient supine or sitting, simultaneously palpate the brachial and radial pulses in one upper extremity.

OUTCOME: If the palpable pulses are simultaneously felt:
- ◆ aortic sclerosis
- ◆ aortic stenosis, mild

If radial pulse is delayed, relative to the brachial pulse:
- ◆ aortic stenosis, severe

Sensitivity of procedure: 100% (17/17) for severe aortic stenosis; 25% (6/16) for mild aortic stenosis.[1]

Auscult base after patient stands from squatting position

PROCEDURE: With the patient squatting and breathing at baseline, auscult using the diaphragm over the base, then auscult again 30 seconds after the patient assumes a standing position.

OUTCOME: If murmur intensity is increased (louder):
- ◆ asymmetric septal hypertrophy (ASH; also known as IHSS or HOCUM)

If decreased (softer):
- ◆ aortic stenosis
- ◆ aortic sclerosis

Auscult base after patient squats from standing position

PROCEDURE: With the patient standing and breathing at baseline, auscult using the diaphragm over the base, then auscult over the base, then auscult again after the patient assumes a squatting position.

OUTCOME: If murmur intensity increases with squatting (louder):
- ◆ aortic stenosis

If there is no change with squatting: ◆ aortic sclerosis
If murmur intensity decreases with squatting (softer):
- ◆ ASH (also known as IHSS or HOCUM)

Auscult heart and palpate carotid artery for pulse

PROCEDURE: With patient supine and breathing at baseline, gently palpate over the right carotid artery; concurrently, auscult using diaphragm over apex.

OUTCOME: If there are two short staccato beats—palpated/ausculted heart tones (pulsus bisfiriens):
- ◆ ASH (also known as IHSS or HOCUM)
- ◆ aortic stenosis with aortic insufficiency (combination)

If no such finding: ◆ normal

Auscult base and listen for murmur after extrasystole

PROCEDURE: With the patient supine and breathing at baseline, auscult using the diaphragm over the base, paying special attention to the murmur in the beat immediately after an extrasystole.

OUTCOME: If murmur intensity decreases after an extrasystole (softer):
♦ **ASH (also known as *IHSS* or *HOCUM*)**
If increases after an extrasystole (louder): ♦ **aortic stenosis**

Palpate carotid or radial artery for pulse after extrasystole

PROCEDURE: With the patient supine and breathing at baseline, palpate the pulse in the carotid or radial artery, or both, noting the pulse intensity immediately after an extrasystole.

OUTCOME: If there is a decrease in the palpable pulse after extrasystole: (Brockenbrough sign): ♦ **ASH (also known as *IHSS* or *HOCUM*)**
If no change in the palpable pulse after extrasystole:
♦ **aortic stenosis**

APPROACH TO A PATIENT WITH A DIASTOLIC MURMUR LOUDEST AT BASE

Calculate pulse pressure

PROCEDURE: Take the blood pressure by auscultation. Measure the difference between the systolic and diastolic blood pressure to arrive at the pulse pressure.

OUTCOME: If <40 mm Hg:
♦ **aortic insufficiency, mild**
♦ **normal**
If >40 mm Hg: ♦ **aortic insufficiency, severe**

Palpate carotid and femoral arteries for pulse wave form

PROCEDURE: With the patient supine and breathing at baseline, gently palpate the right carotid artery, feeling for the pulse wave form. Repeat, using the femoral arteries. Use your own corresponding pulses as controls.

OUTCOME: If there is bounding (short waves, high amplitude) (see Fig 4-5C):
♦ **aortic insufficiency**
♦ **hyperdynamic state**

Observe uvula for Mueller's sign

PROCEDURE: Instruct the patient to open mouth. Use a direct light source to inspect the uvula at rest for 10 seconds.

OUTCOME: If there are no rhythmic movements: ♦ **normal**
If rhythmic movements with each systole (Mueller's sign):
♦ **aortic insufficiency**

Auscult at apex for Austin Flint sign

PROCEDURE: With the patient supine and breathing at baseline, auscult over the apex (see Fig 4-2D,E) with the diaphragm.

OUTCOME: If there is a mid-late diastolic murmur at the apex and a concurrent diastolic murmur loudest at the base (Austin Flint sign):
◆ **aortic insufficiency, severe**
If no such finding: ◆ **aortic insufficiency, mild**

Auscult before and after sphygmomanometer is inflated over systolic blood pressure

PROCEDURE: With the patient supine and breathing at baseline, place a sphygmomanometer on the arm at 20 to 40 mm Hg above the systolic blood pressure for 20 seconds. Auscult over the base using the diaphragm before and during maneuver.

OUTCOME: If the murmur is increased after the maneuver:
◆ **aortic insufficiency, moderate to severe**
If murmur is unchanged:
◆ **aortic insufficiency, mild**
◆ **another diagnosis**

Observe head for de Musset's sign

PROCEDURE: While the patient sits with head forward in a relaxed position, visually inspect the patient's head for any involuntary movements.

OUTCOME: If there is head-bobbing—a forward movement at the beginning of each heartbeat: ◆ **aortic insufficiency, severe**
If no head-bobbing movements: ◆ **normal**

Examine nail beds for Quincke's sign

PROCEDURE: Exert pressure on the edge of a fingernail or toenail, so as to barely blanch the nail bed. Visually observe the movements of the pink/white interface.

OUTCOME: If there are pulsations at the red/white border (Quincke's sign):
◆ **aortic insufficiency, moderate to severe**
If no pulsations at the border: ◆ **normal**

APPROACH TO A PATIENT WITH A DIASTOLIC MURMUR LOUDEST AT APEX

Auscult apex, paying attention to diastole

PROCEDURE: With patient in 20-degree left lateral decubital position (see Fig 4-1) and breathing at baseline, auscult over the apex using the diaphragm. Listen specifically during the time before the diastolic murmur.

OUTCOME: If there is a diastolic snap sound early in diastole (opening snap): ◆ **mitral stenosis**
If no such sound: ◆ **another diagnosis**

Inspect skin of face

PROCEDURE: Visually inspect the skin of the patient's face.

OUTCOME: If there is a rhythmic malar flush with each systole:
♦ **mitral stenosis**
If no such flush: ♦ **another diagnosis**

APPROACH TO A PATIENT WITH A SYSTOLIC MURMUR LOUDEST AT APEX

Auscult in left axilla

PROCEDURE: With the patient in 20-degree left lateral decubitus position (see Fig 4-1) and breathing at baseline, auscult using the diaphragm in the left axilla.

OUTCOME: If there is no radiation of the murmur: ♦ **tricuspid regurgitation**
If radiation of the murmur: ♦ **mitral regurgitation**

Auscult apex during held inspiration (Rivero-Carvallo maneuver)

PROCEDURE: With the patient supine and breathing at baseline, auscult over the apex with the diaphragm at end of expiration and then during a deep, held inspiration.

OUTCOME: If murmur intensity is increased with inspiration (Rivero-Carvallo sign): ♦ **tricuspid regurgitation**
100% sensitivity, 88% specificity; PPV: 67%[2]
If remains the same or is diminished:
♦ **mitral regurgitation**
♦ **MVP**
♦ **VSD**

Auscult apex, palpate over liver

PROCEDURE: With the patient supine and breathing at baseline, auscult over the apex with the diaphragm before and during the placement of pressure on the liver using the right hand for 15 to 20 seconds.

OUTCOME: If there is an increase in murmur intensity (Vitum's sign):
♦ **tricuspid regurgitation**
56% sensitive, 100% specific[3]
If no change in the murmur:
♦ **mitral regurgitation**
♦ **MVP**

Visually inspect jugular venous pulsations

PROCEDURE: With the patient supine and at rest, visually inspect the jugular venous pulsations (JVP), paying attention to the end of the pulsations (i.e., the y descent; Fig 4-6).

OUTCOME: If there are large v waves with great y descents on the jugular venous pulsation (Lancisi's sign):
♦ **tricuspid regurgitation (Fig 4-6C)**
If no such large v waves:
♦ **mitral regurgitation (Fig 4-6A)**
♦ **MVP**

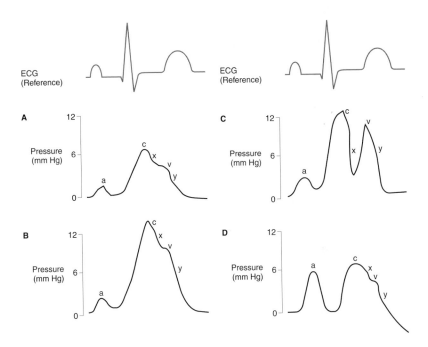

Figure 4-6 **Jugular venous pressure tracing. A.** Normal: *a* wave, atrial contraction; *c* wave, bulging of tricuspid cusps into the right atrium at the beginning of each systole; *x* descent, relaxation of the right atrium; *v* wave, volume of blood that enters the right atrium during ventricular systole; *y* descent, rapid flow of blood into the right ventricle upon opening of the tricuspid valve. **B.** Right ventricular failure: overall increase in jugular venous pulsations and merging of *c* and *v* waves. **C.** Tricuspid regurgitation: overall increase in pressure and marked increase in the magnitude of the *x* descent, resulting in separate *c* and *v* waves. **D.** Canon *a* waves: marked increase in *a* wave intensity with no increase in jugular venous pulsations (found in AV dissociation).

Palpate liver for pulsations

PROCEDURE: With the patient supine and breathing at baseline, place your hands with fingers outstretched around the entire liver with the fingers on the periphery, palpating for any liver pulsations.

OUTCOME: If the liver is pulsatile (rhythmically expansile):
◆ **tricuspid regurgitation**
If nonpulsatile:
◆ **mitral regurgitation**
◆ **mitral valve prolapse**

Inspect right earlobe

PROCEDURE: With the patient sitting upright, visually inspect the right earlobe.

OUTCOME: If the right earlobe bobs or "blinks" with each heartbeat (blinking right earlobe sign): ◆ **tricuspid regurgitation**
If there is no such finding:
◆ **mitral regurgitation**
◆ **MVP**

Auscult apex: systolic sounds

PROCEDURE: With the patient in 20-degree left lateral decubital position (see Fig 4-1) and breathing at baseline, auscult using the diaphragm over the apex, listening for sounds around the systolic murmur.

OUTCOME: If there is a click before the murmur in systole: ◆ **MVP**
If no systolic click:
◆ **mitral regurgitation**
◆ **tricuspid regurgitation**

Auscult apex, supine then standing

PROCEDURE: With the patient in 20-degree left lateral decubital position (see Fig 4-1) and breathing at baseline, auscult using the diaphragm over the apex. Then instruct the patient to assume a standing position, wait 15 seconds, and auscult over the apex with the diaphragm.

OUTCOME: If the click and the murmur increase with standing: ◆ **MVP**
If there is no change in the murmur with standing:
◆ **mitral regurgitation**
◆ **tricuspid regurgitation**

APPROACH TO A PATIENT WITH SECOND HEART SOUND SPLITTING

Auscult base, listening for S_2 variations with respiration

PROCEDURE: With the patient sitting or standing upright and slightly leaning forward (see Fig 4-3), auscult using the diaphragm over the base, specifically in the left second and third intercostal spaces. Instruct the patient to inhale deeply and hold the breath for 10 seconds, then exhale deeply and hold breath.

OUTCOME: If, on inspiration, S_2 splits so that A_2 is earlier and P_2 is later (see Fig 4-4A): ◆ **physiologic splitting**
If, on inspiration, S_2 splits so that P_2 comes before A_2 (see Fig 4-4B): ◆ **paradoxical splitting**
If there is a wide unchanging split during both inspiration and expiration (see Fig 4-4C): ◆ **widely fixed splitting**
If narrow unchanging splitting of S_2 (see Fig 4-4D):
◆ **narrowly fixed splitting**

APPROACH TO A PATIENT WITH GALLOP/DIASTOLIC SOUNDS

Perform basic auscultation: As in Basic Examination.

Auscult apex with bell

PROCEDURE: With the patient in 20-degree left lateral decubital position (see Fig 4-1) and breathing at baseline, auscult over the apex using the bell.

OUTCOME: If there are no diastolic sounds: ◆ **normal**
If there is a low-frequency sound, S_3: ◆ **systolic heart failure**
If low-frequency sound, S_4:
  ◆ **ischemia**
  ◆ **left ventricular hypertrophy (LVH)**
  ◆ **diastolic heart failure**

Palpate apex, point of maximal impulse for gallops

PROCEDURE: With the patient in 20-degree left lateral decubital position (see Fig 4-1) and breathing at baseline, palpate the PMI for any gallops.

OUTCOME: If the gallop is easily palpable: ◆ S_4
If difficult to palpate: ◆ S_3

Auscult gallop and note intensity during extrasystole

PROCEDURE: With the patient in 20-degree left lateral decubital position (see Fig 4-1) and breathing at baseline, auscult using the bell over the apex while listening specifically for the gallop during an extrasystole.

OUTCOME: If the gallop remains: ◆ S_3
If gallop disappears: ◆ S_4

Auscult gallop in patient with atrial fibrillation or VVI pacemaker

PROCEDURE: With the patient in 20-degree left lateral decubital position (see Fig 4-1) and breathing at baseline, auscult using the bell over the apex. Pay attention to the rhythm and its effect on the diastolic sound.

OUTCOME: If the rhythm is irregularly irregular (atrial fibrillation): ◆ S_3
If patient is known to have a VVI-paced rhythm: ◆ S_3

APPROACH TO A PATIENT WITH POTENTIAL PERIPHERAL ARTERIAL DISEASE

Palpate various arteries

PROCEDURE: Place the tips of the index and third fingers on the sites of the arteries. Note the presence and intensity of the pulses, especially in the feet. Use the contralateral side as a control.

OUTCOME: If the pulse is not detectable:
  ◆ **atherosclerosis**
  ◆ **embolic events**
  ◆ **intermittent claudication**

If barely detectable: ◆ **normal**
If easily detectable: ◆ **normal**
If bounding:
   ◆ **hyperdynamic state**
   ◆ **aortic insufficiency**

Auscult carotid arteries

PROCEDURE: While the patient is sitting or supine and at the midpoint of respiration, auscult, using the bell made into a diaphragm by firmly placing it on the skin (Fig 4-7) over the area immediately medial to the sternocleidomastoid muscles. Pay attention to the area inferior to the angle of the mandible.

OUTCOME: If a systolic bruit is present:
   ◆ **atherosclerosis of carotid artery**
   ◆ **systolic murmur, transmitted from the base**
Highly correlated with coronary arterial disease
If there is no bruit: ◆ **normal**

Auscult femoral arteries

PROCEDURE: While the patient is supine with the thighs slightly abducted, auscult gently and without applying any pressure using the diaphragm immediately over the femoral arterial pulse; perform again on the contralateral side.

OUTCOME: If no bruit is present: ◆ **normal**
If a bruit is present: ◆ **atherosclerosis of the femoral artery**
If there are bilateral bruits:
   ◆ **consider abdominal aortic aneurysm (see Chapter 6, p. 131)**

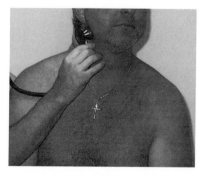

Figure 4-7 Carotid artery auscultation. Note that the bell of the stethoscope is placed gently in the skin overlying the angle formed by the sternocleidomastoid muscle and the inferior mandible.

Auscult abdomen for bruits

PROCEDURE: With the patient supine, auscult using the diaphragm in the areas superior and lateral to the umbilicus, bilaterally.

OUTCOME: If there is a systolic bruit:
   ◆ renal arterial stenosis
   ◆ abdominal aortic aneurysm
If no bruit: ◆ normal

Auscult posterior costovertebral angle

PROCEDURE: With the patient sitting, auscult using the diaphragm, over the costovertebral angles, bilaterally.

OUTCOME: If there is a systolic bruit in the costovertebral angle:
   ◆ renal arterial stenosis
If no bruit: ◆ normal

Measure blood pressure (BP) in both arms

PROCEDURE: Measure BP in the right upper extremity and left upper extremity. Note any differences.

OUTCOME: If there is <10 mm Hg difference between the measured systolic BPs: ◆ normal
If >20 mm Hg difference, with the right arm BP higher than the left arm BP: ◆ coarctation of the aorta

Measure rate of capillary refill

PROCEDURE: Apply direct pressure with a finger so as to blanch a capillary bed on the distal aspect of one of the patient's digits of the involved lower or upper extremity. Measure the time required for the pink color to return.

OUTCOME: If <1 second: ◆ normal
If >3 seconds:
   ◆ consistent with peripheral vascular disease, either atherosclerotic or embolic

APPROACH TO A PATIENT WITH SYNCOPE OR NEAR SYNCOPE

Examine vital signs: See Chapter 1, heart rate and blood pressure procedures; p. 1.

Perform basic cardiac auscultation: As in Basic Examination.

Measure blood pressure using orthostatic parameters

PROCEDURE: With the patient supine, perform a BP measurement and determine the pulse rate. Repeat these measurements after the patient has been standing for at least 1 minute. Query the patient as to any symptoms.

OUTCOME: If the systolic blood pressure (SBP) remains the same or decreases by <10%: ◆ normal

If the pulse increases by <10%: ◆ **normal**
If the SBP decreases by >10% and the pulse increases by >10%: ◆ **intravascular volume depletion**
If the SBP decreases by >10% and the pulse does not increase:
  ◆ **autonomic dysfunction (beta-blockade)**
If the patient subjectively feels weak and dizzy:
   ◆ **intravascular volume depletion**
   ◆ **autonomic dysfunction**

Weigh patient

PROCEDURE: Weigh the patient; compare to his/her weight at baseline.

OUTCOME: If the weight has increased: ◆ **heart failure**
If decreased: ◆ **intravascular volume depletion**
If unchanged: ◆ **nonspecific**

Pinch patient's skin (skin tenting)

PROCEDURE: Gently pinch the skin of the patient to make a "tent." Assess the duration of time required for it to flatten out to baseline.

OUTCOME: If there is tenting with increased time to flatten (poor turgor):
   ◆ **intravascular volume depletion**
   ◆ **increasing age**
If minimal tenting, quickly resolves over time (good turgor):
   ◆ **normal**

Feel for axillary and/or inguinal sweat

PROCEDURE: With a gloved hand, feel for moisture in the axillae and/or inguinal areas.

OUTCOME: If there is sweat in the axillae: ◆ **normal**
If sweat in the inguinal area: ◆ **normal**
If no sweat in the axillae/inguinal area:
   ◆ **intravascular volume depletion**
   ◆ **severe autonomic dysfunction**

APPROACH TO A PATIENT WITH PERIPHERAL EDEMA/VENOUS DISEASE

Inspect and measure jugular venous pulse (central venous pressure)

PROCEDURE: 1. Inspect the right neck with the patient supine, with the head turned slightly to the left. Look for the jugular vein:
Internal jugular vein: Posterior and superior to the medial third of the clavicle, goes deep to the sternocleidomastoid—difficult to see
External jugular vein: Crosses over the top of the sternocleidomastoid

  2. Move the patient from 0 (supine) to 90 degrees (sitting) so as to see the meniscus of the internal or external jugular vein.

3. If you are unable to differentiate the meniscus from carotid pulsation, instruct the patient to inhale deeply, which will either cause the meniscus to increase or decrease and thus facilitate location.

4. Once you have found the meniscus, use a straightedge to measure its height above the sternal angle. Add this height to the cardiologist's constant of 4 cm.

OUTCOME: If the measurement is <10 cm: ◆ **normal**
If the meniscus cannot be seen (i.e., no measured value, even with patient lying flat):
  ◆ **intravascular volume depletion**
  ◆ **profound elevation of central venous pressure (CVP)**
If the measurement is >10 cm: ◆ **elevated CVP**

Inspect pulsations in meniscus

PROCEDURE: Visually inspect the meniscus of the jugular venous pulse on the right by performing the procedure from step 1.

OUTCOME: If the pulsations are as described in Figure 4-6A: ◆ **normal**
If there is a *c*- and *v*-wave merger, that is, the elimination of the *x* descent (see Fig 4-6B): ◆ **right ventricular failure**
If large *v* wave with a great *y* descent on the jugular venous tracing (see Fig 4-6C): ◆ **tricuspid regurgitation**
If there are elevated *a* waves on a few beats, with intermittent normal *a* waves otherwise (see Fig 4-6D):
  ◆ **cannon a waves of atrioventricular (AV) dissociation, for example, third-degree AV block**

Observe veins of hands during von Recklinghausen's maneuver

PROCEDURE: With the patient supine, instruct him or her to place one hand palm down on the thigh and the other hand palm down on the bed (i.e., 5–10 cm inferior to the hand on the thigh). Note the veins in both hands.

OUTCOME: If the veins are engorged in both hands: ◆ **elevated CVP**
If engorged only in the lower hand: ◆ **normal**

Inspect sublingual veins

PROCEDURE: With the patient sitting, instruct him or her to open the mouth. Visually inspect the veins beneath the tongue.

OUTCOME: If the veins are engorged when upright:
  ◆ **elevated CVP**
  ◆ **may be normal variant**
If there are no varicosities: ◆ **normal**

Observe hepatojugular reflux in meniscus (Pasteur's procedure)

PROCEDURE: First, perform the procedure to inspect for the jugular central venous system (see above). After finding the meniscus, use palms of hands to press firmly on the right upper quadrant (liver area) for 30 to 60 seconds while carefully watching the meniscus.

OUTCOME: If there is an increase of the level of the meniscus by <4 cm:
- ◆ **normal**

If an increase of the meniscus by >4 cm: ◆ **right heart failure**

APPROACH TO A PATIENT WITH SUSPECTED PERICARDIAL DISEASE

Visually inspect jugular venous pulsations during inspiration and expiration

PROCEDURE: Visually inspect the jugular venous pulsations during inspiration and expiration. Note level of the venous meniscus and any changes with respiration.

OUTCOME: If the jugular venous pulsations decrease with inspiration:
- ◆ **normal**

If there is an elevation of jugular venous pressure during deep respiration (Kussmaul's sign):
- ◆ **constrictive pericarditis**
- ◆ **right heart failure**

Look for pulsus paradoxus

PROCEDURE: Using the auscultation method (with a sphygmomanometer), measure the patient's SBP at the end of inspiration and expiration.

OUTCOME: If the difference between the two SBP measurements is <10 mm Hg: ◆ **normal**

If >10 mm Hg:
- ◆ **right heart failure**
- ◆ **pericardial effusion, large, approaching tamponade**

Auscult over cardiac area

PROCEDURE: With the patient supine and breathing at baseline, auscult using the diaphragm over the heart.

OUTCOME: If the heart tones are distant: ◆ **pericardial effusion**
If there is a "creaky leather" sound (rub): ◆ **pericarditis**

Keys to Recording Findings

CARDIOVASCULAR

"RR, S1 S2 normal, no murmurs or gallops, PMI non-displaced"

A. Rhythm

Note if irregularly irregular: atrial fibrillation; regularly irregular; regular

B.

Note S1: best heard at apex: Mitral/tricuspid valves

Note S2: best heard at base: aortic/pulmonic valves

Note S2 split: Physiologic versus fixed versus paradoxic

Note Gallops: S3—heart failure; S4—stiff left ventricle; ischemia, hypertrophic

C. Murmurs

- Describe if in systole or diastole
- Describe if loudest in apex or base
- Note radiation of murmur
- Grade intensity of murmur

Without a thrill:

1: softer than S1 and S2 heart tones

2: same intensity as S1 and S2 heart tones

3: louder than the S1 and S2 heart tones

With a thrill:

4: Louder than the S1 and S2 heart tones

5: Very loud, able to hear with stethoscope 1/2 off

6: Can hear without a stethoscope

D. Neck veins

Normal versus not seen versus elevated; if elevated, describe any discernable pulse waves

E. Carotid pulses

Note impulse and any bruit at angle of sternocleidomastoid and mandible

A. Rhythm

Regular	☐
Regularly irregular	☐
Irregularly irregular: atrial fibrillation	☐

B. S1/S2/Gallop/Extra Sounds

S1: Apex: Mitral/tricuspid valves

S2: Base: aortic/pulmonic valves

C. Murmur

$$S_1 \qquad S_2 \qquad S_1$$

Loudest at apex or base; located in systole or diastole; draw on cycle; grade using system of 1 to 6.

D. Neck veins

Unable to see	☐
Not elevated	☐
Elevated	☐

_____ cm

E. Carotid pulses

		Left	Right
Impulse	Normal	☐	☐
	Bounding	☐	☐
	Pulsus parvus et tardus	☐	☐
Bruits present	Carotid	☐	☐

Diagnoses

Aortic insufficiency

Failure of the aortic valve to close completely during diastole because of a bicuspid aortic valve, endocarditis, or rheumatic fever. The condition is asymptomatic until relatively severe; signs include a diastolic murmur loudest at the base (see Fig 4-2A), increased pulse pressure, bounding (Corrigan's) pulse (see Fig 4-5C), positive Mueller's sign, positive de Musset's sign, and positive Quincke's sign. Severe signs include a laterally displaced PMI, S_4, and heart failure. Evaluation includes an echocardiogram to confirm; referral to a cardiologist and preprocedure antibiotic prophylaxis are indicated.

Aortic sclerosis

Calcium deposition in the valve cusps; prevalence is high, but it is quite benign. The condition is asymptomatic; signs include a systolic murmur loudest at the base (see Fig 4-2A), no radiation, no change in S_2, and a physiologic splitting of S_2 (see Fig 4-4A). No change occurs in the murmur with standing or squatting or after an extrasystole. The pulses waves are normal (see Fig 4-5A), and there is no evidence of left ventricular enlargement. Evaluation is clinical recognition; there is no treatment except follow-up examination.

Aortic stenosis

Stiffness and inability of the valve to open completely, with static outflow obstruction due to a bicuspid aortic valve, endocarditis, or rheumatic fever. The condition is asymptomatic until it becomes severe; then angina pectoris (AP), syncope, and heart failure are the prevalent symptoms. Signs include a systolic murmur loudest at the base (see Fig 4-2A) that radiates into the neck (see Fig 4-2F) and infraclavicular (see Fig 4-2G) area, with a decrease in the intensity of S_2 and a paradoxically split S_2 (see Fig 4-4B); the murmur decreases in intensity with standing, increases in intensity with squatting, and increases in intensity after an extrasystole. Signs of severe disease include laterally displaced PMI, S_4, pulsus parvus et tardus (see Fig 4-5B), and brachioradial delay. Evaluation includes an echocardiogram to confirm and demonstrate valve size; referral to a cardiologist and preprocedure antibiotic prophylaxis are indicated.

Asymmetric septal hypertrophy—also known as *IHSS, HOCUM*

Congenital abnormal thickening of the myocardium immediately inferior to the aortic valve in the ventricular septum with dynamic outflow obstruction. When severe, symptoms include AP, syncope, and heart failure; signs include a systolic murmur loudest at the base (see Fig 4-2A) that radiates into the neck (see Fig 4-2A,F), a decrease in the intensity of S_2, and a paradoxically split S_2 (see Fig 4-4B); the murmur increases in intensity with standing, decreases in intensity with squatting, and decreases after an extrasystole. Signs of severe disease include pulsus bisfiriens, a laterally displaced PMI, an S_4, or even an S_3. Evaluation includes an echocardiogram to confirm diagnosis; referral to a cardiologist and preprocedure antibiotic prophylaxis are indicated.

Atherosclerosis
Cholesterol-laden plaques in the arteries; risk factors include increased cholesterol, increased low-density lipoprotein (LDL), decreased high-density lipoprotein (HDL), hypertension, diabetes mellitus, a family history of premature atherosclerotic disease, obesity, smoking, and homocysteinemia. Symptoms include transient ischemic attacks (TIA), AP, and intermittent claudication (IC); signs include S_4, completed cerebrovascular accidents, heart failure, ischemic ulcers on extremities (Plate 24), peripheral arterial bruits, decreased peripheral pulses, and decreased capillary refill of digits. Carotid bruits (see Fig 4-7) are very highly correlated with significant coronary arterial disease. General evaluation and treatment include modification of risk factors and starting aspirin. For TIA, evaluate with a carotid duplex scan and refer the patient to a vascular surgeon; for AP, evaluate with an electrocardiogram (ECG) and stress test and refer the patient to a cardiologist; for IC, evaluate via an ankle-brachial index (ABI) and refer the patient to a vascular surgeon.

Atrial septal defect
Congenital failure of the septum between the atria to close. The condition is asymptomatic; the only signs are a systolic murmur loudest at the base (see Fig 4-2A,B) and a widely fixed split S_2 (see Fig 4-4C). Evaluation includes an ECG to look for incomplete or complete right bundle branch block (RBBB), as well as an echocardiogram to confirm. Treatment includes only clinical recognition; no preprocedure antibiotic prophylaxis is needed.

Atrioventricular dissociation
Atria and ventricles beating in independent rhythms, due to ventricular tachycardia, accelerated idioventricular rhythm, or third-degree (complete) heart block. Symptoms and signs include syncope or near syncope. Heart rate taken by pulse and auscultation may be bradycardic, normal, or tachycardic, and any gallop present is an S_3—never an S_4; JVP assessment is with cannon a waves (see Fig 4-6D). Evaluation includes an ECG to diagnose rhythm; treatment is with admission and emergent referral to a cardiologist for a pacemaker or antidysrhythmic agents.

Autonomic dysfunction
Due to iatrogenic (beta-blockade or end-stage) diabetes mellitus or Shy-Drager syndrome (autonomic dysfunction and Parkinson's disease). Symptoms and signs include dizziness and near syncope or syncope. Orthostatic parameters include a decreased SBP with no increase in heart rate, a lack of

sweating, but moist mucous membranes. In Shy-Drager syndrome, there are concurrent manifestations of Parkinson's disease. Evaluation and treatment include clinical recognition and referral to a neurologist.

Coarctation of the aorta

Narrowing of aorta, often just distal to the origin of the left subclavian artery, due to congenital defect (e.g., Turner's syndrome). Symptoms and signs include disparity in pulse intensity and BP between the left and right arm and between the arms and legs—the right arm has elevated BP, whereas the left arm and legs have a lower BP and diminished pulses. Other signs are palpable collateral arteries at the angles of the scapulae and in the axillae and a midsystolic murmur at the left base (see Fig 4-2A) and in the back between the scapulae. Evaluation includes a chest radiograph to look for inferior notching of the ribs due to collateral arteries and an echocardiogram. Referral to a cardiologist and preprocedure antibiotic prophylaxis are indicated.

Constrictive pericarditis

Thickened, fibrous area within the pericardial sac due to antecedent purulent pericarditis, malignant neoplastic disease, or mycobacterial pericardial disease; may result in heart failure due to a marked decrease in the venous return to the right heart. Symptoms include shortness of breath and platypnea; signs include systolic hypotension, an increase in jugular venous pulsations (see Fig 4-6B), pitting bipedal edema, hepatomegaly, pericardial rub, a pulsus paradoxus, and a positive Kussmaul's sign. Evaluation includes ECG, looking for small QRS complexes and electrical alterans, and an echocardiograph. Treatment includes referral to a cardiologist.

Diastolic heart failure: See Heart failure.

Elevated central venous pressure: See Heart failure.

Endocarditis

Bacterial infection, either with *Staphylococcus aureus*, which is virulent, often in intravenous drug abusers, and requires no antecedent valve damage; or with *Streptococcus* species (spp) that are less virulent, often due to dental procedures, and require a previously damaged valve. Symptoms include fevers, malaise, and back pain; signs include fevers spiking to 103°F, systolic heart failure, tricuspid regurgitation (see Fig 4-2E), and mitral or aortic regurgitation, or both (see Fig 4-2), as well as concurrent hematuria, **Janeway lesions (see p. 294), Osler's nodes,** and **Roth's spots (see p. 67).** Evaluation includes three to four sets of blood culture and an echocardiogram; treatment includes parenteral vancomycin and referral to an infectious disease consultant.

Heart failure

Decreased ability of the heart to pump blood and effectively perfuse the tissues. Specific types are as follows:

Diastolic heart failure: Decreased filling of ventricles; etiologies include left ventricular hypertrophy (LVH) due to severe hypertension, aortic stenosis, or insufficiency, or stiffening of the left ventricle due to ischemia.

Systolic heart failure: Decreased muscle contraction due to myocardial infarctions, drugs (e.g., daunorubicin), or severe chronic ethanol abuse; end stage diastolic failure will evolve into systolic failure.

Usually there are components of both diastolic and systolic failure. Symptoms include shortness of breath, orthopnea, and paroxysmal nocturnal dyspnea; signs such as increased central (jugular) venous pressure (see Fig 4-6B), crackles (rales), and cyanosis indicate backward failure, whereas systolic hypotension, decreased mental status, a Cheyne-Stokes breathing pattern (see Fig 1-1D, p. 2), and oliguria indicate forward failure. Signs for specific types are as follows:

Diastolic heart failure: laterally displaced PMI (see Fig 4-1) and fourth sound (S_4) gallop (see Fig 4-2D), along with concurrent AV nicking and, in long-standing severe hypertension, flame hemorrhages in the retina (Plates 15, 17, and 19); systolic murmur is loudest at base in aortic stenosis; diastolic murmur is loudest at base (see Fig 4-2A) in aortic insufficiency.

Systolic heart failure: laterally displaced PMI, a **heave** or **lift**, and a third sound (S_3) **gallop.**

Evaluation includes an ECG and an echocardiogram to assess the function of the valves, myocardium, and pericardium. The underlying disorder should be treated and the patient referred to a cardiologist.

Heave: See Heart failure.

HOCUM: See Asymmetric septal hypertrophy.

Hyperdynamic state

Dramatic increase in cardiac output due to either an increase in metabolism (hyperthyroidism or fever) or a decrease in resistance to blood flow (anemia or sepsis). Symptoms and signs include tachycardia, increased pulse pressure, bounding pulses, and systolic flow murmurs. Other findings are specific to the underlying etiology: for *hyperthyroidism*, goiter and tremor (see p. 34); for *anemia*, pallor; and for *sepsis*, hypotension and fever. Evaluation includes checking the thyroid-stimulating hormone (TSH), hematocrit, and assessment for any underlying infection; treatment is specific to the underlying etiology.

Idiopathic hypertrophic subaortic stenosis: See Asymmetric septal hypertrophy.

Intravascular volume depletion: See Syncope.

Ischemia: See Atherosclerosis.

Left ventricular enlargement

Overall increase in the size of the left ventricle due to either thickening of the wall **(left ventricular hypertrophy)** as the result of long-standing hypertension or thinning of the wall with increased chamber size (left ventricular dilation) resulting from cardiomyopathy or ischemia. Symptoms and signs of **left ventricular hypertrophy** include a laterally displaced PMI, S_4 gallop, and the retinopathy of long-standing hypertension (Plates 16–18); those of left ventricular dilation include a laterally displaced PMI, S_3 gallop, heave, and often hypotension. Pulmonary edema may be present in either condition. Evaluation and treatment include an echocardiogram and ECG, and referral to a cardiologist.

Left ventricular hypertrophy: See Left ventricular enlargement.

Lift: See Heart failure.

Mitral regurgitation

Failure of the mitral valve to close completely during systole, due to a progression of mitral valve prolapse, ischemia-related papillary muscle dysfunction, and endocarditis. The condition is asymptomatic until severe, then presents with severe heart failure; signs include a systolic murmur loudest at the apex (see Fig 4-2D), radiation into the left axilla and left infrascapular area, negative Rivero-Carvallo sign, negative Vitum's sign, minimal changes to jugular central venous pulsations (see Fig 4-5A), minimal hepatosplenomegaly, and no midsystolic click. Evaluation includes an echocardiogram to confirm diagnosis; referral to a cardiologist and preprocedure antibiotic prophylaxis are indicated.

Mitral stenosis

Failure of the valve to open in diastole due to scarring of the valve from old rheumatic fever, endocarditis, or congenital valve defects. The condition is relatively asymptomatic until late or during the second trimester of pregnancy, when syncope, atrial fibrillation, and heart failure may occur. Signs include diastolic murmur loudest at the apex (see Fig 4-2D) and best heard with the patient in the left lateral decubital position (see Fig 4-1), as well as an **opening snap** in early diastole and malar flush with each systole. Irregularly irregular rhythm indicates atrial fibrillation. Evaluation includes an echocardiogram to confirm diagnosis; referral to a cardiologist and preprocedure antibiotic prophylaxis are indicated.

Mitral valve prolapse

Idiopathic or congenital myxomatous changes to the posterior leaflet of the mitral valve. The condition is asymptomatic; signs include a systolic murmur loudest at the apex (see Fig 4-2D), no radiation, negative Rivero-Carvallo sign, negative Vitum's sign, normal jugular venous pulsations, and no hepatomegaly. A concurrent midsystolic click is heard, and murmur and click become louder on standing. Evaluation includes an echocardiogram to confirm diagnosis; referral to a cardiologist and preprocedure antibiotic prophylaxis are indicated.

Narrowly fixed splitting of S2: See Widely fixed splitting of S_2.

Opening snap: See Mitral stenosis.

Paradoxical splitting of S2
Abnormal delay in aortic valve closure, so that the pulmonic valve (PV) closes before the aortic valve, due to left bundle branch block (LBBB), aortic stenosis, ASH, or severe LVH **(see Fig 4-4B)**. Symptoms and signs include no splitting with inspiration but splitting with expiration, as well as concurrent systolic murmur at the base in aortic stenosis/ASH or an S_4 and laterally displaced PMI in LVH. Evaluation includes an ECG and echocardiogram. Treatment is directed toward the underlying disorder, and referral to a cardiologist may be indicated.

Pericardial effusion
Abnormal quantity of fluid within the pericardial sac due to hypothyroidism, lupus erythematosus, bacterial infections, or malignant neoplasia; an effusion may result in heart failure due to a marked decrease in the venous return to the right heart **(tamponade)**. Symptoms include shortness of breath and platypnea; signs include systolic hypotension and an increase in jugular venous pulsations, pitting bipedal edema, hepatomegaly, distant heart tones, dullness to percussion in the midchest and epigastrium, and a pulsus paradoxus (never a positive Kussmaul's sign). Evaluation includes an ECG, looking for small QRS complexes, and an echocardiogram, looking for effusion with right ventricular end-diastolic collapse, which indicates tamponade. Treatment includes referral to a cardiologist for pericardiocentesis.

Pericardial rub: See Pericarditis.

Pericardial tamponade: See Pericardial effusion.

Pericarditis
Inflammation of the pericardium due to infection, autoimmune disorder, or postinfarction (Dressler's) syndrome. Complications include pericardial effusion/tamponade and constrictive pericarditis. Symptoms include pleuritic pain that decreases with leaning forward; signs include a **pericardial rub** heard in systole or diastole, or both, over the precordium. Specific signs are: for massive pericardial effusion with tamponade—right heart failure, increased jugular venous pressure, and negative Kussmaul's sign; for con-

strictive pericarditis—right heart failure, increased jugular venous pressure, pulsus paradoxus, and positive Kussmaul's sign. Evaluation and treatment include an echocardiogram and ECG and referral to a cardiologist.

Physiologic splitting of S2

Normal splitting of S_2 at the base. The split occurs during inspiration and resolves with expiration, because venous return to the right heart increases during inspiration, causing the pulmonic valve to close later than usual. No symptoms, signs, or intervention necessary.

Pulmonic stenosis

Due to congenital syndrome, either isolated or part of tetralogy of Fallot. Symptoms and signs are minimal until the lesion is severe; they include a systolic murmur loudest at left base (see Fig 4-2B), a systolic click at base, and a widely split S_2 (see Fig 4-4C). Signs of advanced disease include an increased JVP, increased a waves, right lift, hepatomegaly, and decreased P_2 intensity. Evaluation includes an echocardiogram and ECG; referral to a cardiologist and preprocedure antibiotic prophylaxis are indicated.

Rheumatic fever

Immune-mediated systemic process following an infection (usually exudative pharyngitis) with specific types of group A beta-hemolytic streptococci. Symptoms include antecedent sore throat and present polyarticular arthralgias, skin rash, and shortness of breath. Acute signs include chorea or St. Vidus' dance, polyarticular arthritis, nodules on the extensor surfaces of the extremities, erythema marginatum and pericardial rubs, S_3 gallop, and diastolic and systolic murmurs of regurgitant murmurs. Chronic signs include diastolic murmurs of aortic regurgitation and mitral stenosis. Evaluation includes an echocardiogram; the patient should be referred to an infectious disease consultant and a cardiologist.

Right heart failure

Due to right ventricular infarctions, tricuspid insufficiency, or, most commonly, severe left heart failure. Symptoms and signs include dependent pitting edema, especially in the feet and back; elevated jugular venous pressure (see Fig 4-6B); ascites; hepatomegaly; right-sided S_3 gallop; lift; and, if very severe, a Kussmaul's sign. An increased pulsus paradoxus also may be present, along with signs of the underlying etiology. Evaluation and treatment include an echocardiogram and ECG and referral to a cardiologist.

S3 gallop: See Heart failure.

S4 gallop: See Heart failure.

Subclavian steal syndrome: See Syncope.

Syncope

The sudden loss of consciousness due to profound decreased perfusion to the brain, specifically the brainstem; etiologies include cardiac dysrhythmias, forward heart failure, valvular disorders, pericardial disease, **intravascular volume depletion**, **autonomic dysfunction**, and blood loss. Symptoms and signs include acute loss of consciousness along with hypotension, often resulting in a fall. Concurrent signs specific to the underlying etiology are as follows: for dysrhythmia—bradycardia or tachycardia; for valvular disorders—findings of **aortic stenosis, aortic insufficiency, mitral stenosis,** and **mitral insufficiency**; for heart failure—S_3 gallop, displaced PMI, and heave; for **intravascular volume depletion**—decreased turgor and lack of sweat. Evaluation and treatment are directed toward the underlying etiology; if cardiac etiology is suspected, ECG, echocardiogram, and referral to a cardiologist are prudent.

Systolic heart failure: See Heart failure.

Thrill

The palpable component of a murmur if the murmur is intense (i.e., 4/6, 5/6, or 6/6 murmur).

Tricuspid regurgitation

Failure of the tricuspid valve to close completely during systole, due to right-sided endocarditis or right-sided myocardial infarction. The condition is asymptomatic until very severe; signs include a systolic murmur loudest at the apex (see Fig 4-2E), no radiation, positive Rivero-Carvallo sign, positive Vitum's sign, an increase in the JVP with a pronounced *v* wave (see Fig 4-6C), "blinking light" earlobe sign, pitting-dependent edema, and hepatosplenomegaly. Evaluation includes an echocardiogram to confirm diagnosis; referral to a cardiologist and preprocedure antibiotic prophylaxis are indicated.

Ventricular septal defect

A congenital defect in the ventricular septum that may be a complication of a myocardial infarction, with shunting of blood from left to right. A high risk of Eisenmenger's syndrome (i.e., development of secondary pulmonary hypertension) is present. Symptoms and signs include systolic murmur with a thrill at the apex (see Fig 4-2D,E); signs of Eisenmenger's syndrome include a widely fixed splitting of S_2 (see Fig 4-4C), an S_3 gallop, and a lift. Evaluation is with an echocardiogram and ECG; treatment is via referral to a cardiologist and antibiotic prophylaxis.

Widely fixed splitting of S2

Abnormal delay in PV closure so that it closes consistently and significantly later than the aortic valve, due to RBBB, pulmonic stenosis, acute cor pulmonale/pulmonary hypertension; **narrow splitting** has the same pathogenesis but bespeaks chronicity of right heart failure **(see Fig 4-4D)**.

Symptoms and signs include a wide splitting of the S_2 in both inspiration and expiration, as well as concurrent systolic murmur at the base in pulmonic stenosis and in cor pulmonale or right-sided S_3 and increased JVP (see Fig 4-6B). **Narrow splitting** is indicated by narrow fixed splitting in inspiration and expiration. Evaluation includes an ECG and echocardiogram. Treatment is directed toward the underlying disorder, and referral to a cardiologist may be indicated.

Percuss lung fields

PROCEDURE: With the patient sitting up and gently leaning forward:

1. Method of percussion: use two-digit technique (Fig 5-1)

2. Percuss the posterior fields: four pairs (Fig 5-2: sites 1–8) of sites slightly medial to the post-midclavicular line; compare one side to the other; can perform from the top down or from the bottom up

3. Instruct the patient to raise both arms; percuss in the midaxillary line (Fig 5-3: sites 9–12); compare to other side at each level

4. Instruct the patient to resume original position with arms at sides; percuss the anterior upper zones in the anterior midclavicular line (Fig 5-4: sites 13–16)

5. Percuss in the apices, that is, between the lateral neck and the shoulder (Krönig's isthmus; Fig 5-4: sites 17–18)

OUTCOME: If there is a tympanic note:
- ◆ emphysema
- ◆ pneumothorax

If dull note:
- ◆ pleural effusion
- ◆ consolidation

If dull note over left anterior chest: ◆ normal cardiac dullness

Feel for tactile fremitus

PROCEDURE: Instruct the patient to repeat the word "coin" (/*cooiin*/ sound), or the words "toy" or "boy" (the /*eu*/ diphthong). Use the palms of both hands simultaneously on the posterior, lateral, and anterior aspects of the lung fields to feel the transmission of the sound. (See Figs 5-2, 5-3, and 5-4 for the sites and sequence of tactile fremitus.)

OUTCOME: If there is increased transmission over an area of dullness:
- ◆ consolidation with open airways

If decreased transmission over an area of dullness:
- ◆ pleural effusion
- ◆ pneumonectomy
- ◆ consolidation without open airway

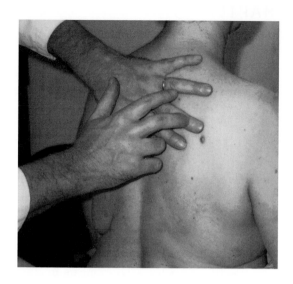

Figure 5-1 Method to percuss. Two-digit technique: Note the position of fingers; use slightly flexed third digit to tap on the distal interphalangeal surface of the other third digit applied to chest wall surface.

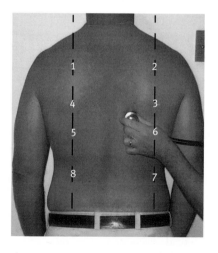

Figure 5-2 Posterior chest sites for percussion, tactile fremitus, and auscultation. Note the four pairs of sites (1–8); use one side to compare with the other at each level. The dashed lines are the posterior midclavicular lines.

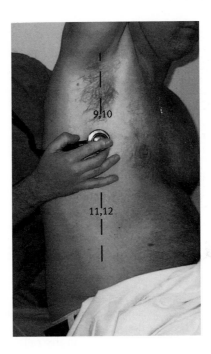

Figure 5-3 Lateral chest sites for percussion, tactile fremitus, and auscultation. Note the two pairs of sites (9–12); use one side to compare with the other at each level. The dashed lines are the midaxillary lines.

Auscult lung fields

PROCEDURE: With the patient sitting up and leaning forward, use the diaphragm to auscult the lung fields. Instruct the patient to inhale and exhale deeply (but not maximally or forcefully). Cover the lung fields as described in Figs 5-2, 5-3, and 5-4 for the sites of auscultation. Describe the intensity of the breath sounds, and note any adventitious, that is, extra, sounds.

OUTCOME: If there is increased intensity of breath sounds over an area of dullness: ◆ **consolidation with open airways**

If decreased intensity of breath sounds over an area of dullness:
- ◆ **pleural effusion**
- ◆ **pneumonectomy**
- ◆ **consolidation with closed airways**

If vesicular breath sounds: ◆ **normal**

If wheezes are present: ◆ **airway obstruction, partial**

If inspiratory wheezes are present: ◆ **chronic bronchitis**

If expiratory wheezes are present: ◆ **asthma**

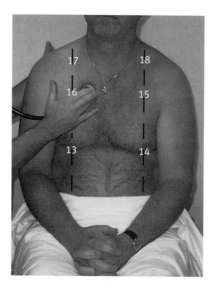

Figure 5-4 Anterior sites for percussion, tactile fremitus, and auscultation. Note the three pairs of sites (13–18); use one side to compare with the other at each level. Sites 17 and 18 are above the clavicles in an area called *Krönig's isthmus*. The dashed lines are the anterior midclavicular lines.

If there is a high-pitched inspiratory sound (stridor):
   ◆ **upper airway obstruction, almost complete**
If there are sounds that could be likened to the rubbing of hairs next to the ears: ◆ **crackles**
If rattling-type sounds that could be likened to something needing to be coughed up (secretions in tubes): ◆ **rhonchi**

Inspect mucous membranes
PROCEDURE: Inspect the mucous membranes and nail beds. Use your own mucous membranes as control.

OUTCOME: If the mucous membranes are pink: ◆ **normal**
If bright red: ◆ **carbon monoxide poisoning**
If blue: ◆ **cyanosis**
If pale: ◆ **anemia**

Observe patient's positioning
PROCEDURE: Instruct the patient to assume a position in which the dyspnea and tachypnea are minimized. Note that position.

OUTCOME: If the patient assumes an upright sitting position, leaning forward with legs dangling over the sides of the table (Fowler's position or severe orthopnea):

> ◆ **pulmonary edema, that is, heart failure**

If the patient assumes a supine position, indicating that it is easier to lie flat than sit up (platypnea):

> ◆ **ASD (see p. 91)**
> ◆ **end-stage liver disease (see p. 132)**

If the patient assumes a left or right decubital position (trepopnea): ◆ **pleural effusion, ipsilateral to the side down**

If the patient has head anteriorly displaced at the neck, nose upward ("sniffing the flowers" position):

> ◆ **upper airway obstruction—epiglottitis or Ludwig's angina**

Inspect chest wall

PROCEDURE: With the patient standing in anatomic position, visually inspect the skeletal components of the chest and chest wall.

OUTCOME: If there is an increased anteroposterior (AP) diameter (i.e., a barrel-shaped chest):

> ◆ **severe chronic obstructive pulmonary disease (COPD)**

If anterior protrusion of the sternum:

> ◆ **pectus carinatum ("pigeon chest")**

If the inferior sternum and xiphoid are inverted (Fig 5-5):

> ◆ **pectus excavatum ("funnel chest")**

If there is a normal AP diameter with the ribs flaring anteriorly and inferiorly (concave) to form a groove bilaterally involving ribs 7 to 10 (Harrison's groove): ◆ **rickets in the past**

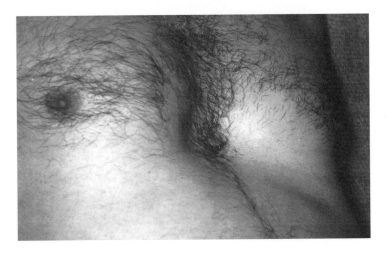

Figure 5-5 Pectus excavatum. Congenital chest wall abnormality in which there is posterior displacement of the lower sternum and xiphoid process; may lead to restrictive pulmonary disease.

Inspect sternocleidomastoid muscles

PROCEDURE: With the patient sitting and breathing at baseline, visually inspect the sternocleidomastoid muscles for contractions during the respiratory cycle.

OUTCOME: If there is a contraction with each inspiration:
   ◆ **COPD**
   ◆ **asthma, acute exacerbation**
   If bilateral muscular hypertrophy: ◆ **COPD, severe**

Inspect thoracic spine

PROCEDURE: With the patient in an upright anatomic position facing away from you, visually inspect the spinal column itself. Repeat after instructing the patient to turn to a profile view.

OUTCOME: If there is a left tilt to the thoracic spine: ◆ **thoracic levoscoliosis**
   If a right tilt (Fig 5-6): ◆ **thoracic dextroscoliosis**

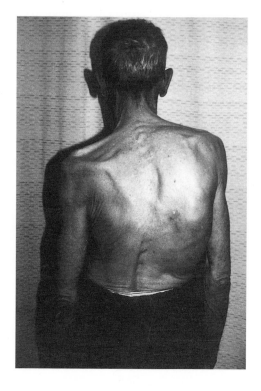

Figure 5-6 Marked thoracic dextroscoliosis. This was accentuated upon forward flexion of the back (not shown); patient had significant restrictive pulmonary disease due to this scoliosis.

If in profile, the cervical spine is lordotic, the thoracic spine kyphotic, the lumbar spine lordotic, and the sacral spine kyphotic: ◆ **normal**

If there is a marked increase in thoracic kyphosis:

   ◆ **dowager's hump of osteoporosis, also known as** *hunch* **or** *humpback*

Inspect intercostal muscles

PROCEDURE: Visually inspect the intercostal muscles for movements in the intercostal spaces during the respiratory cycle.

OUTCOME: If there is diffuse mild inward movement with inspiration and a mild outward movement with expiration: ◆ **normal**

If exaggerated diffuse inward movement with inspiration (retraction) and outward movement with expiration (bulging):

   ◆ **COPD, acute exacerbation**
   ◆ **COPD, severe**

If a focal bulging in inspiration and expiration:

   ◆ **pleural effusion**

Inspect abdomen for movements during respiration

PROCEDURE: With the patient supine, visually inspect the abdominal movements with the patient's breathing at baseline.

OUTCOME: If the abdomen moves outward during inspiration and inward during expiration: ◆ **normal**

If it moves inward during inspiration and outward during expiration (paradoxical respirations):

   ◆ **paralysis of the diaphragm**

Visually inspect expectorated sputum

PROCEDURE: Visually inspect freshly expectorated sputa.

OUTCOME: If clear fluid:

   ◆ **spit**
   ◆ **atypical pneumonia, that is, interstitial**

If yellow-green (purulent):

   ◆ **asthma**
   ◆ **bronchitis**
   ◆ **typical pneumonia, that is, consolidative**

If purulent with red streaks:

   ◆ **bronchitis**
   ◆ **typical pneumonia, that is, consolidative**

If frothy and clear but pink-tinged:

   ◆ **pulmonary edema, that is, heart failure**

If frank blood: ◆ **hemoptysis**

Inspect fingers for signs of clubbing: See Chapter 8, under Advanced Examination (Fig 8-9, p. 184).

Advanced Examination

APPROACH TO A PATIENT WITH CONSOLIDATION OR EFFUSION

Percuss lung fields: As in Basic Examination.

Feel for tactile fremitus: As in Basic Examination.

Auscult lung fields: As in Basic Examination.

Visually inspect expectorated sputum: As in Basic Examination.

Auscult with diaphragm: egophony

PROCEDURE: With the patient sitting and breathing at baseline, use the diaphragm to auscult over the area of presumed consolidation or effusion while the patient is singing the vowel sound /e/: "eeeee." Use the normal lung areas as a control.

OUTCOME: If the /e/ sound remains: ◆ **normal**
If an /e–a/ (an /a/ sound like a bleating sheep, or a hard /a/) is heard throughout the area of dullness: ◆ **consolidation**
If an /e–a/ (an /a/ sound like a bleating sheep, or a hard /a/) is heard, localized to the superior surface of the dullness:
◆ **pleural effusion**
If no sound is transmitted: ◆ **pneumonectomy (lobectomy)**

APPROACH TO A PATIENT WITH SUSPECTED CONGESTIVE HEART FAILURE

Percuss lung fields: As in Basic Examination.

Auscult lung fields: As in Basic Examination.

Inspect mucous membranes: As in Basic Examination.

Observe patient's positioning: As in Basic Examination.

Basic cardiology examination: See Chapter 4, Basic Examination, p. 70.

Auscult after deep cough

PROCEDURE: With the patient sitting in an upright position, use the diaphragm to auscult the area of crackles before and after a deep cough.

OUTCOME: If there are localized, constant crackles that decrease after cough:
◆ **atelectasis**

If localized crackles that do not decrease after a cough:
- ◆ **consolidation**

If diffuse crackles that do not change with a cough:
- ◆ **pulmomary edema, that is, heart failure**
- ◆ **interstitial lung disease**
- ◆ **Atypical pneumonia, that is, interstitial**

Auscult: describe crackles

PROCEDURE: Use the diaphragm to auscult the area of crackles. Attempt to determine the quality of the crackles.

OUTCOME: If the crackles are fine—high pitched, dry, like Velcro being ripped apart: ◆ **interstitial lung disease**

If coarse—low pitched, popping wet, like beer bubbles:
- ◆ **pulmonary edema, that is, heart failure**

APPROACH TO A PATIENT WITH OBSTRUCTIVE LUNG DISEASE

Auscult lung fields: As in Basic Examination.

Inspect sternocleidomastoid muscles: As in Basic Examination.

Inspect intercostal muscles: As in Basic Examination.

Inspect mucous membranes: As in Basic Examination.

Inspect chest wall: As in Basic Examination.

Inspect fingers for signs of clubbing: See Chapter 8, under Advanced Examination (see Fig 8-9, p. 184).

Visually inspect expectorated sputum: As in Basic Examination.

Measure forced expiratory time

PROCEDURE: Place the bell of a stethoscope over the trachea in the jugular notch. Instruct the patient to exhale with maximal effort from the point of deepest inspiration. Measure the time from the beginning to the last point of audible exhalation.

OUTCOME: If <6 seconds: ◆ **normal**

If >6 seconds: ◆ **airway obstruction (i.e., COPD or asthma)**

Study movement of chest and hemidiaphragm

PROCEDURE: With the patient sitting in anatomic position, place both hands on the anterior inferior costal margins with the thumbs on the medial aspects of the cartilages adjacent to the xiphoid, fingers pointing upward and laterally. Instruct the patient to inspire and expire maximally. Note any differences between the two sides.

Perform again on upper anterior chest and once again on lower posterior chest.

OUTCOME: If, during deep inspiration, the fingers symmetrically lateralize and the angle between the thumb and fingers becomes more obtuse: ◆ **normal**

If minimal movement of thumb and fingers:

◆ **Restrictive disease, paralysis of hemidiaphragm**

Keys to Recording Findings

PULMONARY

"Clear to P/A (percussion and auscultation)"

A. Chest wall configuration

Note symmetry of chest to expansion

B. Percussion

Note sites/areas of abnormal dullness (fluid) versus tympany (gas/emphysema) versus normal

C. Tactile fremitus

Note sites/areas of abnormal increased (consolidation) versus decreased (effusion)

E. Breath sounds

Note sites/areas of increased (consolidation) versus decreased (effusion or emphysema)

E. Adventitious sounds

Adventitious sounds and their locations—wheezes, rhonchi, crackles or rubs.

A. Chest wall configuration and symmetry

B. Percussion

Draw on areas of dullness or tympany.

C. Tactile fremitus

Draw on areas of increased or decreased fremitus.

D. Breath sounds

Draw on areas of increased or decreased breath sounds.

E. Adventitious sounds

Draw on location of wheezes, rhonchi, crackles and rubs.

Anterior Chest

Left Chest

Right Chest

Posterior Chest

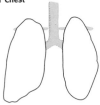

Diagnoses

Airway obstruction: See Asthma, Chronic bronchitis, Emphysema, and Epiglottitis.

Asthma

Reversible hyperactivity of the smooth muscle in the walls of the bronchi with hypoventilation due to atopic or cold/exercise-mediated or reflux of gastric acid mechanisms. Symptoms include cough, shortness of breath, and diffuse chest tightness; may be precipitated in a supine position or by exercise. Signs include diffuse wheezing, intercostal retractions, and use of sternocleidomastoid muscles. If related to atopic disease, may have associated urticaria (Plate 25) or angioedema (see Fig 2-8, p. 15); if severe, may have a paucity of wheezes, diminished breath sounds, and cyanosis. Evaluation is by pulse oximetry and, if severe, arterial blood gas. Treatment includes inhaled β_2-agonists, glucocorticoids, and oxygen supplementation.

Atelectasis

Loss of gas from alveolar sacs in an area of the lung due to partial obstruction or decreased inspiration volume. Symptoms and signs include localized crackles (rales), normal percussion, and mild egophony throughout the area; the crackles usually clear after deep cough. Treat the underlying disorder and perform an aggressive incentive spirometry, especially if in a postoperative patient.

Atypical pneumonia, interstitial

Diffuse inflammation in the lung interstitium due to *Mycoplasma pneumoniae, Legionella* species (spp), viruses including influenza, or *Pneumocystis carinii*. Symptoms include a hacking, nonproductive cough; malaise; and shortness of breath. Signs include diffuse crackles and occasional wheezes and low-grade or spiking fever. Evaluation includes performing chest radiography for diffuse interstitial infiltrate and pulse oximetry for hypoxemia; sputum is scant and thus is of little diagnostic utility. Treatment is with systemic antibiotics—erythromycin-based regimens for *Mycoplasma/Legionella*; trimethoprim (TMP)/sulfa-based regimen for pneumocystitis.

Bronchitis

Acute inflammation of airways due to a viral or bacterial etiology. Symptoms and signs include sputum that is yellow or green with red streaks, low-grade fever, scattered wheezes, and diffuse rhonchi. Chest radiography is often normal. Treatment is with antibiotics and inhaled β_2-agonists.

Chest wall deformities

Congenital or acquired defects in the chest wall that may lead to restrictive lung disease. Symptoms and signs include the deformities themselves: **pectus excavatum, pectus carinatum, thoracic levoscoliosis, thoracic dextroscoliosis** (see Fig 5-6), or **dowager's hump** (thoracic kyphosis). Evaluation includes pulmonary function tests (PFTs), which reveal normal forced expiratory volume in 1 second (FEV_1) and decreased forced vital capacity (FVC; restrictive pattern). Referral to a respiratory therapist/pulmonologist may be indicated, as well as preventive management for osteoporosis.

Chronic bronchitis

Minimally reversible constriction of the bronchi, with hypoventilation and chronic cough: defined as a persistent productive cough for >3 months for 2 consecutive years. Chronic bronchitis is often concurrent to emphysema. Symptoms include a productive cough of purulent sputa and dyspnea. Signs include diffuse scattered wheezes, rhonchi, cyanosis, barrel chest deformity, pursed-lip breathing, and use and even hypertrophy of sternocleidomastoid muscles. An acute increase in symptoms and signs indicates acute exacerbation. Evaluation includes pulmonary function tests (PFTs), which reveal decreased FEV_1, normal FVC, decreased FEV_1/FVC ratio to <60%, and normal residual volume and diffusing capacity. Treatment includes inhaled anticholinergic agents such as ipratropium and cessation of smoking.

Chronic obstructive pulmonary disease: See Emphysema and Chronic bronchitis.

Clubbing: See Hands, Fingers in Chapter 8, p. 197.

Consolidation: See Typical pneumonia.

Crackles

Discrete finding on auscultation indicative of interstitial lung disease, pulmonary edema, or atypical pneumonia.

Cyanosis

Elevated deoxyhemoglobin due to profound hypoxemia from hypoventilation, pulmonary hypertension, pulmonary edema, or interstitial lung disease. Symptoms and signs include blue lips, mucous membranes, and nail beds, along with concurrent manifestations of the underlying etiology. Evaluation includes arterial blood gases. Treatment includes supplemental oxygen and is directed toward the underlying etiology.

Dowager's hump: See Chest wall deformities.

Emphysema

Destruction of the alveolar septa with expansion of the air spaces and a decrease in lung compliance due to smoking cigarettes or α_1-antitrypsin deficiency, or both; usually concurrent to chronic bronchitis. Symptoms include a nonproductive cough, mild to modest dyspnea, and dyspnea on exertion. Signs include barrel chest deformity, flattened diaphragms, pursed lipped breathing, tympany to percussion, diffusely decreased breath sounds, rare cyanosis, or wheezing. Acute increase in symptoms and signs indicates acute exacerbation. Evaluation includes PFTs, which reveal decreased FEV_1, normal FVC, decreased FEV_1/FVC ratio to <60%, increased residual volume, and decreased diffusing capacity. Treatment includes inhaled anticholinergic agents such as ipratropium and cessation of smoking.

Epiglottitis

Inflammation due to infection of the larynx superior to the vocal cords with *Staphylococcus aureus*, *Streptococcus pneumoniae*, ß-hemolytic streptococci in adults, or *Haemophilus influenzae* in children. Symptoms include sore throat, fever, dysphagia, and odynophagia with drooling. Signs include "sniffing the flower" position of head, drooling, and auscultable and even audible stridor. Do not use a tongue depressor in examination, as this may precipitate complete **upper airway obstruction**. Evaluation includes lateral neck films, which may reveal a narrowed epiglottis. Treatment includes emergency referral to an ear, nose, and throat surgeon and parenteral antibiotics.

Hemoptysis

Blood in sputa due to acute bronchitis, mycobacterial disease, or neoplastic disease. Symptoms and signs are specific to the underlying etiology: in acute bronchitis, wheezing; in mycobacterial disease, upper lobe cavitary disease and tympany. Evaluation includes a chest radiograph to assist in localization. Treatment is directed toward the underlying etiology.

Hydropneumothorax: See Pneumothorax.

Interstitial lung disease

Infiltration of lung tissue by fibrous tissue, infection (mycobacterium or atypical pneumonia), or an inhaled agent (silicosis). Symptoms and signs include shortness of breath and dyspnea during exercise; clubbing (see Fig 8-9, p. 184); cyanosis; dry, "Velcro-sounding" crackles; and right heart failure are also present. Evaluation and treatment include arterial blood gases, chest radiography, and referral to a pulmonologist.

Large cavity/bullous disease: See Emphysema and Hemoptysis.

Paralysis of hemidiaphragm

Damage to the phrenic nerve, often after surgery or trauma, or high (C3/C4) cervical cord damage, resulting in restrictive-type pulmonary disease. Symptoms and signs, which are usually minimal unless bilateral, include rapid shallow breathing, use of accessory muscles, and cyanosis. No adventitious sounds are present, but minimal movement of the diaphragm with inspiration may be detected by percussion. Concurrent findings related to quadriparesis or quadriplegia are not uncommon. Evaluation includes PFTs, which reveal normal FEV_1 and decreased FVC (restrictive pattern). Management includes using a tilting bed.

Pectus carinatum: See Chest wall deformities.

Pectus excavatum: See Chest wall deformities.

Pleural effusion
Abnormal quantity of fluid in the pleural space, either transudative—due to nephrosis, cirrhosis, congestive heart failure (CHF), or hypoalbuminemia, or exudative—due to infection, neoplasia, or a connective tissue disorder. Symptoms include dyspnea, orthopnea, and trepopnea. Signs include dullness to percussion, decreased tactile fremitus, decreased to absent breath sounds throughout the area of dullness, and egophony at the superior surface of the dullness. Evaluation with chest radiographs reveals blunting of the costophrenic angle; if it is quite large, radiographs also reveal a diffuse fluid area with a meniscus at the superior side without any air bronchograms. A thoracentesis should be performed and the fluid sent for total protein and lactic dehydrogenase (LDH) testing. Total protein and LDH levels should also be drawn on the patient's plasma. Treatment is of the underlying condition.

Pneumonectomy/lobectomy
Surgical removal of a lung (called *lobectomy* if one lung is removed). Symptoms and signs include a scar, dullness to percussion, and an absence of all breath sounds. Obtain patient history and a chest radiograph for confirmation.

Pneumothorax
Leakage of air into the pleural space. The leakage may be iatrogenic (as a complication of thoracentesis or central line placement), traumatic (from rib fractures or penetrating chest wounds), or spontaneous (with panacinar emphysema or *P. carinii* pneumonitis). Two types of pneumothoraces are recognized: simple—maximal at outset; tension—progressive, leading to mediastinal shift. Symptoms include pleuritic chest pain, dyspnea, tachypnea, and hiccups. Signs include pleural rub and tympany, with marked decreased breath sounds over the site. Other symptoms and signs are specific to diagnosis: a shift of the mediastinum and trachea to the contralateral side, along with progressive cyanosis and respiratory embarrassment in tension pneumothorax. Evaluation includes a chest radiograph. With symptomatic cases of pneumothorax or any tension pneumothorax, emergent placement of a chest tube is indicated.

Pulmonary edema: See Heart failure in Chapter 4.

Restrictive lung disease: See Chest wall deformities.

Rhonchi
Discrete finding on auscultation indicating fluid, phlegm, or foreign material in the airways.

Rickets
Poor bone formation due to vitamin D deficiency in childhood. Signs include Harrison's sulcus sign and bowing of the tibiae. Treatment is through prevention—adequate vitamin D during childhood.

Thoracic levo-/dextroscoliosis: See Chest wall deformities.

Typical pneumonia
Consolidation in the alveoli in one or more of the lobes due to *S. pneumoniae, H. influenzae,* and anaerobes. Symptoms include fever, productive cough with yellow-green sputa, malaise, and shortness of breath. Signs include dullness to percussion, increased tactile fremitus, bronchial breath sounds, and egophony, both throughout the area of dullness. The sputa will be fetid sputa if the agent is anaerobes. Evaluation includes chest radiography, which reveals lobar infiltrate; pulse oximetry, which demonstrates hypoxemia; and sputum culture, which reveals multiple PMNs and organisms. Treatment includes systemic antibiotics, including a second- or third-generation cephalosporin and a macrolide or a fluoroquinolone.

Upper airway obstruction: See Epiglottitis and Ludwig's angina in Chapter 2.

CHAPTER 6
Abdomen

Auscult abdomen

PROCEDURE: With the patient supine, auscult the abdomen using the diaphragm for 30 to 60 seconds. *Perform this procedure before any other abdominal examination.*

OUTCOME: If there are high-pitched bowel sounds (tinkles):
- ◆ **small bowel obstruction (SBO)**

If periods of markedly increased bowel sounds, intermittent in nature (rushes):
- ◆ **normal**
- ◆ **early SBO**

If periods of markedly increased bowel sounds that are recurrent and heard without a stethoscope (borborygmi):
- ◆ **normal**
- ◆ **early SBO**

If decreased or absent bowel sounds: ◆ **ileus**

If there is a systolic bruit in the epigastrium:
- ◆ **abdominal aortic aneurysm**

If systolic bruit in the right or left upper quadrant:
- ◆ **renal arterial stenosis**

If sound likened to two pieces of leather being rubbed together (rubs): ◆ **localized peritonitis**

Perform general visual inspection of abdomen

PROCEDURE: Visually inspect the abdomen with the patient supine (Figs 6-1 and 6-2). Observe for masses, movement; note the skin.

OUTCOME: If the abdomen is diffusely enlarged:
- ◆ **ascites (Fig 6-3)**
- ◆ **fat**
- ◆ **gas (bowel obstruction)**
- ◆ **abdominal mass; nonspecific finding**

If abdomen is scaphoid: ◆ **emaciation/cachexia**

If there are rhythmic contractions of the diaphragm and abdominal wall: ◆ **hiccups**

If ecchymosis on one or both flanks (Grey Turner's sign):
- ◆ **retroperitoneal bleed (see Fig 14-6, p. 295)**

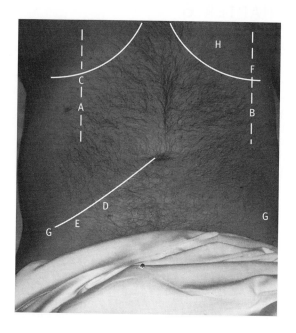

Figure 6-1 Abdominal landmarks. A. Right midclavicular line (MCL), used to assess the liver. B. Left anterior axillary line, used to assess the spleen. C. Murphy's point—the intersection of right MCL and the tenth rib, used to assess the gallbladder. D. McBurney's line—between the anterior superior iliac spine (ASIS) and the umbilicus. E. McBurney's point—3 cm medial to the ASIS on the line, used to assess the appendix. F. Castell's point—site of intersection of anterior axillary line and the tenth rib, used to assess the spleen. G. Anterior superior iliac spine. H. Traube's space—space formed by the left costal margin, the seventh rib, and the anterior axillary line, used to assess the spleen.

Palpate abdominal quadrants

PROCEDURE: Have the patient lie supine, with a pillow under the head and shoulders and the knees and hips slightly flexed, breathing at baseline. Use your dominant hand, the palm adjacent to the skin, to palpate the abdomen directly in all four quadrants and around the umbilicus (see Fig 6-2). Always palpate the painful area last.

OUTCOME: If there is a mass in the right upper quadrant (see Fig 6-2A):
  ◆ **gallbladder enlargement (Courvoisier's sign)**
  ◆ **hepatomegaly**

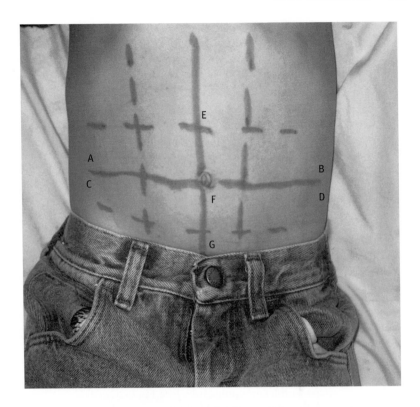

Figure 6-2 Abdominal landmarks. Note the four quadrants (double lines through the umbilicus mark the boundaries). A. Right upper. B. Left upper. C. Right lower. D. Left lower. Of the nine sections of surface anatomy, the most important three are: epigastric (E), periumbilical (F), and suprapubic (G). These sites are useful in defining and locating the sites of pain and tenderness and the location of any other findings.

If tenderness in the right upper quadrant (see Fig 6-2A):
- ◆ **hepatitis**
- ◆ **cholecystitis**
- ◆ **peptic ulcer disease**

If a mass in the left upper quadrant (see Fig 6-2B):
- ◆ **splenomegaly**

If tenderness in the left upper quadrant (see Fig 6-2B):
- ◆ **pancreatitis**

If a mass in the epigastrium (see Fig 6-2E):
- ◆ **abdominal aortic aneurysm**

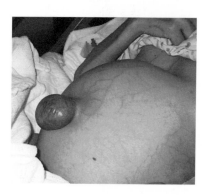

Figure 6-3 End-stage liver disease with ascites. Concurrent umbilical hernia, abdominal venous distention, and icterus in this patient.

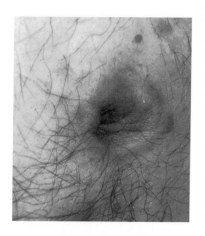

Figure 6-4 Sister Mary Joseph's nodule. Nodular lesions in and about the umbilicus; a metastasis from a primary adenocarcinoma in the gastrointestinal tract.

If a mass in the suprapubic area (see Fig 6-2G):
- ◆ **distended urinary bladder**
- ◆ **gravid uterus (pregnancy)**
- ◆ **leiomyomas (see Chapter 15, p. 355)**

If tenderness in the left lower quadrant (see Fig 6-2D):
- ◆ **diverticulitis**
- ◆ **pelvic inflammatory disease (PID; see Chapter 15, p. 357)**

If tenderness in the right lower quadrant (see Fig 6-2C):
- ◆ **appendicitis**
- ◆ **PID (see p. 357)**
- ◆ **diverticulitis**

If a nontender nodule in the skin in and about the umbilicus:
- ◆ **Sister Mary Joseph's nodule (Fig 6-4)**

If there are nontender, firm masses in the periphery of the abdomen: ◆ **stool in the colon**

If there is tenderness to deep palpation (i.e., pain produced by direct pressure): ◆ **nonspecific finding**

If voluntary guarding (i.e., the patient voluntarily contracts muscles to prevent palpation): ◆ **nonspecific finding**

If involuntary guarding (i.e., abdominal wall is rigid to palpation): ◆ **peritonitis**

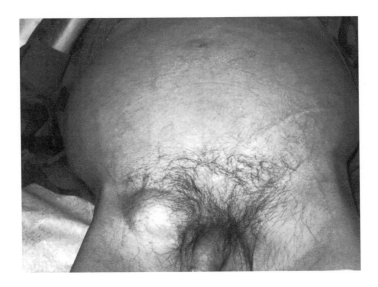

Figure 6-5 Femoral hernia. Note the location, in the medial anterior thigh, under the inguinal ligament. The patient has concurrent ascites as manifested by the bulging flanks.

If a soft mass in the umbilicus (see Fig 6-3): ◆ **umbilical hernia**
If a soft mass in the scrotum or labia majorum: ◆ **inguinal hernia**
If a soft mass in the proximal medial anterior thigh, deep to the inguinal ligament (Fig 6-5): ◆ **femoral hernia**
If a soft mass adjacent to a scar: ◆ **incisional hernia**

Palpate abdomen for rebound tenderness

PROCEDURE: Have the patient lie supine, with a pillow under the head and shoulders, with knees and hips slightly flexed, and breathing at baseline. Using your dominant hand, palm adjacent to the skin, directly palpate in all four quadrants and around the umbilicus. Rapidly withdraw the hand from the point of maximal deep palpation. Always palpate the painful area last.

OUTCOME: If there is no discomfort on withdrawal of the hand: ◆ **normal**
If there is discomfort (rebound tenderness): ◆ **peritonitis**

Perform liver scratch test

PROCEDURE: With the patient supine, use the diaphragm to auscult over the area inferior to the xiphoid process. Concurrently, scratch the skin lightly in the right midclavicular line (see Fig 6-1A), starting at the right nipple and moving inferiorly. Note the levels at which the scratching sound starts and stops and measure the distance between the two.

OUTCOME: If 10 to 12 cm: ◆ **normal size**
If >14 cm: ◆ **hepatomegaly**
If <8 cm: ◆ **cirrhosis**

Advanced Examination

APPROACH TO A PATIENT WITH ABDOMINAL MASSES

Auscult abdomen: As in Basic Examination.

Perform general visual inspection of abdomen: As in Basic Examination.

Palpate abdominal quadrants: As in Basic Examination.

Perform liver scratch test: As in Basic Examination.

Palpate epigastric area for a pulsatile mass

PROCEDURE: Have the patient lie supine, with knees and hips flexed and breathing at baseline. Using the dominant hand, palm adjacent to the skin, gently yet firmly palpate deeply into the abdomen about and superior to the umbilicus (see Fig 6-2E,F). The umbilicus is at L2, which corresponds with aortic bifurcation.

OUTCOME: If there is a pulsatile area <3 cm in diameter: ◆ **normal**
If a pulsatile area >3 cm in diameter:
 ◆ **probable abdominal aortic aneurysm**

Palpate sides of pulsatile mass

PROCEDURE: With the patient supine, knees and hips in a relaxed flexed position, gently yet firmly palpate on both sides of the pulsatile mass.

OUTCOME: If it expands laterally: ◆ **probable abdominal aortic aneurysm**
If expands anteriorly: ◆ **nonspecific finding**

Auscult over pulsatile mass

PROCEDURE: With the patient supine, knees and hips in a relaxed flexed position, use the diaphragm to auscult over the pulsatile mass.

OUTCOME: If a bruit is heard over the mass:
 ◆ **probable abdominal aortic aneurysm**
If no bruit is heard: ◆ **nonspecific finding**

Palpate any hernia

PROCEDURE: Attempt to palpate the hernia gently, assessing for tenderness and reducibility.

OUTCOME: If the hernia is easily and freely movable through the anatomic defect: ◆ **reducible hernia (see Chapter 16, pp. 366, 367)**

If does not return to its normal position spontaneously or by external manipulation:
- ◆ **incarcerated hernia (see Chapter 16, pp. 366, 367)**

If incarcerated and quite tender:
- ◆ **strangulated hernia (see Chapter 16, pp. 366, 367)**

APPROACH TO A PATIENT WITH SUSPECTED HEPATOMEGALY

Perform liver scratch test: As in Basic Examination.

Percuss upper edge of liver

PROCEDURE: With the patient supine, at rest, and breathing at baseline, percuss superior to inferior from the level of the nipple to the costal edge in the right midclavicular (see Fig 6-1A) line. Mark the level at which normal resonance changes to dull.

OUTCOME: This location: ◆ **superior border of the liver**

Palpate lower edge of liver

PROCEDURE: With the patient supine, directly palpate using a hooking maneuver (Fig 6-6) at the inferior site determined by the scratch test. If the liver edge is not discernible, repeat the procedure while the patient maximally inhales. The lower liver edge is best palpated in the right midclavicular line (see Fig 6-1A).

OUTCOME: If the edge is smooth and nontender: ◆ **normal**
If can be palpated across the midline:
- ◆ **Reidel's lobe (normal variant, prominent right lobe)**
- ◆ **hepatomegaly**
- ◆ **splenomegaly**

If there is one or more firm nodules on the liver edge:
- ◆ **rule out primary hepatocellular carcinoma**

If the liver is pulsatile:
- ◆ **tricuspid regurgitation (see Chapter 4, p. 97)**

Measure size of liver

PROCEDURE: Measure the distance between the upper and lower surfaces of the liver as determined by the scratch test and confirmed by percussion and palpation.

OUTCOME: If 10 to 12 cm: ◆ **normal**
If >14 cm: ◆ **hepatomegaly**
If <8 cm: ◆ **cirrhosis**

Auscult liver

PROCEDURE: With the patient supine, instruct him or her to hold the breath at midpoint. Concurrently, use the diaphragm to auscult over the right upper quadrant.

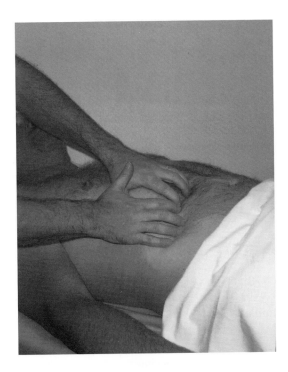

Figure 6-6 Liver span assessment. Palaption of the liver using the hooking maneuver to determine and palpate its lower edge. Hooking is superior to direct palpation.

OUTCOME: If a systolic bruit and/or rub is heard over an enlarged nodular liver: ◆ **primary hepatocellular carcinoma**
If there is no such sound: ◆ **normal**

APPROACH TO A PATIENT WITH SUSPECTED SPLENOMEGALY

Percuss spleen during inspiration and expiration

PROCEDURE: With the patient supine and after instructing the patient to hold a maximal inhalation, percuss over the lowest intercostal space in the left anterior axillary line (Fig 6-1B) (Castell's point) (Fig 6-1F). Repeat, instructing the patient to hold a maximal exhalation.

OUTCOME: If there is a dullness in inspiration that resolves with expiration:
◆ **splenomegaly**
If no dullness in either inspiration or expiration:
◆ **normal**
◆ **splenectomy**

Percuss over Traube's semilunar space

PROCEDURE: With the patient supine with left arm passively abducted, percuss medially to laterally over several levels of Traube's space (Fig 6-1H) (a triangle defined by the sixth rib superiorly, the left midaxillary line laterally, and the left costal margin inferiorly). The examination is best done in the morning, as the patient should have no food or drink for 4 hours before the examination.

OUTCOME: If there is tympany throughout: ♦ **normal**
If dullness throughout: ♦ **splenomegaly**
Sensitivity 62%; specificity 72%[4]

Palpate inferior to superior abdomen with patient supine

PROCEDURE: With the patient supine and in deep full inspiration, directly palpate in the left anterior axillary line (see Fig 6-1B). Feel the spleen edge: Start in the inferior abdomen and palpate at 1-cm intervals in a cephalad direction to the costal margin to catch the lower edge of the spleen. To increase the specificity and sensitivity, place the other hand in the left subcostovertebral area (Middleton maneuver).

OUTCOME: If no edge is felt:
♦ **normal**
♦ **previous splenectomy**
If there is a palpable edge: ♦ **splenomegaly**
Sensitivity 58%; specificity 92%[4]

Palpate with patient in right lateral decubital position

PROCEDURE: With the patient in a right lateral decubital position, place one hand on the inferolateral aspect of the area beneath the left ribcage and palpate with the other hand at the level of the umbilicus, pressing the two hands toward each other. Concurrently, instruct the patient to inhale deeply and maximally. Repeat the procedure four times, moving the right hand several centimeters craniolaterally each time.

OUTCOME: If there is no mass: ♦ **normal**
If a mass: ♦ **splenomegaly**
Sensitivity 71%; specificity 90%[4]

APPROACH TO A PATIENT WITH ABDOMINAL PAIN

See also Chapters 15 and 16.

Palpate abdominal quadrants: As in Basic Examination.

Palpate abdomen for rebound tenderness: As in Basic Examination.

Murphy's sign: right upper quadrant

PROCEDURE: With the patient supine with knees and hips flexed, gently press in the right upper quadrant (see Fig 6-2A), specifically at Murphy's point (see Fig 6-1C), and ask the patient to inhale deeply.

OUTCOME: If inspiration is inhibited due to pain (Murphy's sign):
- ◆ **cholecystitis**

If not inhibited: ◆ **normal**

Gently stroke or lightly pinch right flank skin

PROCEDURE: With the patient supine and relaxed, gently stroke or pinch the skin of the right flank.

OUTCOME: If there is pain:
- ◆ **cholecystitis**
- ◆ **herpes zoster (see Chapter 14, p. 326)**

If no discomfort: ◆ **normal**

Percuss symptomatic side: Murphy's punch

PROCEDURE: With the patient sitting in anatomic position, use your index finger to percuss over the costophrenic angle on the symptomatic side. Use the contralateral side as a control. A variant of this procedure is to punch the costophrenic angle gently with the ulnar aspect of a closed fist from 6 inches back. Use the contralateral side as a control.

OUTCOME: If there is tenderness on the symptomatic side (Murphy's punch sign):
- ◆ **pyelonephritis, ipsilateral**
- ◆ **nephrolithiasis**

If no tenderness: ◆ **normal**

Perform deep/rebound palpation at McBurney's point

PROCEDURE: With the patient supine and hips and knees slightly flexed, perform deep and rebound palpation at McBurney's point. McBurney's point (see Fig 6-1E) is a one finger point that is 1.0 to 1.5 inches medial to the anterior superior process of the ilium on a straight line drawn from it to the umbilicus (see Fig 6-1D).

OUTCOME: If there is tenderness to deep or rebound palpation, or both, at McBurney's point: ◆ **acute appendicitis**

If no such pain: ◆ **normal**

Deeply palpate left lower quadrant: Rovsing's sign

PROCEDURE: With the patient supine, knees and hips flexed, deeply palpate the left lower quadrant, specifically in the left iliac fossa.

OUTCOME: If there is tenderness on the contralateral side, specifically at McBurney's point (see Fig 6-1E; Rovsing's sign):
- ◆ **acute appendicitis**

If no tenderness: ◆ **normal/nonspecific**

Observe patient actively flexing thigh: psoas sign

PROCEDURE: With the patient supine and the knee extended, instruct the patient to actively flex his or her right thigh against your hand. Repeat, using the contralateral side as a control.

OUTCOME: If there is unilateral tenderness in right lower quadrant (psoas sign; see Fig 6-2C):
- ◆ **nonspecific ipsilateral pelvic inflammation (e.g., appendicits, PID)**

If no tenderness: ◆ **normal**

Internally and externally rotate hip: obturator sign

PROCEDURE: With the patient supine and the thigh passively flexed to 90 degrees, internally and externally rotate the patient's right hip. Repeat the procedure on the contralateral side.

OUTCOME: If there is medial tenderness on internal rotation in right lower quadrant (see Fig 6-2C; obturator sign):
- ◆ **nonspecific ipsilateral pelvic inflammation**

If no tenderness: ◆ **normal**

APPROACH TO A PATIENT WITH ABDOMINAL ENLARGEMENT

Visually inspect flanks

PROCEDURE: With the patient supine, visually inspect the flanks.

OUTCOME: If there are bilateral bulging flanks (see Fig 6-5): ◆ **ascites (fluid)** Sensitivity 93%; specificity 54%[5]

If there is no such bulging: ◆ **normal**

Percuss abdomen

PROCEDURE: With the patient resting supine, percuss (use two-finger technique in Fig 5-1, p. 100) the abdomen in an inferolateral arc from the umbilicus. Listen for any change in the percussion note, and mark the site of that change.

OUTCOME: If the sound is tympanic throughout:
- ◆ **gas, consistent with bowel obstruction**

If dull throughout:
- ◆ **adipose tissue (fat)**
- ◆ **ascites (fluid)**

If resonant superiorly then dull in a circle pattern in the flanks (flank dullness): ◆ **ascites (fluid)**
Sensitivity 80%; specificity 69%[5]

Percuss abdomen for shifting dullness

PROCEDURE: With the patient supine, percuss the abdomen in an inferolateral arc from the umbilicus. Note any change from resonant to dull and the level of that change. Mark that level, then instruct the patient to assume a left or right lateral decubital position. With the patient in the decubital position, percuss the abdomen in a superolateral arc from the umbilicus. Note and mark the site of change from resonant to dull.

OUTCOME: If there is a change (shift) in the level of dullness (shifting dullness): ◆ **ascites (fluid)**
Sensitivity 60%; specificity 90%[5]
If no such change: ◆ **fat**

Percuss abdomen for fluid wave

PROCEDURE: With patient supine, tap with a sharp, staccato motion over the inferolateral aspect of the left or right abdomen. Concurrently place the palmar side of the contralateral hand on the inferior aspect of the contralateral side of the distended abdomen. If possible, ask an assistant to gently place the ulnar aspect of his or her hand longitudinally over the abdominal midline.

OUTCOME: If there is a wave through the skin, quite fast and visually discerned, starting from the point of percussion and migrating circumferentially: ◆ **skin wave**
If palpable fluid wave slightly behind the skin wave: ◆ **ascites**
Sensitivity 80%; specificity 92%[5]

Palpate abdomen for rebound tenderness: As in Basic Examination.

Visually inspect venous pattern of skin over abdomen

PROCEDURE: With the patient supine, visually inspect the skin over the abdomen and lower chest for distended veins. Control is "normal/baseline" skin areas (e.g., the thighs).

OUTCOME: If the veins are enlarged, engorged (see Fig 6-3):
◆ **venous obstruction, usually portal hypertension**
If veins are not demonstrable: ◆ **normal**

APPROACH TO A PATIENT WITH ANORECTAL DYSFUNCTION

Perform digital anorectal examination/anoscopy

PROCEDURE: 1. Place the patient in a right or left lateral decubital position with knees and thighs flexed.

2. Visually inspect and palpate the anal and perineal structures.

3. With a gloved hand and water-soluble lubricant on the index finger, gently insert the extended index finger with the palmar side of the digit positioned posteriorly.

4. Palpate the mucosa and the submucosal structures by sweeping laterally right, laterally left, then anteriorly.

5. Note and describe any lesions, relative to the pectinate line.

6. If any lesions are present, repeat the procedure using a clear anoscope.

OUTCOME

Anus: If there is one or more superficial blue-colored structures distal to the pectinate line: ◆ **external hemorrhoids, first degree**

If one or more blue-colored, easily compressed structures distal to the pectinate line: ◆ **external hemorrhoids, second degree**

If one or more blue-colored, firm, tender, nonreducible structures distal to the pectinate line: ◆ **external hemorrhoids, third degree**

If one or more flesh-colored tags on the anal skin:
◆ **external hemorrhoids, fibrosed**

If a tender, blue, swollen, bleeding nodule distal to the pectinate line (Fig 6-7): ◆ **external hemorrhoids, thrombosed**

If one or more nontender, blue, soft lesions proximal to the pectinate line: ◆ **internal hemorrhoids**

If a tender, superficial longitudinal laceration of the distal anus:
◆ **anal fissure**

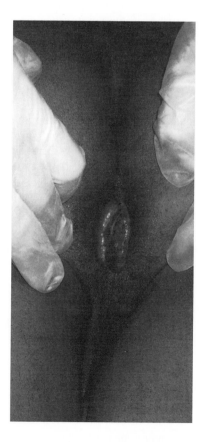

Figure 6-7 Thrombosed external hemorrhoids, quite tender and tense.

If an orifice at the perianal skin: ◆ **anal fistula**

If there are multiple pigmented macules in the mucosa of the anus/rectum: ◆ **Peutz-Jeghers syndrome**

If there is an area of tender fluctuance between the anus and the ischial tuberosity: ◆ **perirectal abscess**

Prostate: If the prostate gland is smooth and nontender, and has the consistency of a contracted thenar muscle: ◆ **normal**

If smooth, enlarged, tender, and boggy:
  ◆ **prostatitis (see Chapter 16, p. 368)**

If smooth, nontender, and has the consistency of cartilage:
  ◆ **benign prostatic hypertrophy (see Chapter 16, p. 365)**

If one or more nodules have the consistency of the nasal bone:
  ◆ **prostatic nodule (see Chapter 16, p. 368)**

Perform guaiac test on stool

PROCEDURE: Place a small sample of stool on a guaiac card. Place a drop of guaiac reagent on the sample and observe any change in color.

OUTCOME: If there is a blue color (see Plate 26):
  ◆ **hemoglobin in stool—gastrointestinal bleeding**

If no change in color:
  ◆ **inorganic iron present**
  ◆ **normal**

Keys to Recording Findings

ABDOMEN

"Soft, Nontender, BS present, no masses or hepatosplenomegaly"

A. Inspection

Note any distention, any scaphoid contour; and location of any scars or any masses

B. Auscultation

High pitched, tinkling bowel sounds; decreased; absent; note any bruits—renal versus midline

C. Palpation

Soft versus rigid; note sites of tenderness—direct (deep) versus rebound; note sites of any nodules or masses; any hernia—note location reducible, incarcerated or strangulated

D. Percussion

Especially if abdomen is distended—tympany versus dull

E. Liver

Span in right mid-clavicular line (normal: 10-12 cm), lower edge smooth, soft, nontender; note presence and location of any bruits, rubs, tenderness, nodules and masses

F. Spleen

Not enlarged by percussion in left anterior axillary line, not palpable; note size and lower edge if enlarged

A. Inspection

Draw on scars, masses, hernia.

B. Auscultation

Bowel sounds (BS), bruits, rubs

C. Palpation

Draw on location of masses, direct tenderness, rebound tenderness

D. Percussion

Areas of dullness, versus tympany

E. Liver size

F. Spleen size

Draw location either on 4 quadrant figure or 9 area figure.

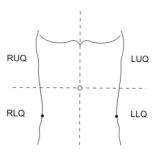

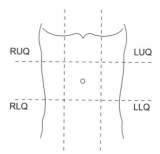

Abdominal aortic aneurysm

Abnormal aortic dilation to >3 cm in diameter, often as a result of long-standing uncontrolled hypertension. The natural history is a progressive increase in aneurysm diameter; with increasing diameter there is increasing risk of rupture; once rupture occurs, death from exsanguination is rapid. The symptoms are minimal, often limited mild lower back pain, even when the aneurysm is large. Signs include a pulsatile mass in the epigastrium (see Fig 6-2E), often with a bruit over the mass. An ultrasound of the abdomen helps in screening and evaluation. If the diameter exceeds 4 cm, semiannual follow-up with ultrasound imaging is indicated. In nonruptured aneurysms, surgical repair is required when the aneurysm diameter exceeds 5 cm. If rupture is imminent or suspected, advanced cardiac life support/advanced trauma life support (ACLS/ATLS) protocol and immediate/emergent vascular surgical intervention are mandated.

Anal fissure

Superficial longitudinal laceration of the distal anus. Risk factors include constipation and anal intercourse. Symptoms and signs include severe anal pain exacerbated by each bowel movement, and hematochezia. Anoscopy will reveal a longitudinal laceration at one site of anus crossing the dentate line. Evaluation and treatment include warm sitz baths, stool softeners, and, if persistent, referral to a gastroenterologist.

Anal fistula

Due to **Crohn's disease** or **squamous cell carcinoma** and characterized by a fistula between the lumen at the base of the crypt of Morgagni at dentate line and the perianal skin or a **perirectal abscess**. Symptoms and signs include acute anal pain, a tender nodule, a sinus in perineal skin, and discharge (at times purulent) from the orifice. A tender fluctuant mass deep indicates a **perirectal abscess**—anoscopy is confirmatory. Treatment includes urgent referral to a general surgeon and, in the case of an abscess, urgent I and D and systemic antibiotics.

Appendicitis

Inflammation of the appendix, which may be caused by obstruction. Symptoms include periumbilical (see Fig 6-2F) discomfort that over several hours migrates to the right lower quadrant, pain specific to McBurney's point (see Fig 6-1E), and often nausea, but minimal vomiting. Signs include deep and rebound tenderness at McBurney's point (see Fig 6-1E) and positive Rovsing's, psoas, and obturator signs. The patient may have a fever and signs of intravascular volume depletion. Evaluation and treatment include performing a pelvic or genitourinary examination, a computed tomographic

(CT) scan of the abdomen and pelvis, and emergent referral to a general surgeon.

Ascites

Abnormal presence of excess fluid within the peritoneal cavity, often due to end-stage liver disease or severe hypoalbuminemia. Symptoms include dependent edema and subjective increased abdominal size. Signs include abdominal distention (see Fig 6-3), bulging flanks (see Fig 6-5), shifting dullness, and a fluid wave. Concurrent internal hemorrhoids, abdominal venous distention (see Fig 6-3), small liver, icterus (Plate 14), an umbilical hernia (see Fig 6-3), asterixis, and/or gynecomastia may be present. Evaluation includes serum albumin and liver function tests. Treatment is of the underlying cause and may include diuretics, high-volume paracentesis, and referral to a gastroenterologist. When deep or rebound tenderness is present, spontaneous bacterial peritonitis (SBP) is likely. In SBP, test the ascitic fluid for cell count and culture, and administer systemic antibiotics, for example, a combination of ampicillin, gentamicin, and metronidazole.

Cholecystitis

Inflammation of the gallbladder due to choledocholithiasis or cholelithiasis, or both. Symptoms include right upper quadrant pain, nausea, and vomiting; the pain is often exacerbated by meals rich in fat. Signs include tenderness over the right upper quadrant (see Fig 6-2A), positive Murphy's sign (see Fig 6-1C), and a normal liver span. Patients may exhibit icterus and dark urine in obstruction of the common bile duct and fever and acute abdomen in ascending cholangitis; a palpable gallbladder (Courvoisier's sign) is indicative of carcinoma of the pancreatic head. Evaluation includes liver function tests for increased alkaline phosphatase and total bilirubin and ultrasound of the gallbladder for stones and ductal dilation. Treatment is by referral to a general surgeon.

Cirrhosis (end-stage liver disease)

Destruction and fibrosis of the liver parenchyma; severe embarrassment of the production of coagulation factors, albumin, and the processing of nutrients absorbed from the small intestine. Symptoms and signs include an enlarged or small liver, usually nontender; icterus (Plate 14); purpura (Plate 27); and ecchymoses (Plate 28). The patient may exhibit abdominal venous distention (see Fig 6-3), spider angiomas, gynecomastia, dependent edema and ascites (see Fig 6-2), asterixis, and encephalopathy. Evaluation includes obtaining a serum total bilirubin, albumin, ammonia, prothrombin time, and plasma glucose tests; in addition, viral hepatitis serologic tests for A, B, and C should be obtained. Treatment includes proscription of hepatotoxic agents (ethanol) and referral to a hepatologist.

Distended urinary bladder

Retention of urine in the bladder due to obstruction or autonomic dysfunction or medication related. Symptoms and signs include fullness in the suprapubic area (see Fig 6-2G) with dullness to percussion; a concurrent enlarged prostate is not uncommon in men. Evaluation and treatment include a postvoid residual (>50 mL is abnormal) via catheter placement, attempting to discontinue any agent that exacerbates dysfunction, and referral to a urologist.

Diverticulitis

Acquired sacs in the wall of the colon, which may form abscesses or perforate. Symptoms include subacute to acute onset of right or left lower quadrant pain (see Fig 6-2C,D); signs include deep and rebound tenderness and guarding. Rectal examination may reveal hematochezia. Evaluation includes a CT scan of the abdomen and pelvis to evaluate for any abscess cavity. Treatment is with systemic antibiotics and referral to a gastroenterologist for colonoscopy and a surgeon for potential resection of affected area of colon.

Emaciation/cachexia

Profound wasting due to malnutrition, malabsorption, or end-stage chronic disease [e.g., cancer, acquired immunodeficiency syndrome (AIDS), heart failure]. Symptoms and signs include loss of fat, a scaphoid abdomen, and atrophy, especially in the temporomandibular areas and intrinsic hand musculature. Treatment is directed toward the underlying etiology and includes adequate nutritional support.

External hemorrhoids

Dilated anal veins external to the dentate line. Risk factors include pregnancy and straining upon defecation. Symptoms include anal pruritus, soiling of underpants, anal pain, and hematochezia. The signs include nontender purple skin tags distal to the dentate line; blood and a tender fluctuant nodule (see Fig 6-7) in the area indicate acute thrombosis—anoscopy is confirmatory. Treatment includes warm sitz baths, topical anal steroids, stool softeners, and, if severe or refractory, referral to a general surgeon for removal.

Gallbladder enlargement

Due to chronic mild chronic obstruction of the biliary tree, usually due to a tumor of the pancreatic head. Symptoms and signs include jaundice, scleral icterus (Plate 14), cachexia, often clay-colored stools, and a palpable nontender gallbladder. Evaluation and treatment include a CT of the abdomen and referral to a gastroenterologist for endoscopic retrograde cholangiopancreatography (ERCP).

Gastrointestinal bleeding

Hemorrhage as a result of upper (peptic ulcer disease, gastritis, varices) or lower (diverticulosis, colon polyps) gastrointestinal sites. Symptoms and signs depend on the rate of bleeding. Slow bleeding is characterized by minimal symptoms until pallor, angular cheilosis, koilonychia, and brown guaiac-positive stool manifest. Rapid bleeding results in tachycardia, orthostatic parameters, and hypotension, with black guaiac-positive (melena; Plate 26) or even red (hematochezia) stool. Treatment includes stabilizing the patient with fluids and blood products as needed and emergent referral to a gastroenterologist for endoscopic assessment of the upper and lower tracts.

Hepatitis: See Hepatomegaly.

Hepatomegaly

Abnormal enlargement of the liver due to inflammation (ethanol abuse or viral hepatitis), right heart failure, infiltration with iron in hemochromatosis, or neoplasia (**hepatocellular carcinoma** or metastatic colon carcinoma). Symptoms and signs include an enlarged liver that may be tender or nontender, smooth or nodular (see Fig 6-6). Other symptoms and signs are specific to the underlying diagnosis: tender liver (see Fig 6-2A), jaundice (Plate 14) in acute hepatitis; nontender smooth liver with new-onset diabetes mellitus, diffusely bronze skin pigment, and right heart failure in hemochromatosis; nontender nodular liver with rubs or bruits, or both, in neoplastic process; mildly tender expansile liver with an increased jugular venous pressure, significant pitting peripheral edema, and an S_3 gallop in right-sided heart failure. Evaluation includes imaging with CT scan of the abdomen and an echocardiogram. The treatment is specific to the underlying cause.

Ileus

Acquired hypofunctioning of the small and large bowel due to inflammation, electrolyte disturbances, surgery, or medications. Symptoms and signs of nausea, intermittent vomiting, anorexia, and decreased to no flatus. The abdomen is soft and nontender but has a paucity of bowel sounds. Concurrent signs are present of the underlying cause—for example, a fresh surgical scar or left upper quadrant tenderness of pancreatitis. Evaluation is with a radiographic abdominal series, which reveals a nonspecific bowel gas pattern. Treatment includes bowel rest, fluid support, and correction of electrolytes.

Incisional hernia

A defect in a suture line, usually due to poor wound healing. Risk factors for poor wound healing include uncontrolled diabetes mellitus, the use of high-dose steroids, or chronic increases in intra-abdominal pressure. Symptoms and signs include a nontender, reducible soft mass adjacent to a suture line; mass may be quite large. Treatment is referral to a general surgeon.

Internal hemorrhoids

Dilated anal veins, proximal to the dentate line. The main risk factor is hepatic portal venous hypertension. Symptoms include hematochezia without anal pruritus or pain. Signs include prolapse of a nontender mass through the anus but minimal to no tenderness—anoscopy is confirmatory. Other signs include those of end-stage liver disease (ESLD): ascites (see Fig 6-3), abdominal venous redistribution, icterus (Plate 14), and small liver. Treatment is of the underlying liver disease. Look for varices, consider the initiation of a beta-blocker to decrease portal hypertension; the patient should be referred to a gastroenterologist.

Nephrolithiasis
Development of stones, such as calcium phosphate/apatite, calcium oxalate, uric acid, or struvite crystals, within the urinary tract. Symptoms include flank pain that radiates into the ipsilateral groin, hematuria, and a past history of stones. Signs include tenderness in the left or right flank and a positive Murphy's punch sign. Evaluation with a urinalysis reveals crystals, pyuria, and/or hematuria. All urine should be strained in order to collect any passed stone, and when the stone is passed it should be sent to the laboratory for crystal analysis. A KUB (kidneys, ureters, bladder) demonstrates all stone types except for uric acid, which is radiolucent. Treatment is with fluids, analgesia, and referral to a urologist or nephrologist.

Pancreatitis
Inflammation of the pancreas most commonly due to choledocholithiasis or chronic ethanol abuse. Symptoms include epigastric or left upper quadrant pain, nausea, vomiting, and dizziness on arising. Signs include tenderness to deep and rebound palpation in the left upper quadrant (see Fig 6-2B); if very severe, necrosis with retroperitoneal hemorrhage may develop with a positive Cullen's and Grey Turner's signs (see Fig 14-6). **Steatorrhea** is common in chronic pancreatitis. Evaluation with KUB reveals calcifications of chronic disease; serum amylase and lipase are elevated; obtaining an abdominal series demonstrates an ileus or, if severe to chronic, pancreatic calcifications. Treatment is with intravenous (IV) fluids, rest of the gastrointestinal (GI) tracts, and referral to a gastroenterologist for potential endoscopic retrograde cholangiopancreatography (ERCP).

Peptic ulcer disease
Ulcer in either the stomach or duodenum owing to excess acid, nonsteroidal anti-inflammatory drug (NSAID) use, or *Helicobacter pylori* infection. Symptoms include epigastric pain that improves with oral intake, early satiety, and black stools. Signs include epigastric tenderness (see Fig 6-2E) and any of the manifestations of complications: With bleeding, the rectal examination may reveal black, guaiac-positive stool (Plate 26); with perforation, there may be involuntary guarding and rebound tenderness; and with pyloric stenosis, there may be a prolonged percussion splash. Evaluation includes performing a hematocrit, an upper GI study, and/or an esophagogastroduodenoscopy (EGD). Treatment includes referral to a gastroenterologist, proscribing NSAIDs, and administering H$_2$-blockers or H-pump inhibitors. With *H. pylori* infection, the patient should receive systemic antibiotics.

Perirectal abscess: See Anal fistula.

Peritonitis

Inflammation of the peritoneum due to infection either from bowel perforation, or SBP, or ascending cholangitis or related to diverticulitis or appendicitis. Symptoms include nausea, vomiting, and generalized abdominal
pain, often after the localized pain episode. Signs include diffuse deep and
rebound tenderness, involuntary guarding, and fevers. Signs of concurrent
processes include McBurney's point sign (see Fig 6-1E) in appendicitis,
tender adnexal mass in PID (see Fig 6-2C,D), or positive Murphy's sign (see
Fig 6-1C) in cholecystitis. Evaluation with abdominal series may reveal free
air if there is a bowel perforation, but in all cases, a CT scan of the abdomen
and pelvis is clearly indicated. Treatment is with systemic antibiotics and
emergency referral to a general surgeon.

Portal hypertension: See Cirrhosis (end-stage liver disease), Venous
obstruction.

Primary hepatocellular carcinoma: See Hepatomegaly.

Peutz-Jeghers syndrome: See p. 37.

Pyelonephritis

Inflammation of the renal parenchyma, calyces, and pelvis due to ascending
urinary tract infection from the urinary bladder. The most common organisms involved are gram-negative rods from the GI tract. Symptoms and signs
of nausea, increased frequency, dysuria, hesitancy, fever, and tender right or
left flank (Murphy's punch sign). Evaluation and treatment are with urinalysis and culture/sensitivity and systemic antibiotics.

Sister Mary Joseph's nodule

Metastatic deposit in the umbilicus from an internal adenocarcinoma,
often gastric or pancreatic. Symptoms and signs include one or more
plaques in the umbilicus (see Fig 6-4), which may ulcerate; concurrent
weight loss, cachexia, early satiety, and postprandial vomiting; and jaundice.
Evaluation is with a CT scan of the abdomen and/or an upper GI study for
a pancreatic or gastric mass. Treatment is referral to a surgeon and/or
oncologist.

Small bowel obstruction

Blockage in the small intestine as a result of adhesions from old surgery,
hernia (see Fig 6-5), intussusception, or volvulus. Symptoms include abdominal pain, moderate nausea, vomiting, and markedly decreased flatus. The
distention is tympanic, with no fluid wave or shifting dullness. Concurrent
manifestations of intravascular volume depletion are present. Evaluation
includes obtaining a set of orthostatic parameters and an abdominal series,
which may reveal air-fluid levels and small bowel distention; CT scan of the

abdomen and pelvis is indicated in most cases; electrolyte abnormalities occur from vomiting of a contraction alkalosis and hypokalemia. Treatment includes intravenous normal saline, repletion of electrolytes, nasogastric decompression, and referral to a general surgeon.

Splenomegaly

Enlargement of the spleen due to passive congestion (liver or heart failure) or extravascular hemolysis. Evaluate the spleen size by percussion: Castell's maneuver (see Fig 6-1F), Traube's sign (dullness over Traube's space; see Fig 6-1H), and palpation, best performed with patient in the right decubital position. A concurrent S_3 gallop and pulsatile liver indicate right heart failure. Evaluation includes imaging with CT scans of the abdomen and/or an echocardiogram. The treatment is specific to the underlying cause.

Steatorrhea: See Pancreatitis.

Umbilical hernia

A defect in the umbilicus due to chronic increase in intra-abdominal pressure, usually related to pregnancy or ascites. Symptoms and signs include a nontender reducible soft mass in the umbilicus (see Fig 6-3); concurrent manifestations of ascites or pregnancy are often evident. Treatment is of the underlying condition; the patient should be referred to a general surgeon.

Venous obstruction: See Cirrhosis (end-stage liver disease), Gastrointestinal bleeding, and Internal hemorrhoids.

CHAPTER 7
Neurology

Basic Examination

Assess strength (power) and/or patterns of weakness in specific muscles

PROCEDURE: Instruct the patient to perform the following activities actively (specific muscles are listed):

Abduction of arm at glenohumeral joint from 30 degrees of abduction: deltoids (C5)

Adduction/abduction of fingers: interossei (T1)

Extension at the knee: quadriceps femoris (L4)

Extension at the great toe: extensor pollicis (L5)

OUTCOME: If there is no active movement: ◆ **0: paralysis**
If a twitch movement: ◆ **1: weakness**
If the patient is able to move but not to overcome gravity:
◆ **2: weakness**
If able to move to overcome gravity: ◆ **3: weakness**
If able to move to overcome mild resistance (2 fingers):
◆ **4: weakness**
If able to move to overcome significant resistance: ◆ **5: normal**

Patterns of If an entire side of the body is weak: ◆ **hemiparesis**
weakness: If an entire side of the body is paralyzed: ◆ **hemiplegia**
If the lower extremities are weak: ◆ **paraparesis**
If lower extremities are paralyzed: ◆ **paraplegia**
If upper and lower extremities are weak:
◆ **quadriparesis (i.e., tetraparesis)**
If upper and lower extremities are paralyzed:
◆ **quadriplegia (i.e., tetraplegia)**
If deltoid and quadriceps are weak but the fingers and toes have normal strength: ◆ **proximal muscle weakness**

Assess tone during passive range of motion

PROCEDURE: Perform a passive range of motion (ROM) about several joints, such as the elbow, wrist, knee, ankle. Repeat on the contralateral side for control. The motion must be passive; if the patient is unable to relax, provide distraction by instructing him or her to tap the contralateral hand on the thigh.

OUTCOME: If there is increased stiffness about the joint due to increased muscle tone: ◆ **hypertonicity (spasticity or rigidity)**

If increased stiffness about joint, with some muscles affected more than others (i.e., agonists more affected than antagonists):
   ◆ **spasticity: upper motor neuron (UMN) damage**
If increased stiffness about joint that is maximum at initiation of passive ROM but decreases with continuation of passive movement (clasp-knife phenomenon): ◆ **spasticity: UMN damage**
If increased stiffness about joint, with all muscles affected equally (i.e., antagonists same as agonists):
   ◆ **rigidity: lead-pipe (if severe)**
   ◆ **rigidity: cogwheel (if moderate)**
If decreased stiffness about joint such that it is floppy:
   ◆ **hypotonicity**

Check reflexes: wrist extensor, triceps, patellar, Achilles

PROCEDURE:

Wrist extensor reflex: Position the patient's forearm on a flat surface. Use a plexor to strike briskly over the middle of the muscle (Fig 7-1). Use the contralateral side or yourself as a control.

OUTCOME: If there is wrist clonus or crossover to other side:
   ◆ **4+: marked hyperreflexia**

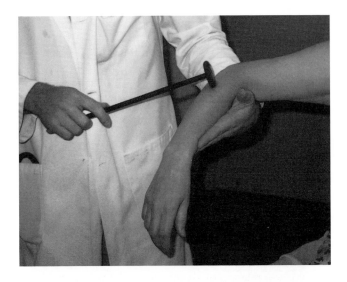

Figure 7-1 Forearm extensor reflex (C7). This deep tendon reflex consists of extension of the wrist or finger on striking the proximal forearm distal to the lateral epicondyle.

If there is marked extension at the wrist: ◆ **3+: hyperreflexia**
If moderate extension at the wrist: ◆ **2+ normal**
If mild extension at the wrist: ◆ **1+ normal or hyporeflexia**
If no movement: ◆ **0 areflexia**

Triceps reflex: Grasp the patient's upper extremity at the elbow and passively abduct the arm at the glenohumeral joint. Flex the arm at the elbow so that the forearm is dangling. Strike the triceps muscle briskly with the plexor, approximately 2 to 3 cm proximal to the olecranon. Use the contralateral side or yourself as control.

OUTCOME: If there is elbow clonus or crossover to other side:
◆ **4+: marked hyperreflexia**
If there is marked extension at the elbow: ◆ **3+**
If moderate extension at the elbow: ◆ **2+**
If mild extension at the elbow: ◆ **1+**
If no movement: ◆ **0**

Patellar (knee) reflex:
1. Have the patient sit with the knees passively flexed and legs dangling (Fig 7-2). Palpate the infrapatellar portion of the patellar ligament. Briskly strike over that site using the plexor. Use the contralateral side or yourself for comparison; *or*

2. Have the patient lie supine. Passively flex the patient's knee to 20 degrees. Palpate the infrapatellar portion of the patellar lig-

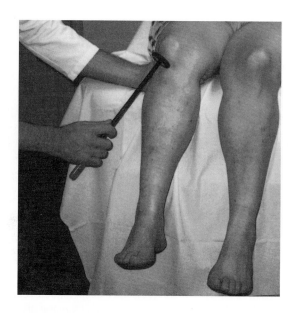

Figure 7-2 Quadriceps reflex (L4). This deep tendon reflex consists of extension of the knee on striking the patellar ligament.

ament. Briskly strike using the plexor over that site. Use the contralateral side or yourself for comparison.

OUTCOME: If there is knee extensor clonus or crossover to other side:
* **4+: marked hyperreflexia**
If there is marked extension at the knee: ◆ **3+**
If moderate extension at the knee: ◆ **2+**
If mild extension at the knee: ◆ **1+**
If no movement: ◆ **0**

Achilles Have the patient kneel on a chair (Fig 7-3). Palpate for the
(ankle) Achilles tendon. Passively dorsiflex the foot at the ankle and
reflex: briskly strike the tendon with the plexor. Use the contralateral side or yourself as control.

OUTCOME: If there is marked plantar flexion with repetitive involuntary plantar/dorsiflexion: ◆ **4+ (clonus; profound hyperreflexia)**
If marked plantar flexion: ◆ **3+**
If moderate plantar flexion: ◆ **2+**
If mild plantar flexion: ◆ **1+**
If no movement: ◆ **0**

Perform Jendrassik's maneuver

PROCEDURE: Have the patient clasp the hands together (or grab wrists tightly) in front of herself or himself and forcefully contract the musculature of both upper extremities. Concurrently perform deep

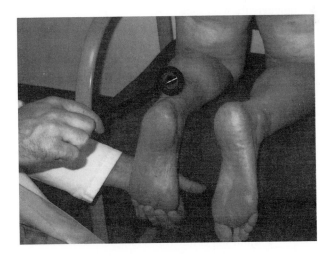

Figure 7-3 Achilles reflex (S1). This deep tendon reflex consists of plantar flexion of the ankle on striking the Achilles ligament.

tendon reflexes on the patella and/or the Achilles. This should be performed on 0 and 1+ reflexes.

OUTCOME: Maneuver increases the sensitivity of deep tendon reflexes.

Assess stance

PROCEDURE: Have the patient stand in place in anatomic position with feet together and eyes open.

OUTCOME: If the patient is able to bring the feet together: ◆ **normal**
If able to stand with feet apart but unable to stand with feet together: ◆ **ataxia, cerebellar**

Perform Romberg's test

PROCEDURE: Have the patient standing in anatomic position with feet together; observe the patient for 20 to 30 seconds. Then tell the patient to close his or her eyes and extend the arms to 90 degrees for another 30 seconds. Visually observe the movement of the body. (Note: Romberg's test requires a normal stance.)

OUTCOME: If the patient stays in midline (no swaying with eyes open or closed): ◆ **normal**
If patient stays in midline with eyes open but sways to the left or right with eyes closed: ◆ **unilateral proprioceptive ataxia**
If patient stays in midline with eyes open but is bilaterally unsteady with eyes closed:
◆ **ataxia, proprioceptive, for example, tabes dorsalis**

Assess arm movements with gait

PROCEDURE: Ask the patient to walk at a normal pace, looking straight ahead. Observe the patient's arm movements.

OUTCOME: If there are pendulum arm movements in concert with the contralateral lower extremity: ◆ **normal**
If no pendulum arm movements with ambulation (Wartenberg's sign): ◆ **ataxia, cerebellar**

Assess gait

PROCEDURE: Ask the patient to walk at a normal pace, looking straight ahead. Visually inspect the patient's position, arm movements, lower extremity placement, and lower extremity movements.

OUTCOME: If there is normal-based foot placement, the hips posteriorly displaced with an accentuated lumbar lordosis, a marked increase in hip wiggle when walking, not unsteady:
◆ **waddling gait**
If narrow-based foot placement; a stiff, straight back; tentative steps, as if painful to the patient; not unsteady: ◆ **poker gait**

If narrow-based foot placement; one arm is immobile and close to the side in an attitude of involuntary flexion at the elbow and involuntary supination at the wrist; the ipsilateral leg is involuntarily extended; the foot is plantar flexed, swept forward with each step, and is involuntarily circumducted at the ankle; and the patient sways to side of weakness: ◆ **spastic hemiparetic gait**

If narrow-based foot placement; both arms are held close to the sides in an attitude of involuntary flexion at the elbow and involuntary supination at the wrist; the legs are involuntarily extended; the foot is plantar flexed, swept forward with each step, and is involuntarily circumducted at the ankle; the patient sways from side to side with thighs crossing in front with each step: ◆ **scissors gait**

If narrow-based foot placement; the knee actively flexes to elevate the foot (unilateral or bilateral); not unsteady:

  ◆ **steppage gait**

If narrow-based foot placement; the patient is stooped, head forward; the hips and knees are slightly flexed, with stiff shuffling; and there is a fenestrating gait (the patient appears to be running with small discrete steps):

  ◆ **parkinsonian gait**

If the lower extremity placement is wide based, with sways to either or both sides: ◆ **ataxia**

Test vibratory sensation

PROCEDURE: Use a 256-Hz tuning fork and always strike the fork in a reproducible manner.

1. Place the vibrating fork on the patient's sternum to give the patient a sensation reference.

2. Place the base of the tuning fork over the bony prominence of the site to be tested. Tell patient to state when the vibratory sensation starts and stops.

3. If the toes have a deficit in vibratory sensation, move proximally to find a level. In the routine examination, only the index toes need to be assessed; if a deficit is present at the lateral malleolus, assess the anterior tibial surface.

OUTCOME: If there is a vibratory sensation at the tips of the second digits of hands and feet: ◆ **normal**

If decreased vibratory sensation in a stocking-glove distribution:

  ◆ **peripheral neuropathy (Fig 7-4A)**

If decreased sensation on one side, beneath a level ipsilateral to a site of spinal cord trauma:

  ◆ **Brown-Séquard syndrome (Fig 7-4B)**

If bilateral absent sensation, no sparing:

  ◆ **cord transection (Fig 7-4C)**

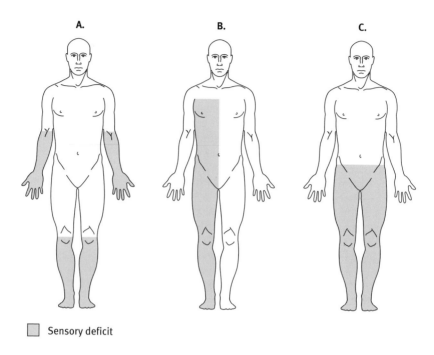

Sensory deficit

Figure 7-4 Vibratory assessment. A. Peripheral neuropathy. B. Right-sided Brown-Séquard syndrome. C. Cord transection—note no sacral sparing.

Superficial pain assessment

PROCEDURE: Tell the patient to close his or her eyes. Break the wooden handle of a cotton-tipped swab; use the broken side, which is pointed, to touch the skin gently on the great toe, metatarsals, heels; then apply to fingertips, metacarpals, and Lister's tubercle (see Fig 8-11D).

OUTCOME: If the patient can sense superficial to all four extremities:
　　　　　◆ **normal**
If a loss of or decrease in sensation in a stocking-glove distribution: ◆ **peripheral neuropathy (Fig 7-5A)**
If a loss of or decrease in sensation on the side, beneath a level contralateral to side of cord lesion and one dermatome at level ipsilateral: ◆ **Brown-Séquard syndrome (Fig 7-5B)**

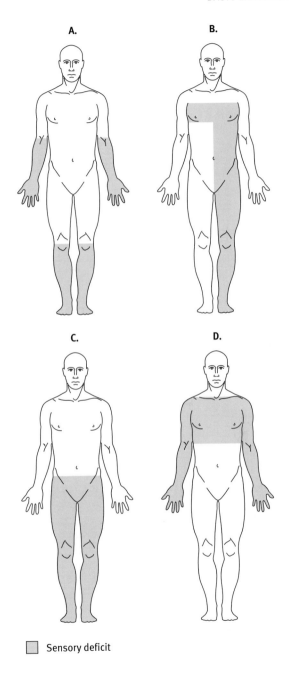

Figure 7-5 Superficial pain assessment: A. Peripheral neuropathy. B. Right-sided Brown-Séquard syndrome. C. Cord transection. D. Syringomyelia.

If loss of sensation with a bilateral level of anesthesia:
◆ **spinal cord transection (Fig 7-5C)**
If bilateral loss of sensation in upper extremities greater than lower extremities: ◆ **syringomyelia (Fig 7-5D)**

Assess cranial nerves: CN I to XII

CN I. Perform vanilla test.

PROCEDURE: Instruct the patient to close the eyes. Place vanilla extract or freshly ground coffee near the patient's nasal orifice. Use yourself as a control.

OUTCOME: If there is sensation: ◆ **normal**
If no sensation: ◆ **abnormal**

CN II. Test visual field: See Chapter 3, as in Basic Examination, p. 46.

CN III. Assess pupil size: See Chapter 3, as in Basic Examination, p. 45 (see Fig 3-2).

CN III. Test extraocular muscle (EOM) movement.

PROCEDURE: Tell the patient to gaze forward, then to follow your finger in six directions: medial, lateral, diagonal superotemporal, diagonal superonasal, diagonal inferonasal, and diagonal inferotemporal (Fig 7-6).

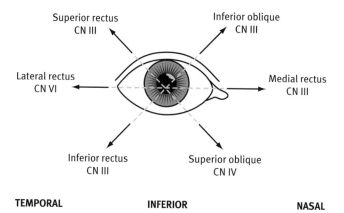

SUPERIOR

Superior rectus
CN III

Inferior oblique
CN III

Lateral rectus
CN VI

Medial rectus
CN III

Inferior rectus
CN III

Superior oblique
CN IV

TEMPORAL   **INFERIOR**   **NASAL**

Figure 7-6 Extraocular movements. Method here used to demonstrate the active range of motion of the eye. CN, cranial nerve.

OUTCOME: If there is no movement of eye except in lateral and inferonasal directions: ◆ **CN III defect (see also Strabismus; p. 68)**
If movement in all axes of gaze: ◆ **normal**

CN III. Check for ptosis.
PROCEDURE: Have the patient gaze forward. Examine the location of the upper eyelids relative to limbus.
OUTCOME: If the eyelid is at the level of the limbus of the cornea: ◆ **normal**
If the eyelid is covering the superior aspect of the cornea (ptosis):
◆ **Horner's syndrome**

CN III. Check for Argyll Robertson sign.
PROCEDURE: In a dimly lit room, have the patient gaze forward. Place your finger approximately 20 cm in front of the patient's gaze. Tell the patient to follow your finger, then slowly move it toward the patient's face. Observe the pupils as the eyes converge.
OUTCOME: If there is no miosis with convergence: ◆ **CN III defect**
If miosis is present, that is, the pupil accommodates (Argyll-Robertson sign; see Fig 3-2C, p. 45): ◆ **tabes dorsalis**

CN IV. Test EOM movement, superior oblique muscle.
PROCEDURE: Have the patient gaze forward. Tell the patient to follow your finger in six directions: medial, lateral, diagonal superotemporal, diagonal superonasal, diagonal inferonasal, and diagonal inferotemporal (Fig 7-6).
OUTCOME: If there is loss of inferomedial (SO4) movement: ◆ **CN IV defect**
If inferomedial movement is present: ◆ **normal**

CN V. Assess masseter strength.
PROCEDURE: Have the patient bite down on a sterile tongue blade placed in between the patient's molar teeth. Palpate the masseter and the temporalis muscles on that side; repeat on other side.
OUTCOME: If there is unilateral weakness of the masseter muscle:
◆ **CN V defect**
If good strength in both masseter muscles: ◆ **normal**

CN V. Test facial skin touch.
PROCEDURE: With the patient looking forward, lightly touch the skin with a cotton swab on one side of the frontal area (V1), the maxillary area (V2), and the mandibular area (V3). Use the other side as a control.
OUTCOME: If there is decreased sensation over the frontal skin: ◆ **V1 defect**
If decreased sensation over the maxillary skin: ◆ **V2 defect**
If decreased sensation over the mandibular skin: ◆ **V3 defect**

CN VI. Test EOM movement, lateral rectus muscle.

PROCEDURE: Have the patient gaze forward. Tell the patient to follow your finger in six directions: medial, lateral, diagonal superotemporal, diagonal superonasal, diagonal inferonasal, and diagonal inferotemporal (see Fig 7-6).

OUTCOME: If there is loss of lateral movement: ◆ **CN VI defect**
If normal lateral movement: ◆ **normal**

CN VII. Test eyelid closure

PROCEDURE: Have the patient tightly close both eyes and keep them closed, even against resistance (Fig 7-7).

OUTCOME: If both eyes are kept closed against moderate resistance:
◆ **normal**
If one eye cannot be closed or there is weakness of the orbicularis oculus: ◆ **peripheral CN VII palsy (Bell's palsy), ipsilateral**

CN VII. Observe smile (nasolabial folds)

PROCEDURE: Tell the patient to smile. Visually inspect the movement of the nasolabial folds and the angles of the mouth (Fig 7-8).

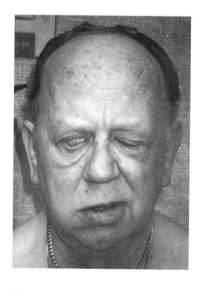

Figure 7-7 Cranial nerve VII palsy, peripheral. Patient instructed to close the eyes tightly, unable to close right eye. In addition, right eye retracts upward as a synkinesis (Bell's phenomenon).

Figure 7-8 Cranial nerve VII palsy, peripheral. Patient instructed to smile, unable to turn right corner of mouth upward, orbicularis oris weakness on the right.

OUTCOME: If the nasolabial folds are accentuated and the sides of the mouth are upturned: ◆ **normal**
If there is a unilateral decrease in nasolabial fold and no upturn of the angle:
- ◆ **peripheral CN VII palsy, ipsilateral**
- ◆ **central CN VII palsy, contralateral side**

CN VII. Observe forehead wrinkle

PROCEDURE: Tell the patient to elevate the eyebrows so as to wrinkle the fore-head skin (Fig 7-9).

OUTCOME: If the forehead skin wrinkles bilaterally: ◆ **normal**
If there is a unilateral decrease in forehead wrinkling:
- ◆ **peripheral CN VII palsy, ipsilateral**

CN VIII. Perform Weber's test for hearing

PROCEDURE: Place the base of a vibrating 512-Hz tuning fork on the skull vertex (the highest point in the midline of the skull). Ask the patient to state when the sound of the tuning fork can no longer

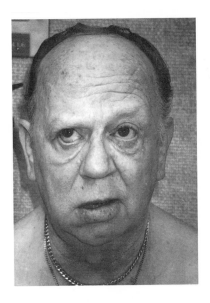

Figure 7-9 Cranial nerve VII palsy, peripheral. Patient instructed to look upward with moving head; note no frontalis movement, that is, a lack of right-sided wrinkling.

be heard in each ear. Note the duration and lateralization. (Lateralization is the side on which the tuning fork is heard longest.)

OUTCOME: If >30 seconds, no lateralization: ◆ **normal hearing**
If the patient hears no sound of the tuning fork from the outset:
◆ **bilateral neurosensory hearing loss**
If no sound of the tuning fork in one ear from the outset:
◆ **neurosensory hearing loss in that ear**
If the sound lateralizes to the deaf ear: ◆ **conductive hearing loss**
If lateralizes to the normal ear: ◆ **neurosensory hearing loss**

CN VIII. Perform the Dix-Hallpike-Nylen-Bárány maneuver

PROCEDURE: 1. Have the patient lie supine with the head at approximately 20 degrees of extension and turned to the right or left for 30 to 90 seconds.

2. Tell the patient to assume a sitting position for 5 minutes.

3. Repeat with the head turned to the contralateral side.

4. Ask the patient whether vertigo develops, and visually inspect the eyes for any nystagmus.

OUTCOME: If vertigo and nystagmus with the rapid phase to the "downward" placed ear develop, nystagmus resolving after 15 to 30 seconds: ◆ **benign positional vertigo**
If there is no nystagmus and no vertigo: ◆ **another etiology**

CN IX, X. Observe active uvula

PROCEDURE: Have the patient open his or her mouth. Visually inspect the uvula at rest and while the patient says "Ahhh" (Fig 7-10).

OUTCOME: If the uvula is at the midline at rest, and elevated in the midline with "Ahhh" (Fig 7-10A): ◆ **normal**
If uvula is deviated toward the nondiseased side at rest and elevated and deviated to the nondiseased side with "Ahhh" (Fig 7-10B): ◆ **unilateral plegia of CN IX, X**
If uvula is at the midline at rest and elevated and deviated to the nondiseased side with "Ahhh" (Fig 7-10C):
◆ **unilateral paresis of CN IX, X**
If uvula is at the midline at rest, and there is no movement with "Ahhh" (Fig 7-10D): ◆ **bilateral plegia of CN IX, X**

CN XI. Assess trapezius muscle

PROCEDURE: Place your hands on the patient's shoulders. Tell the patient to shrug the shoulders upward.

OUTCOME: If the patient is able to shrug against resistance: ◆ **normal**
If there is unilateral weakness:
◆ **CN XI defect (trapezius muscle; pseudobulbar palsy)**
If bilateral weakness: ◆ **proximal muscle weakness**

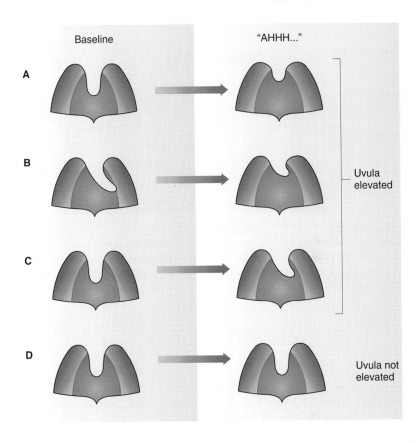

Figure 7-10 Uvula examination used to assess cranial nerves IX and X. A. Normal. B. Right plegia. C. Right paresis. D. Bilateral plegia.

CN XI. Assess sternocleidomastoid muscle

PROCEDURE: Place your hands on both sides of the patient's head. Tell the patient to rotate the head right and left against resistance.

OUTCOME: If the patient can rotate bilaterally: ◆ **normal**
If patient is unilaterally weak:
  ◆ **CN XI defect (sternocleidomastoid; pseudobulbar palsy)**
If patient is bilaterally weak: ◆ **proximal muscle weakness**

CN XII. Observe tongue protrusion

PROCEDURE: Tell the patient to protrude the tongue actively from an open mouth (Fig 7-11).

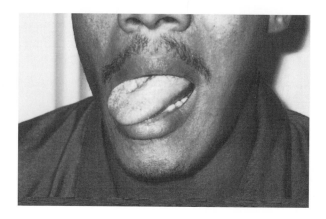

Figure 7-11 Cranial nerve XII, lower motor neuron defect. Tongue deviates to the right on active protrusion, indicative of an ipsilateral lower motor neuron lesion. Patient had sustained a gunshot wound to right neck several years before this photograph was taken.

OUTCOME: If the tongue is protruded in the midline: ◆ **normal**

If tongue is deviated to one side (Dinkler's sign) (see Fig 7-11):

◆ **LMN CN XII defect**

Advanced Examination

APPROACH TO A PATIENT WITH WEAKNESS

Assess strength (power) and/or patterns of weakness in specific muscles: As in Basic Examination.

Observe tone during passive range of motion: As in Basic Examination.

Check reflexes: wrist extensors, triceps, patellar, Achilles: As in Basic Examination.

Assess gait: As in Basic Examination.

Inspect muscles
PROCEDURE: Visually inspect the muscle group being tested.

OUTCOME: If fasiculations, that is, involuntary twitches, are present—an entire motor unit contracting spontaneously:
- ◆ **lower motor neuron (LMN) defect**

If atrophy:
- ◆ **LMN defect**
- ◆ **primary muscle defect**

Palpate muscles
PROCEDURE: Palpate the individual muscle groups.

OUTCOME: If there is muscle tenderness: ◆ **polymyositis/dermatomyositis**
If flabby enlargement of the calf muscles (pseudohypertrophy):
- ◆ **Duchenne's dystrophy**
- ◆ **Becker's muscular dystrophy**

If no inappropriate enlargement: ◆ **nonspecific**

Check for pronator drift sign
PROCEDURE: Have the patient actively place the upper extremities in a position of extension and supination, then maintain that position for 30 seconds. Visually inspect the position of the upper extremities.

OUTCOME: If the patient is able to maintain position: ◆ **normal**
If one upper extremity involuntarily drifts inferiorly and pronates (pronator drift sign): ◆ **UMN defect: spastic paresis**

Observe standing from sitting
PROCEDURE: Have the patient sit in a chair, then stand without the use of the upper extremities.

OUTCOME: If the upper extremities are not used:
- ◆ **normal**
- ◆ **distal muscle weakness**

If upper extremities are used: ◆ **proximal muscle weakness**

Perform anal wink test

PROCEDURE: With the patient in a lateral decubitus position, stroke or scratch the skin adjacent to the anus in the perineum with a gloved finger or tongue depressor. Use a gloved finger to palpate in the anal canal for a reflexive contraction of the anal sphincter.

OUTCOME: If there is anal sphincter contraction: ◆ **normal**

If no anal sphincter contraction:
- ◆ **cord compression/cauda equina syndrome (see p. 244)**
- ◆ **spinal cord transection**

Check for ankle clonus

PROCEDURE: Have patient lie supine or sit at rest. Grasp the ankle and passively flex/extend at the tibiotalar joint three times, the last time in full extension for several seconds. Feel for any involuntary movements in the foot.

OUTCOME: If there is rhythmic resistance (>2 beats) to maintained passive extension: ◆ **4+ reflexes: clonus, UMN damage**

If no involuntary movement: ◆ **normal**

Check for wrist clonus

PROCEDURE: Have patient lie supine or sit at rest. Grasp the hand and passively flex/extend at the wrist joint three times, the last time in full extension for several seconds. Feel for any involuntary movements in the hand.

OUTCOME: If there is rhythmic resistance (>2 beats) to maintained passive extension: ◆ **4+ reflexes: clonus; UMN damage**

If no involuntary movement: ◆ **normal**

Check for Babinski's sign

PROCEDURE: Have the patient lie supine. Stroke the sole of the foot with a plexor or tongue depressor in an arc from the posterolateral aspect extending over the metatarsal heads to the great toe (Fig 7-12). Visually inspect for involuntary movements in the foot/ankle. Use the contralateral side for control.

OUTCOME: If there is involuntary dorsiflexion and spreading of the toes (Babinski's sign): ◆ **UMN defect**

If plantar flexion: ◆ **normal**

If no movement: ◆ **nonspecific finding**

Check for Oppenheim's sign

PROCEDURE: Firmly stroke the medial/anterior tibial surface, superior to inferior, using a plexor or finger (Fig 7-13B). Visually inspect for

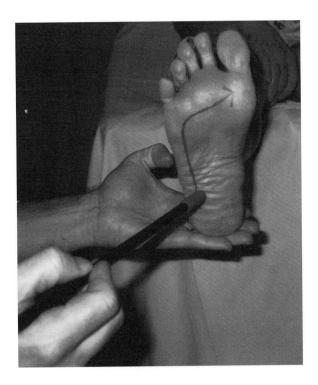

Figure 7-12 Involuntary dorsiflexion and flaring of the toes in response to a noxious stimulus indicative of an upper motor neuron lesion (Babinski's sign).

involuntary movements in the foot/ankle. Use the contralateral side for control.

OUTCOME: If there is involuntary dorsiflexion and spreading of the toes (Oppenheim's sign): ◆ **UMN defect**
If plantar flexion: ◆ **normal**
If no movement: ◆ **nonspecific finding**

Check for Chaddock's sign

PROCEDURE: Using a plexor, repeatedly tap at several sites from the lateral malleolus distally on the lateral dorsum of the foot (see Fig 7-13A). Visually inspect for involuntary movements in the foot/ankle. Use the contralateral side for control.

OUTCOME: If there is involuntary dorsiflexion and spreading of the toes (Chaddock's sign): ◆ **UMN defect**
If plantar flexion: ◆ **normal**
If no movement: ◆ **nonspecific finding**

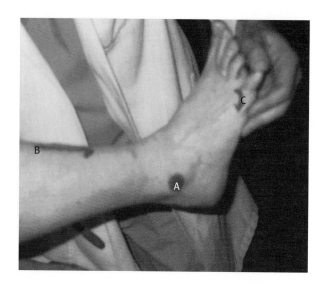

Figure 7-13 Babinski equivalents. A. Chaddock's: tapping over the lateral malleolus. B. Oppenheim's: rubbing the anterior tibia. C. Stransky's: passive abduction of the fifth digit. These are often superior to the Babinski test itself.

Check for Stransky's sign

PROCEDURE: Passively but firmly abduct the fifth digit for 2 seconds, then acutely let it go (see Fig 7-13C). Visually inspect for involuntary movements in the foot/ankle. Use the contralateral side for control.

OUTCOME: If there is involuntary dorsiflexion and spreading of the toes (Stransky's sign): ◆ **UMN defect**
If plantar flexion: ◆ **normal**
If no movement: ◆ **nonspecific finding**

Check for Tromner's sign (a variant of Hoffman's)

PROCEDURE: Have the patient place the hand in a neutral position. Briskly tap or strike over the palmar distal aspects of the third digit. Visually observe and feel for any involuntary movements in the digits.

OUTCOME: If there is involuntary flexion of the digits (Tromner's sign):
◆ **UMN defect**
If no such involuntary movement:
◆ **normal**
◆ **LMN defect**

APPROACH TO A PATIENT WITH TREMOR

Determine location of tremor

PROCEDURE: With patient sitting and at rest, visually inspect the predominate location of the tremor.

OUTCOME: If the tremor affects hands, head, and neck, circular component in hands/digits: ◆ **parkinsonian tremor**

If the tremor affects hands, head, and neck without a circular component in hands/digits: ◆ **essential tremor**

If the head bobs in a horizontal or vertical fashion (yes/yes or no/no): ◆ **essential tremor**

If tremor affects the lower extremities and trunk:
◆ **orthostatic tremor**

Assess intensity of tremor

PROCEDURE: Throughout the entire neurologic examination, visually inspect and palpate the intensity of the tremor.

OUTCOME: If the tremor is detected only by palpation (very fine, low amplitude): ◆ **orthostatic tremor**

If tremor is visibly present (low amplitude, quite fine):
◆ **physiologic tremor**

If tremor is of moderate amplitude:
◆ **parkinsonian tremor**
◆ **essential tremor**

If tremor is of high amplitude and coarse: ◆ **cerebellar tremor**

Assess impact of activities on tremor

PROCEDURE: Visually inspect the tremor while the patient performs a voluntary activity.

OUTCOME: If the tremor is worse at rest, then resolves with voluntary activity: ◆ **parkinsonian tremor**

If tremor while maintaining a specific posture (e.g., standing with hands outstretched, palms down, fingers abducted):
◆ **essential tremor**
◆ **physiologic tremor**
◆ **orthostatic tremor**
◆ **parkinsonian (in addition to resting tremor)**

If tremor only during voluntary, active movement:
◆ **cerebellar tremor**

If tremor during voluntary, goal-directed movement:
◆ **cerebellar tremor**

Assess gait: As in Basic Examination.

Check hands for asterixis

PROCEDURE: Have the patient actively extend the arms at elbows to 0 degrees, then actively maximally dorsiflex hands at wrists and spread out the fingers; maintain the position for 60 to 90 seconds. Visually inspect the hands for any movement(s).

OUTCOME: If there are nonrhythmic, flapping movements of the hands at wrists: ◆ **asterixis**

If there are no movements: ◆ **normal**

APPROACH TO A PATIENT WITH SUSPECTED DEMENTIA

Assess for apraxia

PROCEDURE: Ask the patient to perform a motor activity. Choose an activity that the patient knows and is able to perform (i.e., no anatomic defect will preclude performance), such as "close the door," "kick the ball," "shake my hand."

OUTCOME: If the patient can perform the activity: ◆ **normal**

If patient cannot perform the activity: ◆ **apraxia**

Test for grasp reflex (frontal)

PROCEDURE: Place your extended second and third digits transversely onto the palm of the patient's hand.

OUTCOME: If there is slow involuntary flexion of fingers (grasp reflex):
◆ **marked dementia**

If no such action: ◆ **normal**

Test for snout reflex

PROCEDURE: Use the tip of a finger to rub, lateral to medial, on the vermilion border of the patient's upper lip. Repeat on the lower lip.

OUTCOME: If there is involuntary puckering and protrusion of the lips (snout reflex): ◆ **marked dementia**

If no such action: ◆ **normal**

Test for sucking reflex

PROCEDURE: Use the tip of a finger to rub, lateral to medial, on the patient's upper lip. Repeat on the lower lip.

OUTCOME: If there is involuntary sucking movement (sucking reflex):
◆ **marked dementia**

If no such action: ◆ **normal**

Test for palmomental reflex

PROCEDURE: Use a finger tip to rub on the patient's palm. Visually observe the patient's face.

OUTCOME: If there is involuntary wrinkling of the skin on the face (palmomental reflex): ◆ **marked dementia**

If no such action: ◆ **normal**

Test for plantar grasp

PROCEDURE: Place two fingers firmly and transversely on the plantar aspect of the foot for 5 to 10 seconds. Inspect the foot for any involuntary movement. Repeat on the contralateral side.

OUTCOME: If there is involuntary flexion and adduction of the toes (plantar grasp): ◆ **marked dementia**
If no such action: ◆ **normal**

APPROACH TO A PATIENT WITH A WADDLING GAIT

Assess strength (power) and/or patterns of weakness in specific muscles: As in Basic Examination.

Inspect muscles: As in Approach to a patient with weakness.

Observe tone during passive range of motion: See under Basic Examination.

Observe standing from sitting: As in Approach to a patient with weakness.

Inspect and palpate anterior neck: As in Chapter 2, under Advanced Examination.

Assess handshake

PROCEDURE: Tell the patient to grasp both of your hands in a firm grip, as if firmly shaking hands. Then instruct the patient to release the grip.

OUTCOME: If the grip is not released in a rapid fashion—contraction persists after the voluntary component has stopped (myotonia):
◆ **myotonic dystrophy**
If released in a rapid fashion: ◆ **normal**

APPROACH TO A PATIENT WITH A POKER GAIT

Perform FABERE (Patrick's) test: As in Chapter 11, under Basic Examination (see Fig 11-1, p. 235).

Palpate sacroiliac joints: As in Chapter 11, under Approach to a patient with suspected ankylosing spondylitis.

Perform Schober's maneuver: As in Chapter 11, under Approach to a patient with suspected ankylosing spondylitis.

Measure chest circumference during expiration/inspiration: As in Chapter 11, under Approach to a patient with suspected ankylosing spondylitis.

APPROACH TO A PATIENT WITH A SPASTIC/SCISSORS GAIT

Assess strength (power) and/or patterns of weakness in specific muscles: As in Basic Examination.

Check reflexes: wrist extensors, triceps, patellar, Achilles: As in Basic Examination.

Assess cranial nerve: CN VII: As in Basic Examination.

Observe tone during passive range of motion: As in Basic Examination.

Check for Babinski's sign: As in Approach to a patient with weakness.

Check for Oppenheim's sign: As in Approach to a patient with weakness.

Check for Chaddock's sign: As in Approach to a patient with weakness.

Check for Tromner's/Hoffman's sign: See under Approach to a patient with weakness.

APPROACH TO A PATIENT WITH A STEPPAGE GAIT

Perform sensory examination

PROCEDURE: Perform a sensory examination of the lower extremity, using a cotton-tipped swab, monofilament, or tuning fork (see Figs 7-4 and 7-5).

OUTCOME: If there is a deficit in sensation along the dorsal and lateral foot:
   ◆ **foot-drop syndrome, that is, anterior compartment problem (see Chapter 13, p. 285)**
If no such deficit: ◆ **normal**

Actively dorsiflex great toe

PROCEDURE: Perform an active dorsiflexion of the great toe, apply resistance to dorsum of great toe with index finger.

OUTCOME: If there is weakness of great toe extension:
   ◆ **foot-drop syndrome, that is, anterior compartment problem (see p. 285)**
If no such weakness: ◆ **normal**

APPROACH TO A PATIENT WITH AN ATAXIC, CEREBELLAR GAIT

Assess stance: As in Basic Examination.

Perform Romberg's test: As in Basic Examination.

Assess gait: As in Basic Examination.

Perform tandem walk

PROCEDURE: Have the patient walk in a straight line, heel to toe, with eyes open and looking straight ahead. Assist the patient with the maneuver to prevent a fall.

OUTCOME: If the patient is unable to walk a straight line:
   ◆ **cerebellar ataxia, including multiple sclerosis**
   If able to walk a straight line (tandem walk): ◆ **normal**

Assess gait while patient looks ahead/looks at floor

PROCEDURE: Tell the patient to walk at a normal pace, looking straight ahead. Visually inspect the patient's gait. Repeat this procedure with patient looking at the feet or floor.

OUTCOME: If gait improves when the patient is looking at floor:
   ◆ **ataxic, proprioceptive gait**
   If there is no improvement when looking at floor:
   ◆ **ataxic, cerebellar gait**

Test for finger dysdiadochokinesis

PROCEDURE: Tell the patient to actively touch the tips of his or her fingers (5, 4, 3, 2) to the thumb in rapid repetitive fashion. Use the contralateral side or yourself, or both, for control.

OUTCOME: If the patient is able to perform fine repetitive movements, rapidly and smoothly: ◆ **diadochokinesis (normal)**
   If unable to perform fine repetitive movements unilaterally:
   ◆ **dysdiadochokinesis: ipsilateral cerebellar defect**
   If unable to perform fine repetitive movements bilaterally:
   ◆ **dysdiadochokinesis: bilateral cerebellar defect**
   ◆ **multiple sclerosis**

Test for forearm dysdiadochokinesis

PROCEDURE: Have the patient actively supinate and pronate forearm in a rapid, repetitive fashion. Use the contralateral side or yourself, or both, for control.

OUTCOME: If the patient is able to perform fine repetitive movements, smoothly and rapidly: ◆ **diadochokinesis, normal**
   If unable to perform fine repetitive movements unilaterally:
   ◆ **dysdiadochokinesis: ipsilateral cerebellar defect**
   If unable to perform fine repetitive movements bilaterally:
   ◆ **dysdiadochokinesis: bilateral cerebellar defect**
   ◆ **multiple sclerosis**

Perform finger-to-finger test for dysmetria

PROCEDURE: Have the patient look forward. Hold one finger approximately 2 feet in front of the patient's face. Tell the patient to touch your finger then touch his or her own finger using the second finger of one hand. Repeat this five to six times, relocating the finger each time. Repeat using the patient's contralateral hand.

OUTCOME: If the patient deftly touches finger to nose, alternating with your finger (no past pointing, no dysmetria): ◆ **normal**

If patient has jerky movements, missing the nose and/or fingers using either upper extremity (terminal overshoot, bilateral dysmetria):

- ◆ **bilateral cerebellar disease**
- ◆ **multiple sclerosis**

If patient has jerky movements, missing the nose and/or fingers using one upper extremity (terminal overshoot, unilateral dysmetria): ◆ **unilateral, ipsilateral cerebellar disease**

Perform heel-to-shin test for asynergia

PROCEDURE: Have the patient sit or lie in a supine position. Instruct the patient to place the heel of one foot actively on the opposite knee, then actively extend it so that the heel slides down the shin to the great toe. Tell the patient to repeat this rapidly. Repeat the procedure on the contralateral side and compare them.

OUTCOME: If the patient is able to perform this action smoothly and rapidly:
- ◆ **normal**

If the patient has unilateral decreased ability (asynergia):
- ◆ **ipsilateral cerebellar ataxia**

If bilateral decreased ability (asynergia):
- ◆ **bilateral cerebellar disease**
- ◆ **multiple sclerosis**

Observe writing

PROCEDURE: Have the patient write a statement on a sheet of paper. Use an old sample of the patient's handwriting as a control.

OUTCOME: If the writing is coarse, unsteady (asynergia of this complex motion): ◆ **cerebellar ataxia**

If steady and neat: ◆ **normal**

Assess amplitude of tremor

PROCEDURE: Observe the patient's hands and fingers at rest. Ask the patient to use a finger to point at various sites on a wall or ceiling.

OUTCOME: If there is no tremor: ◆ **normal**

If the tremor increases in amplitude with activity, especially at motion end points: ◆ **intention tremor of cerebellar disease**

If tremor decreases in amplitude with activity:
- ◆ **tremor of Parkinson's disease**

Check for rebound

PROCEDURE: Ask the patient to forward flex the arms to a point where they are straight in front. Tell the patient to close his or her eyes and hold that position. Place force downward, upward, laterally, or medially on the arms, and then suddenly release the force. Visually inspect the activity of the arms on release.

OUTCOME: If the arms go past baseline (rebound):
- ◆ **ipsilateral, cerebellar disease**

If return to baseline: ◆ **normal**

Test for dysarthria

PROCEDURE: Have the patient rapidly repeat words starting with the sounds *k*, *t*, and *cu*.

OUTCOME: If the patient is unable to repeat the words rapidly:
- ◆ **dysarthria of cerebellar ataxia**
- ◆ **multiple sclerosis**

If able to repeat the words with precision and alacrity: ◆ **normal**

Note speech pattern

PROCEDURE: During the course of taking the patient's history, note his or her pattern of speech.

OUTCOME: If the patient's speech is irregular, jerky, slow, with intermittent periods of fast, forced speech:
- ◆ **cerebellar dysfunction speech pattern**
- ◆ **multiple sclerosis**

Sit next to patient on bed

PROCEDURE: Have the patient sit up on the side of a bed, with legs dangling over the side, and actively maintain an upright midline position. Then, after first asking the patient's permission, sit down next to him or her on the bed. Observe the patient's position.

OUTCOME: If the patient is able to maintain an upright position in the midline: ◆ **normal**

If sways back and forth, unable to adjust (truncal ataxia):
- ◆ **midline cerebellar (archeocerebellar) dysfunction**

APPROACH TO A PATIENT WITH AN ATAXIC, PROPRIOCEPTIVE GAIT

Test vibratory sensation: As in Basic Examination.

Test sensation with monofilament: As in Basic Examination

Assess stance: As in Basic Examination.

Perform Romberg's test: As in Basic Examination.

Test proprioception

PROCEDURE: Have the patient sit down and close his/her eyes. Passively move the individual toes and fingers up and down on both sides. Repeat this procedure on seven different toes and/or fingers on each side.

OUTCOME: If the patient knows up from down (7 correct out of 7 movements): ◆ **normal**

If the patient's sense of up and down is decreased in lower and upper extremities (<6/7 correct):
- ◆ **diabetes mellitus**
- ◆ **tabes dorsalis**
- ◆ **vitamin B$_{12}$ deficiency**

Assess gait while patient looks ahead/looks at floor

PROCEDURE: Tell the patient to walk at a normal pace, looking straight ahead. Visually inspect the patient's gait. Repeat this procedure with the patient looking at the feet or floor.

OUTCOME: If the gait improves when looking at the floor:
- ◆ **ataxic, proprioceptive gait**

If no improvement when looking at floor:
- ◆ **ataxic, cerebellar gait**

APPROACH TO A PATIENT WITH AN ATAXIC, VESTIBULAR GAIT

Assess stance: As in Basic Examination.

Perform Romberg's test: As in Basic Examination.

Perform the Dix-Hallpike-Nylen-Bárány maneuver: As in Basic Examination.

APPROACH TO A PATIENT WITH A PARKINSONIAN GAIT

Assess gait: As in Basic Examination.

Test for elbow dysfunction/cogwheel rigidity

PROCEDURE: Grasp the distal forearm and passively flex it over 3 to 4 seconds. Then extend the forearm at the elbow over 3 to 4 seconds. Repeat this procedure several times. Tell the patient to tap on his or her thigh with the contralateral hand. Feel for any resistance to movement at the elbow.

OUTCOME: If stiffness and a marked decrease in ROM are present:
- ◆ **elbow joint dysfunction**

If there is little or no resistance to passive flexion and extension:
- ◆ **normal**

If jerky movement with muscular resistance alternating with periods of rest during passive extension/flexion (cogwheel rigidity): ◆ **Parkinson's disease**

Test for wrist dysfunction/cogwheel rigidity

PROCEDURE: Grasp the tips of the patient's three middle fingers and passively circumduct the hand at the wrist. Instruct the patient to tap on his or her thigh with the contralateral hand. Feel for any resistance to movement at the wrist.

OUTCOME: If stiffness and a marked decrease in ROM are present:
    ◆ **wrist joint dysfunction**
If there is little or no resistance to passive circumduction:
    ◆ **normal**
If jerky movement with muscular resistance alternating with periods of rest during the passive circumduction (cogwheel rigidity): ◆ **Parkinson's disease**

Assess gait attributes

PROCEDURE: Have the patient walk. Visually observe the positioning of the body.

OUTCOME: If there is narrow-based placement, and the patient is stooped with head forward and hips and knees slightly flexed, shuffling stiffly (marche à petit pas): ◆ **Parkinson's disease**
If the strides are very small, so that the patient appears to be running with small discrete steps (festination):
    ◆ **Parkinson's disease**

Observe face and facial expressions

PROCEDURE: Visually observe the patient's face and facial expressions.

OUTCOME: If there is a paucity of facial expressions and the patient's tongue is chronically protruded: ◆ **Parkinson's disease**
If significant decrease in blinking: ◆ **Parkinson's disease**
If the patient is slow to manifest and fade smile:
    ◆ **Parkinson's disease**

Listen to patient's speech

PROCEDURE: Listen to the characteristics and quality of the patient's voice.

OUTCOME: If slow and of low volume: ◆ **hypophonia of Parkinson's disease**

Check glabellar reflex for Myerson's sign

PROCEDURE: Tell the patient to look forward. With the tip of a distal digit, gently but briskly tap on the midpoint of the lower forehead at a rate of 20 to 30 taps per minute. Ensure that the tapping is of reproducible intensity and regular rhythm. Visually inspect the eyes for blinking with each tap.

OUTCOME: If the patient blinks after each of the first three to five taps but ceases to blink thereafter (glabellar reflex): ◆ **normal**
If patient does not blink in relation to tapping: ◆ **blindness**
If patient continues to blink after each tap for greater than 5 taps (especially if >15 taps):
    ◆ **Myerson's sign of Parkinson's disease**

Keys to Recording Findings

NEUROLOGY

"Power, 5/5 to all four extremities; reflexes, 2+ and symmetric to all 4 extremities; cranial nerves 2–12 intact bilaterally; gait normal based, steady; sensory intact to vibration and fine touch to all 4 extremities and to face."

"Alert and oriented to person, place and time (X3)"

A. Power and Reflexes

• Power: Note strength to all four extremities—elbow flexion, shoulder abduction, knee extension, hip forward flexion. Note any asymmetry, any difference between proximal and distal and any difference between upper and lower body.

    Grading

        5:    normal

        4:    Gravity and 2 fingers of resistance

        3:    Gravity only

        2:    Partial ability

        1:    twitch

        0:    absent

• Reflexes: Note reflexes to all four extremities—wrist extension, triceps, patellar, Achilles (plantar). Note any asymmetry or difference between upper and lower extremities.

    Grading

        ++++   Increased, clonus and/or cross over

        +++   Increased

        ++   Normal, present

        +   Decreased

        0   absent

B. Tone

Passive resistance at the joints: elbows, wrists.

A. Power and reflexes

- Triceps/Biceps Reflex
- Flexion at Elbow
- Abduction at Shoulder
- Forward Flexion at Hip
- Patellar Reflex
- Extension at Knee
- Achilles

/2 /2 /5 /5 /5 /5 /5 /5 /2 /2 /5 /2 /2 /5

B. Tone

Normal	❏
Decreased	❏
Increased	❏
Spastic (location _____)	
Rigid (location _____)	

C. Cranial Nerve

	Normal Left	Normal Right	If abnormal, findings:
2: Vision	❏	❏	_____
3: All extraocular movement except lateral and medial/down movement	❏	❏	_____
4: Eye movement down and medial	❏	❏	_____
5: Masseter	❏	❏	_____
V1: Frontal skin	❏	❏	_____
V2: Maxillary skin	❏	❏	_____
V3: Mandible skin	❏	❏	_____
6: Eye movement lateral	❏	❏	_____
7: Smile, grimace	❏	❏	_____
Close eyes	❏	❏	_____
Wrinkle forehead	❏	❏	_____
9 and 10: Ahh-uvula	❏	❏	_____
11: Shrug shoulders	❏	❏	_____
12: Stick out tongue	❏	❏	_____

C. **Cranial nerves (CN)**

2: Vision-visual acuity

3: All eye movements except lateral and downward/nasal movement

4: Downward/nasal eye movement (superior oblique)

5: Jaw closure (masseter)

Sensory: facial skin—V1: forehead, V2: maxillary, V3: mandibular

6: Lateral eye movement (Lateral rectus)

7: Smile (orbicularis oris), grimace (lower facial muscles), close eyes (orbicularis oculus), and wrinkle forehead (frontalis)

Sensory: taste, earlobe

8: Auditory acuity

9 and 10: Uvular movement with AHHH

11: Shrug shoulders (trapezius); turn head side-to-side (sternocleidomastoid)

12: Tongue protrusion

D. **Gait**

Note if normal, wide or narrow-based; note swinging of arms, any unsteadiness, note any listing to left or right

E. **Sensory**

Note and report any deficits to vibratory and/or fine touch

F. **Mental status examination**

Note and report any deficits to alertness or errata to person, place time. Note components missed on a mental screening examination.

• Other: Note pathologic reflexes, e.g., Babinski's or Chaddocks: upgoing or downgoing toes.

D. **Gait**   Normal-based ❏

Wide-based ❏

Narrow-based ❏

Steady ❏   Unsteady ❏

E. **Sensation**

Monofilament or cotton-tipped swab (Note/draw any defects)

Vibration (Note/draw any defects)

Draw findings and or sensory deficits:

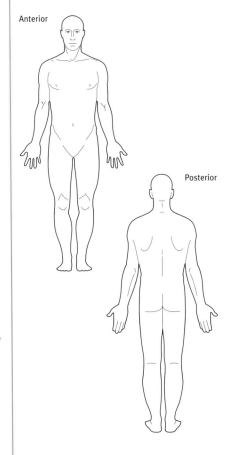

Anterior

Posterior

Diagnoses

Aphonia: See Pseudobulbar palsy.

Apraxia: See Dementia.

Asterixis
Encephalopathy-related inability to maintain a posture actively; this often accompanies end-stage liver disease, exacerbated by protein loads in the gastrointestinal tract and by constipation. Symptoms and signs include liver flap of feet/hands, decreased level of consciousness, concurrent small liver, ascites (see Fig 6-3, p. 118), and gynecomastia. Evaluation includes a serum ammonia level test, which, if elevated, confirms the clinical suspicion. Treatment includes lactulose, titrated to two to three bowel movements per day, and dietary restrictions of protein.

Ataxia, cerebellar gait: See Ataxia.

Ataxia
Unsteady, poor coordination gait due to cerebellar dysfunction, that is, cerebellar ataxia; sensory defects, that is, proprioceptive ataxia; or inner ear dysfunction, that is, vestibular ataxia. Symptoms and signs include an unsteady, wide-based gait in which the patient sways to either or both sides. Signs are specific to type: a decrease in arm swing, poor stance, decreased Romberg's, dysmetria, **dysdiadochokinesis**, cerebellar tremor, nystagmus, and **hypotonia, in cerebellar ataxia;** if one cerebellar hemisphere is involved, the manifestations are unilateral and ipsilateral. If the patient has normal cerebellar function and a marked decrease in sensation in a stocking-glove distribution (see Figs 7-4A and 7-5A), the gait markedly improves when the patient looks at the floor while walking in proprioceptive ataxia; if the patient has vertigo, tinnitus, nausea, and nystagmus consistent with vestibular ataxia. Evaluation and treatment for cerebellar ataxia consist of an emergent computed tomographic (CT) scan of the head, referral to a neurologist, and physical therapy; for proprioceptive ataxia, as outlined in peripheral neuropathy (see p. 172); for vestibular ataxia, referral to a neurologist and/or an ear-nose-throat (ENT) specialist.

Ataxia, proprioceptive: See Ataxia.

Ataxia, vestibular: See Ataxia.

Becker dystrophy: See Muscular dystrophy.

Brown-Séquard syndrome

Unilateral hemidissection of the spinal cord due to trauma (e.g., a gunshot wound to the spinal cord). Symptoms and signs include ipsilateral hemiplegia, ipsilateral loss of proprioceptive and fine touch (see Fig 7-4B), and contralateral loss of pain sensation (see Fig 7-5B), all inferior to the wound level. Evaluation includes CT or magnetic resonance imaging (MRI) of the spinal cord at that level. Treatment includes referral to a neurologist or neurosurgeon and to physical therapy.

Central cranial nerve VII palsy

Palsy due to an intracranial event (e.g., cerebrovascular accident). The upper face and eyes receive UMN cranial nerve VII from both sides of the brain, whereas the lower face receives UMN cranial nerve VII from the contralateral side only. Unilateral damage affects the contralateral lower face only. Symptoms include unilateral facial droop; signs include an inability to curve the contralateral angle of the mouth upward or grimace (see Fig 7-7) but a normal ability to close both eyes; contralateral **spastic hemiparesis** is concurrent. Evaluation includes a CT scan of the head and, if indicated, an MRI/magnetic resonance angiography (MRA) of the head. Treatment is immediate referral to a neurologist.

Cerebellar tremor: See Ataxia.

Cerebrovascular accident: See Central cranial nerve VII palsy and Upper motor neuron defects.

Delirium

An acute deterioration in mental status from a previously stable baseline. Evaluation of the patient requires an extensive history, but ironically, the patient will be unable to give a credible one and may confabulate (create answers). Evaluation includes a mental status examination and a urine toxicologic screen, ethanol level, and a stat fingerstick glucose. In addition, due to the fact that head trauma may result in delirium or coma, see Coma and Head Trauma (Chapter 2, p. 32). Treatment may include thiamine and, if the patient is hypoglycemic, glucose. If no etiology is determined, inpatient evaluation with CT of the head and lumbar puncture may be indicated.

Dementia

Nonspecific, insidious, progressive deterioration in intellectual and cognitive functioning. Symptoms and signs are very subtle early in the course, including abnormal mental status examinations. Later, frontal release signs are present. Evaluation includes serum B_{12}, VDRL (Venereal Disease Research Laboratory), and thyroid-stimulating hormone (TSH) tests to assess for treatable etiologies. Treatment includes referral to occupational, physical, and speech therapy; the patient's family should be referred to support groups.

Dermatomyositis: See Proximal muscle weakness.

Diabetes mellitus: See Peripheral neuropathy.

Duchenne's dystrophy: See Muscular dystrophy.

Dysarthria

Damage to CN XII or the tongue muscle it innervates. Symptoms and signs include an acquired thickness of speech (slurred speech with a loss of exactness in diction and locution), positive Dinkler's sign—lower CN XII palsy (see Fig 7-11), loss of lateral tongue movement—upper CN XII palsy, and concurrent pseudobulbar palsy. Evaluation includes an emergent noncontrast head CT scan and later an MRI/MRA of the head and posterior fossa. Treatment includes immediate referrals to a neurologist and speech therapist.

Dysdiadochokinesis: See Ataxia.

Dysphonia: See Pseudobulbar palsy.

Essential tremor

Idiopathic tremor. Symptoms include a quivering tone to the voice that may improve after ingestion of ethanol; signs include a postural tremor, repetitive flexion/extension of the hands, and/or yes-yes or no-no bobbing of the head. Evaluation and treatment are largely supportive. If the tremor is severe, beta-blockers, benzodiazepines, primidone, and referral to a neurologist can be considered.

Hearing loss

Due to either conductive disorders—those of the canal, for example, cerumen impaction; middle ear bones; or the middle ear itself, for example, acute otitis media; or neurosensory disorders—those of the cochlea or CN VIII, for example, presbycusis or medication. Symptoms and signs include Weber's sign lateralized to the diseased ear in a conductive disorder, whereas Weber's test is either lateralized to the nondiseased ear or, more commonly, bilateral in a neurosensory disorder. Concurrent findings of vertigo and nystagmus may be present in non–age-related neurosensory loss. Evaluation includes audiometry, treatment of the underlying etiology, and potentially a hearing aid.

Horner's syndrome

Damage to superior sympathetic ganglion in lateral neck due to neck trauma (e.g., gunshot wound to neck or Pancoast's tumor involving one lung apex). Symptoms and signs include unilateral ptosis, unilateral miosis, and unilateral facial anhidrosis, all ipsilateral to the lesion. Evaluation includes chest radiography to look for an apical mass. Treatment for an apical mass is referral to a pulmonary specialist or obtaining a CT scan–guided biopsy of the lung.

Hyperreflexia: See Upper motor neuron defects.

Hyporeflexia: See Lower motor neuron defects.

Hypotonicity: See Ataxia.

Lower motor neuron defects

Defect caused by trauma, infiltration, entrapment of one or more peripheral nerves (spinal or cranial), or damage to anterior horn cells via amyotrophic lateral sclerosis or poliomyelitis. Symptoms and signs include flaccid tone (hypotonia), **hyporeflexia** (see Figs 7-1 to 7-3), and a waddling or steppage gait. The affected musculature exhibits significant atrophy and fasciculations. Concurrent sensory defects and a positive Tinel's sign (see Fig 8-17) over an area of entrapment are common in peripheral entrapment neuropathies. Evaluation includes MRI of the lumbar or cervical spine when lumbar or cervical radicular findings are present. Treatment includes rest with splintage and referral to an orthopedic surgeon or neurosurgeon.

Multiple sclerosis

Idiopathic scarring and plaque formation in central nervous system (including CN II) due to demyelination with reactive gliosis. Symptoms and signs are quite diverse and disparate: focal weakness, diplopia, urinary frequency or hesitancy, or both; blurred vision as the result of optic neuritis (Plate 15), intranuclear ophthalmoplegia, nystagmus; unsteadiness, ataxic gait, dysmetria, dysdiadochokinesis, spastic paresis; positive Tromner/Hoffman's and Babinski's signs and hyperreflex with clonus, that is, significant cerebellar and upper motor neuron defects. Findings are perplexing, as there is no pattern and no solitary focal site, but this in itself defines multiple sclerosis. Evaluation includes CT and MRI of the head and a lumbar puncture to assess for myelin base protein and oligoclonal bands. Treatment includes referral to a neurologist and occupational and physical therapy.

Muscular dystrophy

Congenital and progressive destruction of striated muscle. **Duchenne's dystrophy:** X-linked recessive, rapidly progressive; **Becker's dystrophy:** X-linked recessive, less rapidly progressive; **myotonic dystrophy:** autosomal dominant dystrophy. Symptoms and signs of dystrophies include a waddling gait and an increased time to stand from a seated position. Other signs are specific to the underlying diagnosis: pseudohypertrophy, especially of the calves, and profound proximal muscle weakness in Duchenne's and Becker's muscular dystrophy; proximal muscle weakness with myotonia; frontal balding; atrophy of the sternocleidomastoid and temporalis muscles; bilateral ptosis; cataracts; and cardiomyopathy in myotonic dystrophy. Evaluation and treatment include referral to a neurologist and to occupational and physical therapy.

Myotonic dystrophy: See Muscular dystrophy.

Orthostatic tremor

Idiopathic tremor. Symptoms and signs include a postural tremor, fast in rate, that is present when the patient stands unsupported but resolves when he or she leans against a structure or sits. Evaluation and treatment are largely supportive. If the tremor is severe, clonazepam and referral to a neurologist can be considered.

Paresis/plegia: See Weakness (paresis).

Parkinsonian tremor: See Parkinson's disease.

Parkinson's disease

Decrease in the neurotransmitter dopamine, with a resultant imbalance of acetylcholine to dopamine in the basal ganglia, following influenza or neuroleptic-mediated or idiopathic Parkinson's disease. The predominant symptom is **parkinsonian tremor**, that is, a tremor at rest that resolves with movement and exhibits pill-rolling [fingers and metacarpophalangeal (MCP) joints in flexion/extension and abduction/adduction]; the tremor involves distal upper extremities initially but may generalize. Concurrent signs include parkinsonian gait, bradykinesia, **cogwheel rigidity**, micrographia, immobile face, and positive Myerson's sign. Evaluation and treatment include referral to a neurologist, for initiation of levo-/carbidopa, and occupational and physical therapy.

Peripheral cranial nerve VII palsy

Damage peripheral to the cranium due to trauma, surgery, neoplasia, herpesvirus infection, or idiopathic, that is, Bell's palsy. The lower motor neuron component innervates the entire ipsilateral side of the face. Symptoms include unilateral dry eye, facial droop, and ringing in the ear. Signs include a unilateral inability to curve the angle of the mouth upward or grimace (see Fig 7-7), completely close the eye (see Fig 7-7), or wrinkle the forehead (see Fig 7-7) on the ipsilateral side. Concurrent conjunctivitis may be present on the ipsilateral side due to dryness of the eye. Evaluation and treatment include empiric systemic acyclovir, patching of the eye at night, and applications of lubricating eye drops.

Peripheral neuropathy

Damage due to uncontrolled diabetes mellitus, profound long-term deficiency of vitamin B_{12}, tabes dorsalis, radiculopathy (disk herniation, facet disease), entrapment (e.g., carpal or tarsal tunnel), or multiple sclerosis. The peripheral nerve has sensory components and the lower motor components. Symptoms and signs are: in **diabetes mellitus** or **vitamin B_{12} deficiency**—a stocking-glove sensory deficit (see Figs 7-4A and 7-5A) with minimal motor defects, and, in radiculopathy and entrapment neuropathy—sensory deficits and flaccid paresis with hyporeflexia in the affected muscle groups. Possible concurrent manifestations include retinopathy (Plates 18 and 20) in **diabetes mellitus**, a positive Romberg's test, aortic insufficiency and Argyll Robertson

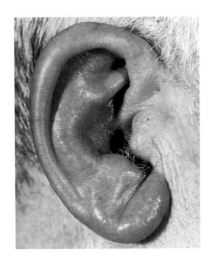

Plate 1. Otitis externa maligna. Diffuse tenderness and swelling in entire ear; infection with *Pseudomonas* species.

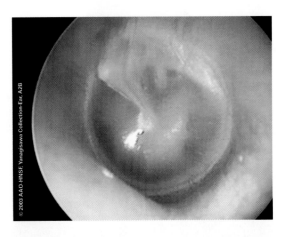

Plate 2. Normal tympanic membrane. Note that the tympanic membrane is gray, pale and translucent. The umbo and triangle-shaped cone of light are normal features. (Reprinted with permission of the American Academy of Otolaryngology—Head and Neck Surgery Foundation, copyright © 2003. All rights reserved.)

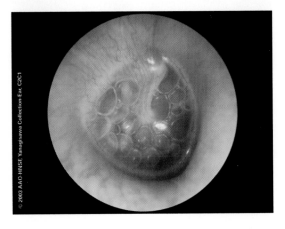

Plate 3. Serous otitis media. Note that the tympanic membrane is retracted, fluid and air bubbles are behind the TM. The cone of light is absent. (Reprinted with permission of the American Academy of Otolaryngology—Head and Neck Surgery Foundation, copyright © 2003. All rights reserved.)

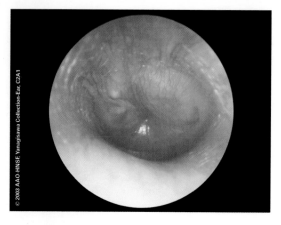

Plate 4. Purulent otitis media. Note the bulging of the tympanic membrane with a circumference of red. The umbo and cone of light are not demonstrable. (Reprinted with permission of the American Academy of Otolaryngology—Head and Neck Surgery Foundation, copyright © 2003.

© 2003 AAO-HNSF Yanagisawa Collection-Ear, C2A1

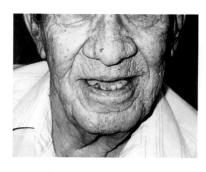

Plate 5. Rendu-Osler-Weber syndrome. Multiple small vascular lesions on face, nose, mucous membranes, and tongue.

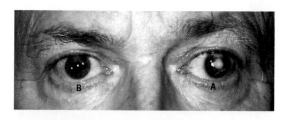

Plate 6. Corneal opacity. A. Scarring in the cornea, left eye, concurrent. B. Iridotomy with poikiloscoria (right eye).

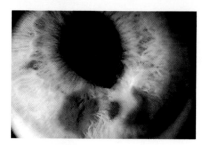

Plate 7. Iris malignant melanoma. Note the poikiloscoria and pigment clumping.

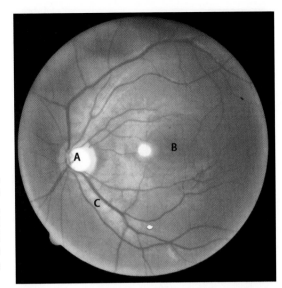

Plate 8. Fundus. Normal. Note the (A) cup-to-disc ratio is at upper side of normal, disc is creamy white, (B) macula is pigmented and located where the vessels terminate, (C) vessels are paired (artery and vein).

Plate 9. Purulent conjunctivitis with ectropion. Bacterial etiology of the infection.

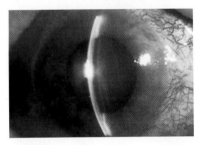

Plate 10. Angle closure glaucoma. Inspection of the anterior chamber from the side demonstrating shallow anterior angle and moderate edema in the cornea itself.

Plate 11. Subconjunctival hemorrhage. Marked hemorrhage in this patient's left eye.

Plate 12. Corneal abrasion. Macule of uptake on the cornea, takes up the fluorescein stain.

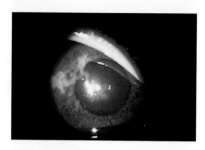

Plate 13. Herpes keratitis. Dendritic pattern of ulcers on the cornea, takes up the fluorescein stain.

Plate 14. Scleral icterus. Patient with end-stage liver disease.

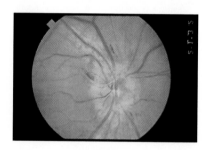

Plate 15. Fundus. Optic neuropathy with papillitis.

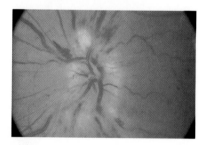

Plate 16. Fundus. Papilledema with elevated disc; concurrent findings of flame-shaped hemorrhages and engorged veins.

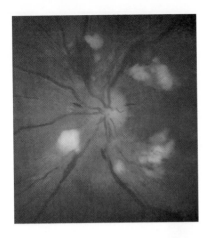

Plate 17. Fundus. Changes in long-standing severe hypertensive (KWB III), with arteriovenous (AV) nicking and multiple blot hemorrhages in the retina. Multiple soft exudates are also present.

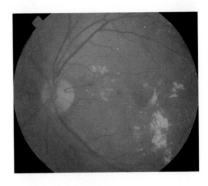

Plate 18. Fundus. Nonproliferative phase of diabetic retinopathy. Hard exudates and microaneurysms are present.

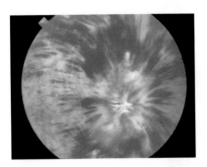

Plate 19. Fundus. Retinal vein thrombosis. Blood and thunder appearance of the fundus in a patient with long-standing hypertension and now with engorged veins and a suffused retina.

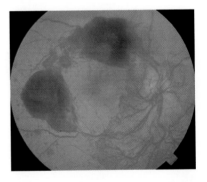

Plate 20. Fundus. Proliferative changes of diabetic retinopathy. Neovascularization, especially about the areas of soft exudates; note sites of vitreous bleeding.

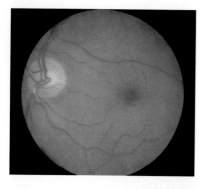

Plate 21. Fundus. Retinal artery occlusion. The retina is pale relative to the contralateral retina; arteries are smaller; a cherry-red macula.

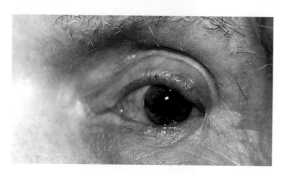

Plate 22. Blepharitis. Seborrheic with scales and erythema on the edges of the eyelids; note also the early sty on upper lateral eyelid.

Plate 23. Preseptal cellulitis. Edema and redness in eyelids superficial to the tarsal plate of the right eye; patient had an antecedent hordeolum.

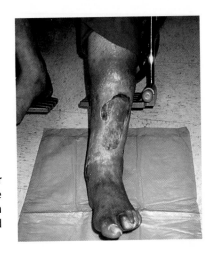

Plate 24. Arterial insufficiency ulcer: lower extremity. Deep ulcer in the skin over the anterior tibia, with concurrent loss of all skin appendages, lack of palpable pulses and coolness of skin.

Plate 25. Urticaria. Pruritic, erythematous papules and plaques, sometimes with an annular pattern.

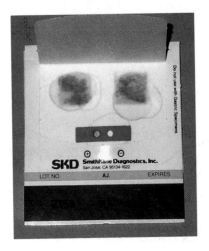

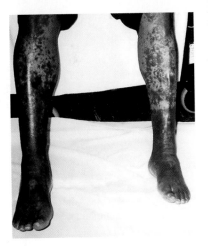

Plate 26. Guaiac-positive stool. Blue color indicates organified iron, that is, hemoglobin.

Plate 27. Purpura. Skin of the lower extremities, here quite advanced and confluent in this patient with vasculitis.

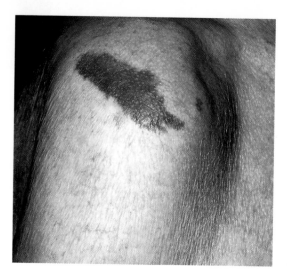

Plate 28. Ecchymosis. Skin of right shoulder, nonpalpable, nonblanching purple patch. Also known as a *bruise* or *contusion* or *black and blue mark*.

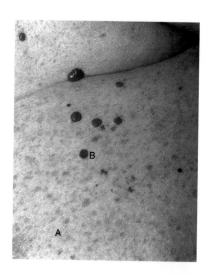

Plate 29. A. Macules—freckles and B. papules—hemangioma. Skin of the right upper chest.

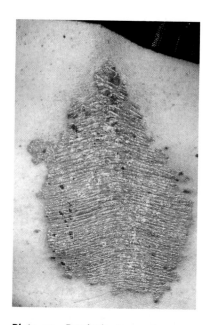

Plate 30. Psoriasis. Large plaque on the back with scales and minute bleeding sites (Auspitz's sign).

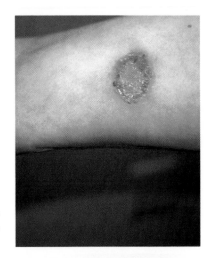

Plate 31. Tinea corporis. Annular erythematous lesion with central clearing and peripheral rim of scales.

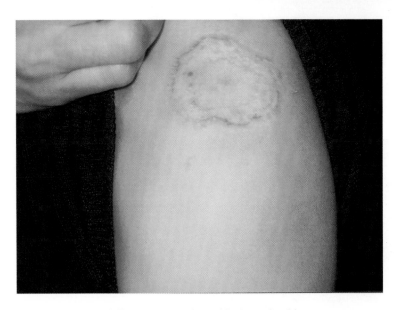

Plate 32. Erythema multiforme. Target-shaped lesions shoulder.

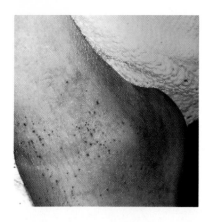

Plate 33. Petechiae. Skin of the left ankle. Multiple nonpalpable, nonblanching purple lesions, all <1 cm.

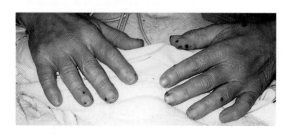

Plate 34. Janeway lesions. Multiple purple lesions and splinter hemorrhages in the fingernails; due to endocarditis.

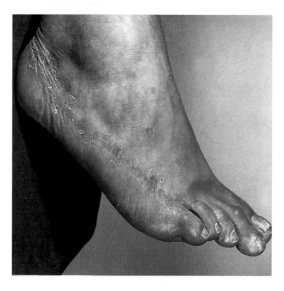

Plate 35. Tinea pedis. A moccasin distribution of a red rash with scales; note clear line of demarcation.

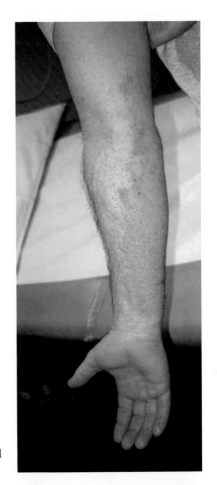

Plate 36. Atopic dermatitis. Antecubital skin: red, itchy rash on the flexor surfaces.

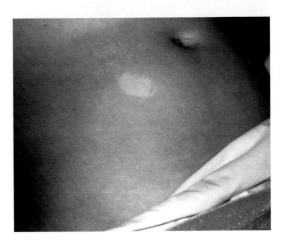

Plate 37. Photodermatitis, that is, sunburn. Diffuse blanching erythema due to overexposure to sun (ultra-violet) light.

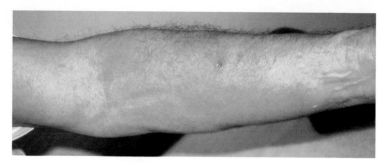

Plate 38. Cellulitis with streaking.

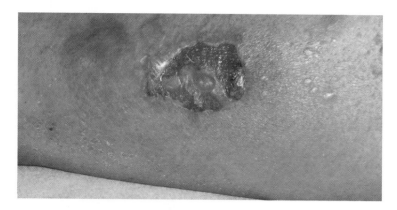

Plate 39. Bullous impetigo.

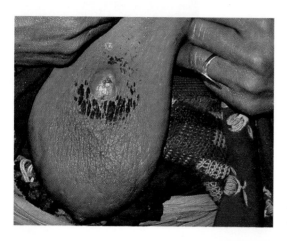

Plate 40. Breast abscess. Fluctuant nodule in breast in this lactating, postpartum woman.

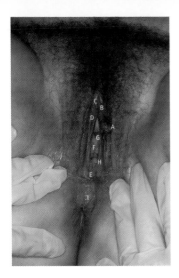

Plate 41. External genitalia.
A. Labia majora. B. Labia minora.
C. Clitoris. D. Urethra. E. Fourchette. F. Vagina. G. Skene's adenitis. H. Bartholin's glands. I. Anus.

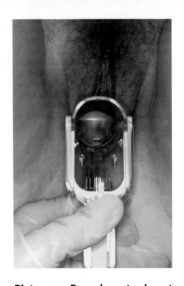

Plate 42. Procedure to insert the speculum into vagina. Here a clear plastic speculum is used. Note that the cervix is visible, as are the lateral vaginal walls.

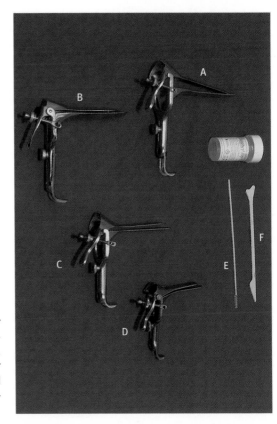

Plate 43. Various tools for pelvic examination. A. Pederson's speculum (narrow bill). B. Grave's speculum (wider bill). C and D. Pediatric and adolescent specula. E. Cytobrush. F. Cervical spatula.

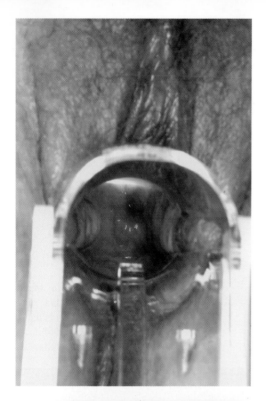

Plate 44. Cervix: Parous os; mild ectropion.

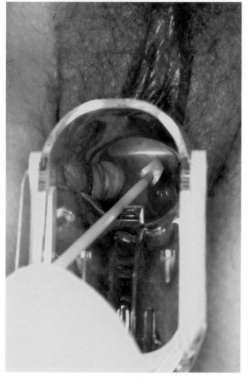

Plate 45. Cytobrush technique. Brush is inserted in the os, brush rotated so as to collect cell sample from line of demarcation (transition).

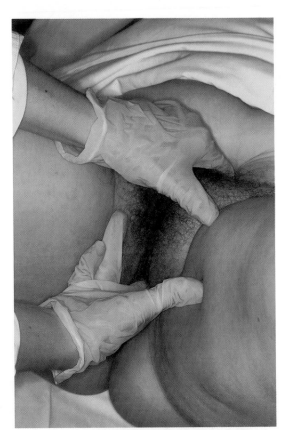

Plate 46. Bimanual examination. After lubricant is applied to fingers and inserted to palpate the cervix/ proximal vagina, other hand used to palpate using a "hooking" maneuver to feel the uterus, then left and then right lower quadrant to feel the adnexa.

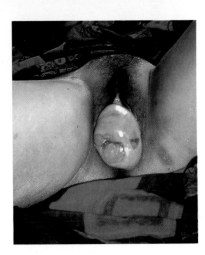

Plate 47. Uterine prolapse. Severe case in which the cervix and uterine corpus have descended through the introitus.

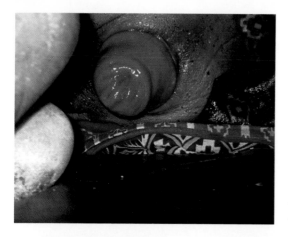

Plate 48. Rectal prolapse. Eversion of the rectum through the anus in a patient with pelvic laxity.

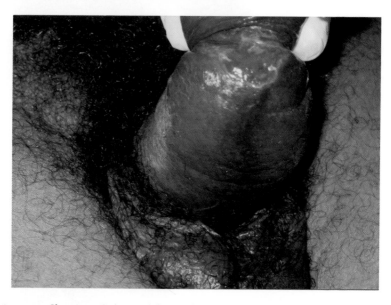

Plate 49. Chancre. Quite painless ulcer located on distal shaft of penis. VDRL (Venereal Disease Research Laboratory test for syphilis) and FTA-abs (fluorescent treponemal antibody absorption test) are nonreactive; spirochetes are present on dark-field analysis.

pupil (see Fig 3-2C, p. 45) in **tabes dorsalis**, low back or neck pain in radiculopathy, and a positive Tinel's sign (see Fig 8-17, p. 192) in entrapment neuropathy. Evaluation and treatment are directed toward the underlying process and etiology.

Physiologic tremor

Enhancement of a normal, usually imperceptible, tremor as a result of anxiety, medications (e.g., ethanol, caffeine), hyperthyroidism, fevers, or hypoglycemia. Symptoms include anxiety and signs of a postural tremor (i.e., increased by instructing the patient to maintain a voluntary position) that is generalized and fast. Evaluation and treatment are largely supportive; if the tremor is severe, beta-blockers can be considered.

Poker gait

Manifestation of a primary back disorder: musculoskeletal strain or ankylosing spondylosis. Symptoms and signs include a narrow-based gait; a stiff, straight back; and tentative steps, as if each step is painful. Other signs are specific to the underlying disorder: tenderness in the lumbar paraspinal muscles in musculoskeletal strain and a straight lumbar and thoracic spine, tenderness over the sacroiliac joints, and a positive Schober's test in ankylosing spondylitis. Evaluate the condition with imaging of the lumbar spine and pelvis. Refer the patient with ankylosing spondylitis to a rheumatologist.

Proximal muscle weakness

Weakness in large motor groups of the pectoralis and pelvic girdles as a result of primary muscle disorders, for example, muscular dystrophy; inflammatory muscle diseases such as dermatomyositis; endocrinopathies such as hyperthyroidism or Cushing's disease; and electrolyte abnormalities such as hypophosphatemia and hypokalemia. Symptoms and signs include decreased reflexes (see Figs 7-1 to 7-3), a waddling gait, and an inability to arise from a sitting position without using the arms. Other signs are specific to the underlying disorder: profound weakness and calf pseudohypertrophy in muscular dystrophy; muscle tenderness, periorbital heliotropic-colored rash, and Gottron's plaques and papules on the dorsum of digits in dermatomyositis. Evaluation includes serum electrolytes, TSH, PO_4, and creatine phosphokinase (CPK) tests and a genetic/family assessment when muscular dystrophy is suspected. Treatment is of the underlying cause, with referral to a neurologist.

Pseudobulbar palsy

One or more infarcts from vertebrobasilar insufficiency that occur in the brainstem, impacting on the nuclei of CN IX, X, XI, and XII. Symptoms and signs of acute contralateral spastic hemiparesis, dysarthria (XII), dysphagia and uvular defect (IX, X; see Fig 7-10), and paresis of the sternocleidomastoid and trapezius (XI). Evaluation includes an emergent noncontrast head CT scan and later an MRI/MRA of the posterior fossa structures. Treatment includes urgent/emergent referral to a neurologist.

Rigidity: See Parkinson's disease.

Scissors gait: See Upper motor neuron defects.

Spastic hemiparetic gait: See Upper motor neuron defects.

Spasticity: See Upper motor neuron defects.

Spinal cord transection

Injury from motor vehicle accidents, gunshot wounds, falls, or other violent trauma. Symptoms and signs depend on the time after injury, the site of cord damage, and whether the cord transection is complete or incomplete. Specific symptoms and signs are as follows:

> *Acute manifestations* (<5 days after injury): flaccid paresis and rectal and urinary retention
>
> *Late manifestations:* spastic paresis/plegia and overflow or reflex incontinence
>
> *C5 or above:* quadriplegia and loss of all sensation
>
> *C5 to T1:* upper extremity paresis and lower extremity plegia, with loss of all sensation below that level (see Figs 7-4D and 7-5D)
>
> *T2 or below:* paraparesis or paraplegia, with loss of sensation below that level (see Figs 7-4D and 7-5D)

Concurrent autonomic hyperreflexia occurs in high cervical lesions. Acute evaluation and treatment include immobilization, imaging with radiographs and CT, parenteral high-dose glucocorticoids, and immediate referral to a neurosurgeon. Chronic treatment is multidisciplinary.

Steppage gait

Damage to the common peroneal nerves, either due to trauma or to peripheral neuropathy. Symptoms and signs include the fact that in this gait, the patient must flex leg at knee to elevate foot, either unilaterally or bilaterally; severe manifestations include atrophy of the anterior leg compartment (deep peroneal nerve) and lateral leg compartment (superficial peroneal nerve), weakness to great toe extension and foot eversion, and a decrease in sensation dorsum of the foot; the patient may and often does have a concurrent proprioceptive gait. Evaluation and treatment are as described in peripheral neuropathy.

Syringomyelia

Idiopathic progressive necrosis and cavitation of the central cervical spinal cord; effects anterior (LMN) and lateral (pain and temperature) aspects of the cord before the dorsal columns (proprioception). Symptoms include an insidious, progressive weakness and numbness bilaterally in upper and then lower extremities. Signs include bilateral loss of pain and temperature sensation (see Fig 7-5E); bilateral flaccid paralysis with atrophy and fasciculations inferior to the site but paradoxical sparing of vibratory and proprioceptive sensations. Evaluation includes CT or MRI of the spinal cord at the appropriate level. Treatment is referral to a neurologist.

Tabes dorsalis: See Peripheral neuropathy.

Upper motor neuron defects

Defects caused by **cerebrovascular accidents**, direct trauma to the central nervous system, or multiple sclerosis. Symptoms and signs include **spasticity** (increased tone), **hyperreflexia** (see Figs 7-1 to 7-3); clonus; paresis, or even plegia; and abnormal reflexes—Oppenheim's (see Fig 7-13B), Babinski's (see Fig 7-12), Chaddock's (see Fig 7-13A), Stransky's (see Fig 7-13C), and/or Tromner/Hoffman's signs. The patient manifests **spastic hemiparetic** or **scissors gait** but no atrophy or fasciculations. Evaluation includes an emergent noncontrast head CT scan and later an MRI/MRA of the head. Treatment includes immediate referral to a neurologist and referral to an occupational/physical therapist.

Vertigo

Rotatory illusion of movement due to unilateral dysfunction of the vestibular branches of CN VIII or of the vestibulocochlear system, or both. Symptoms include illusory movement ("bed spins"). Signs include nystagmus and an ataxic gait. Signs specific to the underlying diagnosis include a positive Dix-Hallpike-Nylen-Bárány test in benign positional vertigo, unilateral tinnitus, and decreased unilateral auditory acuity and a positive Weber's test and a negative Dix-Hallpike-Nylen-Bárány maneuver in an intracranial tumor, especially at the cerebellopontine angle. Evaluation includes auditory testing; if tinnitus is present (hearing loss or intractable), imaging with MRI of the cerebellopontine angle is indicated. Treatment includes meclizine and referral to an ENT specialist or a neurologist, or both.

Vitamin B$_{12}$ deficiency: See Peripheral neuropathy.

Waddling gait

Profound bilateral proximal muscle weakness. Symptoms and signs include a normal-based, stooped gait with posteriorly displaced hips; accentuated lumbar lordosis. The patient is unable to arise from a seated position without using the hands. See **Proximal muscle weakness** for concurrent manifestations, evaluation, and treatment.

Weakness (paresis)

A decrease in power due to a primary muscle disease, for example, muscular dystrophy; a neuromuscular junction disorder, for example, myasthenia gravis; an LMN disorder, for example, peripheral neuropathy; or a UMN disorder, for example, cerebrovascular accident. Weakness is best known as *paresis*; paralysis is best known as *plegia*. A **paresis** (weakness) or **plegia** (paralysis) of the affected areas is present. Determining the pattern of weakness is important—if weakness is proximal, the underlying etiology is more likely to be a primary muscle or neuromuscular junction disorder, whereas if weakness is specific and distal, an LMN or UMN disorder is more probable. Symptoms and signs are specific to the underlying disorder and include pseudohypertrophy in muscular dystrophy; tenderness in polymyositis; progressive weakening with repetitive actions in myasthenia gravis; atrophy, fasciculations, and hyporeflexia of LMN (flaccid) disorders; and contractures, hyperreflexia, clonus, and both Tromner/Hoffman's and Babinski's signs (see Fig 7-12) or Chaddock's sign (see Fig 7-13) in UMN (spastic) disorders. Evaluation and treatment are directed toward the underlying etiology.

CHAPTER 8
Finger, Thumb, Hand, and Wrist

Test sensation of hands, wrists, and fingers

PROCEDURE: While the patient's eyes are closed, use a cotton-tipped swab or monofilament to lightly touch the palmar aspect of digits 1, 2, and 3; the dorsal aspect of digits 1, 2, and 3; and the ulnar aspect of the hand. Repeat on the contralateral hand for control.

OUTCOME: If there is decreased sensation on the ulnar aspect of the hand and skin of digits 4 and 5 (Figs 8-1B and 8-2B):
♦ **ulnar nerve damage**
If decreased sensation on the palmar skin of digits 1, 2, and 3 (Fig 8-2A): ♦ **median nerve damage, nonspecific to site**
If decreased sensation on the dorsal skin of digits 1, 2, and 3 (Fig 8-1A): ♦ **radial nerve damage, nonspecific to site**

Observe active abduction of digits

PROCEDURE: Instruct the patient to abduct all the fingers maximally against resistance (Fig 8-3). Repeat on the contralateral hand for control.

OUTCOME: If there is weakness: ♦ **ulnar nerve damage**
If power is good and equal: ♦ **normal**

Observe active dorsiflexion of hand at wrist

PROCEDURE: Instruct the patient to dorsiflex the hand actively at the wrist (Fig 8-4) against resistance. Repeat on the contralateral side for control.

OUTCOME: If there is weakness: ♦ **radial nerve damage**
If strength is good and equal: ♦ **normal**

Test the tip-to-tip "OK" sign

PROCEDURE: Instruct the patient to make an "OK" sign by flexing the thumb and second digit together (Fig 8-5). Place your index fingers inside the OK space at the tip of the thumb and index fingers and attempt to move the thumb away from the second digit.

OUTCOME: If there is weakness at tip: ♦ **median nerve damage**
If strength is good and equal: ♦ **normal**

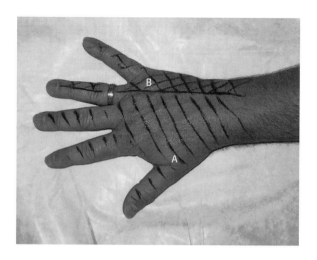

Figure 8-1 Dorsal hand, wrist, and forearm. Sensory sites for radial nerve (A) and ulnar nerve (B).

Figure 8-2 Palmar hand, wrist, and forearm. Sensory sites for median nerve (A) and ulnar nerve (B).

Perform active and passive range of motion of all joints

PROCEDURE: Perform active and passive range of motion (ROM) of all the patient's joints.

OUTCOME: See Table 8-1.

If there is a decrease in active but not passive ROM:

♦ **muscle, tendon, or nerve damage**

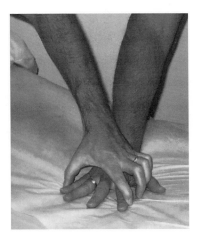

Figure 8-3 Basic motor examination: ulnar nerve. Active finger abduction against resistance.

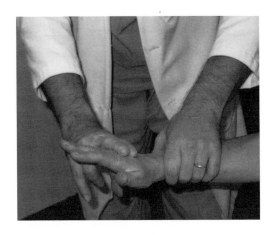

Figure 8-4 Basic motor examination: radial nerve. Active wrist extension against resistance.

If decrease in passive and active ROM:
- ◆ **arthritis**
- ◆ **contracture**

If there is an increase in ROM, especially extension:
- ◆ **hyperextensible joints**

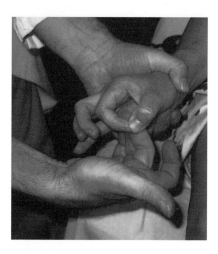

Figure 8-5 Basic motor examination: median nerve. Active tip-to-tip "OK" against resistance at the tips of thumb and second digit.

◆ **Table 8-1 Range of motion of small joints of hand, thumb, and fingers**

	Extension	Flexion	Abduction	Adduction	Circumduction
DIP finger	0 degrees	40–50 degrees	0 degrees	0 degrees	0 degrees
PIP finger	0 degrees	120 degrees	0 degrees	0 degrees	0 degrees
MCP finger	0 degrees	90 degrees	10 degrees	10 degrees	10 degrees
IP thumb	0 degrees	80 degrees	0 degrees	0 degrees	0 degrees
MCP thumb	0 degrees	30 degrees	Flexion: 10 degrees Extension: 0 degrees	Flexion: 10 degrees Extension: 0 degrees	0 degrees
Base thumb	0 degrees	70 degrees	90 degrees	90 degrees	30 degrees
Wrist	45 degrees	90 degrees	(Radial) 20 degrees	(Ulnar) 20 degrees	20 degrees

DIP, distal interphalangeal; PIP, posterior interphalangeal; MCP, metacarpophalangeal; IP, interphalangeal.

Examine skin color: Allen's test

PROCEDURE: 1. Instruct the patient to clench his or her fist.

2. Manually compress both the radial and the ulnar arteries at the wrist.

3. Tell the patient to actively extend his or her fingers.

4. Release the ulnar artery, maintain pressure on radial.

5. Observe the color of the patient's palms.

OUTCOME: If a pink flush occurs in <6 seconds, ulnar side to radial side:
   ◆ **ulnar artery is patent, that is, normal**
   If pink flush occurs in >6 seconds or is absent:
   ◆ **ulnar artery not patent**

| Advanced Examination |

APPROACH TO A PATIENT WITH FINGER DYSFUNCTION / TRAUMA

Visually inspect digits and perform active and passive range of motion

PROCEDURE: Visually inspect the digits and hands, distal to proximal. Perform active and passive ROM (see Table 8-1).

OUTCOME: If there are nontender nodules on the dorsal interphalangeal (DIP) joints (Heberden's nodes):
- ◆ **degenerative joint disease (DJD)**

If the baseline attitude of flexion at the DIP joint is 10 degrees:
- ◆ **mallet finger**

If a very tender collection beneath the nail plate (see Fig 14-26, p. 317): ◆ **subungual hematoma**

If an exquisitely tender, erythematous swelling on palmar distal digit: ◆ **felon**

If contracture of hyperextension at the posterior interphalangeal (PIP) joint, flexion at the metacarpophalangeal (MCP), and flexion at the DIP (Fig 8-6): ◆ **swan neck deformity**

If contracture of flexion at the PIP, hyperextension at the MCP, and hyperextension at the DIP (Fig 8-6):
- ◆ **boutonnière deformity**

If nontender nodules on the PIP joints (Bouchard's nodes): ◆ **DJD**

If tender swelling over the lateral or medial PIP:
- ◆ **collateral ligament sprain**

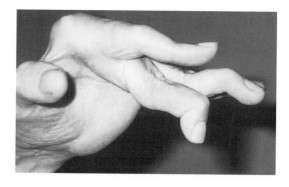

Figure 8-6 Boutonnière deformity in the second finger and swan neck deformity on the third and fourth digits in this patient with advanced severe rheumatoid arthritis.

If the middle phalanx is dorsally displaced on the proximal phalanx: ◆ **PIP joint dislocation**

If there are ulnar deviations of digits with subluxation at the MCPs (Fig 8-7): ◆ **rheumatoid arthritis**

If flexion contractures of the affected digits, especially digits 5 and 4 (Fig 8-8): ◆ **Dupuytren's contracture**

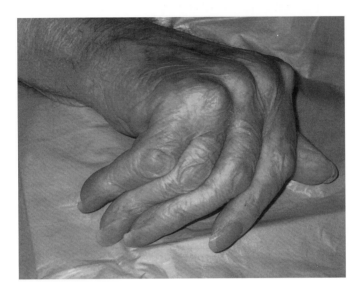

Figure 8-7 Metacarpophalangeal subluxations with ulnar deviation in rheumatoid arthritis.

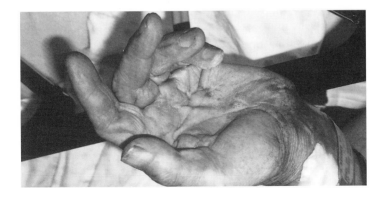

Figure 8-8 Dupuytren's contracture. Quite advanced case: contractures of flexion in digits 5, 4, 3, with discrete palpable fibronodular nodules in the palmaris fascia.

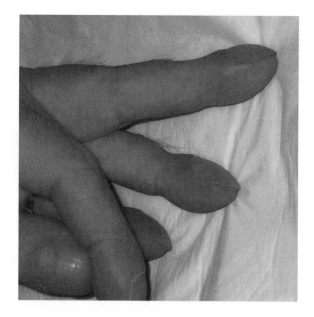

Figure 8-9 Clubbing. Classic appearance of clubbing; both criteria were present in this patient: the angle between the nail plate and the proximal nail fold (Lovibond's angle) is ›170 degrees, and the plates are resting on a spongy nail bed.

If there is intermittent inability to extend the digit at the PIP (locking): ◆ **flexion tenosynovitis (trigger finger)**
If an attitude of mild flexion at the MCP, PIP, and DIP involving all digits: ◆ **diffuse tenosynovitis**

Inspect nail plate angle and nail fold

PROCEDURE: Inspect the angle between the proximal nail fold and the nail plate.

OUTCOME: If the angle is 160 degrees: ◆ **normal**
If >170, approaching 180 degrees (Lovibond's angle sign; Figs 8-9 and 8-10): ◆ **clubbing**

Press over base of nail plate

PROCEDURE: Press over the base of the nail plate.

OUTCOME: If there is sponginess of the nail plate on the nail bed: ◆ **clubbing**
If no nail plate sponginess: ◆ **normal**

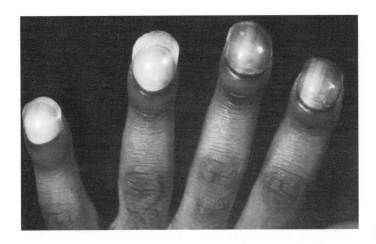

Figure 8-10 Clubbing. Note that the plates appear to be "floating" on the nail beds.

Check for Schamroth's sign

PROCEDURE: Instruct the patient to place the dorsal aspects of two digits together. Inspect the geometric pattern made by the space between the nail plates and the proximal nail folds.

OUTCOME: If no light is visualized—the plates are completely apposed:
> ◆ **clubbing**

If a rhomboid-shaped figure is made by the plates and proximal folds: ◆ **normal**

Palpate palmaris fascia

PROCEDURE: Palpate over the palmaris fascia of the affected digits.

OUTCOME: If painless nodular structures are present in the fascia:
> ◆ **Dupuytren's contracture**

If no nodular structures: ◆ **another diagnosis**

APPROACH TO A PATIENT WITH THUMB DYSFUNCTION/TRAUMA

Perform range of movement and inspect thumb

PROCEDURE: Visually inspect and palpate the thumb. Perform passive and active ROM of the thumb (see Table 8-1)

OUTCOME: If decreased active and passive ROM: ◆ **arthritis**

If passive ROM normal but decreased active ROM:
> ◆ **nerve, muscle, or tendon problem**

If tenderness and crepitus in the radial side of the trapeziometacarpal joint line: ◆ **osteoarthritis of thumb base**

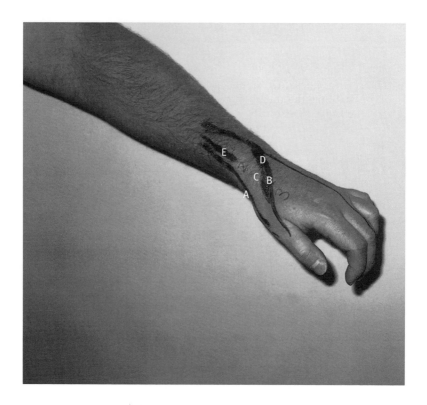

Figure 8-11 Thumb and snuffbox surface anatomy. A. Compartment 1: abductor pollicis longus and extensor pollicis brevis. B. Compartment 3: extensor pollicis longus. C. Scaphoid bone. D. Lister's tubercle of the distal radius. E. Compartment 2: extensor carpi radialis.

If swelling at the thumb base and tenderness on the ulnar, dorsal, and palmar aspect of the MCP joint:
> ◆ **ulnar collateral ligament (UCL) injury (skier's thumb)**

If tenderness to palpation over the tendons of the anatomic snuffbox (abductor pollicis longus, extensor pollicis longus, and extensor pollicis brevis; Fig 8-11A,B): ◆ **de Quervain's disease**

If tenderness at the base of the anatomic snuffbox, extending into the palmar side of the wrist (Fig 8-11C): ◆ **scaphoid fracture**

Actively extend the thumb

PROCEDURE: Instruct the patient to extend the thumb actively from a neutral position. Repeat the extension passively.

OUTCOME: If the patient is not able to extend the thumb, actively or passively: ◆ **arthritis of thumb**

If able to extend the thumb passively but not actively:
- ◆ **radial nerve problem**

Passively abduct at MCP joint

PROCEDURE: With the patient's hand in a neutral position, use one hand to stabilize the thumb metacarpal bone and use the other hand to grasp and passively abduct the thumb at the MCP joint. This is performed with the MCP and IP in full flexion and then in full extension. Repeat in the contralateral thumb for control.

OUTCOME:

Flexion: If there is <30 degrees of abduction: ◆ **normal**
If >30 degrees of abduction: ◆ **UCL tear**

Extension: If there is <10 degrees of abduction: ◆ **normal**
If 10 to 30 degrees of abduction: ◆ **UCL tear (partial)**
If >30 degrees of abduction: ◆ **UCL tear (complete)**

Examine for Finkelstein's sign

PROCEDURE: Instruct the patient to make a fist with the thumb opposed; examiner then passively ulnarly deviates the hand at the wrist (Fig 8-12). Repeat on the other side for comparison.

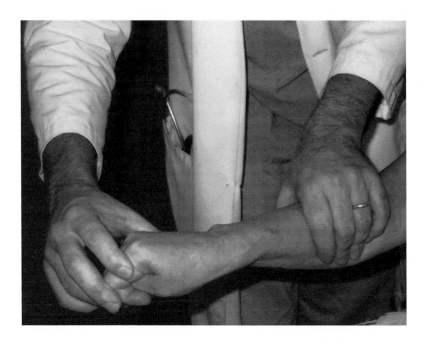

Figure 8-12 Finkelstein's sign. Useful in de Quervain's tenosynovitis and intersection syndrome. Note the patient makes a fist about opposed thumb, examiner gently ulnarly deviates the hand at the wrist.

OUTCOME: If there is pain over the tendons of the anatomic snuffbox:
  ◆ de Quervain's disease
If no pain over the anatomic snuffbox: ◆ normal
If tender over the base of snuffbox into the palmar wrist:
  ◆ scaphoid fracture

APPROACH TO A PATIENT WITH HAND AND WRIST DYSFUNCTION

Visually inspect and palpate hand and wrist

PROCEDURE: Visually inspect and palpate the hand and wrist for masses, lesions, or tenderness. Perform this distal to proximal.

OUTCOME: If pain and swelling over the ulnar side of the hand, especially with a history of antecedent trauma: ◆ boxer's fracture
If a palpable, fluctuant nodule adjacent to a tendon sheath:
  ◆ ganglion cyst
If tenderness or paresthesia in the ulnar aspect of the hand, completely distal to the ulnar (Guyon's) tunnel:
  ◆ ulnar tunnel syndrome, that is, distal ulnar nerve mischief
If atrophy of interosseous muscles:
  ◆ ulnar tunnel syndrome (distal site)
  ◆ cubital tunnel syndrome (proximal site)
If atrophy of interosseous muscles and ulnar wrist flexors in the forearm: ◆ cubital tunnel syndrome (proximal site)
If atrophy of the thenar eminence:
  ◆ carpal tunnel syndrome (distal median site)
If atrophy of wrist extensors in the forearm:
  ◆ radial nerve problem
If tenderness and swelling in the distal radius and dorsal displacement of the distal radius on the proximal radius (Fig 8-13):
  ◆ Colles' fracture

Figure 8-13 Colles' fracture. Note the marked deformity of the distal wrist, in which there is dorsal displacement of the bones distal to fracture; deformity referred to as a *dinner fork position*, with tongs down.

Transilluminate any masses or nodules

PROCEDURE: Apply a light source to the skin adjacent to the nodule or mass. Visually inspect the mass for transmission of light.

OUTCOME: If the lesion is thoroughly illuminated (transilluminable):
◆ **ganglion cyst**
If nontransilluminable: ◆ **any other entity**

Examine for Finkelstein's sign: As in Approach to a patient with thumb dysfunction or pain.

APPROACH TO A PATIENT WITH SUSPECTED ULNAR NEUROPATHY

Inspect for Froment's sign

PROCEDURE: Place a piece of paper between the thumb and second digit so that the thumb and index fingers are completely adducted (Fig 8-14). Ask the patient to attempt to prevent the movement of the paper as you pull on it (Fig 8-14). Repeat on the contralateral side for a control.

OUTCOME: If the paper can be held steady: ◆ **normal**
If paper can be moved:
◆ **ulnar tunnel syndrome**
◆ **cubital tunnel syndrome**

Actively flex digits from a neutral position; that is, make a fist

PROCEDURE: Have the patient hold the hand in a neutral position. Ask him/her to actively flex digits 2 through 5 as if "making a fist." Inspect the movement and the hand musculature. Use the contralateral hand as control.

OUTCOME: If the patient is able to flex all digits: ◆ **normal**

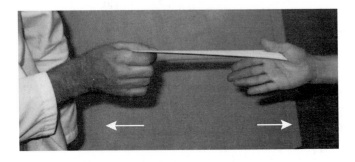

Figure 8-14 Froment's sign to assess the ulnar nerve. Note that the patient is actively adducting the thumb against the second digit. This stresses the furthest domain of the ulnar nerve.

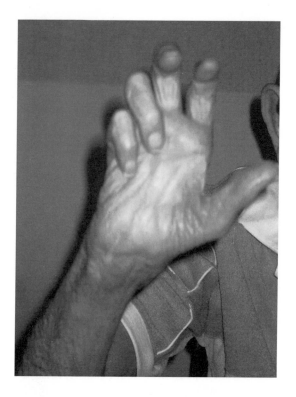

Figure 8-15 Papal hand. Severe median nerve damage. Note patient is instructed to actively make a fist from a neutral baseline; unable to flex second and third digits, with a resulting hand position of benediction.

If there is weakness to flexion of digits 4 and 5:
- ♦ ulnar nerve damage, end stage, nonspecific to site

If weakness to flexion of digits 2 and 3 (papal hand; Fig 8-15):
- ♦ median nerve damage, end stage, nonspecific to site

Inspect hand and wrist muscles

PROCEDURE: Inspect the size of the muscles in the hands and wrist. Use the other hand as a control.

OUTCOME: If there is atrophy of the hypothenar area (Dimple sign):
- ♦ ulnar nerve damage, nonspecific to site

If atrophy of the interosseous musculature:
- ♦ ulnar nerve damage, nonspecific to site

Inspect forearm muscles

PROCEDURE: Inspect the size of the muscles in the forearm. Use the other forearm as a control.

OUTCOME: If there is no atrophy of the flexor carpi ulnaris:
◆ **ulnar tunnel syndrome**
If atrophy of the flexor carpi ulnaris:
◆ **proximal ulnar nerve damage**

Percuss over ulnar (Guyon's) tunnel for Tinel's sign

PROCEDURE: Have patient place the hand at rest with the digits passively extended. Using a plexor or the index finger, tap for 15 to 20 seconds over the palmar/ulnar side (Fig 8-16C) of the patient's affected hand. Repeat on the contralateral side as a control (Fig 8-17).

OUTCOME: If paresthesia and pain of skin are present on the ulnar side of the hand and digits 4 and 5 (see Figs 8-1B and 8-2B):
◆ **ulnar tunnel syndrome (distal site)**
If no paresthesia: ◆ **proximal ulnar nerve problem**

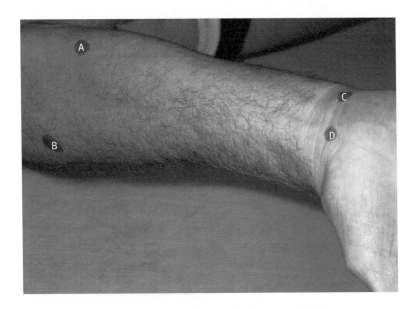

Figure 8-16 Sites of peripheral nerve entrapment. Palmar forearm and hand. A. Pronators, proximal median nerve. B. Brachioradialis/canal of Frohse, radial nerve. C. Loge de Guyon (ulnar tunnel), distal ulnar nerve. D. Carpal tunnel, distal median nerve.

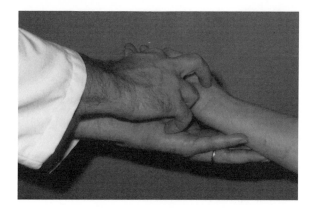

Figure 8-17 Tinel's sign over carpal tunnel site. Note examiner using the tip of second digit to tap over the carpal tunnel; tingling in median nerve distribution indicates carpal tunnel syndrome.

APPROACH TO A PATIENT WITH SUSPECTED RADIAL NEUROPATHY

Actively extend the thumb against resistance

PROCEDURE: Instruct the patient to extend the thumb actively against resistance. Use the contralateral thumb as a control.

OUTCOME: If there is weakness in thumb extension: ◆ **radial nerve problem**
If strength/power is 5/5: ◆ **normal**

Actively abduct the thumb against resistance

PROCEDURE: Instruct the patient to abduct the thumb actively against resistance. Use the contralateral thumb as a control.

OUTCOME: If there is weakness in thumb abduction: ◆ **radial nerve problem**
If strength/power is 5/5: ◆ **normal**

Perform sensory examination over the snuffbox

PROCEDURE: Apply cotton-tipped swab or monofilament to skin overlying the anatomic snuffbox (see Fig 8-1A).

OUTCOME: If sensation present: ◆ **normal**
If decreased sensation: ◆ **radial nerve problem**

APPROACH TO A PATIENT WITH SUSPECTED MEDIAN NEUROPATHY

Active flexion of thumb at interphalangeal joint

PROCEDURE: Instruct patient to flex thumb tip actively [at interphalangeal (IP) joint]; apply resistance to palmar tip.

OUTCOME: If good strength (power): ◆ **normal**
If weakness: ◆ **median nerve problem**

Actively flex fingers from a neutral position (actively make a fist)

PROCEDURE: With the patient's hand in a neutral position, instruct the patient to actively flex digits 2 through 5. Inspect finger movement.

OUTCOME: If the patient is able to flex digits: ◆ **normal**
If there is weakness to flexion of digits 2 and 3 (papal hand; see Fig 8-15): ◆ **median nerve damage, end stage, nonspecific to site**
If weakness to flexion of digits 4 and 5:
◆ **ulnar nerve damage, end stage, nonspecific to site**

Inspect thenar musculature

PROCEDURE: Inspect the size of the muscles in the hands and wrist. Use the other hand as a control.

OUTCOME: If there is atrophy of the thenar area:
◆ **median nerve damage, nonspecific to site**

Inspect forearm musculature

PROCEDURE: Inspect the size of the muscles in the forearm. Use the other forearm as a control.

OUTCOME: If there is no atrophy of the flexor carpi radialis:
◆ **carpal tunnel syndrome**
If atrophy of the flexor carpi radialis: ◆ **proximal median nerve**

Percuss carpal tunnel for Tinel's sign

PROCEDURE: Use the tip of a finger (see Fig 8-17) or a plexor to percuss at the midpoint of a line transversely placed at the base of the thenar and hypothenar eminences (see Fig 8-16D). Continue to tap for greater than 10 to 12 consecutive times or until paresthesia develops. Use the contralateral side as a control.

OUTCOME: If there is paresthesia or dysesthesia in the median nerve distribution: ◆ **carpal tunnel syndrome**
Sensitivity 60%; specificity 67%[6]
If no dysesthesia/paresthesia: ◆ **normal**

Examine hands for Phalen's sign

PROCEDURE: Ask the patient to palmarflex (Phalen's) the hands actively and maximally for 30 seconds (Fig 8-18).

OUTCOME: If there is paresthesia in the median nerve distribution:
◆ **carpal tunnel syndrome**
Sensitivity 75%; specificity 47%[6]
If paresthesia/dysesthesia in the ulnar nerve distribution:
◆ **ulnar tunnel syndrome**
If no paresthesia/dysesthesia: ◆ **normal**

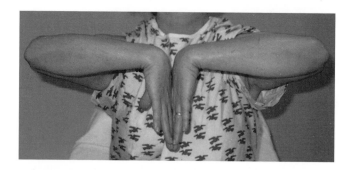

Figure 8-18 Phalen's maneuver. The patient fully palmarflexes hands at the wrist for 30 seconds; tingling in a median nerve distribution indicates carpal tunnel syndrome. Tingling in the ulnar nerve distribution indicates ulnar tunnel syndrome.

Palpate directly over transverse carpal ligament

PROCEDURE: Instruct the patient to place his or her hands in a neutral position. Use your thumbs to press directly on the transverse carpal ligament.

OUTCOME: If there is paresthesia in the median nerve distribution:
◆ **carpal tunnel syndrome**
If paresthesia in the ulnar nerve distribution:
◆ **ulnar tunnel syndrome**

Keys to Recording Findings

HANDS

"Unremarkable" "Allen ‹ 6 seconds"

- Sites of swelling, pain, tenderness on fingers/hands or in joints

- Active and passive ROM at joints; document degrees of the motion if abnormal

- Contractures, e.g. Swan neck or mallet finger

- Any sensory deficits: Thenar skin: median nerve; hypothenar skin: ulnar nerve; snuffbox skin: radial nerve

- Sites of muscle atrophy and/or fasiculations: interossei: ulnar nerve, thenar eminence: median nerve

- If Tinel's performed record site, ulnar tunnel versus carpal tunnel, location of tingling and number of taps required to precipitate finding

- If Phalen's performed record location of tingling and number of seconds required to precipitate findings

- If Allen (ulnar side) performed record number of seconds required for the pink flush to reach the radial side of hand (thenar base)

Sensation: Draw on any deficits.

Range of motion (ROM): At DIP, PIP, MCP and wrist. Draw on any joint swelling; state degrees of motion if abnormal.

Draw on any sites of swelling.

Draw on sites of muscle atrophy.

Dorsal

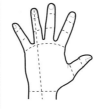

Palmar

Tinel's # of taps _____; draw on location of tingling

Phalen's # of seconds _____; draw on location of tingling

Allen Test	Left	Right
	‹ 6 seconds ☐	‹ 6 seconds ☐
	› 6 seconds ☐	› 6 seconds ☐
	# of seconds	# of seconds
	_____	_____

Diagnoses

Arthritis of thumb base

Caused by recurrent joint trauma or collateral ligament laxity, or both, for example, from skier's thumb. Symptoms include pain that is better in the morning. Signs include decreased range of motion (ROM) flexion, extension, abduction, adduction, circumduction, and opposition (see Table 8-1 for normal); crepitus; tenderness at the trapeziometacarpal joint; pain increased at thumb base specifically with Finkelstein's test (see Fig 8-12). Severe cases feature a contracture of flexion and subluxation at the carpometacarpal joint and hyperextension in the MCP joint. Evaluation and treatment include radiographs, rest, functional splints, intra-articular steroids, and referral to an occupational therapist and hand surgeon.

Boutonnière deformity

Disruption of the central slip of the extensor digitorum tendon due to laceration on the dorsum at the PIP or tenosynovitis. Symptoms include PIP pain and swelling. Early signs are tenderness and swelling at the dorsal PIP; late signs are flexion contracture of the PIP and hyperextension contractures of MCP and PIP (see Fig 8-6), with concurrent PIP lateral/medial laxity. Radiographs can help rule out concurrent avulsion fracture. Treatment includes splinting the PIP joint in full extension. The patient may need referral to a hand surgeon.

Boxer's fracture

Simple fracture of the fifth metacarpal bone due to the patient hitting an object with a closed fist. Symptoms and signs include pain, tenderness, and swelling over the ulnar side of the hand. The function of the ulnar nerve (see Figs 8-1B, 8-2B, and 8-3) and artery should be assessed, as these can be damaged. Radiographs can confirm the fracture. Treat the injury with splint placement and nonemergent referral to a hand surgeon.

Carpal tunnel syndrome

Entrapment of median nerve in the carpal tunnel (see Fig 8-16D). Symptoms include pain and numbness on palmar side of digits 1, 2, and 3 (see Fig 8-2A), which often increase at night. Signs include weakness of flexion of digits 2 and 3 (see Fig 8-15), abnormal tip-to-tip "OK" sign (see Fig 8-5), weakness to thumb IP flexion, and positive Tinel's (see Fig 8-17) and Phalen's (see Fig 8-18) signs. No weakness of wrist flexion is found in carpal tunnel syndrome; weakness of wrist flexion can occur in proximal lesions (see Fig 8-16A). Evaluation includes confirmation with electromyogram/nerve conduction (EMG/NC). Treatment includes a wrist splint in mild hyperextension, nonsteroidal anti-inflammatory drugs (NSAIDs), and, if no improvement, referral to a hand surgeon.

Clubbing

Abnormal accumulation of connective tissue at the tip of each affected digit due to hypertrophic pulmonary osteoarthropathy, chronic mycobacterial disease, bronchiectasis, cystic fibrosis, endocarditis, or inflammatory bowel syndrome. Clubbing is generally asymptomatic. Signs include an increase in the angle formed by the nail plate and the proximal nail fold, approaching or even exceeding 180 degrees (see Fig 8-9), and an abnormal sponginess at the base of the nail plate (see Fig 8-10). (Both features are required to make the diagnosis of clubbing.) Schamroth's sign will be present. The patient may manifest symptoms of the underlying chronic disease. Evaluation includes a chest radiograph. The treatment is specific to the underlying cause.

Collateral ligament sprain of the proximal interphalangeal joint

This sprain is due to twisting or radial/ulnar deviation of the finger. Symptoms and signs include acute-onset pain and swelling about the PIP, point tenderness at the collateral ligament, and increased laxity of the PIP. Evaluation and treatment include radiographs, which are normal; splint PIP in 30 degrees of flexion and refer to occupational therapy.

Colles' fracture

Fracture of the distal radius due to a fall on an outstretched, dorsiflexed hand. Symptoms and signs include distal radius deformity (see Fig 8-13) and swelling. The patient should be assessed for acute damage to the flexor pollicis longus tendon and the median nerve (see Figs 8-2A and 8-5). Radiographs reveal a fractured distal radial styloid with dorsal displacement. Treatment includes reduction, application of a dorsal wrist splint in palmar flexion and ulnar deviation, and referral to a hand surgeon.

Degenerative joint disease

Osteoarthritis of the hands and fingers. Symptoms include pain with some stiffness during activity, which is worse in the afternoon. Signs include minimal joint swelling and the presence of Heberden's (DIP joint) or Bouchard's (PIP joint) nodes, or both. Treatment includes rest, acetaminophen, and referral for physical therapy.

de Quervain's disease

Inflammation of the tendons (abductor pollicis longus, extensor pollicis longus, extensor pollicis brevis) in the anatomic snuffbox (see Fig 8-11) due to inflammatory arthritis, occupation, and/or pregnancy. Symptoms include pain in the snuffbox; signs are tenderness in the snuffbox tendons (see Fig 8-11A,B) and positive Finkelstein's sign (see Fig 8-12). Radiographs are normal. Treatment includes a wrist splint applied with mild dorsiflexion and radial deviation of the wrist.

Dupuytren's syndrome

Idiopathic flexion contractures of the digits due to shortening of palmaris fascia; associated with ethanol abuse, hepatic disease, and diabetes mellitus.

Symptoms and signs include painless flexion contractures of one or more digits (usually digit 4 or 5) and concurrent palpable, nontender nodules in the palmaris fascia (see Fig 8-8). Evaluation and treatment include referral of the patient to a general surgeon.

Ganglion cyst

Fluid-filled, synovial-lined cysts adjacent to tendons. Symptoms and signs include fluctuant, nontender nodules on the hand/wrists that wax and wane in size. Treatment includes observation; referral to a hand surgeon for resection if compression of nerve or if patient desires.

Mallet finger

Rupture of the extensor tendon at the DIP caused by forced flexion of the DIP joint when the digit is fully extended, for example, when a ball hits the tip of a finger. Symptoms are pain and swelling of the DIP; signs are of a decrease in active but not passive extension at the DIP. Evaluation with a radiograph may reveal an avulsion fracture at the DIP. Treatment includes splint with distal phalanx in full or slight hyperextension for 8 weeks (splint only the DIP joint). Referral to a hand surgeon is not always required.

Proximal interphalangeal joint dislocation

Dislocation from forced hyperextension at the PIP joint, often occurs during games of catch. Symptoms include acute onset of severe pain and swelling at the joint. Signs include a visually and palpably evident dislocation of middle phalanx from the proximal phalanx. Radiographs can confirm the dislocation. Treatment includes reduction of the dislocation, applying a splint with the PIP flexed to 30 degrees, and referral to a hand surgeon.

Radial nerve damage

Damage to the radial nerve normally due to a fracture of the humerus (proximal damage) or entrapment in the radial tunnel, that is, in the brachioradialis muscle (distal site of damage; see Fig 8-16B); the proximal damage has an impact on motor and sensory functions, whereas the distal damage impacts only on sensory. Signs include weakness to extension at the wrist (see Fig 8-4), thumb, and finger with normal passive wrist, thumb, and finger extension and decreased sensation on the dorsum of the forearm and hand focused on the anatomic snuffbox skin (see Fig 8-1A). Evaluation includes radiographs of the wrist, forearm, and arm and, to confirm diagnosis, obtaining an EMG and NC study. The patient can be referred to an orthopedic surgeon and occupational therapist (OT).

Rheumatoid arthritis: See Swan neck deformity and Boutonnière deformity.

Scaphoid fracture

Fracture from a fall on an outstretched, dorsiflexed hand with impact at the midwrist. Symptoms and signs include tenderness in the snuffbox base (see Fig 8-11C) and on the palmar radial wrist. Radiographs of the wrist are often negative, but a fracture may still be present. Because of a high risk of nonunion, treatment must be aggressive: thumb spica splint/cast and referral to a hand surgeon.

Swan neck deformity

Volar plate disruption at the PIP joint from an acute forced hyperextension of the PIP or from tenosynovitis. Symptoms include PIP pain and swelling. Early signs include tenderness and swelling at the volar PIP; late signs include hyperextension contracture of the PIP and flexion contractures of the MCP and PIP (see Fig 8-6). Radiographs can rule out a concurrent avulsion fracture. Treatment includes splinting the PIP in 30 degrees of flexion and referral to a hand surgeon.

Ulnar collateral ligament injury of the thumb (skier's thumb)

Forced abduction of the thumb with ulnar collateral ligament (UCL) damage at its insertion on the proximal phalanx; also known as *gamekeeper's thumb* or *skier's thumb* because it often occurs in skiers when they fall while holding onto a pole. Symptoms include pain and swelling at the MCP joint of the thumb. Signs include tenderness and effusion on the ulnar aspect of the MCP and inappropriate laxity to passive thumb abduction. Radiographs may confirm a concurrent avulsion fracture. Treatment includes a thumb spica splint and referral to a hand surgeon.

Ulnar tunnel syndrome

Entrapment of the ulnar nerve or artery in the ulnar tunnel (loge de Guyon), or both. The ulnar tunnel (see Fig 8-16C) is on the ulnar/palmar aspect of the hand, with boundaries that include the pisiform, the transverse carpal ligament, the volar carpal ligament, and the hook of the hamate. It is 4.0 to 4.5 cm in length and contains the ulnar nerve and artery. Etiologies include edema, crush injury, boxer's fracture, hamate fracture, ganglion cyst in the canal, or hypothenar hammer syndrome. Symptoms include weakness in grasp and tingling on the ulnar side of the hand (see Figs 8-1B and 8-2B). Signs include weakness to digit abduction (see Fig 8-3), positive Froment's sign (see Fig 8-14), decreased sensation on the palmar and dorsal aspect of digits 4 and 5 (see Figs 8-1B and 8-2B), positive Phalen's (see Fig 8-18) and Tinel's signs over the ulnar tunnel, and an Allen's test >6 seconds if the ulnar artery is damaged. Evaluation includes radiographs, which may reveal a fifth metatarsal or hamate fracture, and, if indicated, electromyography (EMG) and nerve conduction (NC) studies to confirm the diagnosis. Treatment includes a wrist splint, NSAIDs, and referral to a hand surgeon.

CHAPTER 9
Elbow

Basic Examination

Inspect active and passive range of motion: flexion and extension

PROCEDURE: Perform active and passive flexion and extension range of motion (ROM) of the elbow.

OUTCOME: If flexion is 140 degrees: ◆ **normal ulnar/humeral joint**
If extension is 0°: ◆ **normal ulnar/humeral joint**
If extension/flexion are decreased:
◆ **degenerative joint disease (DJD)**
If cubitus valgus: ◆ **normal**
If cubitus varus (Fig 9-1): ◆ **humeral fracture**

Inspect active and passive range of motion, supination, and pronation

PROCEDURE: With the patient's elbow passively flexed to 90 degrees, perform active and passive supination and pronation ROM of the elbow.

OUTCOME: If pronation is 80 degrees: ◆ **radial/ulnar joint normal**
If supination is 75 degrees: ◆ **radial/ulnar joint normal**
If supination/pronation is decreased:
◆ **DJD**
◆ **radial head fracture**
If there is pain with active supination:
◆ **lateral epicondylitis**
◆ **radial tunnel syndrome**
If pain with active pronation: ◆ **medial epicondylitis**

Palpate structures in and around elbow

PROCEDURE: Visually inspect and palpate the skin and the bony structures of the elbow. Palpate the medial epicondyle, the cubital groove and tunnel, the olecranon process, the groove between the humerus and ulna, and the lateral epicondyle (Fig 9-2).

OUTCOME: If there is tenderness over the medial epicondyle (Fig 9-2A):
◆ **medial epicondylitis**
If paresthesia in the ulnar side of the forearm and hand, with pressure on the cubital tunnel (Fig 9-2B):
◆ **cubital tunnel syndrome (proximal ulnar problem)**
If there is a nontender nodule over and proximal to the olecranon process (Fig 9-2C):
◆ **rheumatoid nodule**
◆ **tophus (Fig 9-3)**

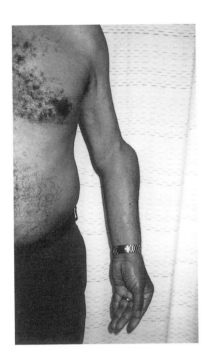

Figure 9-1 Cubitus varus. The elbow is inappropriately and abnormally in a position of varus, usually as a result of trauma in the past. Also known as *gun stock deformity*.

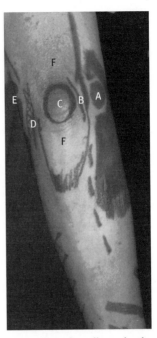

Figure 9-2 Posterior elbow, landmarks. A. Medial epicondyle. B. Cubital tunnel (proximal ulnar nerve site). C. Olecranon and overlying bursa. D. Ulnar/humeral articulation. E. Lateral epicondyle. F. Triceps muscle and its aponeurosis.

Figure 9-3 Tophi over olecranon. Patient with a long history of recurrent attacks of gout in feet and hands; in addition, he had tophi on the auricles and fingers.

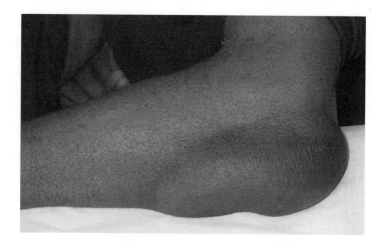

Figure 9-4 Olecranon bursitis. Fluctuant mass over the olecranon that has little if any tenderness and has no associated limitation of elbow range of motion but is transilluminable.

If there is tender swelling over the olecranon process (Fig 9-4):
♦ **olecranon bursitis**
If tenderness over the triceps muscle (Fig 9-2F):
♦ **triceps muscle strain**
If tenderness over the lateral epicondyle (Fig 9-2E):
♦ **lateral epicondylitis**
If there is a palpable nodule in the area immediately proximal to the medial epicondyle: ♦ **epicondylar lymph node enlargement**

| Advanced Examination |

APPROACH TO A PATIENT WITH MEDIAL (ULNAR) ELBOW PAIN

Inspect active and passive range of motion, supination, and pronation:
As in Basic Examination.

Palpate structures in and around elbows: As in Basic Examination.

Perform valgus stress test

PROCEDURE: Position the patient's elbow to be passively flexed to 30 degrees. Grasp the midforearm with one hand and the elbow with the other hand. Apply valgus stress to the joint (Fig 9-5). Palpate the joint for any laxity, and ask the patient if pain develops and, if so, the exact location.

OUTCOME: If <5 degrees of valgus movement:
- ◆ **normal**
- ◆ **medial epicondylitis**

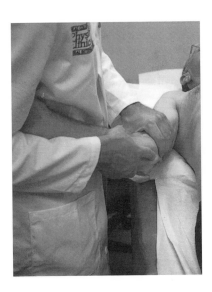

Figure 9-5 Valgus stress test for assessment of the ulnar collateral ligament of elbow. Note that the examiner is placing valgus stress on elbow while palpating the medial elbow for laxity.

If >5 degrees of valgus movement:
- ◆ **medial (ulnar) collateral ligament tear**

Test the tip-to-tip "OK" sign: See p. 177, in hand exam, Approach to patient with median nerve dysfunction.

APPROACH TO A PATIENT WITH POSTERIOR ELBOW PAIN

Palpate over ulnar olecranon
PROCEDURE: Directly palpate over and around the olecranon of the ulna.

OUTCOME: If there is tenderness and swelling over the olecranon (may be large and/or fluctuant) (see Fig 9-2C): ◆ **olecranon bursitis**
If tenderness immediately proximal, that is, in triceps muscle (see Fig 9-2F): ◆ **triceps strain**
If no tenderness: ◆ **normal**

Transilluminate any mass over the olecranon
PROCEDURE: Using a light source (either penlight or otoscope), attempt to transilluminate any nodule or mass.

OUTCOME: If the structure is transilluminable: ◆ **olecranon bursitis, serous**
If structure is opaque:
- ◆ **tophus**
- ◆ **rheumatoid nodule**
- ◆ **olecranon bursitis, blood or purulent**

Apply direct pressure over cubital groove
PROCEDURE: Directly palpate the cubital groove (i.e., apply digital pressure over the ulnar groove; see Fig 9-2B).

OUTCOME: If pain and/or tingling develop on the medial (ulnar) side of the forearm, hand, and digits 4 and 5:
- ◆ **cubital tunnel syndrome (proximal ulnar nerve)**
If no tenderness or paresthesia: ◆ **normal**

Percuss over the cubital groove for Tinel's sign
PROCEDURE: Tap over the cubital groove (see Fig 9-2B) with a finger or plexor for 10 to 12 taps. Ask the patient if paresthesia, pain, or numbness develops. Use the contralateral side as a control.

OUTCOME: If there is pain and/or tingling on the medial (ulnar) side of the forearm, hand, and digits 4 and 5:
- ◆ **cubital tunnel syndrome (proximal ulnar nerve)**
If no tenderness or paresthesia: ◆ **normal**

APPROACH TO A PATIENT WITH LATERAL (RADIAL) ELBOW PAIN

Inspect active and passive range of motion, flexion, and extension: As in Basic Examination.

Inspect active and passive range of motion, supination, and pronation:
As in Basic Examination.

Palpate structures in and around elbows: As in Basic Examination.

Palpate lateral epicondyle
PROCEDURE: With the patient's elbow extended, palpate the lateral aspect of the elbow and forearm, including the lateral epicondyle of the humerus and all structures adjacent to the radius. Use the contralateral side as a control.

OUTCOME: If there is tenderness over the lateral epicondyle:
◆ **lateral epicondylitis (tennis elbow)**
If tenderness over an area 3 to 4 cm distal to the lateral epicondyle: ◆ **radial nerve problem, probably radial tunnel**

Test fine touch of dorsum of fingers and hand, radial side
PROCEDURE: With the patient's arm extended at the elbow, use a cotton-tipped swab to test the fine touch sensation of the forearm, radial side, then ulnar side, and of the hands and digits. Repeat on the contralateral side as a control (see Fig 8-1, p. 178).

OUTCOME: If sensation is decreased on the radial forearm and dorsal hand and digits (see Fig 8-1):
◆ **radial nerve problem , probably radial tunnel**
If there is no decreased sensation: ◆ **lateral epicondylitis**

Inspect for Cozen's sign
PROCEDURE: Instruct the patient to make a fist and position the forearm in a pronated manner. Grasp the pronated fist with both hands and tell the patient to push superiorly (i.e., dorsiflex at the wrist) against resistance. Repeat on the contralateral side as a control.

OUTCOME: If there is tenderness over the lateral epicondyle:
◆ **lateral epicondylitis**
If no tenderness over the lateral epicondyle: ◆ **normal**

Percuss over radial tunnel site (Tinel's)
PROCEDURE: Use a finger or plexor to tap over the lateral proximal forearm for 10 to 12 reproducible taps. Ask the patient if parethesia, pain, or numbness develops. Compare to the contralateral side.

OUTCOME: If pain and tingling on the dorsal, radial side of the forearm and wrist, focused on the skin overlying the anatomic snuffbox:
◆ **radial nerve problem due to entrapment at the radial tunnel**
If no pain or paresthesia: ◆ **normal**

Keys to Recording Findings

ELBOW

"Unremarkable, normal ROM extension/flexion, supination/ pronation, no pain swelling or tenderness"

• Note sites of swelling, pain, tenderness

• Note active and passive ROM at joints-flexion and extension; supination/pronation; document degrees of the motion if abnormal

• Note any sensory deficits

• Note any sites of muscle atrophy and/or fasiculations

	Left	Right
Supination	_____	_____
Pronation	_____	_____
Extension	_____	_____
Flexion	_____	_____

Draw on sites of tenderness.

Draw on sites of swelling.

Draw on sites of muscle atrophy.

Draw on sites of sensory deficits.

Anterior

Right   Left

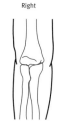

Posterior

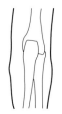

Lateral

Cubital tunnel syndrome

Entrapment of the ulnar nerve in the cubital tunnel (between the medial epicondyle and the olecranon; see Fig 9-2B), most often due to inflammation and/or recurrent mild trauma. Symptoms include progressively worsening pain and tingling on the medial (ulnar) side of the forearm, hand, and palmar and dorsal aspects of digits 4 and 5 (see Figs 8-1 and 8-2, p. 178). Signs include positive Tinel's sign over the cubital tunnel; if severe, weakness of finger abduction/adduction (see Fig 8-3, p. 178); and atrophy of the interosseous, hypothenar, and flexor wrist musculature. Evaluation and treatment include an elbow sling, nonsteroidal anti-inflammatory drugs (NSAIDs), and physical therapy. Referral to an orthopedic surgeon may be indicated if there is atrophy or if any manifestations are refractory to standard treatment.

Degenerative joint disease

Degeneration of the radioulnar and/or humeroulnar joint due to repetitive trauma. The risk factors for this condition include ulnar (medial) collateral ligament damage (see Fig 9-2A) and Little Leaguer's elbow as a child (see below). Symptoms and signs include diffuse pain, decreased ROM with crepitus to pronation/supination (radioulnar) and extension/flexion (ulnohumeral), mild joint swelling, and joint locking if cartilaginous loose body is present. Evaluate the condition with elbow radiographs; osteophytes may appear in the affected articulations. Treatment includes rest, physical therapy, and intra-articular steroids.

Epicondylar lymph node enlargement

Due to an infection in the hand. Symptoms and signs include a node on the medial aspect of the elbow, often enlarged and tender, immediately proximal to the medial epicondyle. Evaluate for and treat any underlying infection.

Lateral/radial epicondylitis (tennis elbow)

Overuse and trauma of wrist extensor and forearm supinator muscles that originate at the lateral epicondyle. Risk factors include playing tennis or racquetball, swimming with crawl stroke, overhand throwing a baseball, and antecedent rotator cuff weakness. Symptoms and signs include pain, tenderness over the lateral epicondyle (specifically at origin of extensor carpi radialis and extensor digitorum muscles; see Fig 9-2E), and positive Cozen's test. Evaluation may include elbow radiographs. Treatment includes rest, referral for physical therapy, and a tennis elbow strap to limit forearm muscle extension.

Medial (ulnar) collateral ligament tear

Tear from valgus displacement on elbow. Primary risk factor is overhand ball pitching. A variant of this condition is Little Leaguer's elbow: damage to the apophysis of the ulnar collateral ligament (UCL) found in adolescent pitchers. Symptoms include pain that worsens with repeated activity. Signs include tenderness over the medial elbow (see Fig 9-2A) and a positive valgus stress test (see Fig 9-5). Evaluation and treatment include rest and referral to an orthopedic surgeon.

Medial/ulnar epicondylitis (golf elbow)

Overuse and trauma of wrist flexors and forearm pronator muscles that originate at the medial epicondyle (see Fig 9-2A). Risk factors include throwing footballs or baseballs, swinging golf clubs, and swimming the crawl stroke. Symptoms and signs include pain and tenderness over the medial epicondyle (see Fig 9-2A), but no swelling or redness. Evaluation may include elbow radiographs. Treatment includes rest and referral for physical therapy.

Olecranon bursitis

Inflammation of the bursa superficial to the olecranon process (see Fig 9-2C) of the humerus, due to infection [*Streptococcus* species (spp), *Staphylococcus* spp], trauma, or crystal formations (gout, pseudogout). Symptoms and signs of pain and fluctuant swelling over the olecranon process (see Fig 9-4); no decreased ROM of the elbow occurs, but there may be overlying erythema and warmth if the cause is infection. Evaluation may include elbow radiographs. Treatment includes compressive dressings and rest; if the cause is an infection, treatment includes incision, drainage, and systemic antibiotics.

Radial head fracture

Due to a fall with impact on an outstretched hand. Symptoms and signs include acute elbow pain, swelling, and tenderness; normal flexion/extension; and markedly decreased supination/pronation. Evaluation includes a radiograph to confirm. Treatment includes splinting and referral to an orthopedics specialist.

Radial neuropathy

Entrapment of the deep branch of the radial nerve as it crosses the elbow at the arcade of Frohse (a connective tissue structure, 3–4 cm distal to the lateral epicondyle, in the proximal brachioradialis muscle; see Fig 8-16B). Symptoms include distal lateral elbow pain and discomfort and paresthesiae in the lateral proximal forearm extending into the anatomic snuffbox area, the dorsum of the thumb, and digits 2 and 3. Signs include a positive Tinel's sign over the proximal brachioradialis muscle (Fig 8-16B); no lateral epicondyle tenderness. Evaluation includes confirmation by electromyography (EMG) and nerve conduction (NC) studies. Treatment includes rest, NSAIDs, and physical therapy and referral to an orthopedic surgeon if the condition is refractory to first-line therapy.

Radial tunnel: See Radial neuropathy.

Rheumatoid nodule

Due to rheumatoid arthritis in which nodules have a proclivity to form in the aponeurosis of the olecranon. Ninety-five percent of such nodules are over the olecranon process of the ulna over tendons such as the olecranon of the ulna. Symptoms and signs include the presence of a nontender, nontransilluminable nodule, with concurrent signs of rheumatoid arthritis. Evaluation and management include rest and the appropriate evaluation and management of rheumatoid arthritis including referral to a rheumatologist.

Tophus

Collection of uric acid crystals in severe (i.e., tophaceous) gout. Tophi can develop anywhere but are commonly found on the auricles, nose, and distal appendages, including over the olecranon process of the ulna (see Fig 9-3). Concurrent tophi on other sites and a history of recurrent podagra or monarticular arthritis are very common. Evaluation and treatment include obtaining a serum uric acid and the initiation of NSAIDs, colchicine, and chronic allopurinol.

Triceps strain

Muscle strain from overuse of the arm in activities that require elbow extension. Symptoms and signs include pain and tenderness in the triceps muscle itself, that is, immediately proximal to the olecranon process (see Fig 9-2F); the pain may radiate into the shoulder and be exacerbated by active elbow extension. Evaluation and treatment include rest, NSAIDs, and referral for physical therapy.

CHAPTER 10
Shoulder

Basic Examination

Inspect and palpate shoulder structures

PROCEDURE: Palpate the various structures of the shoulder. Start at the anterior and medial structures (Fig 10-1) and move to the lateral (Fig 10-2) and posterior (Fig 10-3) structures. Use the contralateral shoulder as a control.

OUTCOME: If there is tenderness and/or swelling at the sternoclavicular joint (see Fig 10-1F): ◆ **sternoclavicular separation**
If swelling of the clavicle (see Fig 10-1G): ◆ **clavicular fracture**
If separation of the lateral clavicle from the acromion (see Fig 10-1E): ◆ **acromioclavicular separation**
If tenderness on or at the bicipital groove (see Fig 10-1C):
◆ **bicipital tendonitis**
If swelling deep to the lateral aspect of the deltoid muscle (see Fig 10-2B): ◆ **subacromial/subdeltoid bursitis**
If tenderness and/or spasm of muscles overlying the posterior scapula: ◆ **trapezius strain**
If tenderness and/or spasm in the posterior shoulder, medial to the inferior vertebral border of the scapula (see Fig 10-3F):
◆ **rhomboid strain**

Passive crank test

PROCEDURE: Patient sitting or standing, hand and forearm in a neutral position, arm at side, elbow flexed to 80 degrees; the examiner grasps forearm with one hand, elbow with the other hand (Fig 10-4). The examiner passively internally rotates arm to 30 degrees; then after returning to baseline, externally rotates the arm to 30 degrees, then again after returning to baseline, abducts the arm to 30 degrees.

OUTCOME: If able to perform without any pain: ◆ **normal**
If pain or unable to perform:
◆ **problem at glenohumeral (GH) joint (e.g., a humeral fracture, frozen shoulder, or anterior glenohumeral dislocation)**

Active crank test

PROCEDURE: Patient sitting or standing, hand and forearm in a neutral position, arm at side, elbow flexed to 80 degrees, the examiner grasps forearm with one hand, elbow with the other hand

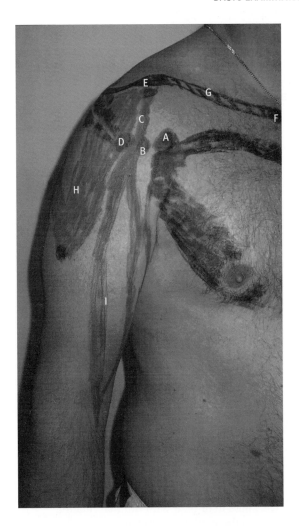

Figure 10-1 Anterior shoulder, landmarks. A. Coracoid process of the scapula. B. Lesser tuberosity (insertion of the subscapularis). C. Bicipital tendon in bicipital groove (long head). D. Greater tuberosity (insertion site of the supraspinatus and infraspinatus muscles). E. Acromioclavicular joint. F. Sternoclavicular joint. G. Clavicle. H. Deltoid muscle. I. Biceps muscle.

(Fig 10-5); instruct patient to actively externally rotate; then, after returning to baseline, internally rotate; and then again, after returning to baseline actively, abduct. All of these actions are made against gentle resistance.

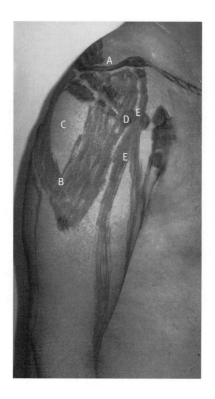

Figure 10-2 Lateral shoulder, landmarks. A. Acromial rum. B. Deltoid muscle. C. Subdeltoid bursa. D. Greater tuberosity. E. Bicipital tendon.

OUTCOME: If able to perform in all three actions without pain: ◆ **normal**
If weakness to or pain with external rotation:
◆ **infraspinatus problem**
If weakness to or pain with internal rotation:
◆ **subscapularis problem**
If weakness to or pain with abduction: ◆ **supraspinatus problem**

Assess the motor function of each nerve root (C5–T1): See Table 10-1; Figures 10-6 to 10-11.

Observe range of motion in shoulder
PROCEDURE: With the patient's arms in neutral position at the sides, perform passive and active range of motion (ROM) in the GH joint while stabilizing the scapulothoracic joint. Use the contralateral side as a control.
OUTCOME: See Table 10-2.
If there is complete loss of passive and active abduction:

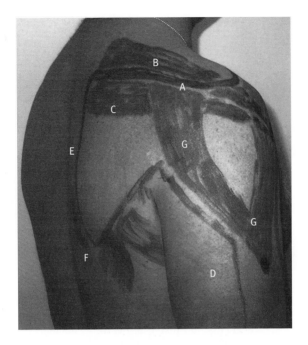

Figure 10-3 Posterior shoulder, landmarks. A. Spine of the scapula. B. Supraspinatus muscle. C. Infraspinatus muscle. D. Triceps muscle. E. Vertebral border of the scapula. F. Rhomboid muscle. G. Deltoid muscle.

> ◆ **anterior GH dislocation**
> ◆ **humeral head fracture**

If a marked decrease in ROM without pain:

> ◆ **adhesive capsulitis (frozen shoulder)**

If limitation of passive and active abduction:

> ◆ **supraspinatus tendonitis**

If limitation of active abduction but not of passive abduction (Codman's sign) (Fig 10-12): ◆ **supraspinatus tendon tear**

If crepitus in the joint: ◆ **nonspecific finding**

Observe active range of motion: Note contributions of scapulothoracic and glenohumeral joints.

PROCEDURE: Visually inspect the patient's shoulder from the posterior aspect as he or she actively abducts and then flexes the arm. Note the movement at the GH joint and the thoracoscapular joint. Use the contralateral side as a control (see Fig 10-7).

OUTCOME: See Table 10-2 for normal.

Overall: If passive ROM is less painful than active ROM:

> ◆ **rotator cuff tear**

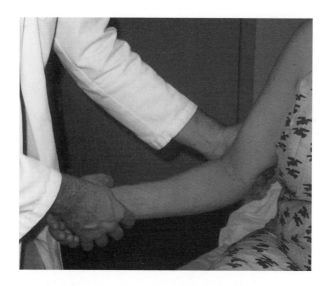

Figure 10-4 Passive crank test. Arm in neutral position, examiner passively internally rotates, externally rotates, then abducts the arm in the glenohumeral joint to 20 to 30 degrees. Excellent first-line test to assess the glenohumeral joint. Here the examiner is externally rotating the arm.

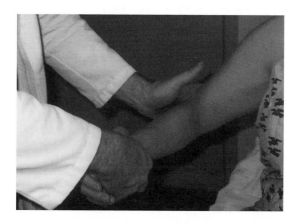

Figure 10-5 Active crank test. Arm in neutral position, patient actively internally rotates, externally rotates, then abducts the arm in the glenohumeral joint to 30 degrees. Excellent first-line test to assess the rotator cuff. Here the examiner is actively abducting the arm.

◆ **Table 10-1 Motor examination for roots C5 to T1**

Root	Muscle	Action	Main nerve to muscle	Figure
C5	Biceps brachii	Flexion at elbow	Musculocutaneous	Fig 10-6
C5	Deltoid	Abduction at GH	Axillary	Fig 10-7
C6	Extensor carpi radialis	Extension at wrist (radial side)	Radial	Fig 10-8
C6	Brachioradialis	Supination, forearm	Musculocutaneous	Fig 10-8
C7	Triceps	Extension at elbow	Radial	Fig 10-9
C8	Wrist and finger flexors	Make a fist, finger flexion	Median/ulnar	Fig 10-10
T1	Interossei	Abduction and adduction of fingers	Ulnar	Fig 10-11

GH, glenohumeral.

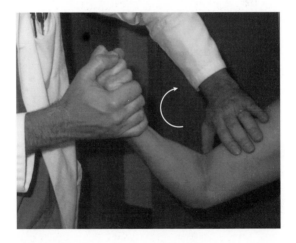

Figure 10-6 Active flexion at elbow, against resistance; excellent test to assess C5 root.

Abduction: If the first 30 degrees of abduction uses the GH joint exclusively: ◆ **normal**

If 30 to 100 degrees of abduction uses the thoracoscapular joint, 1 degree for each 2 degrees of GH joint: ◆ **normal**

If 100 to 170 degrees of abduction exclusively uses the thoracoscapular joint: ◆ **normal**

If most abduction of the shoulder is thoracoscapular, with minimal GH movement: ◆ **frozen shoulder**

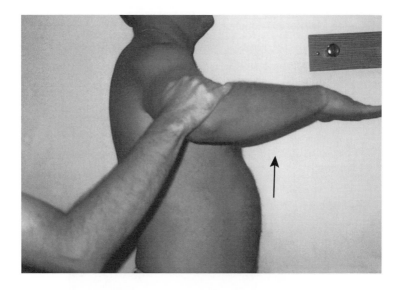

Figure 10-7 Active abduction of arm at glenohumeral joint, against resistance; excellent test to assess C5 root.

Figure 10-8 A. Active supination. B. Radial side wrist extension, against resistance; excellent test to assess C6 root.

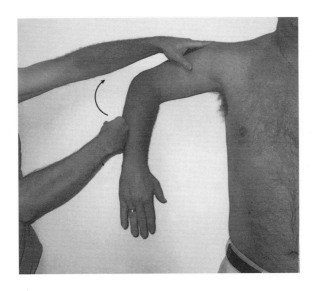

Figure 10-9 Active elbow extension, against resistance; excellent test to assess C7 root.

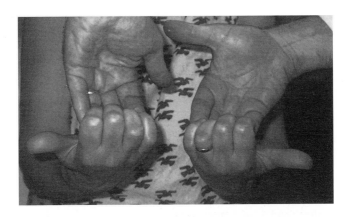

Figure 10-10 Active claw, against resistance; excellent test to assess C8 root.

Forward	If the first 140 degrees of forward flexion exclusively uses the
flexion:	GH joint: ◆ **normal**
	If 140 to 170 degrees uses the thoracoscapular joint more than
	the GH joint: ◆ **normal**

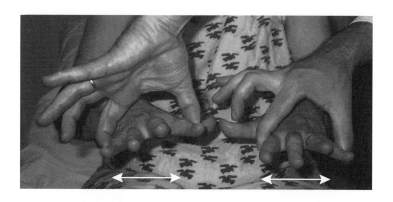

Figure 10-11 Active finger abduction, against resistance; excellent test to assess T1 root.

◆ Table 10-2 Range of motion, shoulder joint: overall and glenohumeral		
Motion	**Passive**	**Active**
External rotation	80	80
	GH: 80	GH: 80
Internal rotation	75	75
	GH: 75	GH: 75
Backward flexion	50	50
	GH: 50	GH: 50
Forward flexion:	170	170
	GH: 140	GH: 140
Abduction	170	170
	GH: 100	GH: 100
Adduction:	50	50
	GH: 20	GH: 20

GH, glenohumeral.

Perform Apley scratch test from bottom

PROCEDURE: With the patient's arms in neutral position at the sides, instruct the patient to actively "scratch the back," or "undo the bra strap," attempting to reach highest point on back bilaterally (Fig 10-13).

OUTCOME: If the thumbs can reach the T7 to T8 level bilaterally:
- ◆ **normal internal rotation of GH joint**
- ◆ **normal subscapularis function**

If one thumb is lower than the other: ◆ **subscapularis problem**

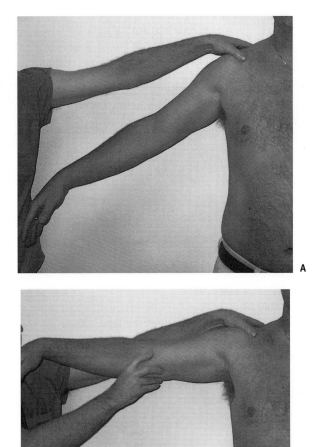

A

B

Figure 10-12 Codman's maneuver. The examiner places one hand over the top of the acromion. A. Patient instructed to abduct arm at glenohumeral joint maximally; here it is limited, indicative of a supraspinatus tear or tendonitis. B. Examiner grasps distal humerus to attempt passive abduction; if, as here, the passive is greater than the active, consistent with a tear; if passive no greater than active, tendonitis.

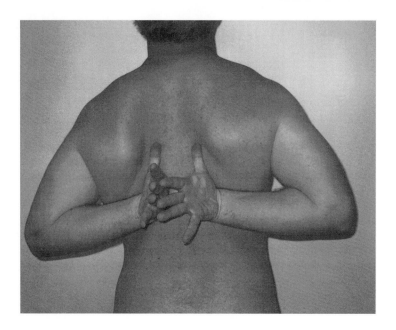

Figure 10-13 Apley from below. Functional test of the subscapularis, that is, internal rotation. Here examination findings are normal.

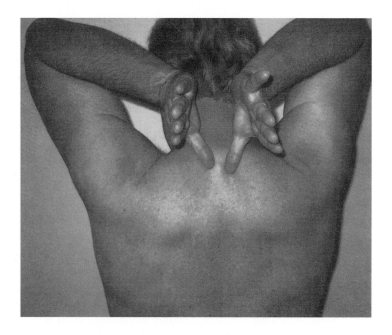

Figure 10-14 Apley from above. Functional test of the infraspinatus and teres minor, that is, external rotation. Here the findings are quite normal.

Perform Apley scratch test from top

PROCEDURE: With the patient's arms in neutral position at the sides, instruct him or her to actively "comb your hair," attempting to reach the lowest point on the back bilaterally (Fig 10-14).

OUTCOME: If the thumbs can reach the T4 to T5 level bilaterally:
- ◆ **normal external rotation of GH joint**
- ◆ **normal infraspinatus/teres minor function**

If one thumb is higher than the other:
- ◆ **infraspinatus/teres minor problem**

Advanced Examination

APPROACH TO A PATIENT WITH ANTERIOR SHOULDER PAIN

Perform the passive crank assessment: As in Basic Examination.

Perform the active crank assessment: As in Basic Examination.

Perform Apley scratch test from bottom: As in Basic Examination.

Inspect and palpate shoulder structures: As in Basic Examination.

Palpate sternoclavicular joint
PROCEDURE: Visually inspect and palpate the clavicle at the sternoclavicular joint (see Fig 10-1F). Use the contralateral joint as a control.

OUTCOME: If there is no tenderness over the sternoclavicular joint: ◆ **normal**
If there is tenderness or ecchymosis, or both:
◆ **sternoclavicular dislocation**

Palpate and visually inspect clavicle
PROCEDURE: Visually inspect and palpate the ipsilateral clavicle (see Fig 10-1G). Use the contralateral clavicle as a control.

OUTCOME: If there is bony step-off: ◆ **clavicular fracture**
If no step-off or tenderness: ◆ **normal**

Palpate acromioclavicular joint
PROCEDURE: Visually inspect and directly palpate the lateral clavicle at the site where it attaches to the acromion (see Fig 10-1E). Use the contralateral side as a control.

OUTCOME: If there is springing movement of the clavicle with marked tenderness over the site:
◆ **first-degree acromioclavicular (AC) separation**
If space between the lateral clavicle and acromion (Fig 10-15):
◆ **second- or third-degree AC separation**
If no springing and no palpable separation: ◆ **normal**

Check for Yergason's sign
PROCEDURE: Have patient place the arms in neutral position. Palpate gently over the anterior humeral head as the patient actively flexes the arm at the elbow and supinates at the forearm ("make a muscle with the biceps") against resistance. Passively externally rotate the humerus to accentuate the bicipital groove.

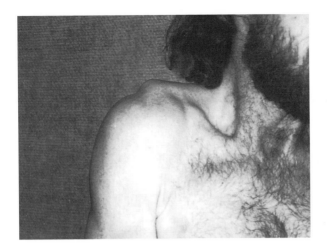

Figure 10-15 Acromioclavicular separation. Severe separation of the clavicle from the acromion as the result of an injury 5 years before presentation.

OUTCOME: If there is tenderness (Yergason's sign): ◆ **bicipital tendonitis**
If no tenderness: ◆ **normal**

Palpate and inspect biceps muscle

PROCEDURE: Visually inspect and palpate the belly of the biceps muscle both at rest and during active, resisted flexion and supination of the forearm at the elbow. Use the contralateral arm as a control.

OUTCOME: If there is a firm belly of muscle throughout: ◆ **normal**
If single hump of soft, noncontractile fleshy tissue:
◆ **biceps tendon rupture**
If there are two humps of soft, noncontractile fleshy tissue:
◆ **biceps muscle rupture**
If there is marked ecchymoses in the area about the fleshy mass:
◆ **biceps tendon rupture (acute)**

APPROACH TO A PATIENT WITH LATERAL SHOULDER PAIN

Observe range of motion in scapulothoracic and glenohumeral joints: As in Basic Examination.

Perform Apley scratch test from top: As in Basic Examination.

Perform the crossover test

PROCEDURE: Instruct the patient to adduct the arm actively across the trunk (i.e., actively touch the contralateral shoulder) and maintain this position. Palpate over the ipsilateral AC joint, the acromion, the subacromial space, and the humeral head. Repeat on the contralateral side for a control.

OUTCOME: If there is tenderness in the AC joint: ◆ **AC separation**
If tenderness in the lateral subacromial space:
> ◆ **rotator cuff tear, specifically the supraspinatus**
> ◆ **supraspinatus tendonitis**

Abduct GH area while palpating subacromial area

PROCEDURE: Passively abduct the arm at the GH joint while palpating directly deep to the lateral acromion. Use the contralateral side as a control.

OUTCOME: If there is tenderness specific to the greater tuberosity (see Fig 10-2D):
> ◆ **supraspinatus problem**
> ◆ **infraspinatus problem**

If no tenderness:
> ◆ **normal**
> ◆ **problem extrinsic to the GH joint**

Examine for Neer and Welsh impingement signs

PROCEDURE: Passively hold the patient's hand upward so that the entire upper extremity is vertical, with fingers pointing to the ceiling and palm directed medially. Push on the groove anterior to the deltoid muscle (the greater tuberosity of the humerus) with an anterior-inferior force. Use the contralateral arm as a control.

OUTCOME: If there is tenderness over the greater tuberosity:
> ◆ **impingement syndrome**
> ◆ **supraspinatus tear**
> ◆ **subacromial/subdeltoid bursitis**
> ◆ **supraspinatus tendonitis**

If no tenderness: ◆ **different etiology**

Steadily, actively adduct the abducted arm (drop test)

PROCEDURE: Passively abduct the patient's arm to the horizontal (90 degrees). Ask the patient to actively, but slowly and steadily, adduct the arm at the GH joint. Use the contralateral arm as a control.

OUTCOME: If the patient can slowly, steadily, actively adduct arm from horizontal:
> ◆ **normal**
> ◆ **partial supraspinatus tear**

If patient has sudden fall adduction (a drop):
> ◆ **supraspinatus tear**

Actively, then passively abduct the arm (Codman's sign)

PROCEDURE: As shown in Figure 10-12A, with 1) the patient sitting or standing and the arm externally rotated at the GH joint, 2) a hand placed on the ipsilateral superior aspect of the shoulder to prevent pectoralis girdle movement. Instruct the patient to 3) actively and maximally abduct the arm at the GH joint. As shown in Figure 10-12B, when the maximum active abduction is reached, 4) passively abduct the upper extremity farther. Note the degree of abduction in both active and passive modes. Use the contralateral upper extremity as a control.

OUTCOME: If passive and active abduction at the GH joint are limited to <90 degrees: ◆ **supraspinatus tendonitis/impingement syndrome**
If there is limitation of active, but not passive, abduction at the GH joint (Codman's sign): ◆ **supraspinatus tear**
If no limitation of passive and active abduction to 120 to 130 degrees: ◆ **normal**

Actively abduct arm from 0 to 30 degrees (Jobe's sign)
PROCEDURE: With the patient standing or sitting in a neutral position, perform passive abduction of the arm at the GH joint to 90 degrees, then passively place the arm back in neutral position. Instruct the patient to perform active abduction of the affected arm at the GH joint from 0 to 30 degrees. Use the contralateral arm as a control.

OUTCOME: If the patient is unable to abduct the arm at the GH joint for the first 30 degrees but once passively placed at 30 degrees can actively abduct the arm farther: ◆ **supraspinatus tear**
If patient is able to actively abduct the first 30 degrees but no farther: ◆ **deltoid muscle paresis**
If patient is able to actively abduct at the GH joint to 90 degrees: ◆ **normal**

APPROACH TO A PATIENT WITH NECK AND SHOULDER PAIN

Before any examination, if there is any history of neck trauma or any suspicion of a cervical spine (C-spine) injury, one *must* immobilize the neck with a Philadelphia collar and immobilize the back as appropriate and radiographically assess the spine, especially the C-spine, to rule out any fracture(s) before performing the following examination.

Inspect and palpate shoulder structures: As in Basic Examination.

Palpate posterior neck and shoulder
PROCEDURE: Palpate the muscle of the neck, trapezius, deltoid, and rhomboid areas. Use the contralateral side as a control (see Fig 10-3).

OUTCOME: If there is tenderness and/or spasm of the cervical paraspinous muscles: ◆ **paraspinous muscle strain**
If tenderness over the trapezius muscle:
◆ **trapezius muscle strain**
If tenderness over the rhomboid muscle (see Fig 10-3F):
◆ **rhomboid muscle strain**

Palpate spinous processes

PROCEDURE: Immobilize the patient's neck. Palpate directly over the individual spinous processes of the C-spine.

OUTCOME: If there is tenderness over one or more spinous processes:
◆ **increased suspicion of bony involvement**
If no tenderness: ◆ **normal**

Apply direct pressure to anterior scalene triangle

PROCEDURE: Place direct pressure with your hand over the patient's anterior scalene triangle (immediately posterior to the clavicular head of the sternocleidomastoid muscle). Concurrently, instruct the patient to bend the head actively and laterally to the contralateral side. Repeat on the contralateral side as a control.

OUTCOME: If pain and paresthesia develop in the symptomatic upper extremity: ◆ **brachial plexus problem**
If there is no discomfort: ◆ **normal**

Perform neck compression (Spurling's) test

PROCEDURE: Place one hand on the top of the patient's head. Examiner passively extends the neck, rotates the head toward the symptomatic side, and exerts downward pressure on the head. Repeat to the contralateral side for control.

OUTCOME: If there is no discomfort: ◆ **normal**
If pain radiates into the affected upper extremity:
◆ **cervical radiculopathy**

Inspect scapular placement while patient pushes against wall with palms

PROCEDURE: Have the patient standing facing a wall. Tell the patient to place both palms on the wall and push against the wall with the upper extremities (as if performing a "pushup" in a vertical position). Visually inspect the scapulae during this maneuver.

OUTCOME: If the scapulae remain in place, with the vertebral edge remaining at the spinous processes: ◆ **normal**
If one scapula posteriorly is displaced: ◆ **winged scapula**

Keys to Recording Findings

SHOULDER

"Unremarkable, normal ROM, no pain swelling or tenderness; C5-T1 nerve roots intact bilaterally"

A. Active and passive ROM, document degrees if abnormal; overall and at GH joint.

B. Note sites of increased pain with ROM.

C. Note sites of swelling, pain and tenderness.

D. Note sites of muscle atrophy and/or fasiculations.

E. Motor function:

C5: Shoulder abduction

C6: Forearm supination

C7: Elbow extension

C8: Flexion of fingers

T1: Abduction of fingers

		Degrees	
		Left	Right
A. ROM	Abduction	——	——
	Adduction	——	——
	Forward flexion	——	——
	Backward flexion	——	——
	Internal rotation	——	——
	External rotation	——	——

ROM, limited to the glenohumeral joint	Degrees	
	Left	Right
External rotation	——	——
Internal rotation	——	——
Abduction	——	——

B./C./D. Draw on sites of pain, tenderness, atrophy, swelling.

Anterior shoulder

Posterior shoulder

T1

		Normal		If abnormal
		Left	Right	
E.	C5: Biceps flexion	❏	❏	_____
	C6: Forearm	❏	❏	_____
	C7: Elbow extension	❏	❏	_____
	C8: Finger flexion	❏	❏	_____
	T1: Abduction fingers	❏	❏	_____

Diagnoses

Acromioclavicular separation

Separation following trauma after force has been placed on the shoulder with an inferoposterior thrust (as when running into a door). Symptoms and signs include pain and tenderness over the acromioclavicular joint (see Fig 10-1E) and painful abduction at the GH joint with limitation in the most extreme 20 degrees; palpable springing movement of the clavicle or a space between the lateral distal clavicle and the acromion, or both (see Fig 10-15) bespeaks a more severe separation. Evaluation includes radiographs of the shoulder, and treatment includes immobilization and referral to a physical therapist; severe cases can be referred to an orthopedic surgeon. Complications include axillary nerve damage and, thus, deltoid muscle atrophy.

Adhesive capsulitis (frozen shoulder)

Nonspecific end result of severe, recurrent trauma or inflammation, or both, of the GH joint. Symptoms include chronic, diffuse mild pain in the GH joint; signs include a severe decrease in all ROM, both passive and active; all abduction of the shoulder is confined to the thoracoscapular joint. Evaluation includes radiographs of the shoulder that reveal osteolysis of the affected bones. Treatment is by prevention, demonstrating the technique and need to perform Codman's exercises and, if the problem develops, referral to a physical therapist for ROM and to an orthopedic surgeon.

Biceps tendon rupture

Rupture from trauma or iatrogenic causes (e.g., after steroid injection). Symptoms and signs include acute painful snap in the biceps, weakness in forearm supination, and flexion. Active flexion reveals a single "hump" of flaccid muscle in the area of the biceps muscle. Evaluation with shoulder radiographs will be unremarkable. Treatment includes rest, a sling, and referral to an orthopedic surgeon.

Bicipital tendonitis

Inflammation of the long head of the biceps in the bicipital groove due to a rotator cuff tear or tendonitis or repeated over-the-head throwing activities. Symptoms and signs include pain in the anterior shoulder, tenderness over the bicipital groove (see Fig 10-1C), and positive Yergason's signs. Concurrent subacromial bursitis or impingement syndrome may be present. Radiographs are of little diagnostic benefit. Treatment includes rest, a sling, and referral to a physical therapist for Codman's exercises.

Brachial plexus problem: See Cervical spine disease.

Cervical spine disease
Due to cervical spinal stenosis, spondylolisthesis, or posterior herniation of the cervical disks; may also be a problem involving the brachial plexus. Symptoms and signs include chronic pain and occipital headaches, pain that may radiate into the shoulder or hand, decreased ROM of the neck, and positive compression and Spurling's tests; C5 to T1 nerve roots must be assessed (see Table 10-1 and Figs 10-6 to 10-11). Evaluation includes obtaining C-spine radiographs first in routine fashion, then repeated in neck flexion and neck extension; if any abnormalities or any weakness on examination with magnetic resonance imaging (MRI), the C-spine area is suspected to be the site of mischief. Treatment is rest, acetaminophen, a soft cervical collar, and referral to a physical therapist and a neurosurgeon.

Clavicular fracture
Fracture following a direct trauma to the anterior shoulder (e.g., a fall in ice hockey or football). Symptoms and signs include an inability to abduct or elevate the entire upper extremity proximal to the elbow, a visible or palpable bony step-off of the clavicle, and adjacent ecchymosis and tenderness. Radiographs of the shoulder confirm the diagnosis. Treatment includes a sling for 6 to 8 weeks and referral to an orthopedic surgeon.

Deltoid muscle paresis: See Acromioclavicular separation.

Glenohumeral dislocation
Dislocation from excessive forward flexion of the arm (often from overhand throwing or sliding into second base with arm outstretched). Symptoms include acute pain and a severely restricted/decreased ROM. Signs include dead-arm sign, a marked decrease in ROM of the humerus, an inappropriately prominent acromion, and an anteriorly and medially displaced head of the humerus to a position inferior or even medial to the coracoid process (see Fig 10-1A). The roots of C5 to T1 (see Table 10-1 and Figs 10-6 to 10-11) and the radial, median, and ulnar nerve functions must be tested and Allen's test performed. Radiographs of the shoulder can be obtained to rule out concurrent humeral fracture. Treatment is effective analgesia; emergency reduction can be performed by an orthopedic surgeon.

Impingement syndrome (painful arc syndrome)
Swelling in the subacromial space from GH laxity, subacromial bursitis, or osteophytes on the lateral acromion, accompanied by lateral impingement at the supraspinatus insertion site or anterior impingement (i.e., swelling about the long head of the biceps tendon), or both. Symptoms and signs are of significant pain throughout the abduction arc, positive anterior impingement sign, positive Neer-Welsh sign, and a decrease in active

and passive abduction. Radiographs may reveal an osteophyte on the inferior aspect of the acromion. Treatment is of the underlying process: a rotator cuff tear, bicipital tendonitis (see Fig 10-1C), subacromial bursitis (see Fig 10-2C), or supraspinatus tendonitis (see Fig 10-2D). Paradoxically, the patient may also have laxity. The patient should be referred to an orthopedic surgeon.

Infraspinatus/teres minor tear

Tears from rotatory trauma; infraspinatus inserts on the greater tuberosity of the humerus, often associated with a supraspinatus tear. Symptoms and signs include lateral pain, tenderness deep to the deltoid, a positive active crank test (see Fig 10-5) to external rotation, a positive Apley scratch test with external rotation (see Fig 10-14); concurrent assessment of the supraspinatus muscle is indicated. Radiographs are of little diagnostic value, but MRI demonstrates the tear. Treatment includes rest and referral to a physical therapist for Codman's exercises and to an orthopedic surgeon.

Paraspinous muscle strain: See Trapezius muscle strain.

Rhomboid strain

Strain from falling on an outstretched arm or lifting an object with an outstretched arm. Symptoms and signs include minimal pain and stiffness immediately after incident that slowly and progressively worsen and discrete tenderness and spasm over the rhomboid (see Fig 10-3F). No sensory or motor defects and no tenderness over the spinous processes are present. Radiographs are unremarkable. Treatment includes rest, NSAIDs, and referral to a physical therapist.

Rotator cuff tear: See Infraspinatus/teres minor tear, Subscapularis tear, and Supraspinatus tear.

Sternoclavicular separation

Separation following blunt trauma to the medial clavicle. Symptoms and signs of severe pain, tenderness, and swelling and ecchymosis around the sternoclavicular joint (see Fig 10-1F); in severe cases, a gap forms between the sternum and clavicle; a clicking sensation may be present with upper extremity movement. Radiographs should be taken of the shoulder and of the chest for concurrent fractures or sequelae (e.g., pneumothorax). Treatment includes immobilization and immediate referral to an orthopedic surgeon.

Subacromial/subdeltoid bursitis: See Impingement syndrome (painful arc syndrome).

Subscapularis tear

Tear from rotatory trauma; the subscapularis inserts on the lesser tuberosity of the humerus. Symptoms and signs include anterior pain, a positive active crank test (see Fig 10-5) to internal rotation, and a positive Apley scratch with internal rotation (see Fig 10-13). Radiographs are of little diagnostic benefit, but MRI demonstrates the tear. Treatment includes rest and referral to a physical therapist for Codman's exercises and to an orthopedic surgeon.

Supraspinatus tear

Tear from rotatory trauma; the supraspinatus inserts on the greater tuberosity of the humerus. Symptoms and signs include lateral/posterior pain, tenderness deep to the deltoid, and weakness of abduction of the humerus; the passive crank test (see Fig 10-4) to abduction results in lateral pain; active crank test (see Fig 10-5) to abduction results in weakness and pain. Passive range of motion of the arm at the GH joint is normal, but active abduction is limited; the patient will have positive Jobe's and adductor glide signs. Radiographs are of little diagnostic value, but MRI demonstrates the tear. Treatment includes rest and referral to a physical therapist for Codman's exercises and to an orthopedic surgeon.

Supraspinatus tendonitis

Tendonitis from trauma or overuse. Significant overlap of this process is found with subdeltoid bursitis and impingement syndrome. Symptoms and signs include pain in the lateral shoulder exacerbated by abduction; the passive crank test (see Fig 10-4) to abduction results in lateral pain; the active crank test (see Fig 10-5) to abduction results in pain but no weakness; lateral/posterior shoulder tenderness, specifically at the humeral greater tuberosity; marked restriction to passive and active abduction of the humerus at the GH joint; and a positive Codman's sign (see Fig 10-12). Radiographs of the shoulder may demonstrate calcified tendons. Treatment includes rest and referral to a physical therapist for Codman's exercises and to an orthopedic surgeon.

Trapezius strain

Strain from rapid movement forward then backward of the head (e.g., a motor vehicle accident "whiplash" injury). Symptoms and signs include minimal pain and stiffness immediately after an accident that slowly and progressively worsen and discrete tenderness and spasm over the trapezius and even the sternocleidomastoids. Concurrent **paraspinous strain** (indicated by tenderness and even spasm in these muscles located lateral to the vertebral spinous processes) is common. No sensory or motor defects and no tenderness over the spinous processes are present. Radiographs may reveal a straightened C-spine and rarely a spinous process avulsion fracture. Treatment includes rest, a soft cervical collar, and referral to a physical therapist.

Winged scapula

Caused by damage to the long thoracic nerve or by cervical radiculopathy involving C5/6 (e.g., plexopathy, radiculopathy) with resulting paresis of the serratus anterior muscle. Evaluate with C-spine radiographs and MRI of C5/6; refer the patient to a neurologist.

CHAPTER 11
Hip/Back

Perform active range of motion of the hip

PROCEDURE: Have the patient lie supine. Passively, then actively, perform range of motion (ROM) at the hip joint. Repeat the examination with the knee passively flexed to 90 degrees. Use the contralateral side as a control.

OUTCOME: If ROM, with knee straight, is:
Flexion: 90°
Extension: 15°
Abduction: 45 to 60°
Adduction: 30° ◆ **normal**

If ROM, with knee flexed, is:
Flexion: 120°
Extension: 0°
Abduction: 40°
Adduction: 40° ◆ **normal**

If the ROM is decreased: ◆ **hip degenerative joint disease**

Perform active range of motion of the spine

PROCEDURE: Have the patient stand in an upright anatomic position facing away from you. Visually inspect the spinal column as the patient flexes, extends, internally rotates, externally rotates, and laterally bends to the left and right. Measure the ROM.

OUTCOME: If the ROM is:
Flexion: 70 to 100°
Extension: 15 to 20°
Lateral bending: 20°
Rotation of 60°: ◆ **normal**
If decreased: ◆ **nonspecific finding for low back dysfunction**

Observe gait

PROCEDURE: Observe the patient's gait.

OUTCOME: If steppage gait: ◆ **radiculopathy (often L5)**
If poker gait:
◆ **ankylosing spondylitis**
◆ **musculoskeletal low back strain**
If proprioceptive, ataxic gait:
◆ **radiculopathy (often S1 or multiple defects)**
If the thigh and leg are adducted and externally rotated to minimize any discomfort (antalgic gait):
◆ **hip degenerative joint disease**

Inspect erect back

PROCEDURE: Have the patient stand in an upright anatomic position. Visually inspect the spinal column. Repeat after patient turns to the right or the left 90 degrees to reveal the profile.

OUTCOME:

Erect: If there is a left tilt of thoracic spine: ◆ **levoscoliosis**
If right tilt of thoracic spine (see Fig 5-6): ◆ **dextroscoliosis**

Profile: If the cervical spine is lordotic, thoracic is kyphotic, lumbar is lordotic, and sacral is kyphotic: ◆ **normal**
If there is a marked increase in the thoracic kyphosis:
◆ **dowager's hump of osteoporosis**

Inspect reversal lumbar lordosis

PROCEDURE: Have the patient stand erect in upright anatomic position. Visually inspect the degree of lumbar lordosis in the lumbar spinal column itself. Repeat with patient in full back forward flexion.

OUTCOME: If there is lumbar lordosis when erect: ◆ **normal**
If the lumbar lordosis becomes kyphotic with back flexed:
◆ **normal**
If lumbar spine is flat or kyphotic when erect:
◆ **ankylosing spondylitis**
◆ **compression fractures**
If lumbar spine is lordotic when erect and remains so with full back forward flexion: ◆ **musculoskeletal low back strain**

Palpate structures of hip and back

PROCEDURE: Have the patient stand erect in upright anatomic position. Palpate the spinous processes, the paraspinous muscles, the skin, the sacroiliac (SI) joints, the ischiogluteal area, the greater trochanteric area, and the costovertebral angles.

OUTCOME: If there is tenderness over the spinous process(es):
◆ **compression fracture**
◆ **metastatic disease (infectious or neoplastic)**
If tenderness over the paraspinous musculature:
◆ **musculoskeletal low back strain**
◆ **radicular low back pain**
If tenderness over the skin, unilaterally:
◆ **herpes zoster (see Chapter 14, p. 326)**
If tenderness over the SI joints: ◆ **ankylosing spondylitis**
If tenderness in the ischiogluteal area, specifically at the ischial tuberosity: ◆ **ischiogluteal bursitis**
If tenderness posterior to the greater trochanter, deep to the gluteal muscles: ◆ **greater trochanter bursitis**
If tenderness over the costovertebral angle:
◆ **pyelonephritis**
◆ **nephrolithiasis**

Percuss spinous processes

PROCEDURE: Gently percuss over the spinous processes.

OUTCOME: If there is no tenderness: ◆ **normal**

If tenderness: ◆ **compression fracture of a vertebral body**

Perform FABERE (Patrick's) test

PROCEDURE: For the FABERE (flexion, abduction, external rotation) test, have the patient lie supine. Passively flex, abduct, and externally rotate the lower extremity at the hip so that the lateral malleolus (Fig 11-1) touches the contralateral patella. Then place downward force on the ipsilateral knee. Repeat on the contralateral side for control.

OUTCOME: If there is pain in the lateral lumbar area with radiation into the leg: ◆ **radicular low back pain**

If pain in the midline back over a specific site:

◆ **compression fracture**

If pain in the SI joint: ◆ **ankylosing spondylitis, ipsilateral**

If pain in the affected hip: ◆ **hip degenerative joint disease**

If no exacerbation of pain:

◆ **normal**

◆ **another etiology**

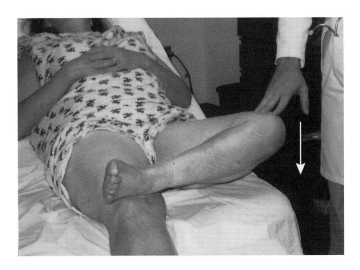

Figure 11-1 FABERE test. Patient supine, passive flexion, abduction, external rotation of the lower extremity; here the left leg is being assessed. Excellent test to assess the function of the hip and to determine the most significant locus of discomfort, thus providing an aid to diagnosis.

Actively extend knee

PROCEDURE: Have the patient lie supine, with legs hanging over the examination table. Instruct the patient to extend the leg actively at the knee. Use the contralateral side as a control.

OUTCOME: If strength is 5/5: ◆ **normal**
If strength is 0/5 to 4/5:
- ◆ **radiculopathy (L4)**
- ◆ **quadriceps tendon/muscle damage**

Actively dorsiflex foot

PROCEDURE: Instruct the patient to dorsiflex the foot actively at the ankle. Use the contralateral side as a control.

OUTCOME: If strength is 5/5: ◆ **normal**
If strength is 0/5 to 4/5:
- ◆ **radiculopathy (L5)**
- ◆ **Anterior compartment problem foot-drop syndrome (see Chapter 13, p. 285)**

Actively plantarflex foot

PROCEDURE: Instruct the patient to plantarflex the foot actively at the ankle. Use the contralateral side as a control.

OUTCOME: If strength is 5/5: ◆ **normal**
If strength is 0/5 to 4/5:
- ◆ **radiculopathy (S1)**
- ◆ **posterior compartment problem**

Test Achilles reflex: See Fig 7-3, p. 141.

Perform sensory examination

PROCEDURE: Have the patient close his or her eyes. Use a cotton-tipped swab or apply a monofilament to check for fine touch. Be certain to check in the middle of the dermatome to optimize the sensitivity.

OUTCOME: If decreased sensation over the medial malleolus and plantar foot: ◆ **radiculopathy (S1)**
If decreased sensation over the medial foot, great toe, and dorsal foot (see Fig 13-1, p. 271): ◆ **radiculopathy (L5)**
If decreased sensation over the lateral malleolus:
- ◆ **radiculopathy (L4)**
If defect is in a saddle distribution (i.e., perineum, superior medial thighs): ◆ **cauda equina/cord compression**

| Advanced Examination |

APPROACH TO A PATIENT WITH HIP TRAUMA

Inspect position of leg

PROCEDURE: Have the patient lie supine. Visually inspect the position of the symptomatic lower extremity. Use the asymptomatic lower extremity as a control.

OUTCOME: If the extremity is shortened and externally rotated to 90 degrees (Fig 11-2): ◆ **femoral neck fracture**
If isolated external rotation: ◆ **femoral shaft fracture**

Check for Auenbrugger's sign

PROCEDURE: Have the patient lie supine. Place the bell of the stethoscope over the symphysis pubis. Concurrently, place a vibrating 128-Hz tuning fork over each medial epicondyle of the femur. Use the contralateral side as a control.

OUTCOME: If conduction is equal: ◆ **normal**
If there is decreased conduction on the symptomatic side:
◆ **femoral fracture or dislocation**

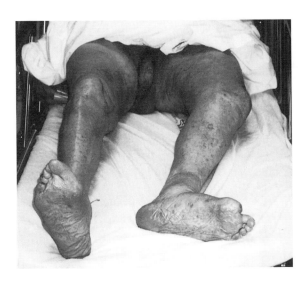

Figure 11-2 Intertrochanteric fracture. Eighty-year-old man with diabetic neuropathy (note great toe amputation) who fell; lower extremity on left short and externally rotated virtually diagnostic of an intertrochanteric femur fracture.

APPROACH TO A PATIENT WITH HIP PAIN OR DECREASED RANGE OF MOTION, OR BOTH

Palpate structures of hip and back: As in Basic Examination.

Perform FABERE (Patrick's) test: As in Basic Examination.

Observe gait: As in Basic Examination.

Perform Laguerre's test

PROCEDURE: Have the patient lie supine. Grasp the heel of the symptomatic leg, and passively flex the leg at the hip and knee. Then passively externally and internally rotate the patient's hip. Ask the patient whether discomfort develops with rotation.

OUTCOME: If there is pain in the hip and groin:
◆ **hip degenerative joint disease**
If pain over the greater trochanter, immediately deep to the gluteus maximus: ◆ **greater trochanteric bursitis**
If no tenderness: ◆ **normal**

Inspect for Trendelenburg's sign

PROCEDURE: Have the patient stand in anatomic position, and place all of weight on the lower extremity opposite of the painful hip. Visually inspect the movement of the buttock musculature before and during the placement of weight upon the symptomatic lower extremity.

OUTCOME: If the buttock on the symptomatic side remains firm and elevated: ◆ **normal**
If buttock on the symptomatic side falls and becomes flaccid (Trendelenburg's sign): ◆ **hip degenerative joint disease (severe)**

Test for Tinel's sign over lateral inguinal ligament

PROCEDURE: Repeatedly tap over the inguinal ligament at the anterior superior iliac spine with a finger or a plexor. Ask the patient whether pain develops.

OUTCOME: If there are tingling and pain in the anterolateral thigh (Fig 11-3B):
◆ **meralgia paresthetica—lateral cutaneous nerve of the thigh (L2, L3)**
If there is no tingling: ◆ **normal**

APPROACH TO A PATIENT WITH LOWER BACK PAIN

Perform FABERE (Patrick's) test: As in Basic Examination.

Perform sensory examination: As in Basic Examination.

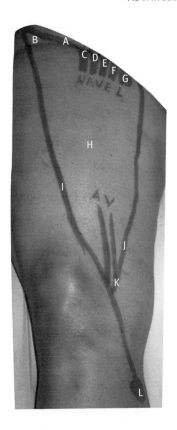

Figure 11-3 Anterior thigh landmarks. A. Inguinal ligament from the anterior superior iliac spine (ASIS) to the symphysis pubis. B. Lateral cutaneous nerve of thigh (L2, L3), the site to perform Tinel's procedure. C. Femoral nerve under the inguinal ligament halfway between the ASIS and the symphysis pubis. D. Femoral artery immediately medial to nerve. E. Femoral vein immediately medial to artery. F. Empty space of femoral canal immediately medial to vein site of potential femoral hernias. G. Lymphatic tissue and nodes. Useful acronym: NAVEL. H. Femoral triangle boundaries: inguinal ligament, sartorius muscle, adductor longus muscle. I. Sartorius muscle. J. Adductor longus muscle. K. Canal of Hunter. L. Pes anserine.

Actively extend knee: As in Basic Examination.

Actively dorsiflex foot: As in Basic Examination.

Actively plantarflex foot: As in Basic Examination.

Test Achilles reflex: As in Basic Examination.

Perform straight-leg raise (Lasègue-Lazarevic's test)

PROCEDURE: With the patient supine, place one hand beneath the lumbar spine, then passively flex the leg on the symptomatic side at the hip to 90 degrees (Fig 11-4). Ask the patient whether and when any discomfort develops. If pain develops, measure and record the angle of the leg at which pain developed. Repeat on the contralateral side as a control.

OUTCOME: If pain occurs that radiates into the posterolateral thigh and leg at <40 degrees: ◆ **radicular lower back pain, usually sciatica**
If pain occurs with/without radiation at >40 degrees:
◆ **radicular lower back pain**
◆ **musculoskeletal lower back strain**
If no pain develops: ◆ **normal**

Perform straight-leg raise with passive dorsiflexion

PROCEDURE: With the patient supine, place one hand beneath the lumbar spine, then passively flex the leg at the hip on the symptomatic

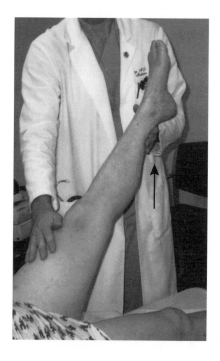

Figure 11-4 Straight-leg raise (SLR) procedure. Examiner passively forward flexes leg at hip to stress the lumbosacral roots, especially L5/S1. Sciatica would manifest with pain radiating into posterior lateral thigh and leg with SLR.

side to an angle slightly acute to the level of pain during the straight-leg raise test. Passively dorsiflex the foot at the ankle.

OUTCOME: If pain occurs that radiates into the posterolateral thigh and leg at <40 degrees: ◆ **radicular lower back pain, usually sciatica**
If pain occurs with/without radiation at >40 degrees:
- ◆ **radicular lower back pain**
- ◆ **musculoskeletal lower back pain**

If no pain develops: ◆ **normal**

Perform crossed straight-leg raise

PROCEDURE: With the patient supine, place one hand beneath the lumbar spine, then passively flex the asymptomatic leg at the hip to 90 degrees. Ask the patient when any discomfort is present; measure that angle.

OUTCOME: If there is pain in the posterolateral side of the symptomatic leg at any angle: ◆ **radicular lower back pain, usually sciatica**
If no pain: ◆ **normal**

Examine anal sphincter tone

PROCEDURE: Perform an anorectal examination (see Chapter 6, p. 127). Ask the patient to squeeze around your gloved finger.

OUTCOME: If the sphincter is lax:
- ◆ **cauda equina syndrome/cord compression**

If sphincter tone is normal: ◆ **normal**

Test anal wink: See Chapter 7, under Approach to a patient with weakness.

APPROACH TO A PATIENT WITH SUSPECTED ANKYLOSING SPONDYLITIS

Palpate structures of hip and back: As in Basic Examination.

Perform FABERE (Patrick's) test: As in Basic Examination (see Fig 11-1).

Observe gait: As in Basic Examination.

Perform sacroiliac compression test

PROCEDURE: Have the patient lie down with the symptomatic side superior. Use a hand to apply direct pressure over the lateral iliac crest.

OUTCOME: If there is pain over the sacroiliac joint: ◆ **sacroiliac etiology**
If pain over the hip: ◆ **hip etiology**

Palpate sacroiliac joints

PROCEDURE: Have the patient lie prone, sit upright, or stand. Directly palpate over each sacroiliac joint.

OUTCOME: If there is tenderness: ◆ **sacroiliac etiology**
If no tenderness: ◆ **normal**

Perform knee-to-chest position test

PROCEDURE: Have the patient lie supine with the legs freely flexed over the end of the table. Passively flex the leg opposite the affected side at the knee and the thigh into a knee-to-chest position.

OUTCOME: If there is pain in the sacroiliac joint: ◆ **ankylosing spondylitis**
If anterior thigh pain: ◆ **radiculopathy (L4)**
If hip pain: ◆ **hip etiology**
If no pain: ◆ **normal**

Measure chest circumference during expiration/inspiration

PROCEDURE: Place a flexible measuring tape around the circumference of the patient's chest. Tell the patient to inhale fully, measure the circumference. Tell the patient to exhale fully, remeasure the circumference. Note the difference between measurements.

OUTCOME: If <2.5 cm difference:
◆ **chest wall restriction of ankylosing spondylitis**
If >2.5 cm difference: ◆ **normal**

Perform Schober's maneuver

PROCEDURE: Patient standing erect, place marks in the patient's midline, at the lumbosacral junction (i.e., at the level of the posterior iliac spines), and 10 cm above. Tell the patient to forward flex maximally at the waist. Remeasure the distance between the marks.

OUTCOME: If increase <5 cm: ◆ **ankylosing spondylitis**
If increase >5 cm: ◆ **normal**

Keys to Recording Findings

HIP/LOW BACK

"Unremarkable, normal ROM to low back and hip, normal thoracic kyphosis and lumbar lordosis, no pain, swelling or tenderness; L2–S1 nerve roots intact bilaterally"

A. Active and passive ROM at joints—low back: forward flexion, backward flexion, lateral bends; hip forward flexion, backward flexion, abduction, adduction, internal and external rotation; document degrees of the motion if abnormal

B. L1–S1 root motor exam

L1/2:	Hip forward flexion
L3/4:	Knee extension
L5:	Great toe extension
	Foot dorsiflexion
S1:	Great toe flexion
	Foot plantarflexion

C. and D. Note sites of swelling, pain, tenderness in back and hip

E. Note sites of increased pain with FABERE

F. Note sites of increased pain with straight leg raise (SLR).

A. ROM hip

| | Degrees | |
	Left	Right
Forward flexion	———	———
Backward flexion	———	———
Internal rotation	———	———
External rotation	———	———
Abduction	———	———
Adduction	———	———

ROM lumbar spine

| | Degrees | |
	Left	Right
Forward flexion	———	———
Backward flexion	———	———
Lateral bend	———	———

B.

| | Normal | | |
	Left	Right	If abnormal
L1/2: Hip forward flexion	❑	❑	———
L3/4: Knee extension	❑	❑	———
L5: Dorsiflexion great toe	❑	❑	———
S1: Plantarflexion great toe	❑	❑	———

C. Posterior Back

Left   Right

D. Anterior Back

E. FABERE Site of tenderness ———

F. SLR (Straight leg raise) to Left ___° Right ___°

Diagnoses

Ankylosing spondylitis

Rheumatoid factor–seronegative polyarticular arthritis. Symptoms include acute to subacute arthritis (for more than 3 months), marked morning stiffness, an onset in the third or fourth decade of life, and pain that decreases with exercise. Signs include sacroiliac joint tenderness with FABERE (see Fig 11-1), moderate tenderness over the SI joints, tenderness to iliac compression, decrease in chest wall expansion, and a positive Schober's maneuver. A concurrent finding may be a diastolic murmur of aortic insufficiency. Evaluation includes radiographs of the lumbar spine and SI joints. Rheumatoid factor and antinuclear antibody (ANA) test results are normal. Treatment includes physical therapy, nonsteroidal anti-inflammatory drugs (NSAIDs) and a referral to a rheumatology specialist.

Cauda equina/cord compression syndrome

Syndrome caused by midline disk herniation, spinal stenosis, and epidural tumor or abscess. Symptoms include significant pain that is worse at night and urinary and/or fecal incontinence. Signs include anesthesia in a saddle distribution, decreased anal sphincter tone, bilaterally decreased reflexes (see Figs 7-1 and 7-2, on pp. 139 and 140) and strength, decrease in the anal wink reflex, and a positive bilateral straight-leg raise test (see Fig 11-4). Evaluate the syndrome with lumbar films and magnetic resonance imaging (MRI). Treatment is emergent referral to a neurosurgeon.

Compression fractures

Due to **metastatic neoplastic disease** (breast, colon), infection (endocarditis), trauma, or, most commonly, osteoporosis. Symptoms and signs include acute onset of pain and tenderness over the affected vertebra. Other signs are specific to the underlying diagnosis: thoracic spine involvement, acute, nontraumatic with the development of dowager's hump in osteoporosis; lumbar spine involvement; a past history of neoplasia in a malignant neoplastic etiology; fever; new heart murmurs; and purpura in endocarditis. Evaluation includes radiographs, and, if there is any neurologic deficit, computed tomography (CT) or MRI; bone scan is "hot" in lesions due to neoplasia or infection. If the patient is unstable or has neurologic deficit, referral to a neurosurgeon is indicated; referral to an oncologist or infectious disease specialist also may be indicated.

Dextroscoliosis: See Scoliosis.

Femoral neck fracture

Most common fracture in the geriatric population, usually caused by a fall. Risk factors include osteoporosis and unsteady gait. Symptoms and signs include pain and inability to bear weight on the affected side, proximal femur tenderness, a marked decrease in ROM, and a shortened leg that is externally rotated to 90 degrees (see Fig 11-2). Auenbrugger's sign is present. Evaluation includes radiographs of the hip, which confirm the fracture. The patient should be immediately referred to an orthopedic surgeon.

Femoral shaft fracture

Due to trauma, either from a fall or motor vehicle accident. Symptoms and signs include trauma, inability to bear weight, and Auenbrugger's sign; the leg is externally rotated but not shortened. Evaluation includes radiographs to confirm and thus needs to include the shaft of the femur in the radiographs. Treatment includes splinting, traction, and referral to an orthopedic specialist.

Greater trochanteric bursitis

This is a large bursa between the greater trochanter and the gluteus maximus muscle. Symptoms include pain over the lateral hip and thigh. Signs include a normal back ROM, a FABERE (see Fig 11-1) with pain over the lateral hip, a negative straight-leg raise test, and discrete tenderness immediately posterior to the greater trochanter. Evaluation and treatment include referral to a physical therapist, NSAIDs, and potentially an injection of the bursa with glucocorticoids.

Herniated disk: See Radicular lower back pain.

Hip degenerative joint disease

Risk factors include increasing age, trauma, Legg-Calvé-Perthes disease, and/or obesity. Symptoms include a chronic dull pain that is exacerbated by bearing weight; the pain often radiates into the ipsilateral inguinal area. Signs include a leg in attitude of adduction, flexion, and external rotation to minimize the pain; decreased ROM of joint; crepitus; and a positive Trendelenburg's sign. Radiographs of the hip reveal joint space narrowing and osteophytes. Treatment includes acetaminophen or NSAIDs, physical therapy, and referral to an orthopedic surgeon.

Ischiogluteal bursitis

Bursa between gluteal muscles and the ischium. Symptoms include pain in the buttock that is exacerbated on sitting or with the Valsalva maneuver; the pain is worse at night and may have associated sciatica. Signs include normal back ROM, a negative straight-leg raise test (see Fig 11-4), a FABERE (see Fig 11-1) with pain over the ischum, and discrete tenderness over the ischial tuberosity. Evaluation and treatment include sitting on a pillow or heating pad, NSAIDs, and referral to a physical therapist.

Levoscoliosis: See Scoliosis.

Meralgia paresthetica

Entrapment of the lateral cutaneous nerve of the thigh beneath the inguinal ligament due to pregnancy, obesity, and/or the wearing of tight jeans. Symptoms include tingling and/or burning on the anterolateral surface of the thigh that increases with prolonged hip extension (standing) and decreases with hip flexion. Tinel's sign is positive at the lateral inguinal ligament (see Fig 11-3B). Evaluation and treatment include modification of clothing, weight loss, and NSAIDs.

Metastatic disease: See Compression fractures.

Musculoskeletal lower back strain

Strain of paraspinal muscles, sprain of ligaments. Acute lower back pain is of less than 6 weeks' duration; subacute lower back pain is more than 6 weeks' duration. Symptoms of acute pain include pain on twisting or lifting, which may have a radicular component. Signs include spasm in the paraspinous muscles, poker gait, a positive straight-leg raise (see Fig 11-4) and FABERE (see Fig 11-1) with pain in the paraspinous area, and no neurologic deficits. Lumbar radiographs are not routinely indicated unless the patient is older than 50 years and/or has a fever, history of malignancy, or objective motor deficit, or if no improvement occurs in weeks of first-line therapy. Treatment is with rest, NSAIDs, and physical therapy.

Radicular lower back pain

Irritation and/or entrapment of one or more nerve roots in the lumbosacral area. Causes include 1) spinal stenosis—the result of degenerative spondylolisthesis (facet disease—anterior displacement of one vertebral body on the one below, usually at L5/S1), 2) **herniated disk**—protrusion of nucleus pulposis through the posterior disk into the cord canal, 3) epidural disease—metastatic abscess or neoplasia, and 4) ischiogluteal bursitis—extraspinal irritation of the sciatic nerve as it passes an inflamed ischiogluteal bursa. Symptoms are those of lower back pain radiating into a specific dermatome or set of dermatomes; in facet disease, there is neuroclaudication—discomfort increases with standing and decreases with rest. Signs include increased pain with the Valsalva maneuver and pain reproduction with the FABERE (see Fig 11-1), straight-leg raise (see Fig 11-4), and crossed straight-leg raise tests. The patient exhibits (S1; see Fig 7-3, p. 141) weakness to the knee extension (L4) and great toe extension (L5) and to ankle plantarflexion (S1), decreased Achilles (S1) and patellar (L4) reflexes (see Fig 7-2, p. 140), concurrent decrease in anal wink, and saddle distribution of anesthesia in cauda equina. Lumbar radiographs may be indicated; if the patient exhibits a motor deficit, lumbar radiographs and an MRI are indicated. Treatment includes rest and physical therapy. Emergent referral to a neurosurgeon is necessary for cord compression/cauda equina; urgent referral can be considered with motor deficits; in both cases strongly consider a course of systemic steroids.

Radiculopathy: See Radicular lower back pain.

Scoliosis

A congenital variant in which the spinal column is arched to the left **(levoscoliosis)** or the right **(dextroscoliosis)**. Symptoms and signs include the fact that it most commonly involves the thoracic spine (see Fig 5-6, p. 104) and is accentuated by the patient forward flexing at the waist. If severe, concurrent restrictive pulmonary disease may be present. Evaluation and treatment include obtaining thoracic and lumbar radiographs, pulmonary function tests, and, if severe, referral to a neurosurgeon for surgical correction.

CHAPTER 12
Knee

| Basic Examination |

Inspect varus/valgus

PROCEDURE: Have the patient stand in anatomic position. Visually inspect the angle of the knee articulation and the position of the feet.

OUTCOME: If the patient can stand with feet and knees touching: ◆ **normal**
If tibia is angled outward, knock-kneed (Fig 12-1): ◆ **genu valgus**
If tibia is angled inward, bow-legged: ◆ **genu varus**
If tibia hyperextends: ◆ **genu recurvatum**
If patellar height >1 cm higher on the affected side: ◆ **patella alta**

Perform a passive range of motion examination

PROCEDURE: Have the patient lie supine or sit. Perform a passive range of motion (ROM) examination. Repeat the examination on the contralateral lower extremity as a control.

OUTCOME: If the passive ROM is as follows:
Flexion: 0 to 130 degrees
Extension: 0 to 5 degrees
Adduction and abduction: <5 degrees
Internal and external rotation: <5 degrees: ◆ **normal**
If there is an increase in adduction or abduction:
   ◆ **ligament damage**
If a decrease in flexion/extension:
   ◆ **joint dysfunction (degenerative joint disease)**

Examine for ballottable patella and bulge sign

PROCEDURE: Have the patient lie supine with the knee extended. Gently press on the suprapatellar area with one hand and on the patella with the other hand. Feel the patella for movement and visually inspect the distal sides of the patella (Fig 12-2).

OUTCOME: If the patella is ballottable: ◆ **knee effusion**
If patella is not ballottable: ◆ **normal**
If there is a bulge at the sides (i.e., interface between the patella and the condyles), medially and/or laterally: ◆ **knee effusion**
If concavity remains at the sides: ◆ **normal**

Inspect for fluid displacement

PROCEDURE: Have the patient lie supine with the knee extended. Gently press on the lateral side of the knee, on distal, deep to the patella.

248

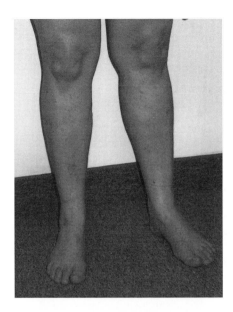

Figure 12-1 Genu valgus. Patient standing, tibial axis pointing lateral relative to the femoral axis. This is particularly evident in patient's left leg.

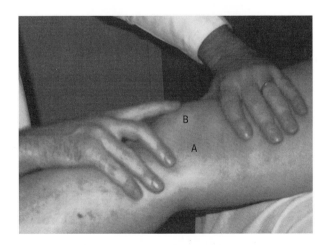

Figure 12-2 Examination for knee effusion. Leg at knee in extension and parallel to floor. A. Site of potential bulge of an effusion—posterior to patella, over joint line. B. Application of pressure on patella to attempt ballottement.

Visually inspect the medial side of the knee. Repeat the procedure on the medial side, visually inspecting the lateral side.

OUTCOME: If a prior concavity remains concave on applying pressure:
♦ **normal**
If there is a loss of concavity or a bulge develops: ♦ **effusion**

Measure Q angle

PROCEDURE: Patient standing in anatomic position, examiner visually inspects and thus measures the Q angle. The Q angle is formed by two lines: One line runs from the anterior superior iliac spine to the patellar center; the other line runs from the center of the patella to the anterior tibial tuberosity.

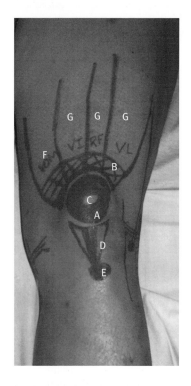

Figure 12-3 Anterior knee landmarks. A. Patella. B. Suprapatellar bursa. C. Prepatellar bursa. D. Infrapatellar bursa. E. Anterior tibial tuberosity. F. Vastus obliquus medialis (VOM) of quadriceps muscle. G. Other components of quadriceps: vastus intermedialis (VI), rectus femoris (RF), and vastus lateralis (VL).

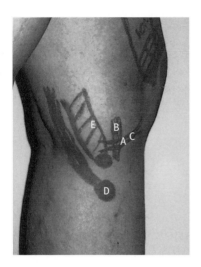

Figure 12-4 Medial knee landmarks. A. Joint line. B. Medial collateral ligament. C. Medial meniscus. D. Pes anserine bursa. E. Semimembranosus muscle.

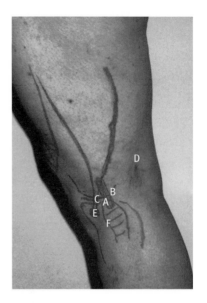

Figure 12-5 Lateral knee landmarks. A. Joint line. B. Lateral collateral ligament. C. Lateral meniscus. D. Biceps femoris muscle. E. Iliotibial band and Gerdy's tubercle. F. Fibula.

OUTCOME:

Women: If Q angle <15 degrees: ◆ **normal**
If Q angle >15 degrees: ◆ **patellofemoral syndrome**

Men: If Q angle <10 degrees: ◆ **normal**
If Q angle >10 degrees: ◆ **patellofemoral syndrome**

Locate condyles and anterior tibial spine

PROCEDURE: Passively flex knee to 30 degrees. Palpate on the medial joint line between the condyles of the tibia and femur, especially the posterior side [medial collateral ligament (MCL) site], and the lateral joint line, especially between the head of the fibula and the tibial condyle [lateral collateral ligament (LCL)]. Also, palpate the anterior tibial tuberosity (Fig 12-3E).

OUTCOME: If medial tenderness (Fig 12-4A):
◆ **MCL sprain**
◆ **medial meniscus (MM) sprain**

If lateral joint line tender (Fig 12-5A):
- ◆ **LCL sprain**
- ◆ **lateral meniscus (LM) sprain**

If no tenderness: ◆ **normal**

If anterior tibial tuberosity bony (Fig 12-3E): ◆ **Osgood-Schlatter**

If tibia subluxed anteriorly on femur: ◆ **ACL sprain**

If tibia subluxed posteriorly on femur:
- ◆ **posterior cruciate ligament (PCL) sprain**

Advanced Examination

APPROACH TO A PATIENT WITH ANTERIOR KNEE PAIN

Inspect varus/valgus: As in Basic Examination.

Examine for ballottable patella and bulge sign: As in Basic Examination.

Inspect for fluid displacement: As in Basic Examination.

Measure Q angle: As in Basic Examination.

Palpate anterior knee structures

PROCEDURE: Have the patient lie supine with the knee extended. Gently palpate superior to, over, and inferior to the patella area. Use the contralateral side as a control.

OUTCOME: If there are swelling and tenderness over the caudad part of the quadriceps femoris musculature (see Fig 12-3):
- ◆ **quadriceps femoris strain/rupture**

If there is swelling with a doughy edema in the area cephalad to the patella (see Fig 12-3B): ◆ **suprapatellar bursitis**

If swelling over the superficial patella (see Fig 12-3C):
- ◆ **prepatellar bursitis**

If tender swelling on one or both sides of the patellar ligament (see Fig 12-3D): ◆ **infrapatellar bursitis**

If tenderness behind the patella on palpation without associated swelling:
- ◆ **patellofemoral syndrome**
- ◆ **degenerative joint disease**

If a nontender bony protuberance on the anterior tibial spine (see Fig 12-3E): ◆ **Osgood-Schlatter disease**

If there are marked tenderness and swelling in the patella itself (see Fig 12-3A): ◆ **patellar fracture**

Perform apprehension test

PROCEDURE: Have the patient sit or lie supine. Passively flex the knee to 30 degrees and apply medial then lateral pressure on the patella. Ask the patient whether any discomfort develops. Visually inspect the quadriceps muscle as the patella is medially and laterally mobilized. Use the contralateral patella as a control.

OUTCOME: If voluntary contraction of the quadriceps muscle on the affected side when attempting to mobilize the patella laterally:
- ◆ **patellofemoral syndrome**

If no difference in patellar mobility and no quadriceps muscle contraction: ◆ **normal**

Measure for quadriceps atrophy

PROCEDURE: Measure the circumference of the thigh. Use the contralateral thigh as a control.

OUTCOME: If the affected side has a smaller diameter:
♦ **quadriceps atrophy of patellofemoral syndrome**
If there is no difference in size: ♦ **normal**

Inspect for vastus obliquus medialis atrophy

PROCEDURE: Visually inspect the size of the quadriceps musculature, specifically the vastus obliquus medialis muscle. Use the contralateral side as a control.

OUTCOME: If there is atrophy of the vastus obliquus medialis muscle (see Fig 12-3F): ♦ **patellofemoral syndrome**
If no atrophy of the vastus obliquus medialis muscle: ♦ **normal**

APPROACH TO A PATIENT WITH POSTERIOR KNEE/POPLITEAL FOSSA COMPLAINTS

Palpate popliteal fossa

PROCEDURE: Have the patient lie supine with the knee extended. Gently palpate the popliteal fossa and adjacent muscles. Use the contralateral knee as a control.

OUTCOME: If tenderness in the medial aspect, in hamstring tendons and muscles: ♦ **hamstring strain**
If a nontender area of fluctuance, not adjacent to a muscle:
♦ **Baker's (Adam's) cyst**
If diffuse tenderness and swelling are present:
♦ **deep venous thrombosis**
♦ **ruptured Baker's cyst**
If there is a pulsatile mass: ♦ **popliteal artery aneurysm**
If no mass or tenderness: ♦ **normal**

Auscult fossa

PROCEDURE: Use the diaphragm of the stethoscope to auscult over the mass.

OUTCOME: If there is a bruit: ♦ **popliteal aneurysm**
If no bruit: ♦ **another etiology**

Transilluminate mass

PROCEDURE: Use a light source to transilluminate the mass.

OUTCOME: If transilluminable: ♦ **Baker's cyst**
If nontransilluminable: ♦ **another etiology**

APPROACH TO A PATIENT WITH MEDIAL KNEE PAIN

Inspect varus/valgus: As in Basic Examination.

Palpate medial knee

PROCEDURE: Have the patient lie supine with knee fully extended; palpate over the medial knee, observing the hamstrings, tibiofemoral joint line, and proximal tibia. Ask the patient whether there is tenderness.

OUTCOME: If there is a tender area over the extreme medial aspect of the knee, 4 cm inferior to the medial femoral condyle (see Fig 12-4D):
◆ **anserine bursitis**
If tenderness in posterior joint line (see Fig 12-4B): ◆ **MCL sprain**
If tenderness in mid- to anterior tibiofemoral joint line (see Fig 12-4C): ◆ **medial meniscus tear**
If tenderness in insertions of the hamstrings, with pain radiating into the posteromedial thigh (see Fig 12-4E): ◆ **hamstring sprain**
If no tenderness or swelling: ◆ **normal**

Hamstring squeeze sign

PROCEDURE: Patient supine, knee extended; examiner places hand over mid-distal hamstrings, gently squeezes the muscles, uses other side as control.

OUTCOME: If no tenderness: ◆ **normal**
If tender to groin and the entire thigh (see Fig 12-4E):
◆ **semimembranosus strain**
If tender in proximal medial tibia (see Fig 12-4D):
◆ **pes anserine bursitis**

Perform valgus stress test

PROCEDURE: Have the patient lie supine with the knee passively flexed at 25 to 30 degrees (Fig 12-6). Maintain the patient's position by placing your flexed knee beneath the patient's knee, and palpate the medial joint line while applying valgus stress on the knee. Inspect and palpate for any laxity in the medial aspect of the joint with valgus force (Fig 12-6). Repeat on the contralateral side for a control.

OUTCOME: If there is no pain or laxity in the medial aspect of knee:
◆ **normal**
If pain without increased laxity in the medial aspect of knee (see Fig 12-4B): ◆ **first-degree MCL tear**
If pain with increased laxity, <5 mm of displacement:
◆ **second-degree MCL tear**
If pain with increased laxity, >5 mm of displacement:
◆ **third-degree MCL tear**
If pain in the lateral compartment (Böhler's sign):
◆ **lateral meniscus tear**

Perform modified valgus stress test

PROCEDURE: Have the patient sit at the edge of the table (Fig 12-7), knee flexed at 25 to 30 degrees and stabilized in this position by placing the

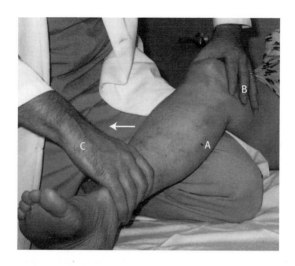

Figure 12-6 Valgus stress procedure. A. Knee stabilized in 30 degrees flexion. B. Palpate over the medial joint line. C. Apply valgus stress on the tibia to assess for medial collateral ligament sprain.

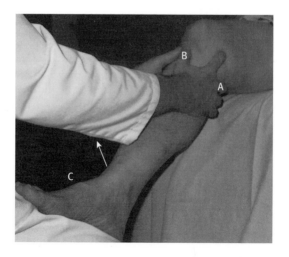

Figure 12-7 Modified valgus stress procedure. A. Knee stabilized in 30 degrees flexion. B. "W" configuration of fingers over the medial and lateral joint line, thumbs over anterior tibial tuberosity. C. Apply valgus stress on the tibia to assess for medial collateral ligament sprain.

patient's foot on examiner's anterior thigh. Examiner places each index finger over the medial and then lateral joint lines with the thumbs on the anterior tibial tuberosity, that is, a classic "W" configuration. Place valgus force on the tibiofemoral (knee) joint. Palpate for laxity in the medial aspect of the joint with valgus force. Repeat on the contralateral side for a control.

OUTCOME: See above, under Perform valgus stress test.

Perform McMurray test: See under Approach to a patient with knee laxity/clicking/locking.

APPROACH TO A PATIENT WITH LATERAL KNEE PAIN

Inspect varus/valgus: As in Basic Examination.

Palpate lateral knee
PROCEDURE: Have the patient lie supine with the knee extended; palpate over the lateral knee, observing the tibiofemoral joint line, biceps femoris, and proximal tibia. Ask the patient about any tenderness.

OUTCOME: If there is tenderness between the lateral femoral condyle and fibular head (see Fig 12-5B): ◆ **LCL sprain**
If tenderness in mid- to anterior tibiofemoral joint line (see Fig 12-5C): ◆ **lateral meniscus tear**
If tenderness over the lateral tibial condyle (Gerdy's tubercle), radiating over the lateral thigh (see Fig 12-5E):
◆ **iliotibial band syndrome**
If tenderness over the fibular head (see Fig 12-5F):
◆ **fibular head fracture**
If no tenderness or swelling: ◆ **normal**

Perform varus stress test
PROCEDURE: Have the patient lie supine with the knee passively flexed at 25 to 30 degrees (see Fig 12-6). Maintain the patient's position by placing your flexed knee beneath the patient's knee; palpate the lateral joint line while applying varus stress on the knee. Inspect and palpate for any laxity in the lateral aspect of the joint with varus force (see Fig 12-6). Repeat on the contralateral side for a control.

OUTCOME: If there is no pain or laxity in the lateral aspect: ◆ **normal**
If pain without increased laxity: ◆ **first-degree LCL tear**
If pain with increased laxity, <5 mm of displacement:
◆ **second-degree LCL tear**
If pain with increased laxity, >5 mm of displacement:
◆ **third-degree LCL tear**
If pain in the medial compartment (Böhler's sign):
◆ **medial meniscus tear**

Perform modified varus stress test

PROCEDURE: Have the patient sit at the edge of the table (see Fig 12-7), knee flexed at 25 to 30 degrees and stabilized in this position by placing the patient's foot on your anterior thigh. Examiner places each index finger over the medial and then lateral joint lines with the thumbs on the anterior tibial tuberosity, that is, a classic "W" configuration. Place varus force on the tibiofemoral (knee) joint. Palpate for laxity in the lateral aspect of the joint (see Fig 12-5B) with varus force. Repeat on the contralateral side for a control.

OUTCOME: See above, under Perform varus stress test.

Perform the Ober test

PROCEDURE: Patient in lateral decubital position, asymptomatic side down. The lower leg is passively forward flexed to 20 degrees; the examiner then passively backward flexes the hip and attempts to adduct the leg at the hip to touch the medial knee to the examination table.

OUTCOME: If unable to perform due to stiffness or pain:
- ◆ iliotibial band syndrome

If able to perform:
- ◆ normal
- ◆ another etiology

Perform McMurray test: See under Approach to a patient with knee laxity/clicking/locking.

APPROACH TO A PATIENT WITH KNEE LAXITY/CLICKING/LOCKING

Locate condyles and anterior tibial spine: As in Basic Examination.

Perform anterior drawer test

PROCEDURE: With the patient supine or seated, hold the patient's knee flexed at 90 degrees (Fig 12-8). Place your knee on the patient's foot (Fig 12-8). Place thumbs over the anterior tibial spine, fingers on sides of knee in a classic "W" configuration; firmly pull on the tibia in an anterior direction so as to sublux it anteriorly (Fig 12-8). Use the contralateral side as a control.

OUTCOME: If the tibia slides anteriorly >2 mm over the femur:
- ◆ anterior cruciate ligament tear

If end point of displacement is soft (i.e., sharpness of cessation of anterior movement is obtuse): ◆ **anterior cruciate ligament tear**
If end point of displacement is firm (i.e., sharpness of cessation of anterior movement is acute): ◆ **normal**
If tibia slides anteriorly <2 mm over the femur:

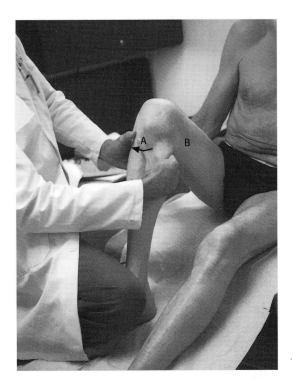

Figure 12-8 Anterior drawer. A. Knee stabilized in 90 degrees flexion. B. Pull anterior on tibia to stress the anterior cruciate ligament.

> ◆ **normal**
> ◆ **false negative**
>
> If medial or lateral condyle alone is displaced:
> ◆ **medial or lateral collateral ligament tear**

Perform Lachman's maneuver

PROCEDURE: With the patient supine, hold his/her knee flexed at 20 to 25 degrees. Stabilize the femur with one hand and attempt to relax the hamstrings; with the other hand, firmly pull on the tibia in an anterior direction. Repeat on the contralateral side as a control.

OUTCOME: If the tibia slides anteriorly >2 mm over the femur (Lachman's sign): ◆ **anterior cruciate ligament tear**
If end point of displacement is soft (Lachman's sign):
◆ **anterior cruciate ligament tear**

If end point of displacement is tight: ◆ **normal**

If tibia slides anteriorly <2 mm over the femur: ◆ **normal**

Perform modified Lachman's maneuver

PROCEDURE: Have the patient lie supine. Place your flexed knee under the patient's knee (Fig 12-9). Maintain the patient's knee in 20 to 25 degrees of flexion. Place thumbs over the anterior tibial tuberosity, fingers on sides of knee, that is, a classic "W" configuration. Firmly pull on the tibia in an anterior direction (Fig 12-9). Repeat on the contralateral side as a control.

OUTCOME: See above, under Perform Lachman's maneuver.

Perform prone modified drawer test

PROCEDURE: Have the patient lie prone. Passively flex the knee to 20 to 30 degrees. Place thumbs on the anterior tibial tuberosity and the fingers over the medial and lateral tibiofemoral joint lines, that is, a classic "W" configuration. Put firm pressure on the posterior proximal gastrocnemius area, attempting to sublux the tibia anteriorly. Repeat on the contralateral side as a control.

OUTCOME: If the tibia slides anteriorly >2 mm over the femur:

◆ **anterior cruciate ligament tear**

If end point of displacement is soft:

◆ **anterior cruciate ligament tear**

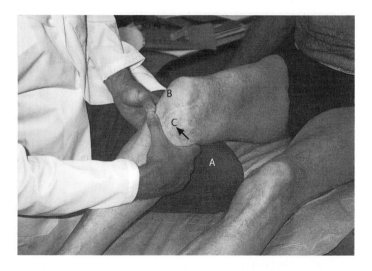

Figure 12-9 Lachman's test. A. Knee stabilized in 30 degrees flexion. B. "W" configuration of fingers over the medial and lateral joint line, thumbs over anterior tibial tuberosity. C. Pull anteriorly on tibia.

If end point of displacement is firm: ◆ **normal**
If tibia slides anteriorly <2 mm over femur: ◆ **normal**

Perform posterior drawer test

PROCEDURE: Have the patient lie prone, with the knee held in a position of flexion at 90 degrees. Place thumbs over the anterior tibial tuberosity, fingers on the medial and lateral joint line; press posteriorly on the proximal tibia. Press on the proximal tibia with an anterior to posterior force and palpate for any movement of the tibia on the femur. Repeat on the contralateral side for a control.

OUTCOME: If there is posterior displacement of the tibia on the femur:
◆ **posterior cruciate ligament tear**
If no posterior displacement: ◆ **normal**

Perform external rotation recurvatum test (Godfrey's test)

PROCEDURE: Have the patient lie supine. Passively flex the patient's lower extremity at the hip with the knee in full extension; provide varus and external rotation by pulling up on the distal foot to 90 degrees. Visually inspect the knee for any displacement.

OUTCOME: If there is posterior displacement of the tibia on the femur:
◆ **posterior cruciate ligament tear**
If no posterior displacement: ◆ **normal**

Perform McMurray test

PROCEDURE: See Figure 12-10. Have the patient lie supine. 1) Passively flex the hip and the knee until the heel touches the buttock. 2) Steady the knee with one hand, and grasp the heel with the other hand, rotating the foot as far lateral (external rotation at ankle) as possible. 3) Then extend the knee to 90 degrees. 4) Repeat this three times. Return to the beginning and rotate the foot as far medial (internal rotation at ankle) as possible, then passively extend the knee to 90 degrees. While performing this, palpate the knee being tested, specifically at the tibiofemoral articulation. 5) Again repeat this three times. Repeat in the contralateral knee as a control.

OUTCOME: If there is a click/thud with or without tenderness over the lateral aspect of the knee: ◆ **LM tear**
If a click/thud with or without tenderness over the medial aspect of the knee: ◆ **MM tear**

Perform Payr's test

PROCEDURE: With the patient sitting cross-legged, apply gentle pressure to the affected knee. Query the patient as to any pain. Repeat, using the contralateral side as a control.

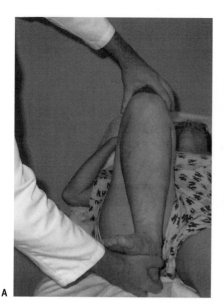
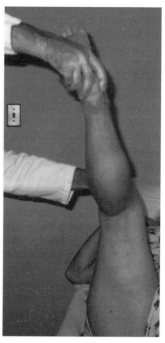

A B

Figure 12-10 McMurray maneuver, here in external rotation. A. Knee inflexion with external rotation applied to the ankle; palpate over the joint line. B. Knee in passive extension. Clicks or thuds in medial or lateral joint lines indicate a meniscal tear.

OUTCOME: If there is medial pain: ◆ **nonspecific**
If no pain: ◆ **normal, makes an MM tear quite unlikely**

Perform varus and valgus stress test: See under Approach to a patient with medial knee pain and Approach to a patient with lateral knee pain.

Keys to Recording Findings

KNEE

"Unremarkable, normal passive and active ROM, mild valgus, Q-angle < 10 degrees, no pain, swelling or tenderness"

A. Active and passive ROM flexion/extension; document degrees of the motion if abnormal

B. Note valgus/varus of each knee

C. Note Q-angle, report in degrees

D. E. F. Note sites of swelling, pain, tenderness in and about the knee

D. E. F. Note any evidence of intraarticular effusion—bulging, ballotable patella, fluid displacement

G. Note sites of increased pain and/or any laxity with

  —Valgus stress test

  —Varus stress test

  —Lachman's stress test

  —Anterior drawer procedure

  —McMurray's manuever

	Degrees	
	Left	Right
A. ROM Flexion	———	———
Extension	———	———
B. Valgus/Varus	———	———
C. Q Angle	———	———

D. Anterior Knee

Right   Left

E. Medial Knee

F. Posterior Knee

	Normal		Abnormal, details:
	Left	Right	
G. Stress Tests			
Valgus stress	❏	❏	_____
Varus stress	❏	❏	_____
Lachman's	❏	❏	_____
Anterior drawer	❏	❏	_____
McMurray's	❏	❏	_____

Diagnoses

Anserine bursitis

Inflammation of the pes anserine bursa (see Fig 12-4D), located on medial knee adjacent to the insertions of the sartorius, gracilis, and semitendinous muscles. The condition is often caused by long-distance running, running in flat shoes, or hyperpronating running. Symptoms and signs include a tender area 3 cm inferior to the medial femoral condyle reproduced with the hamstring squeeze test. Radiographs are unnecessary, and treatment includes rest, proper stretching, and running with shoes that have adequate arch support.

Anterior cruciate ligament sprain

Tear of the anterior cruciate ligament (ACL) due to hyperextension of the knee (e.g., going for a fade-away jumpshot) or a twist, knee flexion at 20 degrees. Symptoms include an acute audible pop; a painful, unstable joint; and a large effusion within 1 hour. Signs include positive anterior drawer (see Fig 12-8) and Lachman's tests (see Fig 12-9); one must assess for concurrent MM or MCL damage (the unhappy triad of O'Donaghue), or both. Evaluation with radiographs of the knee is indicated; treatment includes immobilization of the knee, urgent referral to an orthopedic surgeon, and physical therapy.

Baker's cyst

Herniation of the posterior joint capsule of the knee due to a chronic knee effusion. Symptoms and signs include a mildly painful transilluminable mass in the popliteal fossa with an antecedent concurrent knee effusion. An acute onset of pain and swelling in the posterior knee and calf may indicate acute cyst rupture. Evaluation with radiographs of the knee reveals degenerative joint disease (DJD); ultrasound demonstrates a cyst in the popliteal fossa. The treatment is the same as for DJD.

Deep venous thrombosis

Thrombus formation in the deep venous system of a lower extremity due to immobilization, inflammation, and/or hypercoagulable states. Symptoms and signs include swelling in the affected leg and thigh and fullness in the popliteal fossa. Physical examination is quite to very poor for the diagnosis of deep venous thrombosis (DVT); one should not perform Homan's maneuver. Evaluation includes a duplex ultrasound study of the deep venous system; treatment is with full anticoagulation with low-molecular-weight heparin or with heparin if proximal DVT is present.

Degenerative joint disease

Loss of articular cartilage in the affected knee joint medial and lateral compartment (the risk factors include obesity and recurrent trauma). Chondromalacia patella is DJD specific to the anterior compartment. Symptoms and signs include pain that is worse in the afternoon and after activities but better in the morning, small effusion, and a decreased range of motion of the knee with crepitus upon ROM. Radiographs of the knee reveal narrowing of the articular compartments. Treatment includes acetaminophen, physical therapy, and injection of joint with glucocorticoids. Advanced cases should be referred to an orthopedic surgeon for total knee replacement.

Fibular head fracture
Due to direct trauma or concurrent to a lateral ankle sprain. Symptoms and signs include tender swelling over the proximal fibula (see Fig 12-5F) and possible concurrent tingling, anesthesia, and weakness in distribution of the common peroneal nerve; thus, one needs to assess function of the anterior compartment (i.e., active dorsiflexion) and the lateral compartment (i.e., active eversion). Evaluation and treatment include radiographs of the knee and ankle, the use of crutches, knee immobilization, and referral to an orthopedics surgeon.

Genu recurvatum
Hyperextension at the knee, due to laxity or a posterior cruciate ligament problem. Symptoms and signs include laxity, potentially a positive posterior drawer, and baseline extension at the knee >10 degrees. Evaluation and treatment include referral to physical therapy for quadriceps strengthening.

Genu valgus
Laterally directed tibia ("knock-kneed"); acutely it may be due to a significant MCL tear. Symptoms and signs include valgus of >10 degrees (see Fig 12-1); specific findings include medial knee pain and a positive valgus stress test in MCL tears; medial pain and a normal valgus stress test in DJD. Evaluation and treatment are with knee radiographs if onset is acute, the prescription of rest, nonsteroidal anti-inflammatory drugs (NSAIDs), and referral to orthopedics if an acute MCL tear occurs.

Genu varus
Medially directed tibia ("bow-legged"); acutely, it may be due to a significant LCL tear. Symptoms and signs include varus of >0 degrees; specific findings include lateral knee pain and a positive varus stress test in LCL tears; lateral pain and a normal varus stress test in DJD. Evaluation and treatment are with knee radiographs if onset is acute, the prescription of rest, NSAIDs, and referral to orthopedics if an acute LCL tear occurs.

Hamstring strain (semimembranosus, semitendinosus)
Tearing of the muscle(s) or tendons of semimembranosus/semitendinosus due to inadequate pre-exercise stretching. Symptoms and signs include tenderness and spasm in the lower part of the hamstrings (see Fig 12-4E). The pain radiates into the groin, and the patient has limited active flexion at the knee and a positive hamstring squeeze test. Evaluation with radiographs is

unnecessary. Treatment includes rest, NSAIDs, referral to a physical therapist, and education on stretching exercises.

Iliotibial band syndrome
Inflammation of the iliotibial band, often due to long-distance running without adequate stretching. The band, which is an extension of the gluteus maximus muscle, slides anteriorly with extension and posteriorly with flexion of the knee and inserts on Gerdy's tubercle of the lateral tibia. Symptoms and signs include tenderness at the insertion of the iliotibial band onto the lateral tibial condyle (see Fig 12-5E) and a positive Ober test. Radiographs are unnecessary, and treatment includes rest, proper stretching, and running on flat surfaces.

Infrapatellar bursitis (clergyman's knee)
Inflammation of the bursa immediately inferior to the patella and patellar ligament, usually caused by repetitive dropping onto (and thus hitting) the inferior aspects of the knees. Unilateral bursitis may be due to an infectious etiology; bilateral is most often occupation related. Symptoms and signs include tender swelling deep to the patellar ligament (see Fig 12-3D), bilaterally. If bilateral, radiographs are unnecessary, and treatment includes rest, refraining from the exacerbating activity, and use of knee pads; if unilateral, one must strongly consider a tap of the bursa.

Knee effusion
Excess fluid within the knee joint itself; most commonly due to osteoarthritis, trauma, gout, or other crystal arthropathy or a septic (e.g., gonococcal) etiology. Symptoms and signs include increase or decrease in ROM, swelling in joint lines, ballottable patella (see Fig 12-2B), bulging of fluid (see Fig 12-2A), and fluid displacement. Effusion may be concurrent to fluid in surrounding bursae (e.g., suprapatellar or prepatellar). Evaluation includes arthrocentesis; treatment is of the underlying etiology.

Lateral collateral ligament sprain
Injury from excessive varus bending of the knee. Symptoms include acute onset of lateral knee pain with joint swelling >6 hours after the injury; the patient is able to walk. Signs include tenderness, ecchymosis, and swelling at the lateral joint line (see Fig 12-5A,B). The varus stress test is positive; the McMurray (see Fig 12-10) test is negative. Radiographs of the knee are indicated to rule out a concurrent fracture. Treatment includes immobilization of the knee, referral to an orthopedic surgeon, and physical therapy.

Lateral meniscus sprain
Injury that occurred with lateral twisting while bearing weight with the knee in flexion. Symptoms include pain in the lateral joint line and recurrent knee locking; that is, the knee is stuck in 10 degrees of flexion and cannot completely extend, but no significant joint instability or effusion is present. Signs include positive lateral McMurray (see Fig 12-10), Apley grind, and varus

stress (Böhler's) test, which manifests lateral joint line tenderness (see Fig 12-5A,B). Radiographs of the knee are indicated. Treatment includes immobilization of the knee, referral to an orthopedic surgeon, magnetic resonance imaging (MRI) of the knee, and physical therapy.

Medial collateral ligament sprain

Injury from excessive valgus bending of the knee (most common injury in downhill skiers). Overall this is the most common knee injury. Symptoms include acute onset of medial knee pain with joint swelling 6 hours after the injury; the patient is able to walk. Signs include tenderness, ecchymosis, and swelling at the medial joint line (see Fig 12-4A). The valgus stress test is positive (see Fig 12-6); the McMurray (see Fig 12-10) test is negative. Radiographs of the knee are indicated. Treatment includes immobilization of the knee, referral to an orthopedic surgeon, MRI of the knee, and physical therapy. If the injury is severe, a concurrent MM tear is very likely.

Medial meniscus sprain

Injury that occurred with medial twisting while bearing weight with the knee in flexion. Symptoms include pain in the medial joint line and recurrent knee locking but no significant joint instability or effusion. Signs include positive medial McMurray (see Fig 12-10) and varus stress (Böhler's) test, with medial side (see Fig 12-4A,C) pain. Radiographs of the knee are indicated. Treatment includes immobilization of the knee, referral to an orthopedic surgeon, and physical therapy.

Osgood-Schlatter syndrome: See Traction apophysitis.

Patella alta: See Patellofemoral syndrome.

Patellar fracture

Due to direct trauma to the patella. Symptoms and signs include severe anterior knee pain, along with swelling; patellar tenderness (see Fig 12-3A) with a marked decrease in knee ROM, particularly in extension. Radiographs confirm diagnosis; immobilization and referral to an orthopedic surgeon are indicated.

Patellofemoral syndrome

Abnormal lateral tracking of the patella on knee extension, with wearing of the anterior compartment cartilage. Symptoms include anterior knee pain, especially when climbing down stairs or sitting (moviegoer's knees). Signs include an increased Q angle to >15 degrees, **inappropriate lateral patella in extension, patella alta** (if unilateral), and atrophy of the vastus obliquus medialis muscle (see Fig 12-3F). Severe cases feature a positive apprehension test and lateral subluxation or dislocation of the patella. Evaluation includes radiographs of the knees; treatment includes referral to physical therapy for strengthening of the quadriceps femoris musculature and application of a patellar brace. Severe cases should be referred to an orthopedic surgeon.

Popliteal artery aneurysm

Either due to trauma, particularly a spontaneously reduced tibiofibular dislocation or severe peripheral atherosclerotic disease. Symptoms and signs include a palpable swelling in the popliteal fossa. A bruit is present, and foot pulses may be decreased. Evaluation and management include urgent or, if trauma related, emergent referral to a vascular surgeon.

Posterior cruciate ligament sprain

Injury due to a direct blow to the proximal anterior tibia when the knee is flexed. Symptoms include the acute onset of an unstable knee with an effusion. Signs include positive posterior drawer test, posterior sag, and a positive Godfrey's sign. Evaluation includes radiographs of the knee; treatment includes immobilization of the knee, urgent referral to an orthopedic surgeon, probable need for a knee MRI, and physical therapy.

Prepatellar bursitis (roofer's knee)

Inflammation of the bursa immediately anterior to the patella, due to an extended period of kneeling. Symptoms and signs include tenderness and swelling in the anterior aspect of the patella (see Fig 12-3C) bilaterally. Radiographs are unnecessary, and treatment includes rest and refraining from the exacerbating activity.

Quadriceps femoris strain (see also Quadriceps tendon rupture)

Stretching or tearing of the muscle due to inadequate stretching. Symptoms and signs include tenderness in the lower part of the quadriceps femoris muscle (see Fig 12-3F,G); active extension of the knee reproduces the pain. Radiographs are unnecessary. Treatment includes rest, NSAIDs, referral to a physical therapist, and education on stretching exercises.

Quadriceps tendon rupture

Rupture from a sudden marked contraction of the quadriceps femoris during running or jumping. Symptoms and signs include acute pain and tenderness over the distal quadriceps femoris tendon (see Fig 12-3F,G), a loss of active knee extension, and subluxation of the patella laterally or medially. Evaluation includes radiographs of the knee and an MRI of the distal quadriceps area; treatment includes immobilization of the knee in extension and urgent referral to an orthopedic surgeon.

Suprapatellar plica syndrome ("bursitis")

Inflammation in the suprapatellar plica has synovium that is contiguous to the joint; commonly, but, inappropriately, referred to as a *bursa*. Symptoms and signs include doughy nonpitting swelling with pain in the suprapatellar area (see Fig 12-3B), most often unilateral. Radiographs are unnecessary, and treatment includes rest and refraining from the exacerbating activity.

Traction apophysitis

Inflammatory changes in the attachments of tendons to the bones. **Osgood-Schlatter syndrome** affects the patellar tendon at its insertion on the tibial tuberosity in adolescents. Symptoms and signs include tenderness over the anterior tibial tuberosity with early swelling (see Fig 12-3E); later, nontender bony enlargement occurs. Radiographs reveal heterotopic ossification. Treatment includes rest and prevention.

CHAPTER 13
Foot/Ankle

Assess passive range of motion at tibiotalar and subtalar joints

PROCEDURE: Perform passive range of motion at the ankle (tibiotalar and sub-talar) joints. Note the range in degrees and the presence of pain.

OUTCOME: If passive range of motion (ROM) for each is:
Dorsiflexion of ankle: 30 degrees
Plantarflexion of ankle: 45 degrees
Inversion of foot (great toe side tilted up): 30 degrees
Eversion of foot (great toe side tilted down): 20 degrees ◆ **normal**
If there is decreased eversion/inversion:
◆ **subtalar joint dysfunction**
If decreased dorsiflexion/plantarflexion:
◆ **tibiotalar joint dysfunction**
If painless "bag of bones" feel to the joint: ◆ **Charcot's joint**

Actively dorsiflex great toe

PROCEDURE: Have the patient extend/dorsiflex the great toe against resistance (Fig 13-1). Use the contralateral ankle/foot as a control.

OUTCOME: If there is a decrease in power/strength:
◆ **anterior compartment problem**, for example, exten-sor hallucis longus tendonitis, deep peroneal nerve problem
◆ **first metatarsophalangeal joint deficit**
If strength is 5/5: ◆ **normal**

Actively plantarflex ankle

PROCEDURE: With the patient sitting or supine, passively flex the knee to 90 degrees. Tell the patient to plantarflex the ankle actively (Fig 13-2). Use the contralateral ankle as a control.

OUTCOME: If there is a decrease in strength:
◆ **posterior compartment problem**, for example, gastrocne-mius tear, Achilles tendon rupture/tendonitis, tibial nerve (S1) damage
◆ **ankle sprain (tibiotalar joint)**
If strength is 5/5: ◆ **normal**

Actively dorsiflex ankle

PROCEDURE: Have the patient dorsiflex the ankle against resistance. Use the contralateral ankle as a control.

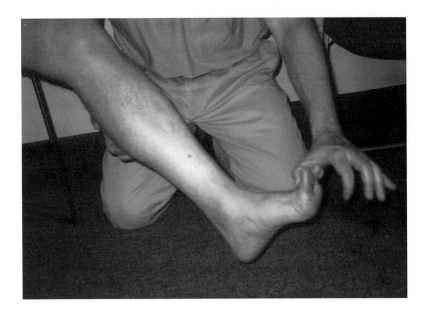

Figure 13-1 Active great toe extension. Assessment of L5, deep peroneal nerve, anterior compartment.

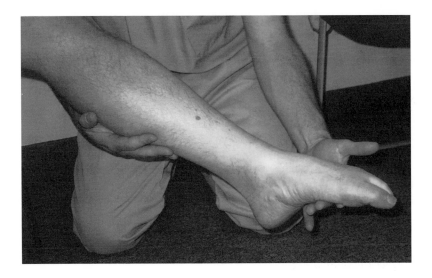

Figure 13-2 Active plantarflexion of foot, against resistance. Assessment of S1, tibial nerve, posterior compartment.

OUTCOME: If there is a decrease in strength:
- **anterior compartment problem**, for example, deep peroneal nerve deficit (L5; foot drop), extensor tendonitis
- **ankle sprain (tibiotalar joint)**

If strength is 5/5: ◆ **normal**

Actively evert foot

PROCEDURE: Have the patient evert the foot against resistance. Use the contralateral foot as a control.

OUTCOME: If there is a decrease in strength:
- **lateral compartment problem**, for example, superficial peroneal nerve deficit, peroneal muscle strain or tendon sprain
- **ankle sprain (subtalar joint)**

If strength is 5/5: ◆ **normal**

Actively invert ankle

PROCEDURE: Have the patient invert the foot against resistance. Use the contralateral foot as a control.

OUTCOME: If there is a decrease in strength:
- **anterior compartment problem**, for example, tibialis anterior tendonitis, deep peroneal nerve (L5) deficit (foot drop)
- **ankle sprain (subtalar joint)**

If strength is 5/5: ◆ **normal**

Inspect anterior compartment muscles

PROCEDURE: Visually inspect and palpate the anterior compartment musculature, specifically the dorsiflexor muscles. Use the contralateral side for control.

OUTCOME: If there is no atrophy: ◆ **normal**
If atrophy:
- **deep peroneal nerve problem (anterior compartment)**

Perform sensory examination of dorsal foot

PROCEDURE: Tell the patient to close his or her eyes. Use a cotton-tipped swab or a monofilament to touch the dorsal aspect of the foot lightly, specifically at the dorsal web between the first and second toes (Fig 13-3C). Use the contralateral foot as a control.

OUTCOME: If there is equal sensation in both feet: ◆ **normal**
If decreased sensation in the affected foot:
- **deep peroneal nerve problem**
- **L5 deficit**

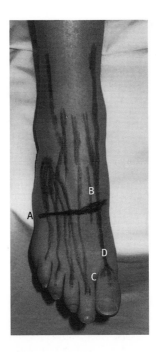

Figure 13-3 Dorsal foot landmarks. A. Lisfranc's joint. B. Dorsalis pedis artery. C. Site for deep peroneal nerve sensation assessment. D. Site of turf toe tenderness, the extensor.

Perform sensory examination of plantar foot

PROCEDURE: Tell the patient to close his or her eyes. Use a cotton-tipped swab to touch the plantar aspect of the foot lightly. Use the contralateral foot as a control.

OUTCOME: If there is equal sensation in both feet: ◆ **normal**
If decreased sensation in the affected foot:
◆ **tibialis nerve problem**
◆ **S1 deficit**

Check reflexes: Achilles: See Chapter 7, under Basic Examination (Fig 7-3, p. 141).

| Advanced Examination |

APPROACH TO A PATIENT WITH FOOT/ANKLE TRAUMA

Visually inspect and palpate structures of foot/ankle

PROCEDURE: Visually inspect and palpate the ankle and foot. Use the contralateral foot and ankle as a control.

OUTCOME: If there is ecchymosis and a discrete area of marked swelling on the lateral fifth metatarsal (Fig 13-4E): ◆ **Jones' fracture**

If discrete swelling and tenderness anterior and inferior to the lateral malleolus (Fig 13-4A): ◆ **lateral sprain**

If discrete tenderness on the posterior rim of the lateral malleolus (Fig 13-4A): ◆ **peroneal sprain**

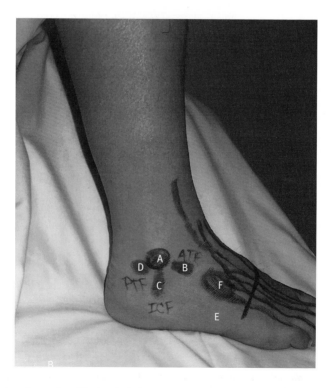

Figure 13-4 Lateral ankle landmarks. A. Lateral malleolus. B. Anterior talofibular ligament (ATF). C. Inferior calcaneofibular ligament (ICF). D. Posterior talofibular ligament (PTF). E. Base of fifth metatarsal. F. Extensor digitorum brevis.

If an area adjacent to the medial malleolus (Fig 13-5A) is tender and swollen:
- ◆ medial sprain
- ◆ syndesmotic sprain, that is, severe lateral sprain

Perform anterior drawer test

PROCEDURE: Have the patient sit with the plantar aspect of his or her foot on your thigh, with the ankle in 0 degrees of plantarflexion. Grasp the patient's distal tibia with one hand and the patient's posterior heel (calcaneus) with the other hand. Apply an anterior force on the calcaneus (Fig 13-6). Repeat on the contralateral side for control.

OUTCOME: If no anterior shift/movement of the calcaneus under the tibia:
- ◆ normal

If the anterior shift of the calcaneus under the tibia is >5 mm:
- ◆ severe ankle sprain (anterior and lateral ligaments damaged)

Perform talar tilt test

PROCEDURE: Have the patient sit with the foot in a neutral position. Hold the midfoot with your thumb on the dorsum and your fingers on the plantar side. Apply gentle passive inversion, especially supination (lateral side of foot down), to the foot and ankle; repeat on other side to compare.

OUTCOME: If the difference between the two ankles is <10 degrees:
- ◆ mild lateral sprain
- ◆ normal

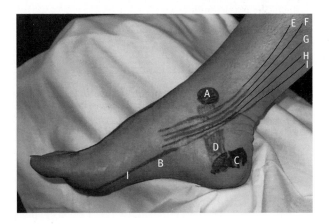

Figure 13-5 Medial foot/ankle: landmarks. A. Medial malleolus. B. Navicular bone. C. Calcaneus bone. D. Flexor retinaculum. E. Tibialis posterior tendon. F. Flexor digitorum tendon. G. Posterior tibial artery. H. Tibialis nerve. I. Flexor hallucis longus tendon.

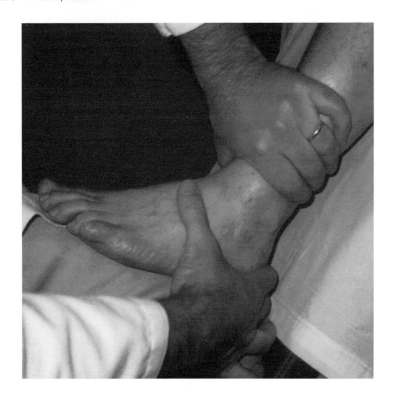

Figure 13-6 Anterior drawer sign. Useful to assess the lateral ligaments of the tibiotalar joint, anterior subluxation (drawer) of the tarsus on the tibia indicative of a moderate to severe sprain.

If the difference between the two ankles is >10 degrees:
- ◆ **moderate to severe lateral sprain**

Perform squeeze test

PROCEDURE: Place your hands around the patient's calf approximately 8 cm inferior to the knee, with your thumbs on the fibula and your fingertips on the medial tibia. Squeeze the leg as if to bring the bones together. Repeat on the contralateral side for a control.

OUTCOME: If there is no pain in the ankle: ◆ **nonsyndesmotic sprain**
If pain in the ankle: ◆ **syndesmotic (very severe) sprain**

Perform external rotation test

PROCEDURE: Place the patient's foot in a neutral position. Passively externally rotate the foot at the ankle. Ask the patient whether this activity increases or decreases the pain.

OUTCOME: If there is no change in pain: ◆ **nonsyndesmotic sprain**
If an increase in pain: ◆ **syndesmotic (very severe) sprain**

Palpate proximal fibula

PROCEDURE: Palpate the lateral knee on the ipsilateral lower extremity, specifically over fibula (see Fig 12-5F, p. 251).

OUTCOME: If there is tenderness to palpation:
◆ **consistent with a concurrent proximal fibular fracture**
If no discrete tenderness over this site:
◆ **no concurrent fracture likely present**

APPROACH TO A PATIENT WITH AN ANTERIOR FOOT COMPLAINT

Visually inspect and palpate forefoot

PROCEDURE: Visually inspect the feet. Use a gloved hand to palpate each foot, paying attention to the joints.

OUTCOME:

Great toe: If there is lateral displacement of the first digit from the site of the first metatarsophalangeal (MTP), often with concurrent corn or callous: ◆ **hallux valgus**
If a firm nodule, which may be tender or nontender over the medial first MTP joint, concurrent to a hallux valgus (Fig 13-7): ◆ **bunion**
If a discrete area of severe swelling tenderness, as well as decreased ROM, and redness in the first MTP:
◆ **trauma**
◆ **podagra**

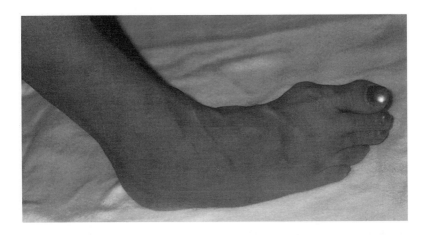

Figure 13-7 Bunion. Marked hallux valgus with an exostosis on medial first metatarsophalangeal joint.

If tenderness over the dorsum of the first MTP (see Fig 13-3):
◆ **turf toe (extensor hallucis longus sprain)**
If tenderness on plantar first metatarsal head, specifically the distal part that articulates with the base of the proximal phalanx:
◆ **flexor hallucis longus tendonitis (sesamoiditis)**

Other toes: If one or more toes have MTP extension contracture, posterior interphalangeal (PIP) flexion contracture, and dorsal interphalangeal (DIP) either flexion or extension contracture:
◆ **hammertoe**
If there is dorsal subluxation of the phalanx at the MTP joint such that the tip of the toe is elevated above any surface on which the foot rests, with the toes spread apart: ◆ **cock-up toes**
If tenderness in the plantar aspect of the forefoot directly over the heads of the metatarsal bones, with a callus over the affected metatarsal heads: ◆ **metatarsalgia**
If tenderness on the dorsal aspect of the metatarsal heads, especially on the second or third digit:
◆ **metatarsal stress fracture**
If tenderness specific to the dorsal aspect of the second or third metatarsal head: ◆ **Freiberg's infarction**
If burning-type dysthetic tenderness on the plantar surfaces of the proximal aspect of the third and fourth toes about the MTP joints: ◆ **Morton's neuroma**
If there are swelling, tenderness, and ecchymosis of the phalanx:
◆ **phalangeal fracture**

Squeeze transverse arch
PROCEDURE: The examiner places a squeeze on the transverse arch on the forefoot by placing pressure on it with the thumb and third digit (Fig 13-8).

OUTCOME: If tenderness is greater on the dorsal side:
◆ **metatarsal stress fracture**
If tenderness is greater on the plantar aspect: ◆ **metatarsalgia**
If tingling and dysthesia: ◆ **Morton's neuroma**

Perform passive great toe flexion
PROCEDURE: With foot and toes in neutral position, passively flex the great toe; ask patient if any tenderness develops.

OUTCOME: If increased pain over the dorsal great toe:
◆ **turf toe (extensor hallucis longus tendonitis)**
If no changes or no pain: ◆ **normal**

Perform passive great toe extension
PROCEDURE: With foot and toes in neutral position, passively extend the great toe; ask patient if any tenderness develops.

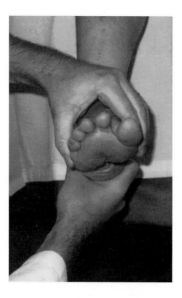

Figure 13-8 Transverse arch squeeze test. Examiner squeezes the forefoot to accentuate the transverse arch. Pain from metatarsalgia or Morton's neuroma will increase on the plantar and dorsal aspects, respectively.

OUTCOME: If increased pain over the plantar great toe:
- **sesamoiditis (flexor hallucis longus tendonitis)**

If no changes or no pain: ◆ **normal**

APPROACH TO A PATIENT WITH LATERAL MIDFOOT/ANKLE PAIN

Palpate lateral ankle and foot

PROCEDURE: Visually inspect the feet. Use a gloved hand to palpate the lateral structures of each foot and ankle.

OUTCOME: If there are swelling and tenderness anterior and/or inferior to the lateral malleolus (see Fig 13-4A):
- **lateral sprain**
- **fibular (distal) fracture**

If there is tenderness at the base of the fifth metatarsal:
- **peroneus brevis sprain**

If tenderness of the fifth metatarsal, several centimeters distal to the base: ◆ **Jones' fracture**

If tenderness at the posterior lateral malleolus:
- **peroneus sprain**

Perform anterior drawer test: See under Approach to a patient with foot/ankle trauma.

Perform talar tilt test: See under Approach to a patient with foot/ankle trauma.

APPROACH TO A PATIENT WITH A PLANTAR FOOT COMPLAINT

Inspect and palpate plantar aspect of foot

PROCEDURE: Visually inspect the structures of the plantar foot. Use a gloved hand to palpate the structures, starting with the great toe and palpating proximally and laterally.

OUTCOME: If there is lateral deviation of the great toe with a prominent first MTP (see Fig 13-7): ◆ **hallux valgus**
If thickening of the skin on plantar foot: ◆ **callus**
If tenderness over the plantar aspect of the metatarsal heads:
◆ **metatarsalgia**
If there is unilateral, ipsilateral loss of longitudinal arch (flatfoot) with dorsal foot swelling: ◆ **deep foot cellulitis**
If flattening of the arch of the foot: ◆ **pes planus**
If tenderness over the plantar/medial aspects of the foot, starting at the anterior calcaneus: ◆ **plantar fasciitis**
If tenderness at the anterior distal plantar aspect of the calcaneus: ◆ **subcalcaneal bursitis**

Palpate plantar aspect with passive toe flexion

PROCEDURE: Directly palpate the central plantar aspect of the foot before and during passive flexion of the toes.

OUTCOME: If tenderness increases: ◆ **plantar fasciitis**
If tenderness does not increase: ◆ **another diagnosis**

Perform passive great toe extension: As in Approach to the anterior foot.

APPROACH TO A PATIENT WITH POSTERIOR HEEL/FOOT PAIN

Inspect joints and structures of heel and posterior foot

PROCEDURE: Visually inspect the structures of the heel. Use a gloved hand to palpate the heel, starting with the Achilles tendon and moving inferiorly to the base of the calcaneus. Use the contralateral side for control.

OUTCOME: If there are tenderness and swelling deep to the Achilles tendon, between the Achilles tendon and calcaneus:
◆ **retrocalcaneal bursitis**
If diffuse tenderness and even palpable swelling within the Achilles tendon: ◆ **Achilles tendonitis**
If a palpable gap in the Achilles tendon: ◆ **Achilles tendon tear**
If tenderness in the posterior tibialis tendon as it enters the foot immediately posterior to the medial malleolus under the flexor retinaculum: ◆ **tibialis tendonitis, posterior**

Check for Simmonds' sign

PROCEDURE: Have the patient lie in a prone position with the legs extended at the knees and the distal halves of the legs over the side of the examining table. Gently but firmly squeeze the mid-distal calf musculature. Visually inspect the passive movement of the foot and ankle. Use the contralateral lower extremity as a control.

OUTCOME: If the foot passively plantarflexes: ◆ **normal**
If foot does not passively plantarflex:
- ◆ **Achilles tendon tear**
- ◆ **gastrocnemius tear**

Check for Thompson's sign

PROCEDURE: Have the patient kneel on a chair with the feet extended over the edge. Squeeze the calf and forcefully push it in a cephalad direction (Fig 13-9). Visually inspect the passive activity of the foot at the ankle. Use the contralateral leg as a control.

OUTCOME: If the foot passively plantarflexes: ◆ **normal**
If foot does not passively plantarflex:
- ◆ **Achilles tendon tear**
- ◆ **gastrocnemius tear**

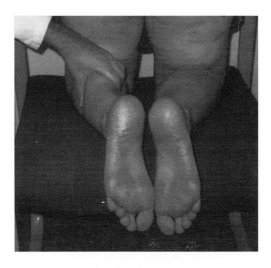

Figure 13-9 Thompson's test. Squeeze the gastrocnemius muscle to assess the integrity of the Achilles tendon. Here foot is plantarflexed with the test and thus is normal.

APPROACH TO A PATIENT WITH MEDIAL ANKLE/FOOT PAIN

Palpate midfoot structures

PROCEDURE: Palpate the structures of the plantar aspect and midfoot (see Fig 13-5). Use the contralateral side as a control.

OUTCOME: If there are tenderness and swelling inferior to the medial malleolus (see Fig 13-5A):
- ◆ **medial ankle sprain**
- ◆ **severe lateral sprain**

If there is tenderness over the navicular tuberosity (see Fig 13-5B): ◆ **navicular tuberosity irritation**

If tenderness posterior and inferior to the medial malleolus, radiating from the medial arch to the medial great toe under the flexor retinaculum: ◆ **flexor hallucis longus tendonitis**

If there are tenderness and swelling in the medial midfoot with pes planus after crush or fall injury: ◆ **Lisfranc's fracture**

If there is tenderness over the medial and plantar aspects of the foot, immediately anterior (distal) to the heel: ◆ **plantar fasciitis**

If there are pain and tingling over the medial and plantar aspects of the foot, distal to flexor retinaculum (see Fig 13-5D):
- ◆ **tarsal tunnel syndrome (distal tibialis nerve)**

Palpate plantar aspect of foot, great toe flexed

PROCEDURE: Directly palpate the central plantar aspect of the foot before and during active flexion of the great toe.

OUTCOME: If there is increased tenderness on active flexion:
- ◆ **flexor hallucis longus tendonitis**

If no increased tenderness: ◆ **other diagnosis**

Tinel's sign

PROCEDURE: Use a plexor or finger to tap repeatedly over the posteroinferior aspect of the medial malleolus, that is, over the flexor retinaculum (see Fig 12-5D, p. 251). Ask the patient whether any symptoms develop.

OUTCOME: If there is reproduction of dysesthesia and pain over the medial and plantar foot (Tinel's sign): ◆ **tarsal tunnel syndrome**

If no paresthesia: ◆ **another diagnosis**

If medial plantar pain (Tinel's sign):
- ◆ **jogger's foot of medial plantar nerve**

Perform squeeze test: See under Approach to a patient with foot/ankle trauma.

Perform external rotation test: See under Approach to a patient with foot/ankle trauma.

APPROACH TO A PATIENT WITH LOWER EXTREMITY SWELLING

Inspect and palpate skin

PROCEDURE: Visually inspect and palpate the skin of the affected lower extremity. Use the contralateral lower extremity as a control.

OUTCOME: If there are small, purple, nonblanching vein-like structures in the skin: ◆ **varicosities**

If there is diffuse erythema and/or warmth:
- ◆ **deep venous thrombophlebitis**
- ◆ **superficial venous thrombophlebitis**
- ◆ **cellulitis**

If pitting edema of the lower extremity:
- ◆ **right heart failure**
- ◆ **deep venous thrombophlebitis**
- ◆ **cellulitis**

If a palpable cord in the site of a vein:
- ◆ **superficial venous thrombophlebitis**

If erythema with discrete margin and/or an associated skin ulcer, fissure, or bite: ◆ **cellulitis**

If bilateral, brawny, hyperpigmented skin with medial malleolar ulcers: ◆ **chronic venous insufficiency**

If there are swelling, ecchymosis, tenderness, and a flaccid area in the gastrocnemius: ◆ **gastrocnemius tear**

Check for Thompson's sign: See under Approach to a patient with posterior heel/foot pain.

Check for Simmonds' sign: See under Approach to a patient with posterior heel/foot pain.

Keys to Recording Findings

FOOT/ANKLE

"Unremarkable, normal passive and active ROM, no pain, swelling or tenderness, normal DP/PT pulses, normal sensation"

A. Note active and passive ROM at foot, ankle and toes; document degrees of the motion if abnormal

B. Note pulses at the dorsalis pedis and posterior tibialis, report using grading system:

+++	bounding
++	present
+	barely palpable
o	absent

C.–E. Sites of swelling, pain, tenderness in and about the foot and ankle (C–F)

C.–F. Note and draw on image, C–F, sites of any sensory deficit

G. Toe nail findings

A. ROM of Foot/Ankle

		Degrees	
		Left	Right
Ankle	Dorsiflexion	———	———
	Plantarflexion	———	———
	Eversion	———	———
	Inversion	———	———
Great Toe	Flexion	———	———
	Extension	———	———
Toe(s)	Flexion	———	———
	Extension	———	———

		Grade	
B. Pulse	Dorsalis pedis	———	———
	Posterior tibialis	———	———

C. Dorsal

Left   Right

D. Plantar

E. Lateral

F. Medial

G. Toneail findings

Achilles tendon tear and gastrocnemis tear

Injury of forced dorsiflexion at the ankle with the knee in full extension. Symptoms include acute pain, swelling, and ecchymosis one-third of the way down the calf. The patient has severe pain with attempted running but is able to walk. Signs include a positive Simmonds' test and Thompson's test (see Fig 13-9), with either a palpable gap in the Achilles tendon or flaccid area in the gastrocnemis. Evaluation includes magnetic resonance imaging (MRI) to define the extent of the tear; treatment includes crutches and referral to an orthopedic surgeon.

Achilles tendonitis/enthesitis

Inflammation of the Achilles tendon (gastrocnemius muscle) due to running in boots or hard-soled shoes. Symptoms and signs include tenderness and swelling in the tendon, 3 to 4 cm superior to the calcaneus or immediately adjacent to the insertion of the tendon on the calcaneus, or both. Radiographs are not necessary; treatment is rest and referral to a physical therapist.

Anterior compartment problem

Damage to common peroneal nerve (L5) from compression or fracture of the proximal fibula. Symptoms and signs include paresthesiae on the dorsum of the foot (see Fig 13-3C) and paresis of foot and great toe dorsiflexion; a steppage gait; and atrophy of the anterior compartment leg musculature. Concurrent eversion **(superficial peroneal nerve)** or inversion **(deep peroneal nerve)** weakness may be present. Radiographs of the knee indicated to rule out a proximal fibula fracture. Treatment includes referral to a physical therapist and to a podiatrist for special shoes.

Bunion

Noninfectious inflammation of the bursa on the great toe from ill-fitting shoes. Symptoms and signs include tenderness and swelling over the MTP of the great toe, with concurrent hallus valgus (see Fig 13-7). Radiographs are not necessary; treatment is by referral to a podiatrist and preventive modalities.

Cellulitis: See Chapter 14.

Charcot's joint

Recurrent trauma to the joints of the feet and ankles from severe neuropathy; often related to uncontrolled diabetes mellitus. Symptoms and signs include nontender swelling with a loss of the arch of the foot (rocker-sole), a "bag of bones" consistency of the ankle/foot, increased ROM of the joint, and concurrent sensory loss. Radiographs reveal severe destruction of the joints, with fragmentation and sclerosis. Treatment is by controlling the underlying etiology and referral to an orthopedic surgeon.

Chronic venous insufficiency: See Varicosities.

Cock-up toes

Deviation often as a result of rheumatoid arthritis. Symptoms and signs include dorsal subluxation of phalanx at MTP; toes are spread apart and do not touch floor. Concurrent signs include those of rheumatoid arthritis— nodules and, in hands, swan necking and ulnar deviation. Treatment includes referral to a physical therapist, a rheumatologist, and a podiatrist.

Fibular fracture: See Lateral ankle sprain and Lateral knee (see Chapter 12).

Flexor hallucis longus tendonitis (sesamoiditis)

Injury from repetitive microtrauma of repeated pronation, as in ballet dancing (sur les pointes position). Symptoms and signs include flat foot and pain and tenderness in the medial aspect of the midfoot and onto the plantar aspect of the great toe if sesamoiditis. The pain increases with passive extension or active flexion of the hallux. Radiographs are not necessary. Treatment is by referral to a podiatrist for a pair of hard-soled shoes.

Hallux valgus

Toe deviation often due to ill-fitting shoes. Symptoms and signs include recurrent pain and tenderness over the medial first MTP head with lateral deviation of the great toe (see Fig 13-7); bunions are concurrent. Radiographs are usually not necessary; treatment is by referral to podiatrist.

Hammertoe

Deformity due to ill-fitting shoes. Symptoms and signs include contracture of DIP hyperextension or flexion, PIP flexion, and MTP hyperextension; corns are concurrent. Radiographs are unnecessary; treatment is referral to a podiatrist.

Jogger's foot: See Tarsal tunnel syndrome.

Jones' fracture

Transverse, nondisplaced fracture of the proximal diaphysis of the fifth metatarsal bone. Symptoms and signs include aching pain and swelling of the lateral foot, specifically the fifth metatarsal. Radiographs of foot reveal the fracture. Treatment includes posterior splintage and, as there is a high incidence of malunion, referral to an orthopedic surgeon.

Lateral ankle sprain

Inversion-related damage to lateral ligaments; in order of severity: mild, anterior talofibular ligament; moderate, calcaneofibular ligament; severe, posterior talofibular ligament; common sprain. Symptoms include lateral ankle pain, swelling, and ecchymosis. Mild sprains: Signs include negative anterior drawer sign (see Fig 13-6) and negative talar tilt test. Moderate sprains: Signs include positive anterior drawer sign (see Fig 13-6) with a firm end point and a negative talar tilt test. Severe sprains: Signs include positive anterior drawer test (see Fig 13-6) without an end point and a positive talar tilt test. Palpation of fibula (see Fig 12-5F) must be performed to assess for fibula fracture. The squeeze and external rotation tests must be performed to evaluate for an unstable ankle, that is, syndesmotic tear. Radiographs can rule out **avulsion fractures**. Treatment includes a posterior splint and elective referral to an orthopedic surgeon.

Lisfranc's fracture: See Pes planus (flat foot).

Medial sprain
Eversion-related damage to the deltoid ligament; comprises fewer than 2% of all sprains; most common reason for medial swelling is severe lateral sprain. Symptoms and signs include medial ankle pain and tenderness, decreased ROM of the ankle joint, and significant medial and lateral swelling. The leg squeeze and external rotation tests must be performed to evaluate for an unstable type syndesmotic tear. Radiographs can rule out avulsion fractures. Treatment includes a posterior splint and elective referral to an orthopedic surgeon.

Metatarsal stress fracture (march fracture)
Fracture from repetitive blunt trauma to the plantar forefoot while marching, especially in the "goose-step" manner; risk factors include soft shoes. Symptoms and signs include tenderness over the affected metatarsal head, especially the dorsal side. Radiographs or MRI, or both, may demonstrate a fracture. Treatment includes crutches and referral to a podiatrist.

Metatarsalgia
Nonspecific inflammation of metatarsal heads due to ill-fitting shoes or acute repetitive trauma, for example, polka dancing. Symptoms and signs include tenderness on the plantar metatarsal heads often with concurrent calluses. Radiographs are not necessary; treatment is by referral to a podiatrist for orthosis.

Morton's neuroma
Chronic damage to the third MTP space with neuroma formation from a plantar nerve, often due to uncontrolled diabetes mellitus. Symptoms and signs include burning pain on the plantar surfaces of the proximal aspect of the third and fourth toes around the MTP joints and a positive transverse squeeze sign. Radiographs are not necessary. Treatment is by referral to a podiatrist for orthosis and neuroma resection.

Navicular tuberosity irritation
Inflammation of the navicular tuberosity, often due to ill-fitting shoes. Symptoms and signs include recurrent pain and tenderness at the proximal aspect

of the navicular bone (see Fig 13-5B) but no decreased ankle or foot ROM. Radiographs are unnecessary. Treatment includes wearing athletic support shoes and referral to a physical therapist and podiatrist.

Peroneal brevis sprain

Sprain from trauma to the peroneus muscles or tendon, or both. Symptoms include lateral foot pain and swelling, specific to the base of the fifth metatarsal. Signs include decreased active eversion and swelling and tenderness on the posterior lateral malleolus and the peroneus brevis muscle. Evaluation with radiographs may reveal a concurrent avulsion fracture of the fifth metatarsal base. Treatment includes a posterior splint and referral to an orthopedic surgeon.

Peroneal nerve defect: See Anterior compartment problem.

Pes cavus

Inappropriately high arches due to congenital abnormalities including Friedreich's ataxia.

Pes planus (flat foot)

Flattening of the longitudinal foot arch due to inappropriate stretching of the ligaments and tendons of the plantar aspect of the foot caused by hypotonicity, **Lisfranc's fracture** (fracture of base of second metatarsal with cuneiform disruption), or flexor hallucis longus tendonitis sprain. Symptoms and signs include flat foot and excessive wear on the medial side of the foot. Radiographs are not necessary unless there is antecedent trauma. Generally, treatment is by referral to a podiatrist. Treatment for Lisfranc's fracture includes a posterior splint and urgent referral to an orthopedic surgeon.

Phalangeal fractures

Direct blunt or crush trauma to the toes, most commonly the great and fifth toes. Symptoms and signs include ecchymosis, edema, and tenderness of the affected toe. Radiographs will confirm the diagnosis. Treatment is with buddy splintage of the toes.

Plantar fasciitis

Noninfectious inflammation of the plantar fascia as a result of excessive use in running (as in long-distance/marathon runners). Symptoms and signs include pain and tenderness on the medial and plantar foot, immediately anterior to the heel. The pain is worse in the morning, usually with the first step, but improves through the day. Passive toe flexion increases the pain. Radiographs may reveal osteophyte on the plantar aspect of the calcaneus. Treatment includes rest and, if severe, referral to a podiatrist.

Podagra

Severe pain due to crystal-induced arthritis, that is, gout. Symptoms and signs include acute pain, swelling tenderness, and erythema in the first MTP;

concurrent tophi on auricles or on the extensor tendon sheaths may be present. Treatment includes arthrocentesis if there is concern for infection and colchicine or a nonsteroidal anti-inflammatory drug (NSAID) for pain relief; vexing cases should be referred to a rheumatologist.

Posterior compartment problem, tibialis nerve
Mischief in the posterior compartment, involves the gastrocnemius or tibialis nerve neuropathy; the tibialis nerve is a large branch of the sciatic nerve—almost exclusively derived from S1. The damage is due to trauma, compartment syndrome, diabetes mellitus, vitamin B_{12} deficiency, or lues venereum. Symptoms and signs include weak foot plantarflexion, atrophy of the gastrocnemius, and decreased sensation of the plantar aspect of the foot. The site must be defined and the underlying cause identified; treatment is then directed toward that etiology.

Retrocalcaneal bursitis
Noninfectious inflammation of the superficial bursa adjacent to the Achilles tendon, usually due to wearing high-heeled shoes. Symptoms and signs include pain and tenderness superficial to the Achilles tendon at its insertion on the calcaneus; a supracalcaneal nodule ("pump-bump") is present. Radiographs are unnecessary. Treatment includes proscription of high heels and referral to a podiatrist.

Sesamoiditis: See Flexor hallucis longus tendinitis (sesamoiditis).

Subcalcaneal bursitis (painful heel cushion syndrome)
Rupture of one or more compartments of fat overlying the heel as a result of mild trauma, often due to ill-fitting shoes. Symptoms and signs include tenderness and pain in areas immediately anterior to the calcaneus. Radiographs are not necessary; treatment is symptomatic relief, modification of shoes, and, if refractory, referral to a podiatrist.

Superficial venous thrombophlebitis: See Varicosities.

Syndesmotic sprain: See Lateral ankle sprain.

Tarsal tunnel syndrome
Entrapment of the posterior tibial nerve (S1) in the tarsal tunnel (under the flexor retinaculum, which is inferior posterior to the medial malleolus). Symptoms and signs include paresthesiae on the plantar side of the foot, paresis of toe adduction and abduction, and a positive Tinel's sign at the flexor retinaculum (see Fig 13-5D). Jogger's foot is a variant in which the medial plantar branch is involved; thus, paresthesia, pain, and tingling is isolated to the medial plantar skin (see Fig 13-5I). Treatment includes NSAIDs and referral to a podiatrist.

Turf toe/great toe sprain

Sprain of the tendon of the extensor hallucis longus. Symptoms and signs include marked decrease in the ROM of the great toe with marked pain, tenderness, and swelling on the dorsum of the great toe (see Fig 13-3D) at the MTP. Radiographs will be unremarkable. Treatment includes buddy splintage and referral to a podiatrist.

Varicosities

Dilation of the venous structures of a particular area of the body, usually the lower extremities. Varicosities are due to chronic venous hypertension and are common with increasing age, right heart failure, and pregnancy. Symptoms and signs include modest edema and dilated purple veins that may be serpiginous; concurrent hyperpigmentation and superficial ulcerations with a loss of hair (manifestations of **venous insufficiency**) are common; a painful, tender cord in a vein site indicates superficial thrombophlebitis. Treatment includes elevation, support stockings, and, if superficial thrombophlebitis is present, NSAIDs. Referral to a general surgeon may be indicated.

CHAPTER 14
Dermatology

Visually inspect and palpate skin lesions

PROCEDURE: Visually inspect and describe any lesions. Use a gloved hand to palpate the lesions.

OUTCOME: If there is a colored lesion <1 cm without induration, elevation, or depression: ◆ **macule (freckle)**

If colored lesion <1 cm with induration and elevation (Plate 29): ◆ **papule**

If colored lesion >1 cm without induration, elevation, or depression (Fig 14-1): ◆ **patch**

If colored lesion >1 cm with induration and elevation (Fig 14-2): ◆ **plaque**

If palpable, dome-shaped lesion >1 cm in the dermis or subcutaneous tissue: ◆ **nodule**

If there is an elevated, clear fluid–containing lesion <1 cm (Fig 14-3): ◆ **vesicle**

If elevated, clear fluid–containing lesion (a blister) >1 cm (Fig 14-4): ◆ **bulla**

If elevated, purulent fluid–containing lesion, any size: ◆ **pustule**

If there is a palpable white or red lesion with peau d'orange and pruritus ("hives"; see Plate 25): ◆ **urticaria**

If superficial loss of skin tissue involving the epidermis: ◆ **erosion/abrasion**

If deep loss of skin tissue involving the dermis: ◆ **ulcer**

If deep abrasion in which tissue is ripped/torn from a deeper level: ◆ **avulsion**

If deep, narrow wound, such as the result of a bite: ◆ **puncture**

If longitudinal crack in skin through the epidermis into the dermis: ◆ **fissure**

If one or more longitudinal erosions, ulcers, or fissures from scratching: ◆ **excoriation**

If longitudinal cut in the skin: ◆ **laceration**

If there is increased skin thickness with accentuation of skin contour, woody by palpation: ◆ **lichenified**

If red discoloration to the skin ("rubor"): ◆ **erythema**

If there is a loss of skin substance, involving one, two, or all three skin layers, and/or decreased pigmentation: ◆ **atrophy**

If there are flesh-colored flakes adjacent and/or superficial to a lesion (see Plate 30): ◆ **scales**

291

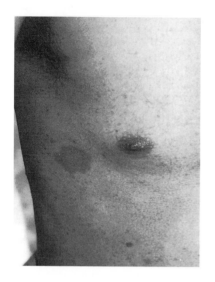

Figure 14-1 Macules and patch. Skin of the right chest: multiple macules (freckles) and a solitary nonpalpable patch >1 cm in size (café au lait spot).

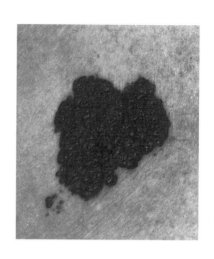

Figure 14-2 Plaque. Pigmented palpable lesion >1 cm in size on the left shoulder.

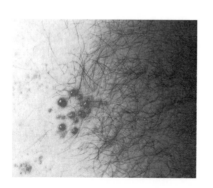

Figure 14-3 Cluster of vesicles. A specific cluster in a patient with herpes zoster in this dermatome.

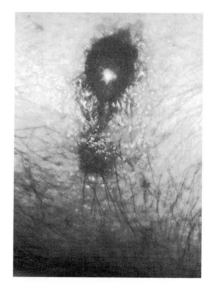

Figure 14-4 Bulla. Fluid-filled structure >1 cm in size, trauma related.

If there is a ring pattern to a rash (see Plate 31):
    ◆ **annular pattern**
If series of concentric rings to a rash (Plate 32):
    ◆ **target pattern**
If cluster of lesions (see Fig 14-3): ◆ **herpetiform pattern**

Advanced Examination

APPROACH TO A PATIENT WITH PURPLE LESIONS

Inspect and palpate skin

PROCEDURE: Visually inspect the skin. Use a gloved hand to palpate the skin.

OUTCOME:

Overall: If there are linear dilated vessels, single or grouped, on the face, trunk, and/or lower extremities: ◆ **telangiectasia**

If there is a spider-like dilated vessel that blanches with pressure on the upper trunk, neck, and/or shoulders:
  ◆ **spider angioma**

If nonblanching macule (Plate 33): ◆ **petechiae**

If nonblanching patch (Plate 28): ◆ **ecchymosis**

If nonblanching, palpable or unpalpable small patch (see Plate 27): ◆ **purpura**

If nonblanching papule, 3 to 5 mm (Plate 29):
  ◆ **cherry/capillary hemangiomas**

If multiple nonblanching papules/nodules anywhere on the skin surface of a patient with acquired immunodeficiency syndrome (AIDS): ◆ **Kaposi's sarcoma**

If multiple discrete telangiectasiae in the skin, especially on the mucous membranes and digits (Plate 5):
  ◆ **Rendu-Osler-Weber syndrome**

Extremities: If there is a fishnet (reticulated) pattern of mottled, purple-blue patches on the lower extremities and trunk: ◆ **livedo reticularis**

If there are circular macules with yellow-white centers on the proximal palms/soles (Plate 34):
  ◆ **Janeway lesion (see Chapter 4, p. 92)**

If tender purple-red nodules on the palmar aspects of the distal digits: ◆ **Osler's nodes (see Chapter 4, p. 92)**

If nonblanching papules/nodules on the feet in an older individual: ◆ **Kaposi's sarcoma**

If intensely pruritic, often violaceous, polygon-shaped papules/plaques, usually on the lower extremities (Fig 14-5):
  ◆ **lichen planus**

Truncal: If there are multiple patches in the lower abdominal wall:
  ◆ **subcutaneous heparin injection sites**

If there is a large ecchymosis on the unilateral flank (Grey Turner's sign; Fig 14-6): ◆ **retroperitoneal bleed**

If an ecchymosis about the umbilicus (Cullen's sign):
  ◆ **retroperitoneal bleed**

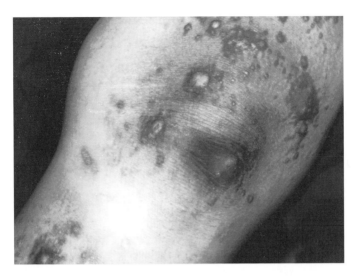

Figure 14-5 Lichen planus. Markedly pruritic papules and plaques, purple to pigmented predominately on extensor surfaces.

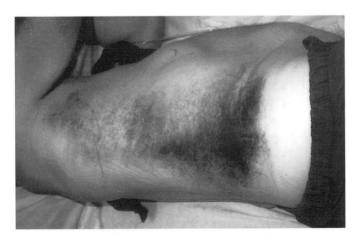

Figure 14-6 Grey Turner's sign. Large ecchymosis on the right flank of this patient with a retroperitoneal bleed.

Place pressure on center of spider angioma

PROCEDURE: Use a cotton-tipped swab to press on the center of the telangiectasia, then release.

OUTCOME: If the lesion collapses (blanches) on pressure, then refills on release of the swab: ◆ **spider angioma**

If there is no collapse: ◆ **telangiectasia**

Inspect purple lesions for Köbner's phenomenon

PROCEDURE: Visually observe if any lesions develop in an area of recent scar or trauma.

OUTCOME: If new lesions develop (Köbner's sign): ◆ **lichen planus**
If there are no new lesions: ◆ **another diagnosis**

APPROACH TO A PATIENT WITH PINK/RED LESIONS

Inspect and palpate lesions

PROCEDURE: Visually inspect and assess the lesions. Use a gloved hand to palpate the lesions. Note their distribution and location.

OUTCOME:

Pruritic: If there is a macerated, well-demarcated, pruritic, moist erythematous rash in intertriginous areas (Fig 14-7): ◆ **tinea cruris**
If patch-like lesion with central clearing and peripheral scales (Plate 31): ◆ **tinea corporis (ringworm)**
If dry, scaly rash in moccasin distribution on the feet with some vesicles, petechiae, and scales (Plate 35):
◆ **tinea pedis (often *Trichophyton rubrum*)**
If macerated, pruritic, wet, erythematous rash with fissuring of the interdigital grooves, especially the fourth space:
◆ **tinea pedis [*Candida* species (spp)]**
If there is an intensely pruritic, linear pattern of papules and even pustules in the finger webs, the toe webs, the elbows, and the groin (Fig 14-8): ◆ **scabies**
If there is an erythematous, scaly, pruritic lesion on one areola and/or nipple: ◆ **Paget's disease of the breast**
If very pruritic patches and plaques with crusting and with

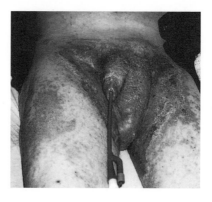

Figure 14-7 Tinea cruris, severe. Macerated rash on the intertriginous areas of groin. Concurrent balanitis and balanoposthitis.

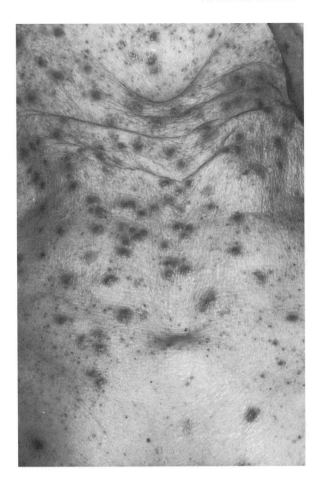

Figure 14-8 Scabies. Multiple markedly pruritic papules and pustules, often in "runs," most commonly in skin folds.

weeping of exudative fluid; some patches are in linear groupings, in an asymmetric distribution, often in one discrete area (e.g., under underpants): ◆ **contact dermatitis**

If lichenified pruritic papules and plaques on the flexor surfaces (Plate 36): ◆ **atopic dermatitis (eczema)**

If there is a mildly pruritic bright red rash, starting on the trunk and spreading to the periphery: ◆ **drug-induced dermatitis**

If diffuse, confluent, flat, warm rash on areas exposed to sun (Plate 37): ◆ **photodermatitis (sunburn)**

If papulosquamous rash, with small fluffy scales, affecting hair

areas, especially eyebrows and head hair (dandruff):
◆ **seborrheic dermatitis**
If there are coin-shaped erythematous plaques with clear centers, with crusting and oozing, in a symmetric distribution on the shoulders, buttocks, and extensor surfaces: ◆ **nummular eczema**
If there is a pigmented-pink rash, with loss of skin appendages on the lower extremities, hyperpigmentation, and pitting edema (Fig 14-9): ◆ **venous stasis dermatitis**

Febrile: If there is an area of painful redness, warmth, and swelling adjacent to a wound; the wound has purulent discharge (Plate 38):
◆ **cellulitis**
If there is a well-demarcated warm, bright red patch, often on the face: ◆ **erysipelas**
If warm patch/plaque with superficial yellow crusting (Plate 39):
◆ **impetigo**

Exanthems: If there is a diffuse evanescent maculopapular rash, with fevers and arthralgia: ◆ **viral exanthem**
If diffuse, lacy then confluent, maculopapular rash on the upper extremities, upper trunk, and face (a "slapped face" appearance), with antecedent fever:
◆ **fifth disease (erythema infectiosum)**
If diffuse, morbilliform (gritty sandpaper) texture on the trunk, back, and upper extremities, with antecedent arthralgia, rhinorrhea, and nonproductive cough:
◆ **rubella**
◆ **rubeola**

Erythema: If there is one flat, red ring with a pale center that is nonpainful and warm and is enlarging centripetally, starting from the site of a tick bite: ◆ **erythema chronicum migrans**
If there are mottled patches over areas chronically exposed to heat, with secondary hyperpigmentation:
◆ **erythema ab igne**
If multiple tender nodules/papules on extensor surfaces of distal extremities, especially lower extremities:
◆ **erythema nodosum**
If multiple wheals and papules, with irregular margins, that may resemble a target (bull's eye) or be confluent or desquamate and are symmetrically distributed on extensor surfaces (Plate 32):
◆ **erythema multiforme**
If multiple discrete, centrally flat patches/plaques with raised peripheries: ◆ **erythema marginatum**

Facial: If there is a chronic diffuse or patchy papular rash on the skin overlying the maxillae, nose, and frontal areas:
◆ **rosacea**
◆ **discoid lupus erythematosus**

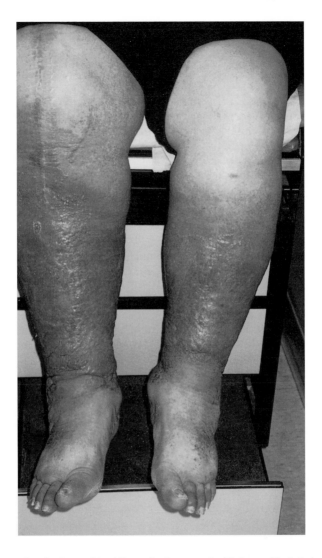

Figure 14-9 Stasis dermatitis, bilateral; pigmented with loss of hair in both lower extremities.

Inspect and palpate nasolabial folds

PROCEDURE: Visually inspect and palpate the nasolabial folds.

OUTCOME: If the nasolabial folds are involved: ◆ **rosacea**
If nasolabial folds are not involved:
◆ **another diagnosis, for example, discoid lupus**

Inspect nose

PROCEDURE: Visually inspect and palpate the nose.

OUTCOME: If diffusely erythematous, indurated, and enlarged (rhino-phyma): ◆ **rosacea**
If only erythematous:
◆ **lupus erythematosus, another diagnosis, for example, lupus**

APPROACH TO A PATIENT WITH CELLULITIS

Inspect and palpate lesions: See under Approach to a patient with pink/red lesions.

Palpate and inspect around cellulitis

PROCEDURE: Palpate the soft tissues about the cellulitis.

OUTCOME: If there is crackling in the subcutaneous tissue:
◆ **crepitus of gas (severe cellulitis)**
If a concurrent fluctuant mass/nodule in the subcutaneous tissue (Fig 14-10): ◆ **furuncle/carbuncle**
If a fissure, cut, or wound in or about the cellulitis:
◆ **potential site of origin of cellulites**
If multiple sites of scars about veins (Fig 14-11): ◆ **tracks**

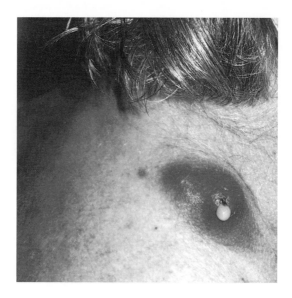

Figure 14-10 Carbuncle, several discrete pus-filled structures interconnected. Here located on the right posterior neck.

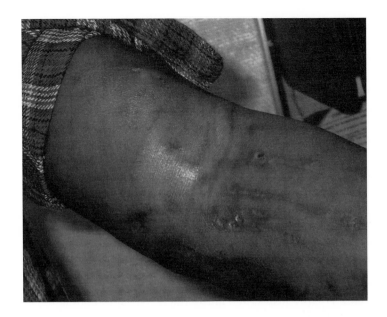

Figure 14-11 Track marks. Scarring and skin breakdown over the veins of arm and antecubital fossa in an intravenous drug abuser.

APPROACH TO A PATIENT WITH A SUSPECTED ERYTHEMA

Inspect and palpate lesions: See under Approach to a patient with pink/red lesions.

Palpate joints

PROCEDURE: Palpate and perform range of motion on the joints of the hands, upper extremities, feet, and lower extremities.

OUTCOME: If there is any evidence of arthritis:
  ◆ **erythema chronicum migrans**
  ◆ **erythema marginatum**
  If no evidence of arthritis: ◆ **nonspecific finding**

Perform cardiac auscultation

PROCEDURE: Auscult the base and apex of the heart, using the diaphragm.

OUTCOME: If there is a new diastolic murmur:
  ◆ **erythema marginatum (rheumatic fever)**
  If any other murmur: ◆ **nonspecific finding**

Examine mucous membranes

PROCEDURE: Visually inspect the mouth and mucous membranes for any desquamation/sloughing.

OUTCOME: If there is sloughing:
- ◆ **erythema multiforme major (Stevens-Johnson syndrome)**

If no involvement: ◆ **erythema multiforme minor**

Determine amount of skin involved in erythema multiforme

PROCEDURE: Visually inspect the extent of skin involvement with the erythema multiforme (Plate 32).

OUTCOME: If there is involvement of >2 discrete areas:
- ◆ **erythema multiforme major**

If involvement of <2 discrete areas:
- ◆ **erythema multiforme minor**

APPROACH TO A PATIENT WITH A SUSPECTED EXANTHEM

Inspect and palpate lesions: See under Approach to a patient with pink/red lesions.

Inspect oral mucosa adjacent to Stensen's duct

PROCEDURE: Visually inspect the mucosa of the mouth opposite the second maxillary molar (i.e., adjacent to Stensen's duct).

OUTCOME: If there is a cluster of whitish macules (Koplik's sign): ◆ **rubeola**

Inspect and palpate lymph nodes

PROCEDURE: Visually inspect and palpate the lymph nodes of the posterior cervical chain (immediately posterior to the sternocleidomastoid), bilaterally.

OUTCOME: If there are enlarged posterior cervical lymph nodes: ◆ **rubella**
If no such nodes: ◆ **another diagnosis**

APPROACH TO A PATIENT WITH NONPIGMENTED, FLESH-COLORED LESIONS

Inspect and palpate flesh-colored lesions

PROCEDURE: Visually inspect the affected skin. Use a gloved hand to palpate the affected skin. Pay attention to distribution and other features of the lesion.

OUTCOME: If there are multiple, nontender, pedunculated papules about the trunk, back, and often the face and genital areas (Fig 14-12):
- ◆ **molluscum contagiosum**

If nontender, well-circumscribed, coarse-textured, punctate black dots on fingers, feet, or toes:
- ◆ **common warts**
- ◆ **plantar warts**

If nontender, coarse-textured, well-circumscribed cauliflower-like papules on mucous membranes of the perianal, vulvar,

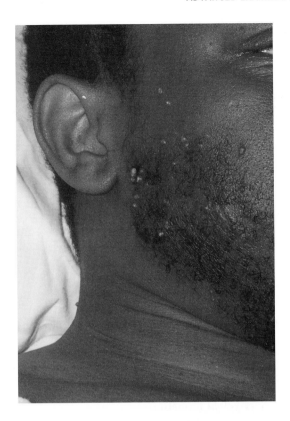

Figure 14-12 Molluscum contagiosum. Face: multiple pedunculated papules, each with a cheesy central core.

penile, or glans area or of the undersurface of the foreskin:
♦ **condyloma acuminatum**
If there is a solitary, nontender, translucent plaque/papule with telangiectases embedded: ♦ **basal cell carcinoma**
If solitary, nontranslucent papule/plaque with central necrotic ulceration and peripheral erythema that may have hyperkeratinized core:
♦ **squamous cell carcinoma (Fig 14-13)**
♦ **keratoacanthoma (Fig 14-14)**
If there are multiple, sandpaper-like, nontranslucent, scaly papules (Fig 14-15): ♦ **actinic keratosis (solar keratosis)**
If there is a keratinized horn (Fig 14-15):
♦ **actinic keratosis**
♦ **squamous cell carcinoma**
If there are multiple nontender, soft, pedunculated nodules:
♦ **neurofibromas**

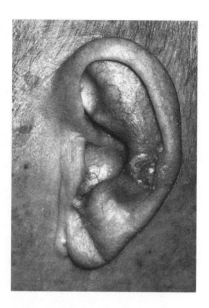

Figure 14-13 Squamous cell carcinoma, auricle. Painless ulcer on the auricle.

If multiple nontranslucent, pedunculated papules (<2 mm in size) on the neck, trunk, and back: ◆ **acrochordons (skin tags)**
If papule/nodules in and/or adjacent to a scar:
◆ **keloid formation**
If multiple tender/nontender, firm nodules on the face, trunk, and back: ◆ **nodular/cystic acne vulgaris**

Determine distribution of lesions

PROCEDURE: Visually observe and define the distribution of the lesions on the face/head.

OUTCOME: If located above a line from the angles of the mouth to the ear lobes: ◆ **basal cell carcinoma**
If located below a line from the angles of the mouth to the earlobes (including the dorsum of the hands and arms; see Fig 14-13):
◆ **squamous cell carcinoma**
◆ **actinic keratosis**

APPROACH TO A PATIENT WITH HYPOPIGMENTED LESIONS IN SKIN AND HAIR

Inspect and palpate areas of hypopigmentation

PROCEDURE: Visually inspect the skin. Use a gloved hand to palpate the skin.

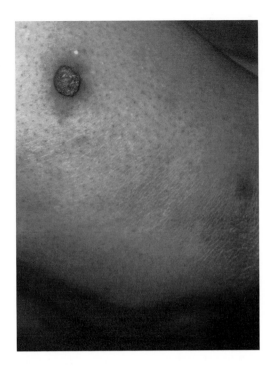

Figure 14-14 Keratoacanthoma. Nontender ulcerating nodule with a keratotic plug. Benign lesion, difficult to differentiate from squamous cell carcinoma on inspection alone.

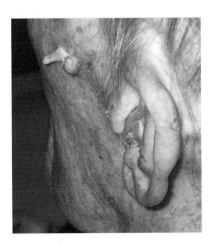

Figure 14-15 Hypertrophic actinic keratosis. Cutaneous horns of keratin present in this 101-year-old man.

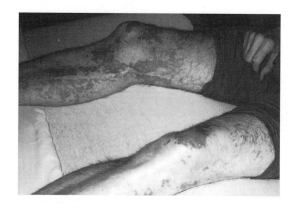

Figure 14-16 Vitiligo. Large areas of pigment loss in this individual.

OUTCOME: If there are well-circumscribed patches of no pigment involving the palms, soles, perioral areas, and genital areas (Fig 14-16): ◆ **vitiligo**
If there is premature graying of some hair, specifically the eyelashes: ◆ **poliosis**
If loss of pigment in macules on the back and trunk:
◆ **tinea versicolor**

Perform Wood's lamp test

PROCEDURE: Visually inspect the affected skin with a Wood's lamp.

OUTCOME: If fluorescent golden: ◆ **tinea versicolor**
If fluorescent coral red: ◆ **erythrasma**
If fluorescent green: ◆ *Pseudomonas* **spp superinfection**

APPROACH TO A PATIENT WITH PIGMENTED LESIONS

Inspect and palpate pigmented lesions

PROCEDURE: Visually inspect and palpate the lesions.

OUTCOME: If the lesions are <5 mm with sharp, well-defined boundaries and uniform pigment: ◆ **benign nevus**
If there are patches on the dorsum of the hands:
◆ **lentigines ("liver spots")**
If multiple small macules over the face and trunk (see Fig 14-1):
◆ **ephelides (freckles)**
If the skin is diffusely brown with tan lines: ◆ **suntan**
If there are waxy, nonpruritic, light to dark brown papules/plaques on the trunk, proximal extremities, and back (Fig 14-17): ◆ **seborrheic keratosis**
If there is a marked increase in number, distribution, and size of seborrheic keratosis: ◆ **Leser-Trélat sign**

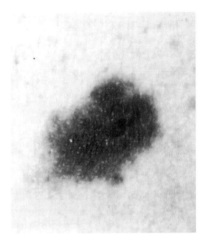

Figure 14-17 Seborrheic keratosis. Low back, multiple pigmented lesions, each with irregular borders, palpable and "stuck on" in appearance.

Figure 14-18 Malignant melanoma: ABCDE descriptors: A. **A**symmetric. B. **B**orders irregular. C. **C**olors multiple. D. **D**iameter >5 mm. E. **E**levated or not, here quite palpable.

If the lesions are >5 mm with ill-defined boundaries and disorganized pigment (often has pink hues) (Fig 14-18, note A, B, C, D, E classes on legend):
- ◆ **dysplastic nevus**
- ◆ **malignant melanoma**

If there are deeply pigmented, velvety plaques in axillae and other intertriginous areas: ◆ **acanthosis nigricans**

If one or more pigmented patches and macules are present in both axillae (Crowe's sign): ◆ **neurofibromatosis**

If there are pigmented, atrophic patches on the anterior surfaces of tibial skin: ◆ **pretibial pigmented patches of diabetes mellitus**

If there are multiple pigmented macules and patches on the tips of digits: ◆ **Peutz-Jeghers syndrome (see Chapter 2, p. 37)**

If there is a focal increase in brown pigment over scars, glans, and areolae: ◆ **Addison's disease**

If pigment changes on the lower extremities begin on toes and extend proximally with alopecia and varicosities: ◆ **venous stasis**
If there are nontender streaks of yellow papules adjacent to the eyelids: ◆ **xanthelasma (see Fig 3-6)**
If pigments from toes proximally with alopecia: ◆ **venous stasis**

APPROACH TO A PATIENT WITH ULCERATING/EROSIVE SKIN LESIONS

Inspect and palpate ulcers/erosions

PROCEDURE: Visually inspect the lesions. Use a gloved hand to palpate the lesions. (Also see Approach to a patient with bullous lesions.)

OUTCOME: If there are painful, necrotizing ulcers with irregular borders, red bases, and pustular material that may be large and may involve the face and upper and/or lower extremities (Fig 14-19):
  ◆ **pyoderma gangrenosum**
If ulcers on the distal lower extremities:
  ◆ **neurotropic ulcers**
  ◆ **arterial insufficiency ulcers (Plate 24)**
  ◆ **venous stasis ulcers**
If ulcers of various depth over pressure sites on the back, hips, lateral malleolus, heel, or lateral edge of foot:
  ◆ **decubital ulcers (Fig 14-20)**
If there is a painless plaque with ulcer on a mucous membrane site such as on the penis, vulva, oral mucosa, cervix, or uvula:
  ◆ **chancre**
If solitary plaque with central necrotic ulceration and peripheral erythema: ◆ **squamous cell carcinoma (see Fig 14-13)**
If deeply ulcerated, relatively painless lesion on the face, especially the nose: ◆ **basal cell carcinoma (rodent ulcer)**

Perform sensory examination of feet

PROCEDURE: See Chapter 7, under Basic Examination. Test vibratory sensation, and test fine touch sensation using monofilaments. Perform the examinations on the dorsal foot (see Fig 13-1C) and the plantar foot, and repeat on the contralateral foot for comparison.

OUTCOME: If there is decreased sensation: ◆ **neurotropic ulcer**
If normal sensation: ◆ **nonspecific finding**

Palpate foot pulses

PROCEDURE: Use the tips of the second and third digits to palpate the dorsal aspect of the skin gently in a line proximal to the crease between

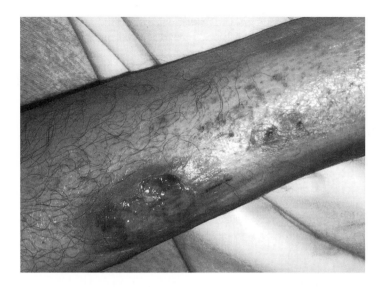

Figure 14-19 Pyoderma gangrenosum. Lower extremity, painful necrotic ulcer with modest purulence present. Patient has an underlying ulcerative colitis.

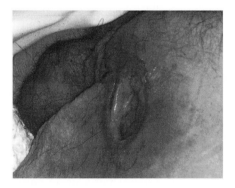

Figure 14-20 Decubitus ulcer. Right buttock, deep ulcer with surrounding cellulitis, in a bed-ridden patient.

the first and second toes (dorsalis pedis artery; see Fig 13-1B). Then palpate at a site immediately posterior and inferior to the medial malleolus (posterior tibialis artery; see Fig 13-7G). Use your pulses or the patient's contralateral extremity as a control.

OUTCOME: If one or both pulses are palpable:
- ◆ **decreased likelihood of arterial insufficiency**

If neither pulse is palpable:
- ◆ **increased likelihood of arterial insufficiency**

Describe location and number of appendages (such as hair)

PROCEDURE: Visually inspect the skin and appendages of the affected extremity. Use the patient's contralateral extremity or your own extremity for comparison.

OUTCOME: If there is a marked decrease in the amount of hair in the affected area: ◆ **arterial insufficiency**

If moderate to marked amount of nonblanching, bluish discoloration: ◆ **venous stasis**

If there are multiple serpiginous, palpable, nontender, purple, distended veins in the distal lower extremities:
- ◆ **varicosities of venous stasis**

APPROACH TO A PATIENT WITH PLAQUE AND PLAQUE-LIKE LESIONS

Inspect and palpate lesions

PROCEDURE: Visually inspect the lesions and assess their location and distribution. Use a gloved hand to palpate the lesions.

OUTCOME: If multiple erythematous plaques with scales on extensor surfaces:
- ◆ **psoriasis (Fig 14-21; Plate 30)**
- ◆ **nummular eczema**

If oval scaling lesions on the trunk and back with central clearing (Plate 31): ◆ **tinea corporis**

If erythematous patches and plaques with scales on flexor surfaces: ◆ **atopic dermatitis (eczema; Plate 36)**

If reddish-yellow atrophic plaques on the anterior surfaces of tibial skin and the dorsal surfaces of the feet:
- ◆ **necrobiosis lipoidica diabeticorum**

If violaceous papules/plaques of polygonal shape with whitish reticulated pattern (Wickstram's striae) often on lower extremities (see Fig 14-5): ◆ **lichen planus**

If there is hard, woody thickening of keratin on the soles of the feet and/or toes: ◆ **callus (tyloma)**

If hard thickening of keratin on the dorsum of the feet and/or toes: ◆ **corn (heloma)**

Inspect nail plates

PROCEDURE: Visually inspect the nail plates using both direct and oblique light sources.

OUTCOME: If there is nail pitting: ◆ **psoriasis**

If no nail pitting: ◆ **another diagnosis**

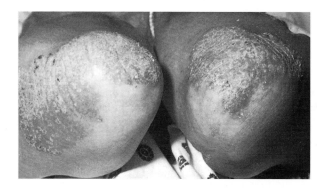

Figure 14-21 Psoriasis. Plaques with silvery scales on the extensor surfaces of the upper extremities.

Check for Köbner's sign

PROCEDURE: Visually inspect and palpate the areas about recent scarring and/or skin trauma. Look for new lesions similar to the original ones.

OUTCOME: If new lesions develop (Köbner's phenomenon):
- ◆ psoriasis
- ◆ lichen planus

If no new lesions develop: ◆ another diagnosis

Remove a scale from plaque

PROCEDURE: Using a gloved hand, gently remove one of the scales from one of the lesions.

OUTCOME: If there is no bleeding or there is one large site of bleeding:
- ◆ atopic dermatitis (eczema)
- ◆ nummular eczema

If there are multiple punctate sites of bleeding (Auspitz's sign; Plate 30): ◆ psoriasis

APPROACH TO A PATIENT WITH URTICARIA

Inspect skin and take vital signs

PROCEDURE: Inspect the patient's skin and check the patient's vital signs (see Chapter 1, under Basic Examination).

OUTCOME: If there is evidence of respiratory distress with stridor:
- ◆ angioedema

If the patient is hypotensive: ◆ **anaphylaxis**
If short of breath with audible wheezes:
◆ **anaphylaxis/status asthmaticus**

Test dermatographism

PROCEDURE: Use a fingertip or a sterile cotton-tipped swab to gently scratch a number or word onto the patient's skin.

OUTCOME: If there is no rash and the writing is not readable: ◆ **normal**
If erythematous tracing of the writing:
◆ **dermatographism (of urticaria)**

Inspect lips

PROCEDURE: Examine the patient's lips and oral mucosa.

OUTCOME: If there is diffuse swelling of the lips and the tissues of the face and neck (see Fig 2-8, p. 15): ◆ **angioedema**

APPROACH TO A PATIENT WITH VESICULAR LESIONS

Inspect skin about vesicles and pattern of distribution

PROCEDURE: Visually inspect the areas adjacent to the vesicles. Use a gloved hand to palpate these areas.

OUTCOME: If there is a unilateral single cluster of vesicles on perioral areas, including the lips (see Fig 2-6, p. 13): ◆ **herpes labialis**
If unilateral or bilateral cluster of vesicles on the genital mucosa (see Fig 16-4, p. 363): ◆ **herpes genitalis**
If there are erythema and vesicles in the region of a unilateral single dermatome (Fig 14-22): ◆ **herpes zoster (shingles)**
If there are multiple vesicles on the trunk, face, proximal extremities, abdomen, or back (Fig 14-23), with antecedent crops of vesicles, fever, malaise, or rhinorrhea:
◆ **varicella (chickenpox)**
If intense erythema, pruritus, and crusting grouped linearly, usually on the legs, abdomen, or feet:
◆ **contact dermatitis (poison ivy)**

APPROACH TO A PATIENT WITH BULLOUS LESIONS

Note: Test for Nikolsky's sign should *never* be performed.

Locate and describe size of bullae and vesicles on skin and mucous membranes

PROCEDURE: Visually assess the location and size of the vesicles and/ or bullous lesions. Note the involvement of the mucous membranes.

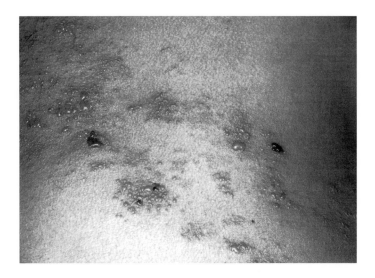

Figure 14-22 Herpes zoster. One dermatome, classic clusters of vesicles. Painful with dysesthesia in the affected dermatome.

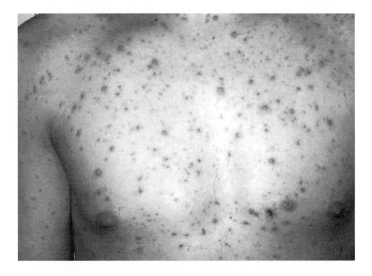

Figure 14-23 Varicella (chickenpox). Multiple vesicles and pustules in crops on the face, trunk, and back.

OUTCOME: If the vesicles/lesions are very superficial and so fragile that they are rarely if ever intact, and there are concurrent erosions with ragged edges on the face, scalp, chest, and back, with no associated erythema at the bases:
◆ **pemphigus vulgaris/foliaceus**
If there are tense, round lesions on the skin, with significant inflammation and erythema at the bases (Fig 14-24):
◆ **bullous pemphigoid**
If bullae at a site of significant, recurrent trauma:
◆ **mechanical trauma bullae**
If bullae after exposure to heat, steam, or very hot water:
◆ **second-degree burn (usually a scald)**
If bullous lesions at a site of exposure to severe cold (on hands, feet, ears, etc.) (Fig 14-25): ◆ **second-degree frostbite**
If there is diffuse tender erythema that evolves into large thin-roofed bullae, then into superficial, large erosions, beginning at

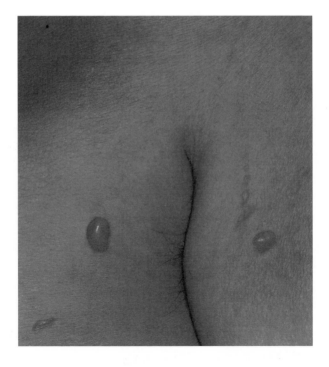

Figure 14-24 Bullous pemphigoid. Tense, discrete blisters. The stability of these lesions shows the depth of the cleavage plane.

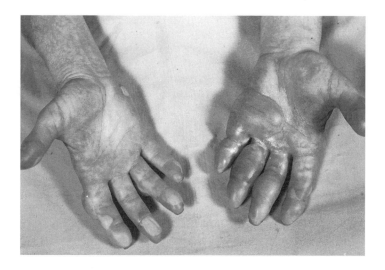

Figure 14-25 Frostbite, severe. Multiple blisters developed after the patient was exposed to the −25°F temperature of the Wisconsin winter without appropriate gloves.

the knees and elbows (i.e., sites stretched with flexion), with no involvement of the palms and soles:
> ◆ **staphylococcal scalded skin syndrome (SSS syndrome)**
If erythema multiforme that evolves into large thin-roofed bullae, then into erosions on extensor surfaces and acral areas, particularly the palms and soles (possible mucous membrane involvement):
> ◆ **erythema multiforme major (Stevens-Johnson syndrome)**
If clear bullae in an area of warm erythema that rupture with a light thin crusting (Plate 39): ◆ **bullous impetigo**
If there is significant oral mucous membrane involvement:
> ◆ **pemphigus vulgaris**
> ◆ **erythema multiforme major**
If the palms and soles are involved:
> ◆ **erythema multiforme major**

APPROACH TO A PATIENT WITH PUSTULES/PURULENT LESIONS

Inspect distribution and features of pustules
PROCEDURE: Visually inspect and palpate the lesions. Describe their distribution and the associated features of the pustules.

OUTCOME: If adjacent to/contiguous with the bases of hair follicles:
◆ **folliculitis**
If there is tender, fluctuant, erythematous nodule on the face, back, or trunk: ◆ **furuncle**
If there are several interconnected tender, fluctuant, erythematous nodules on the back of the neck (see Fig 14-10):
◆ **carbuncle**
If one or more painful, erythematous pustules in the hair follicles of the face: ◆ **tinea barbae**
If there are multiple pustules and comedones on the face and/or back: ◆ **acne vulgaris**
If multiple pustules, all of which were vesicles, concurrent to a new crop of vesicles: ◆ **varicella (chickenpox; see Fig 14-23)**
If multiple, very pruritic pustules and papules about the skin folds, for example, gluteal folds, web spaces between digits (see Fig 14-8): ◆ **scabies**

APPROACH TO A PATIENT WITH HAIR LOSS

Inspect hair pattern and hair loss pattern
PROCEDURE: Visually inspect the hair pattern on the patient's head, face, axilla, body, and pubic area.

OUTCOME: If there is patchy loss of head hair, with no other areas of hair loss:
◆ **tinea capitis (*Trichophyton* spp)**
◆ **alopecia areata**
◆ **trichotillomania**
If loss of temporal and occipital hair: ◆ **androgenic alopecia**
If complete loss of head hair: ◆ **alopecia totalis**
If complete loss of all body hair: ◆ **alopecia universalis**

Perform Wood's lamp test
PROCEDURE: Visually inspect under a Wood's lamp any hair that has recently fallen out and/or that is adjacent to the site of alopecia.

OUTCOME: If the hair is fluorescent green: ◆ **tinea capitis**
If hair is not fluorescent: ◆ **other etiology of hair loss**

APPROACH TO A PATIENT WITH FINGERNAIL AND/OR TOENAIL COMPLAINTS

Inspect the nail plate, nail bed, and nail folds
PROCEDURE: Visually inspect the nail plate, nail bed, and nail folds.

OUTCOME:

Nail plate: If there is one or more transverse furrows, 1 to 2 mm wide, in the plate: ◆ **Beau's lines**

If the plate is thickened and green:
- ◆ *Pseudomonas* **superinfection of nail plate**

If there is partial separation of the plate from the bed, starting at the distal edge and proceeding proximally:
- ◆ **onycholysis (Plummer's nails) of hyperthyroidism**

If the entire plate is separated from the bed, starting proximally and proceeding distally (Fig 14-26):
- ◆ **onychomadesis (nail shedding)**

If plate is thickened to 4 to 5 mm, discolored, brittle, and easily fractured: ◆ **onychauxis**

If there is a grossly elongated nail that may assume a "ram's horn" configuration (Fig 14-27): ◆ **onychogryposis**

If thickened, brittle plate (actual destruction of the plate occurs, starting on the sides): ◆ **onychomycosis**

If there are multiple small (pinhead to pintip in size) shallow depressions/pits within the plate: ◆ **psoriasis**

If there is a concave plate (flared upward) (Fig 14-28):
- ◆ **koilonychia of iron-deficiency anemia**

Nail bed: If one or more longitudinal red lines are present in the beds (see Plate 34):
- ◆ **splinter hemorrhages of trauma, psoriasis, or infectious endocenditis (see Chapter 4, p. 92)**

If painful red-purple area in the bed (see Fig 14-26):
- ◆ **subungual hematoma**

If pair of white transverse bands in the beds, especially on the second, third, and fourth digits: ◆ **Muercke's lines**

If lunulae are deep red: ◆ **Terry's nails**

If there is a longitudinal line of pigment in the bed:
- ◆ **malignant melanoma**
- ◆ **normal variant**

Figure 14-26 Subungual hematoma. A trauma-related, exquisitely tender collection of blood beneath the nail plate. Note also the onychomadesis at the proximal plates.

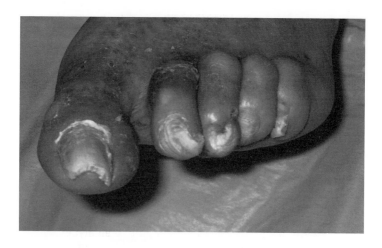

Figure 14-27 Onychogryposis. Ram's horn configuration of the toenails, often due to poor hygiene. Also has thickened nails (onychauxis) and concurrent hammertoe of toes 2 to 5.

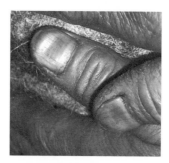

Figure 14-28 Koilonychia. Marked spooning of the nails as the result of profound iron deficiency. This patient from Nepal had chronic iron loss from a hookworm infection.

If the beds are pink: ◆ **normal**
If pale: ◆ **anemia (i.e., hemoglobin <10 g/dL)**
If blue: ◆ **cyanosis (see Chapter 5, p. 111)**

Nail folds: If there is hyperpigmentation of the proximal and lateral folds adjacent to a pigmented lesion in the bed (Hutchinson's sign):
◆ **malignant melanoma**
If the plate grows into the lateral fold: ◆ **onychocryptosis**
If there is redness, warmth, tenderness, swelling, and an area of purulent material in the involved lateral fold (Fig 14-29):
◆ **paronychia**

Figure 14-29 Paronychium. Swelling erythema, tenderness, and fluctuance in and about the lateral nail fold.

If redness, warmth, tenderness, swelling, and an area of purulent material in the involved proximal fold: ◆ **eponychium**

If the angle between the plate and proximal fold is greater than 160 degrees and the plate is spongy on its bed (see Fig 8-9, p. 184): ◆ **clubbing**

Keys to Recording Findings

DERMATOLOGY

"Unremarkable, no specific lesions or entities present on skin or skin appendages (hair, nails)"

• **Descriptors** of specific entities/ lesions: Size, color, pigment, palpable or flat

> macule: < 1cm, flat
>
> papule: > 1 cm, palpable
>
> patch: > 1 cm, flat
>
> plaque: > 1 cm, palpable
>
> petechia: < 5 mm, flat, purple
>
> purpura: 5-15 mm, flat or palpable, purple
>
> ecchymosis: > 15mm, flat, purple
>
> vesicles: < 1 cm, palpable, clear-fluid filled
>
> pustules: < 1 cm, palpable, purulent fluid filled
>
> bulla: > 1cm palpable, clear-fluid filled = blister
>
> erosion: superficial loss of skin
>
> ulcer: deep loss of skin

• **Pattern** of multiple entities/ lesions:

> Flexor surface: e.g. eczema, atopic dermatitis
>
> Extensor surface: e.g. psoriasis
>
> Palms and soles: e.g. Coxsachie
>
> One dermatome: e.g. herpes zoster
>
> Clusters: e.g. herpes zoster/ simplex
>
> Kobner's phenomenon: in scars or sites of trauma: e.g. psoriasis

A. Draw Entity

Location:

Descriptors
_____
_____
_____
_____
_____
_____
_____
_____

Location:

Descriptors
_____
_____
_____
_____
_____
_____
_____
_____

Describe

B. Pattern

		Describe
Extensor surfaces	❏	_____
Flexor surfaces	❏	_____
Unilateral	❏	_____
Clusters	❏	_____
Dermatome	❏	_____
Koebner's	❏	_____

C. Size reference

◯ 6 mm   ◯ 5 mm   ◯ 4 mm   ∘ 2 mm

Diagnoses

Acanthosis nigricans
Skin discoloration due to insulinoma, glucagonoma, adult-onset diabetes mellitus, acromegaly, or a paraneoplastic process. Symptoms and signs include a deeply pigmented, velvety textured plaque/patch in axillae or intertriginous areas. Evaluation and treatment are of the underlying etiology.

Acne vulgaris
Obstruction and infection with *Propionibacterium* spp of pilosebaceous glands on face, neck, upper back, and trunk. Symptoms and signs include one or more tender papules, each with a whitish-yellow center and peripheral erythema, that is, closed comedones or whiteheads, and/or one or more nontender papules, each with a central black area, that is, closed comedones or blackheads. In addition, tender nodules may be present, each with some intermittent purulent discharge in nodular acne. Evaluation and treatment are with topical agents such as benzoyl peroxide and/or topical retinoic acid. Severe cases with infection can be treated with oral antibiotics, for example, tetracycline, and should be referred to a dermatologist.

Acrochordons (skin tags)
Due to exuberant skin growth, benign, and common with increasing age. Asymptomatic pedunculated flesh-colored papules are present. Evaluation and treatment are mainly a cosmetic concern, and they can be removed as per patient desire.

Actinic keratosis
Premalignant form of squamous cell carcinoma. Main risk factor for development is ultraviolet (UV) light exposure, especially in individuals with fair skin and of increasing age. Symptoms and signs include the presence of single or multiple well-demarcated pink papules up to 5 mm in diameter in an atrophic variant of actinic keratosis and the presence of cutaneous "horns" of keratin (see Fig 14-15) in the hypertrophic variant. The lesions occur on the face, neck, and dorsal aspects of the hands and forearms. Evaluation and treatment include performing an excisional biopsy of suspicious sites and/or referring the patient to a dermatologist.

Alopecia areata
Autoimmune inflammatory destruction of the hair follicles. Symptoms and signs include well-circumscribed patches of hair loss, often with concurrent manifestations of systemic lupus erythematosus (SLE) or thyroid disease; the hair may regrow. Evaluation and treatment are of the underlying disorder.

Anaphylaxis: See Urticaria.

Androgenic alopecia

Androgen-mediated hair loss. Symptoms and signs include, in men, alopecia over the crown and temporal surface hair, but the fringes remain intact. In women, hair thins diffusely on the crown, sparing the frontal hair. Evaluation and treatment are primarily patient reassurance and evaluation for any elevated androgen state in a woman.

Angioedema: See Urticaria.

Arterial insufficiency ulcers

Ischemia of skin due to atherosclerotic disease, Raynaud's syndrome, or emboli. Symptoms and signs include painful ulcers on the hands or feet (Plate 24). Decreased pulses, bruits in sites proximal, significant alopecia, cool extremities, decreased capillary refill, and Allen's test result of >6 seconds in the hand are all indications of atherosclerotic disease. Atrial fibrillation and blue or black toes/fingers indicate emboli. Evaluation includes Doppler studies [ankle-brachial index (ABI)], electrocardiogram (ECG), and echocardiogram. Treatment is referral to a vascular surgeon, initiation of aspirin, and consideration to initiate full anticoagulation.

Atopic dermatitis (eczema)

Allergy-related dermatitis. Symptoms and signs include recurrent pruritic erythema with weeping, crusting, and excoriations. Distribution is symmetric: face, neck, trunk, and flexor surfaces of the knees and elbows. Thickening and lichenification indicate chronicity. Concurrent asthma frequently occurs. Treatment includes topical glucocorticoids and systemic antihistamines; referral to a dermatologist in severe cases is indicated.

Basal cell carcinoma

Malignant, invasive, destructive neoplastic disorder of the skin that spreads by contiguous growth, seldom metastasizing. It is one of the most common forms of cancer in the United States today; the risk factors for basal cell carcinoma (BCCA) include fair skin, increasing age, and exposure to UV (A and B) light. Symptoms and signs include a papular lesion with a translucent, pearly margin that may have telangiectases and may secondarily ulcerate. The lesions occur primarily on the face, head, and back of the neck. Evaluation and treatment include performing an excisional biopsy and referring the patient to a dermatologist.

Beau's lines

Transverse furrows in nails as a result of a severe systemic disease process. Symptoms and signs include one or more transverse furrows, 1 to 2 mm in width, in the plates. The finding is nonspecific for diagnoses.

Bullous impetigo

Superficial skin infection with *Staphylococcus aureus*. Infection incidence is highest in the summer and early fall; the infection is extremely contagious, and epidemics are not uncommon. Symptoms and signs include erythema with bullae (Plate 39)—the fluid is clear at first but becomes yellow, thick, and turbid. Evaluation and treatment include systemic, usually oral, antibiotics.

Bullous pemphigoid

Antibody-mediated cleavage of the skin in a subepidermal site; antibasement membrane antibodies lead to the breakdown between the epidermis and the dermis. Symptoms and signs include sturdy, tense bullae on the skin and mucous membranes; the bullae have erythema at their bases and rarely rupture spontaneously (see Fig 14-24). Evaluation includes biopsy and immunofluorescent staining: immunoglobulin G (IgG) and C3 to basal layer of the epidermis. Treatment is referral to a dermatologist.

Callus/corn

Hyperkeratotic area on the skin of the feet due to recurrent mild trauma, use, or irritation. Symptoms and signs include the following: thickened skin on the dorsal aspect (i.e., normally thinly keratinized skin) is a corn; thickened skin on the plantar aspect (i.e., normally thickly keratinized skin) is a callus. Evaluation and management include removal of the corn or callus if it is large and symptomatic or if an associated cellulitis is present. Referral to a podiatrist may be indicated.

Carbuncle: See Furuncle.

Cellulitis

Infection of the deeper layers of the skin with *Streptococcus* spp, *S. aureus*, or anaerobes. Risk factors include lacerations, bite wounds, poorly controlled diabetes mellitus especially in lower extremity cellulitis, and intravenous (IV) drug abuse (tracks, see Fig 14-11). Symptoms and signs include poorly demarcated erythema, nonpitting edema, warmth, and tenderness with a concurrent fever. Treatment is with systemic oral (PO) or IV antibiotics.

Cherry hemangioma

Benign vascular tumors associated only with increasing age. Symptoms and signs include single or multiple, 3- to 5-mm, red to red-purple papules that do not blanch with pressure (Plate 29). Other than clinical recognition, no specific intervention is necessary.

Condyloma acuminatum

Infection of the genital mucous membranes with the human papillomavirus (HPV). Symptoms and signs include one or more rough papules or cauliflower-like lesions on the perianal, vulvar, perineal, scrotal, and/or penile skin. Treatment includes destruction of lesions with trichloroacetic acid (TCA) or liquid nitrogen and patient education in safe-sex techniques.

Contact dermatitis

Dermatitis resulting from cutaneous exposure to an allergen or irritant, such as poison ivy (*Toxicodendron radicans*). Symptoms and signs include acute onset of pruritic erythematous plaques and patches with vesicles and bullae that weep and crust. The distribution is an asymmetric, linear pattern specific to poison ivy. Evaluation and treatment include removal of the inciting agent, topical glucocorticoids, systemic antihistamines, and, in severe reactions, systemic steroids.

Decubital ulcers

Skin ulcers from chronic increased pressure at specific sites, particularly in bedridden or wheelchair-bound individuals. Symptoms and signs include painless to painful, superficial to deep ulcers at pressure points (see Fig 14-20), such as on the back, hips, lateral malleolus, heel, or lateral foot. Treatment is prevention.

Discoid lupus erythematosus

Antibodies against the basal layer of the epidermis due to an autoimmune process. Symptoms and signs of multiple hyperkeratotic red papules and plaques on the face, scalp, ears. The papules and plaques are hyperkeratotic and will heal with severe scarring, profound hypopigmentation, tissue atrophy, and alopecia. Signs of concurrent SLE may be present. Evaluation includes biopsy of the skin lesion; treatment with topical glucocorticoids, oral hydroxychloroquine, and referral to a dermatologist.

Drug-induced dermatitis

Immune-mediated response to a specific medicinal agent, such as sulfa. Symptoms and signs include a bright red rash on the trunk that spreads to the periphery. The rash begins 8 to 10 days after first exposure and 1 to 3 days after subsequent exposures. Treatment includes discontinuing the offending agent and labeling the patient "allergic" to the drug; topical glucocorticoids and systemic antihistamines can be administered.

Dysplastic nevus syndrome

Sporadic or hereditary (autosomal dominant) nevi with significant risk of malignant melanoma. Symptoms and signs include large (>5-mm diameter) nevi with irregular, ill-defined boundaries and disorganized pigment. Patients with the syndrome should perform regular monthly self-examinations; physicians should examine the nevi with comparison photographs every 6 months. Treatment also includes excisional biopsy of any suspicious lesions and referral to a dermatologist.

Eponychium: See Paronychia.

Erysipelas

Superficial skin infection with group A streptococci (GAS). Risk factors include uncontrolled diabetes mellitus, ethanol abuse, prednisone use, and/or neutropenia. Symptoms and signs include a bright red, indurated, tender, and sharply demarcated rash that spreads rapidly over the skin. Fever is concurrent. Treatment includes systemic IV antibiotics.

Erythema ab igne

Irritation from overexposure to a radiant heat source, usually a heating blanket or portable space heater. Symptoms and signs include a flat, mottled, red-brown rash with a reticulated pattern, often with telangiectasia and loss of skin appendages. Treatment is primarily prevention.

Erythema chronicum migrans

Skin manifestation of Lyme disease, caused by the infectious agent *Borrelia burgdorferi*, whose vector is the deer tick, *Ixodes scapularis*. Symptoms and signs include erythematous, asymmetric, well-demarcated, nonpruritic patches with central clearing that occur at the site of a bite usually after 10 to 14 days. The patches usually appear on the trunk, back, or thigh. Concurrent symptoms are arthralgia or peripheral neuropathies (e.g., peripheral cranial nerve VII palsy). Evaluation and treatment include a Lyme titer and systemic antibiotics such as doxycycline.

Erythema infectiosum (fifth disease)

Exanthem of parvovirus B19. Symptoms and signs include erythematous, papular rash on the trunk, back, and face; the characteristic facial involvement gives patients a "slapped-cheek" appearance. Concurrent are spiking fevers, rhinorrhea, and sore throat. Treatment includes acetaminophen and fluids. The patient should have no exposure to pregnant women.

Erythema marginatum

Manifestation of streptococcal infection—one of the five major criteria for the diagnosis of rheumatic fever. Symptoms and signs include erythematous patches with flat pale centers and raised red margins that spread rapidly and become confluent. Concurrent manifestations of rheumatic fever include extensor surface nodules, polyarthralgia, chorea (St. Vitus' dance), and pancarditis with regurgitant (aortic regurgitation, pulmonic regurgitation, mitral regurgitation, tricuspid regurgitation) murmurs. Evaluation and treatment include antistreptolysin O (ASO) titer, systemic penicillin, and referral to an infectious diseases specialist.

Erythema multiforme

Acute eruptions due to mycoplasma or herpes simplex infections or as a side effect of phenytoin and trimethoprim (TMP)/sulfa. Symptoms and signs include multiple target-shaped erythematous wheals and papules of symmetric distribution on the palms and soles. *Erythema multiforme minor:* one set of lesions. *Erythema multiforme major:* two or more sets of lesions.

Stevens-Johnson syndrome: severe desquamation with mucous membrane involvement. Treatment includes systemic acyclovir and referral to a dermatologist. Patients with Stevens-Johnson syndrome should be admitted to a hospital burn unit.

Erythema nodosum

Septal panniculitis due to streptococcal infections, coccidioidomycosis, hepatitis B, mycobacterial infections, sarcoidosis, or ulcerative colitis. Symptoms and signs include tender erythematous nodules on the extensor surfaces of the lower extremities. Evaluation includes chest radiograph and a hepatitis panel. Treatment includes topical glucocorticoids, identifying the underlying etiology, and referral to a dermatologist.

Folliculitis: See Furuncle.

Furuncle

Abscess in the hair-bearing areas of the skin as a result of *S. aureus* infection. Risk factors include eczema, IV drug abuse, scabies, and **folliculitis** (infection of a follicle). Symptoms and signs include a tender, fluctuant, red nodule that may rupture and drain pus. A **carbuncle** is multiple interconnected furuncles (see Fig 14-10). Evaluation and treatment include incision and drainage plus systemic, usually oral, antibiotics.

Herpes genitalis

Infection of mucous membranes and underlying cutaneous nerves of the penis, vulva, and anus with a deoxyribonucleic acid (DNA) virus, herpes simplex 2 (HSV-2). Symptoms and signs include acute onset of a painful cluster of vesicular lesions (see Fig 16-4, p. 363). Treatment includes patient education in safe-sex techniques and administration of systemic acyclovir.

Herpes labialis (cold sore/fever blister)

Infection of the perioral mucous membranes and trigeminal nerve/ganglion with a DNA virus, herpes simplex 1 (HSV-1). Symptoms and signs include acute onset of a unilateral single group of vesicles on the perioral mucosa, which crosses over the vermilion border of the lip to involve the skin (see Fig 2-7, p. 14). Treatment includes prevention via proscription of kissing and administration of systemic acyclovir.

Herpes zoster (shingles)

Infection of a dorsal root ganglion with the DNA virus varicella-zoster (chickenpox virus). Symptoms and signs include acute onset of erythema and vesicles in the region of a unilateral single dermatome (see Fig 14-22), with hyperesthesia and pain. Treatment includes administering systemic acyclovir and effective analgesia.

Impetigo

Superficial skin infection with GAS. Infection incidence is highest in the summer and early fall; the infection is extremely contagious, and epidemics are not uncommon. Symptoms and signs include erythematous, painless, superficial erosions with a "honey-yellow" crust, usually on the face. Treatment includes systemic oral antibiotics or, in mild cases, topical antibiotics.

Kaposi's sarcoma

Malignant neoplasm associated with herpes simplex virus 8 in AIDS patients or as an indolent form in elderly individuals. Symptoms and signs of one or more nontender, nonblanching purple papules/nodules on the skin or mucous membranes; in the indolent form, the lesions are limited to both feet. Evaluation and treatment include performing a biopsy and referral to an infectious diseases specialist and an oncologist.

Keloid formation

Exuberant scar formation. Symptoms and signs include a marked amount of scar tissue in old healed lacerations or surgical scars. The tissue is soft and nontender but may be disfiguring. Treatment is by referral to a plastic surgeon, as desired by the patient.

Keratoacanthoma (pseudocarcinoma)

Nonmalignant neoplastic lesion that spontaneously resolves after reaching maximal size. Symptoms and signs include a papule or plaque with central ulceration and a keratin plug (see Fig 14-14) on the face, dorsal hands, or upper back. Evaluation and treatment include performing an excisional biopsy and referring the patient to a dermatologist.

Koilonychia

Nail deformity highly correlated with severe, chronic iron deficiency. Symptoms and signs include each nail being concave, often, but not always, with concurrent pale nail beds if anemia is present (see Fig 14-28); in addition, cheilosis (angular stomatitis) is commonly present. Evaluation includes a menstrual history, the performance of a pelvic examination, and stool guaiac, hematocrit, and serum iron studies. For men and postmenopausal women, a thorough gastrointestinal tract evaluation is needed. Treatment includes finding the source of blood loss, if present, and iron replacement in all cases.

Leser-Trélat sign: See Seborrheic keratosis.

Lichen planus

Skin eruptions associated with ulcerative colitis, graft-versus-host disease, and medications such as gold, quinine, and tetracycline. Symptoms and signs include multiple pruritic, polygonal papules (see Fig 14-5) in a symmetric distribution on skin and mucous membranes; Wickstram's striae and Köbner's phenomenon are found. Evaluation and treatment include biopsy, topical glucocorticoids, and referral to a dermatologist.

Livedo reticularis

Due to a connective tissue disease, such as SLE or Cushing's syndrome. Symptoms include a chronic, nonpalpable, purple-blue fishnet network on the trunk and lower extremities. Treatment is of the underlying cause.

Malignant melanoma

Malignant neoplasm of the melanocytes of the skin. A direct relationship exists between depth of invasion and distant metastases and an inverse relationship between depth and survival. The risk factors for its development include fair skin; exposure to UV light and intense sunburns, especially as a child; a family history of melanoma; and dysplastic nevus syndrome. Symptoms and signs include large nevi (>5-mm diameter) with irregular, ill-defined boundaries (see Fig 14-18); the lesion has disorganized pigment and may be nodular or even ulcerate. (Use the A,B,C,D,E examination: A = asymmetry, B = borders, C = color, D = diameter, E = elevation.) Evaluation and treatment include performing an excisional biopsy on all suspicious lesions and referring the patient to a dermatologist.

Mechanical or thermal trauma bullae

Damage of the epidermis or dermis from physical forces, such as mechanical trauma, **second-degree burn**, or **frostbite**. Symptoms and signs include tense or flaccid bullae (see Fig 14-25) in the site of damage/exposure that will become avulsions or erosions. Treatment includes cleansing, a tetanus booster, and silver sulfadiazine (Silvadene) application to the wound.

Miliaria (prickly heat)

Heat-related blockage of the sweat glands in children and young adults (more common in summer). Symptoms include a "prickling" sensation when there is sweating and a diffuse, erythematous papular rash on the trunk and extremities that spares the face. The papules are a greater distance from each other than in exanthems. Treatment primarily consists of reassurance.

Molluscum contagiosum

Infection with the DNA virus of the Poxviridae family, transmitted by direct contact. Symptoms and signs include multiple painless umbilicated papules (see Fig 14-12) on the trunk, face, arms, and genitals that slowly increase in number and size. There are no associated systemic symptoms or signs. Treatment includes patient education in safe-sex techniques and electrocautery damage to each papule.

Muercke's lines

Nail sign of profound hypoalbuminemia as the result of nephrotic syndrome, end-stage liver disease, and/or malnutrition, first reported by Muercke in 1956. Symptoms and signs include white, transverse bands across the nail beds, especially in digits 2, 3, and 4, with concurrent ascites (see Fig 6-5, p. 119), dependent pitting edema, and anasarca. Evaluation includes serum albumin, urinalysis, and liver function tests. Treatment is of the specific underlying disorder.

Mycosis fungoides
Cutaneous non-Hodgkin's lymphoma. Symptoms and signs include multiple erythematous, scaly patches and plaques on the trunk and back. Concurrent B symptoms include fevers with a Pel-Ebstein pattern, night sweats, and weight loss. The patient will have no Köbner's sign or nail pitting. Evaluation and treatment include a biopsy and referral to a dermatologist and oncologist.

Necrobiosis lipoidica diabeticorum
Cutaneous eruptions correlated with uncontrolled diabetes mellitus. Symptoms and signs include multiple red papules on anterior and lateral legs that enlarge, flatten, and thicken to form well-circumscribed plaques. The plaques evolve into atrophic yellow-brown areas on the anterior tibial surface. Treatment includes control of the diabetes mellitus and consideration of application of topical low-dose glucocorticoids.

Neurofibromatosis
An autosomal dominant disorder that affects cells of neural crest origin; the two types are NF1 and NF2. The symptoms and signs of NF1 include café au lait spots (see Fig 14-1), Crowe's sign, Lisch nodules, and neurofibromas; tinnitus from an acoustic neuroma or radicular pain from a glioma may also be present. NF2 has few skin findings, only bilateral neuromas or gliomas, or both. There is no treatment beyond clinical recognition. If neurologic findings are present, magnetic resonance imaging (MRI) and referral to a neurosurgeon are indicated.

Neurotropic ulcers
Ulcer from recurrent trauma in an area of decreased sensation most often due to a neuropathy B_{12} deficiency or diabetes mellitus; arterial insufficiency may be a concurrent condition. Symptoms and signs include a painless ulcer on the distal lower extremity; concurrent stocking-glove neuropathy (see Figs 7-4 and 7-5, pp. 144 and 145), Charcot's joint, or diabetes mellitus is common. Treatment includes zealous foot care and glycemic control in patients with diabetes; B_{12} replacement therapy is indicated if the patient has a deficiency.

Nodular acne: See Acne vulgaris.

Nummular eczema
Inflammation of the dermis exacerbated by dry skin. Symptoms and signs include coin-like scaly patches on extensor surfaces of extremities, back, and buttocks that may weep and crust when severe. Treatment includes skin moisturizers, topical glucocorticoids, and systemic antihistamines.

Onychauxis
Nail thickening due to psoriasis, onychomycosis, and/or arterial insufficiency. Symptoms and signs include diffuse thickening of the nail plate that

may reach 4 to 5 mm (see Fig 14-27) and a yellow nail that is brittle and may fracture quite easily. Evaluation and treatment require identifying the underlying cause.

Onychium: See Paronychia.

Onychocryptosis: See Paronychia.

Onychogryphosis
Nail overgrowth following too infrequent pedicures or manicures. Symptoms and signs include a grossly elongated nail that curves laterally, then posteriorly. The nail may attain a ram's-horn configuration (see Fig 14-27). Treatment includes a manicure or pedicure, or both, with optional referral to a podiatrist.

Onychomadesis
Nail shedding after trauma or onychomycosis. Symptoms and signs include separation of the nail plate from the bed (see Fig 14-29), starting proximally and progressing distally, with concurrent subungual hematoma or onychomycosis. Evaluation and treatment require identifying the underlying cause.

Onychomycosis
Chronic infection of the nail plate with a dermatophyte and/or *Candida* spp. Symptoms and signs of onychauxis, onychomadesis, and oncolysis, with concurrent tinea manus or pedis. Treatment includes a manicure or pedicure and systemic itraconazole.

Paget's disease
Malignant neoplastic lesion due to an underlying infiltrating ductal breast carcinoma. Symptoms and signs include one or more pruritic scaly plaques on the areola and/or nipple with a concurrent breast lump. A mammogram reveals the nodule or mass with clustered microcalcification. The patient must be immediately referred to a general surgeon.

Paronychia
Purulent infection of the lateral nail fold owing to trauma, onychomycosis, or **onychocryptosis** (ingrown nail). Symptoms include acute onset of pain and swelling in the lateral nail fold (see Fig 14-27). Signs include erythema, warmth, tenderness, and purulent material in the lateral nail fold. **Eponychium** is the condition in proximal nail fold. **Onychium** applies to the entire nail bed. Treatment includes incision and drainage and systemic oral antibiotics.

Pemphigus vulgaris/foliaceus
Antibody-mediated cleavage of the skin in an intraepidermal site, resulting in breakdown of the desmosomes and superficial skin. Symptoms and signs

include superficial flaccid bullae that often rupture before presentation, thus manifesting as erosions on skin and mucous membranes. **Pemphigus vulgaris** begins around the face and mouth; 90% of cases have oral or pharyngeal involvement. Pemphigus foliaceus affects mainly the face, scalp, central chest, and back. Evaluation includes a biopsy and immunofluorescent staining: IgG and C3 to desmosomes. Refer the patient to a dermatologist.

Photodermatitis (sunburn)
Dermatitis from acute exposure to UV light. Risk factors include lightly pigmented skin, lupus erythematosus, use of systemic tetracycline, and **porphyria cutanea tarda**. Symptoms and signs include diffuse, confluent, nonraised, warm red rash on areas exposed to sunlight (Plate 37); blistering occurs in severe cases of sunburn or with porphyria cutanea tarda. Hypertrichosis is common in porphyria cutanea tarda. Acute treatment includes skin moisturizers, topical glucocorticoids, and aspirin; severe cases may require systemic steroids. With porphyria cutanea tarda, treatment also includes chloroquine or phlebotomy and referral to a hematologist.

Pityriasis rosea
Idiopathic skin condition. Symptoms and signs include multiple oval reddish scaly patches, located on the trunk, back, and chest. The condition is preceded by a herald patch on the back. Treatment includes topical glucocorticoids, antihistamines, and patient reassurance.

Poliosis: See Vitiligo.

Psoriasis
Abnormal increase in the proliferation of the basal epidermal cells; genetic predisposition. Symptoms and signs include multiple mildly pruritic red plaques with silvery scales (see Fig 14-21 and Plate 30). Distribution is symmetric on extensor surfaces, back, and scalp; also a positive Auspitz's sign and Köbner's phenomenon. Nail pitting and asymmetric large joint arthritis are concurrent. Treatment includes high-potency topical glucocorticoids. Vexing cases should be referred to a dermatologist.

Pyoderma gangrenosum
Necrotizing process involving skin due to inflammatory bowel disease. Symptoms and signs include painful, large ulcers with irregular borders and bases with purulent material, usually found on a lower extremity (see Fig 14-19). Lesions heal with scarring. Concurrent conditions are ulcerative colitis or Crohn's disease. Evaluation and treatment include biopsy and referral to a dermatologist and gastroenterologist.

Rendu-Osler-Weber syndrome
Autosomal dominant syndrome involving small blood vessels. Symptoms and signs include multiple telangiectasiae and hemangiomas in the skin, mucous membranes (Plate 5), tongue, lips, and perineal and genital areas.

Recurrent epistaxis, hematuria, and hemoptysis and a guaiac-positive stool are also present (Plate 26). Evaluation and treatment include iron studies and local destruction of any bleeding hemangioma via cautery.

Retroperitoneal bleeds

Hemorrhage from femoral neck fracture, a ruptured ectopic pregnancy, warfarin-related hypocoagulation, or, rarely, hemorrhagic pancreatitis. Symptoms and signs include positive Grey Turner's sign (see Fig 14-6) and Cullen's sign. Concurrent manifestations of acute abdomen (see Chapter 6) or femoral neck fracture (see Fig 11-2, p. 237) are quite evident. Evaluation and treatment include coagulation parameters [activated partial thromboplastin time (aPTT) and prothrombin time (PT)], complete blood count, a computed tomographic (CT) scan of the abdomen, and treatment of underlying etiology.

Rosacea

Idiopathic skin condition, possibly correlated with chronic ethanol ingestion and increasing age. Symptoms and signs include a diffuse papular rash on the maxillary, nasal, and frontal skin with concurrent rhinophyma and multiple telangiectasiae. Treatment includes application of moisturizing cream to affected areas.

Rubella (third disease)

Viral exanthem. Symptoms and signs include a diffuse, light red, and finely papular rash over the back, trunk, abdomen, and upper extremities that never desquamates. Concurrent manifestations are enlarged and tender posterior cervical nodes, fever, bilateral conjunctivitis, and myalgia. Treatment includes fluids and acetaminophen. The patient should be isolated from pregnant women.

Rubeola (first disease)

Viral exanthem. Symptoms and signs include a diffuse, bright red, and finely papular rash over the back, trunk, abdomen, and upper extremities that may desquamate with healing. Antecedent Koplik's spots and concurrent fever, bilateral conjunctivitis, and myalgia also manifest. Treatment includes fluids and acetaminophen.

Scabies

Infestation of the parasite, *Sarcoptes scabiei*, which burrows in skin and spreads easily (epidemics can occur). Symptoms include severe nocturnal pruritus on the trunk, back, and arms. Signs include papules that occur in straight lines (i.e., in "runs"). Excoriations and pustules may be present on the entire body except for the head. Evaluation includes scraping a lesion and demonstrating the organism under a microscope. Treatment is with topical scabicides—the patient's entire family must be treated.

Seborrheic dermatitis

Inflammation of the dermis in areas adjacent to the hair line, exacerbated by emotional stressors. Symptoms and signs include multiple pruritic greasy papules and plaques, located adjacent to hair lines and on central chest. Treatment includes topical glucocorticoids and use of shampoo containing selenium.

Seborrheic keratosis
Nonmalignant hyperkeratotic growths, usually associated with increasing age. **Leser-Trélat sign** is a paraneoplastic increase in seborrheic keratosis associated with an internal adenocarcinoma. Symptoms and signs include a nonpainful, nonpruritic 1.0- to 1.5-cm lesion that is light to dark brown and has a "stuck-on" appearance (see Fig 14-17). Distribution is symmetric on the trunk and proximal extremities. Other than clinical recognition, no specific intervention is necessary.

Second-degree burns: See Mechanical or thermal trauma bullae.

Second-degree frostbite: See Mechanical or thermal trauma bullae.

Spider angioma
Vascular formations following an increase in estrogen as a result of hepatic insufficiency/pregnancy. Symptoms and signs of multiple lesions on the chest and shoulders, each having a pinhead-sized central vessel with small vessels radiating centripetally from it. Evaluation and treatment include clinical recognition and performing a pregnancy test, if indicated.

Squamous cell carcinoma
Malignant neoplastic process involving the skin, the lesions both contiguously, by invading adjacent tissues and by metastasizing to local lymph nodes early in the course of disease, then to the bone, brain, liver, and/or lungs later. Squamous cell carcinoma (SCCA) is of increasing incidence in the United States today; risk factors include exposure to UV light or ionizing radiation, recurrent trauma to the skin, or the viral-related lesions of condyloma acuminatum, HPV, and periungual warts. Symptoms and signs of a nontender, solitary nodular lesion with central ulcer (see Fig 14-13) and peripheral erythema on the face, ears, or dorsum of hands. Evaluation and treatment include performing an excisional biopsy and referring the patient to a dermatologist.

Staphylococcal scalded skin syndrome
Cleavage of the skin in epidermis due to an exfoliative toxin produced by a phage within the *Staphylococcus* bacterium. Bullous impetigo or an abscess usually precedes this syndrome. Symptoms and signs include a diffuse, erythematous, tender rash that evolves into thin-roofed bullae and erosions. Treatment includes systemic antibiotics.

Subungual hematoma
Collection of blood beneath the nail plate after a crush trauma. Symptoms and signs include a reddish-blue collection of blood beneath the nail plate

(see Fig 14-26) and exquisite tenderness. Treatment is to incise and drain the hematoma.

Telangiectasia

Dilated vessels (usually venules in the superficial skin) due to actinic changes, steroid-related atrophy, Rendu-Osler-Weber syndrome, or increasing age. The primary sign is a nonblanching purple vascular structure. Telangiectasiae are mainly of cosmetic concern and can be removed for cosmesis.

Terry's nails

Nail discoloration due to chronic congestive heart failure, first reported by Terry in 1954. Symptoms and signs include red lunulae in fingernails and toenails, with concurrent findings of heart failure—an S_3 gallop, crackles, and peripheral edema. Evaluation places this finding in context with the other more important manifestations salient to congestive heart failure.

Tinea barbae

Fungal infection of the hair and skin of the face. Symptoms and signs include patchy beard alopecia with pruritic scales and erythema at the base of each patch; purulent folliculitis is concurrent. Evaluation and treatment include a potassium hydroxide (KOH) test on scrapings or hair clippings and systemic oral itraconazole.

Tinea capitis

Fungal infection of the hair and skin of the scalp. Symptoms and signs include patchy alopecia with pruritic scales and erythema at the base of each patch. Evaluation and treatment include a KOH test on skin scrapings or hair sample and systemic oral itraconazole.

Tinea corporis (ringworm)

Fungal infection of the skin of any body area. Symptoms and signs include one or more erythematous patches, each with central clearing and peripheral raised scaly margins (Plate 31); distribution is asymmetric on the trunk, back, and thighs. Evaluation and treatment include a KOH test on scrapings and topical clotrimazole.

Tinea cruris (jock itch)

Fungal infection of the intertriginous area of the groin. Symptoms and signs include pruritic, macerated erythematous area in the skin folds of the groin (see Fig 14-7); the rash is sharply demarcated. Evaluation and treatment include a KOH test on scrapings and systemic oral fluconazole or topical clotrimazole.

Tinea pedis

Fungal infection of the feet, especially the plantar aspect of the feet soles. Symptoms and signs include pruritic areas, erythema and vesicles, with weeping on the palms or soles; distribution is moccasin-shaped on both feet, may desquamate (Plate 35). Concurrent candidiasis manifests as cracking and fissuring in the interdigital sites. Evaluation and treatment include a KOH test on scrapings and systemic itraconazole or topical clotrimazole.

Tinea versicolor
Fungal infection of the superficial skin by *Pityrosporum orbiculare* (*Malassezia furfur*). Symptoms and signs include mildly pruritic hypopigmented macules and patches on the trunk, shoulders, and chest. Evaluation includes a KOH test; the agent has a "spaghetti and meatballs" appearance—the spores forming the meatballs and the hyphae the spaghetti. Treatment includes topical clotrimazole or a selenium-containing shampoo.

Trichotillomania
Anxiety-related habit of pulling out one's hair. Symptoms and signs include patchy hair loss on the crown; often accompanied by nail biting (onychophagia). Short hair (i.e., too short to be pulled) is spared. The hair will regrow. Treatment includes patient reassurance.

Urticaria
Wheals from immunoglobulin E (IgE)-mediated release of histamine precipitated by a local (insect bite) or generalized (medication, food) allergen. Symptoms and signs of acute onset include one or more intensely pruritic red papules (colloquially referred to as *hives*; Plate 25) and dermatographism. Concurrent signs include **angioedema** of the lips (see Fig 2-8, p. 15), wheezing from bronchospasm, or **anaphylaxis**. Evaluation and treatment include administration of an antihistamine; epinephrine is administered for anaphylaxis. The patient should be referred to an allergist.

Varicella (chickenpox)
Infection with DNA virus varicella-zoster. The patient inhales the virus (aerosol transmission); the incubation period is 10 to 14 days after exposure. Symptoms and signs include acute onset of fever, malaise, mild rhinorrhea, and multiple pruritic vesicles. The vesicles evolve into pustules and crust over (see Fig 14-23); new crops occur every 2 to 3 days for a total of four to five crops. The first crop occurs on the trunk, and subsequent crops progress peripherally. Treatment includes support and, in severe cases, acyclovir administration.

Venous stasis dermatitis
Dermatitis due to chronic edema and stasis of blood in the lower extremities. Symptoms and signs include thickened dry skin with cracking, erythema, varicosities, and loss of skin appendages. Treatment includes skin moisturizers, topical glucocorticoids, elevation, and support hose.

Viral exanthem: See Erythema infectiosum (fifth disease), Rubella (third disease), Rubeola (first disease).

Vitiligo

Autoimmune-related destruction of melanocytes with a loss of pigment in specific areas of skin; associated with other autoimmune disorders (e.g., SLE, thyroiditis). Symptoms and signs include patches of profound hypopigmentation (see Fig 14-16) on the face and the genital areas; in **poliosis**, there are shocks of gray hair and eyelashes. The patient should be referred to a dermatologist and an endocrinologist as necessary.

Warts: plantar/common (verruca vulgaris)

Infection of keratinized skin with HPV; lifetime prevalence is almost 100%. Symptoms and signs include one or more papules on the fingers or toes, each with rough texture and minute black spots. Common wart: manifest on fingers. Plantar wart: manifest deep on the plantar foot. Treatment includes destruction of the warts with TCA or liquid nitrogen if they are symptomatic.

Xanthelasma

Manifestation of type IIa or type IIb hyperlipidemia, an increase in total cholesterol and low-density lipoprotein (LDL); type IIb also has an increase in very-low-density lipoprotein (VLDL). Symptoms include nontender yellow plaques (see Fig 3-6, p. 54) in and about the periorbital skin and skin structures. Concurrent conditions are arcus juvenilis, tendon xanthomas, and premature atherosclerotic disease. A plasma lipid panel reveals profoundly elevated cholesterol and LDL; in type IIb VLDL is also elevated. Treatment is referral to an endocrinologist.

CHAPTER 15
Gynecology and Obstetrics

Inspect breast and nipples

PROCEDURE: Have the patient sit with her arms at her sides. Visually inspect the breasts for symmetry. Also, visually inspect the nipples and areolae, and the skin overlying the breast. Repeat the inspection while the patient's arms are over her head, then with arms on hips, and then with arms in forward flexion to 90 degrees. Compare one breast with the other (Fig 15-1).

OUTCOME: If the nipples are retracted bilaterally: ◆ **normal**
If retracted unilaterally:
- ◆ **normal**
- ◆ **breast carcinoma**

If there is skin dimpling (peau d'orange): ◆ **breast carcinoma**
If there is an erythematous, sometimes ulcerating plaque:
- ◆ **inflammatory carcinoma**

If there are erythematous, scaly, pruritic lesions on the areola and/or nipple: ◆ **Paget's disease of the breast (see Chapter 14, p. 330)**

Palpate axilla

PROCEDURE: Have the patient sit with her arms at her sides.

1. With one hand, hold the patient's arm at the elbow, and passively abduct and mildly rotate it at the glenohumeral joint.
2. Cup your other hand, insert the digits gently toward the apex of the patient's axilla, and passively adduct shoulder, which allows the examiner to palpate the apex of the axilla easily. Repeat for the anterior wall, then the posterior wall of the axilla. Feel for any nodes or masses adjacent to the walls of the axilla.

Note the number, location, consistency, mobility, tenderness, and size of any nodes or masses in the axilla.

OUTCOME: If there are no masses or nodes palpable: ◆ **normal**
If one or more tender, enlarged lymph nodes are present:
- ◆ **infection**
- ◆ **metastatic malignancy**

If one or more nontender, firm, enlarged lymph nodes:
- ◆ **infection**
- ◆ **metastatic malignancy**

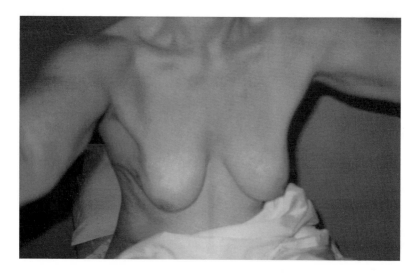

Figure 15-1 Sitting position for breast inspection.

If a nodule fixed to the overlying skin: ◆ **metastatic malignancy**
If an erythematous, fluctuant, tender nodule: ◆ **sebaceous cysts**
If a soft, fleshy, nontender nodule: ◆ **lipoma**

Palpate breasts

PROCEDURE: Have the patient assume a relaxed, supine position, with the ipsilateral arm flexed at the elbow, the arm toward the head, and the head resting on the hand (Fig 15-2). Stand at the patient's side. Palpate the patient's breast with the palmar pads of the distal index and middle fingers, using a combination of kneading and rotatory motion at each site. Perform one of three patterns (Fig 15-3) in this examination to cover the breast area:

Concentric circles (Fig 15-3A). Begin at periphery at the tail of Spence, and rotate in a set of progressively smaller concentric circles, terminating at the nipple.

Wedge/spokes of wheel (Fig 15-3B). Begin at periphery at the tail of Spence, and palpate in a straight line to the nipple. Repeat the procedure in a series of adjacent lines, akin to spokes on a wheel.

Vertical lines (Fig 15-3C). Begin at tail of Spence and cover breast in pattern shown. This is the preferred method.

In each pattern, there should be a slight overlap of the palpation sites. Pay particular attention to the upper outer quadrant (tail of Spence), as breast tissue often extends into the axilla. Palpate over the nipple, note any discharge. Note any masses or tender-

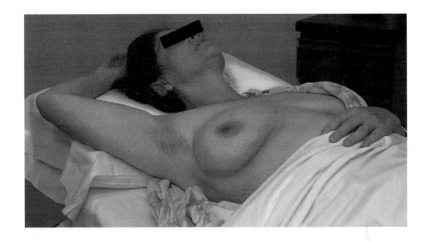

Figure 15-2 Positioning for breast examination and landmarks.

ness. Use the contralateral breast as a control, and take particular heed to any objective difference.

OUTCOME: If there are multiple variably tender nodules:
   ◆ **fibrocystic changes**
If there is a rock-hard nodule or mass, either fixed or mobile:
   ◆ **breast carcinoma**
If nodule immediately deep to the areola:
   ◆ **intraductal papilloma**
If there is bloody nipple discharge:
   ◆ **intraductal papilloma**
   ◆ **breast carcinoma**
If serous nipple discharge:
   ◆ **nonspecific finding**
   ◆ **intraductal papilloma**
   ◆ **breast carcinoma**
If milky nipple discharge: ◆ **galactorrhea**
If a well-demarcated triangular area of warmth, redness, and tenderness, with no nipple discharge or retraction and no areas of fluctuance: ◆ **acute mastitis**
If one or more fluctuant, tender, warm nodules (Plate 40) in the area of mastitis: ◆ **breast abscess**
If there are multiple, mildly tender, pigmented papules in the areolae: ◆ **Montgomery's tubercles (sign of pregnancy)**

Postpartum: If tender enlargement of one portion of the breast, with fluctuance distant from the areola, not warm or red:
   ◆ **milk stasis (normal)**

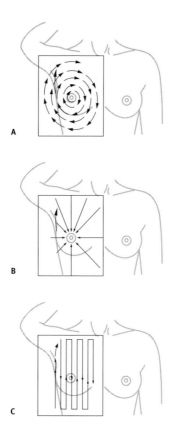

Figure 15-3 Clinical breast examination. Patterns include concentric circles (A), wedges/spokes of a wheel (B), vertical lines (C). Must include the tail of Spence in all palpation patterns.

If tender enlargement of one or both breasts in their entirety, not warm or red: ◆ **milk engorgement (normal)**

Inspect and palpate external genitalia

PROCEDURE: Have the patient lie in the dorsal lithotomy position. Visually inspect and, with a gloved hand, palpate the vulva (labia minora and labia majora), clitoris, urethra, fourchette, and intertriginous areas, bilaterally (Plate 41).

OUTCOME:

Red: If there are red pruritic plaques and patches with oozing, crusting, and vesicles, usually in the distribution of a pad or underpants: ◆ **contact dermatitis**

If there is a macerated, moist red rash in intertriginous areas:
◆ **tinea cruris**

White: If one or more hypopigmented, atrophic, shiny, fragile macules and patches are present that are pruritic, with loss of skin appendages and symmetric distribution:
◆ **lichen sclerosis et atrophicus**

If a hyperkeratotic, superficial plaque on any vulvar site except the labia minora: ◆ **squamous cell hyperplasia**

If lichen sclerosis with concurrent decrease in size, elasticity of vaginal orifice, and fissuring, especially at the fourchette:
◆ **kraurosis vulvae**

If an ulcerated scaly plaque with irregular borders:
◆ **vulvar intraepithelial neoplasia (VIN)**
◆ **squamous cell carcinoma**

Flesh-colored: If multiple umbilicated papules, each with a central core of cheesy material: ◆ **molluscum contagiosum**

If multiple firm, exuberant, cauliflower-like papules that are asymmetric in distribution: ◆ **condyloma acuminatum**

Cyst/ nodules/ swelling: If multiple nontender nodules on the lateral (outer) aspect of the labia majora, usually not exceeding 2 cm in size:
◆ **sebaceous cyst**

If there is a unilateral nodule or mass in the soft tissue deep to the mons pubis or in the labia majora: ◆ **indirect inguinal hernia**

If tender discrete nodule with erythema, posterior and lateral to the urethra: ◆ **Skene's adenitis**

If solitary tender, fluctuant nodule in the posterior third of the labia majora that protrudes medially into the vaginal introitus:
◆ **Bartholin's cyst/abscess**
◆ **Bartholin's adenocarcinoma**

Ulcers/ erosions: If there is a cluster of painful vesicles/erosions/ulcers:
◆ **herpes genitalis**

If solitary, indurated, well-demarcated, relatively painless ulcer:
◆ **chancre (primary lues)**

Discharge: If there is a frothy, clear, fishy-smelling discharge:
◆ ***Trichomonas* infection**

If a creamy, white, chunky discharge: ◆ ***Candida* infection**

If a clear, whitish-gray, homogeneous discharge:
◆ **bacterial vaginosis**

Pregnancy: If there is a bluish hue to the vagina and vulva:
> ◆ **Chadwick sign/Jacquemier sign of early pregnancy**

Examine vagina and vaginal mucosa using speculum

PROCEDURE: Have the patient lie in the dorsal lithotomy position. Insert a speculum into the vagina (Plate 42) and visually inspect the vaginal mucosa. See Plate 43 for various specula, cytobrush, and spatula needed for examination.

OUTCOME:

Discharge: If there is a small amount of mucus or clear discharge: ◆ **normal**
If frothy, clear, fishy-smelling discharge:
> ◆ ***Trichomonas* infection**

If creamy, white, chunky discharge: ◆ ***Candida* infection**
If clear, homogenous, whitish-gray discharge:
> ◆ **bacterial vaginosis**

Nodules/ papules: If there is one or more warty, exophytic, cauliflower-like lesions:
> ◆ **condyloma acuminatum**

If a single indurated, ulcerated, nontender plaque: ◆ **chancre**
If one or more nontender nodules in the anterolateral wall of the vagina: ◆ **Gartner's duct cyst**
If an indurated, friable, ulcering papule/plaque in the vaginal mucosa: ◆ **vaginal adenocarcinoma**
If a reddish, polypoid nodule in the vaginal mucosa:
> ◆ **vaginal adenosis**
> ◆ **vaginal adenocarcinoma**

If a red nodule in the mucosa, most commonly in the posterior fornix: ◆ **endometriosis**

Pregnancy: If a bluish hue to the vagina and vulva:
> ◆ **Chadwick sign/Jacquemier sign of early pregnancy**

Examine cervix using speculum

PROCEDURE: First, explain the procedure to the patient. Then have the patient assume the dorsal lithotomy position. Lubricate the speculum with warm water before insertion.

1. *Insertion:* Close the bill of the speculum, and insert it gently into the vagina. Open the bill of the speculum so that you can see the entire cervix (the bill opening is horizontal; Plate 42).

2. *Adjustment:* If you cannot see the cervix, remove the speculum and reinsert it at a different angle. *Note:* If the uterus is retroverted, the cervix will point more anteriorly, making inspection more challenging. Once the angle is correct, open the bill of the speculum so that you can see the entire cervix (Plate 44). Stabilize the speculum by tightening the instrument's thumbscrew.

3. *Cultures:* If any discharge is present at the os, remove it with a cotton-tipped swab. If the discharge appears purulent, perform the appropriate cultures for *Chlamydia* and *Neisseria*

gonorrhoeae. Also perform a cervical smear, if necessary [see Papanicolaou (Pap) smear technique, below].

4. *Removal:* To remove the speculum, loosen the thumbscrew to allow the bill to close, and gently withdraw the instrument from the vagina. Inspect the vaginal mucosa present.

OUTCOME: If there is demarcation between the pink squamous epithelium of ectocervix and red columnar epithelium of the endocervix:
   ◆ **ectropion (eversion)**

If no red columnar epithelium: ◆ **entropion (inversion)**

If one or more spherical elevations, 2 to 10 mm in size, on the cervix: ◆ **nabothian cysts**

If the os is round:
   ◆ **nulliparous os (no previous vaginal deliveries)**

If slit-like (Plate 44): ◆ **parous os (previous vaginal delivery)**

If there is a bright red, fragile, soft, pediculated lesion in the cervical os: ◆ **cervical polyp**

If a yellow, purulent discharge from the cervical os:
   ◆ **purulent cervicitis**

If one or more warty, exophytic, flesh-colored lesions:
   ◆ **condyloma acuminatum**

If one or more painful vesicular lesions: ◆ **herpes genitalis**

If a single indurated, ulcerated, nontender lesion: ◆ **chancre**

If an ulcerating lesion on the cervix, usually adjacent to the demarcation line between the endocervical (red) and ectocervical (pink) mucosa: ◆ **cervical carcinoma**

If bleeding and friability of cervical tissue around the os:
   ◆ **severe purulent cervicitis**
   ◆ **cervical carcinoma**

If the entire cervix is covered with red columnar epithelium (marked ectropion): ◆ **fetal exposure to diethylstilbestrol (DES)**

Pregnancy: If there is a bluish hue to the cervix:
   ◆ **Goodell's sign (early pregnancy)**

Obtain a Papanicolaou smear

PROCEDURE: Obtain two scrapings of cervical epithelium by:

1. *Spatula:* Place the spatula (Plate 43) on the surface of the cervix, with the longer prong placed into the cervical os. Rotate the spatula 360 degrees. Attempt to obtain a specimen so as to include the margin between the endocervical cells and ectocervical cells.

2. *Cytobrush:* Insert the cytobrush (Plate 43) into the cervical os and rotate it 360 degrees to obtain endocervical cells (Plate 45). Place each specimen on a glass slide and immediately spray the slide with fixative (do not let the sample air dry). Send the slides to the pathology department.

OUTCOME: Interpretation to be provided by cytopathology.

Perform bimanual examination

PROCEDURE: First, explain the procedure to the patient. Then have the patient assume the dorsal lithotomy position. Apply a sterile, water-soluble jelly to the second and third digits on your gloved, dominant hand.

1. Gently insert the second and third digits into the vagina until the cervix is palpable. Palpate the cervix.
2. Place your nondominant hand on the patient's abdomen and directly palpate over the midline of the suprapubic area. Attempt to move the uterus between your two hands (Plate 46).
3. Palpate the adnexa: Move your digits within the vagina superiorly and anteriorly on the left side while using your contralateral hand to palpate directly and deeply in the left lower quadrant. Feel the structures between your hands. Repeat the procedure on the right.

While you are palpating, note any masses, the size and position of the uterus, and the location of any tenderness.

OUTCOME:

Uterus: If the surface of the uterus is smooth: ◆ **normal**
If uterus cannot be palpated:
- ◆ **hysterectomy**
- ◆ **retroverted uterus**
- ◆ **retroflexed uterus**

If uterus is palpable at a level beneath the pubic ramus: ◆ **normal**
If uterus is palpable at a level superior to the pubic ramus, with multiple smooth, globular, nontender, rubbery masses:
- ◆ **leiomyomas (fibroids)**

Pregnancy: If uterus is palpable at a level superior to the pubic ramus and is smooth: ◆ **gravid uterus (pregnancy; Fig 15-4)**

Adnexa: If there are nontender, almond-shaped nodules in the left and right adnexal areas: ◆ **normal ovaries**
If there is a unilateral or bilateral nontender, movable smooth mass, separate from the uterus and <5 cm in size: ◆ **ovarian cyst**
If unilateral, tender movable mass, separate from the uterus:
- ◆ **ovarian torsion**
- ◆ **pelvic inflammatory disease (PID)**
- ◆ **ectopic pregnancy**

If tender or nontender mass (in a postmenopausal woman):
- ◆ **ovarian neoplasia, benign or malignant**

Examine rectovaginal area

PROCEDURE: Perform the rectovaginal examination immediately after you complete the bimanual examination. The patient remains in the dorsal lithotomy position, with the second and third digits of

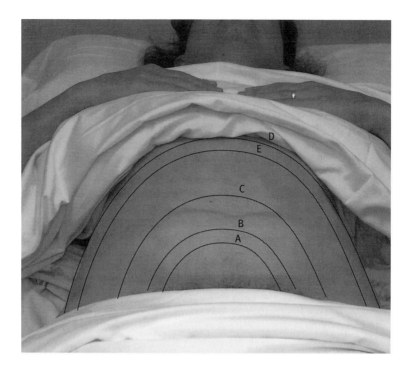

Figure 15-4 Gravid uterus in abdomen, various levels. A. 12 weeks. B. 16 weeks. C. 24 weeks. D. 38 weeks. E. 40 weeks.

your dominant hand still in the patient's vagina. Before you begin, explain the procedure to the patient.

1. Gently remove your third digit from the vagina, and gently insert it into the rectum.
2. Palpate the tissue between the rectum and vagina using the two extended digits. Note the presence and location of any masses and/or any discrete tenderness.
3. Place your nondominant hand on the patient's abdomen and directly palpate over the midline of the suprapubic area. Attempt to move the uterus between your two hands. Note any masses, the size and position of the uterus, and the location of any tenderness.
4. Remove your digits from vagina and rectum. If any stool is present on your gloved third digit, perform a stool guaiac test (Plate 26).

OUTCOME: If no masses or tenderness are present in the area: ◆ **normal**

If there is a nontender mass in the area deep to the posterior fornix, adjacent to the cervix:
- ◆ **endometriosis**
- ◆ **malignant ovarian neoplasia**

If tender fullness in the area: ◆ **PID**

If tender fullness on the lateral aspect of the rectum:
- ◆ **perirectal abscess**

| Advanced Examination |

APPROACH TO A PATIENT WITH VULVAR/EXTERNAL GENITALIA LESIONS

Inspect and palpate external genitalia: As in Basic Examination.

Perform acetic acid test

PROCEDURE: Have the patient assume the dorsal lithotomy position. Place a cotton gauze soaked with 3% to 5% acetic acid on the area of concern in the vulva/perineum. Leave the gauze on for 2 to 3 minutes, then remove it and visually inspect the area of skin.

OUTCOME: If the skin area becomes enhanced (accentuated whitening) and is larger, even with several smaller peripheral macular satellite lesions present: ◆ **condyloma acuminatum**

If there is no enhancement (no accentuated whitening): ◆ **normal**

APPROACH TO A PATIENT WITH URINARY INCONTINENCE

Perform Valsalva maneuver for prolapse

PROCEDURE: Have the patient assume the standard dorsal lithotomy position. Instruct the patient to perform a Valsalva maneuver for 10 to 15 seconds. Visually inspect the perineal structures for movements and/or bulges.

OUTCOME: If there are no bulges or movements of tissue in the perineal structures: ◆ **normal**

If there is caudad displacement of the lateral vaginal walls so that they protrude through the vaginal orifice: ◆ **vaginal prolapse**

If a bulge in the anterior vagina: ◆ **cystocele**

If a bulge in the posterior vagina: ◆ **rectocele**

If caudad displacement of the cervix to level of, but not past, the vaginal introitus: ◆ **first-degree uterine prolapse**

If caudad displacement of the cervix so that it protrudes past the vaginal introitus: ◆ **second-degree uterine prolapse**

If caudad displacement of the cervix and uterus with eversion of the vagina: ◆ **third-degree uterine prolapse (Plate 47)**

If eversion of rectal tissue so that mucosa is demonstrable:
◆ **rectal prolapse (Plate 48)**

Perform speculum examination during Valsalva maneuver

PROCEDURE: Have the patient assume the standard dorsal lithotomy position. Perform the speculum examination, with the following modification: remove the upper blade of the instrument. Gently insert the modified speculum, and gently retract it on each side of the vagina: lateral left, superior, lateral right, then posterior. Visually inspect the contralateral wall of the vagina before and during the Valsalva maneuver. Note any movement or bulging.

OUTCOME: If there is no bulging: ◆ **normal**

If bulging in the superior and anterior wall of the vagina:
◆ **cystocele**

If bulging in the posterior wall in the inferior two-thirds of the vagina: ◆ **rectocele**

Check for urine leakage during Valsalva maneuver

PROCEDURE: The patient must have a full urinary bladder for this test. Have the patient assume the standard dorsal lithotomy position. Instruct the patient to perform a Valsalva maneuver. Visually inspect the urethra and watch for any leakage of urine.

OUTCOME: If there is no leakage: ◆ **normal**

If leakage immediately after Valsalva, but the patient can control the urinary stream: ◆ **stress incontinence**

If leakage 2 to 3 seconds after termination of Valsalva that cannot be controlled for several seconds: ◆ **detrusor dysfunction**

Perform anal wink test: See Chapter 7, under Basic Examination.

APPROACH TO A PATIENT WITH A VAGINAL COMPLAINT

Examine vagina and vaginal mucosa using speculum: See under Basic Examination.

Wet mount a sample discharge

PROCEDURE: Obtain a sample by placing a sterile cotton-tipped swab in the discharge. Place the swab in a test tube containing 3 mL normal saline, and swirl the contents. Pipette out 1 mL of the solution, and place it on a glass microscopic slide. Visually inspect the slide under scanning or low magnification.

OUTCOME: If there are motile organisms, each with antennae:
◆ *Trichomonas* **infection**

If rhomboid-shaped vaginal epithelial cells covered on periphery with clumps (clue cells): ◆ **bacterial vaginosis**

Note odor of wet mount with potassium hydroxide

PROCEDURE: Add 2 to 3 drops of 10% potassium hydroxide (KOH) to the wet mount solution on the glass slide. Note the odor of the solution on the slide.

OUTCOME: If a fishy odor (positive amine test) ◆ **bacterial vaginosis**

If no particular odor: ◆ **another diagnosis**

Examine wet mount with potassium hydroxide under microscope

PROCEDURE: Add 2 to 3 drops of 10% KOH to the wet mount solution on the glass slide. Visually observe the slide using low, then high power.

OUTCOME: If there are hyphae or budding yeast forms: ◆ *Candida* **infection**
If no yeast forms: ◆ **another diagnosis**

Test pH of vaginal secretions

PROCEDURE: Perform a pH dipstick test on the wet mount solution.

OUTCOME: If the pH is 3.8 to 4.2: ◆ **normal**
If 4.0 to 5.0: ◆ *Candida* **vulvovaginitis**
If 4.5 to 6.0: ◆ **bacterial vaginosis**
If >6.0:
  ◆ **atrophic vaginitis**
  ◆ *Trichomonas* **infection**

Keys to Recording Findings

BREAST

"Symmetric, no nipple inversion or discharge, no palpable nodules, masses or tenderness; no palpable axillary, supraclavicular or infraclavicular lymph nodes"

A. Note sites or any nodule (< 4 cm), masses (> 4 cm), or swelling in the breasts

B. Note any skin or nipple changes—peau d'orange, nipple asymmetry, nipple inversion, nipple discharge: bloody, milk-like, clear, purulent.

C. Note any palpable lymph nodes—axillary, supraclavicular or infraclavicular.

A. Draw location and size of nodule or mass.

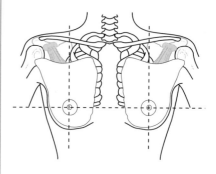

B. Use descriptors for the nodule or mass:

—Hard

—Soft

—Fixed

—Mobile

—Tender

—Non-tender

—Nipple-discharge

—Skin changes

C. Note any palpable axillary or supraclavicular nodes.

GYNECOLOGY/FEMALE GU

"Unremarkable labia majora, labia minora, vagina, fourchette, clitoris; introitus and vagina unremarkable; cervix parous or nonporous os, unremarkable; bimanual examination: no adnexal masses or nodules, uterus nonenlarged, nontender, no masses; rectovaginal without nodules; stool sample obtained brown guaiac negative."

A. Note sites of any papules, vesicles or other skin lesions (see skin descriptors for specifics)

B. Note any vaginal discharge—color—white, clear, purulent; odor—fishy, foul, non; consistency—frothy, serous, thick

B. Note site of any papules, vesicles, etcetera of the vagina

C. Note cervix for any papules, vesicles

D. and E. Bimanual examination: note uterus size and site of any nodules, masses or tenderness; note any adnexal masses or tenderness

F. Rectovaginal examination: note sites of any tenderness or nodules

G. Stool sample—describe color—brown, black, red and guaiac status

A. External Genitalia

Draw on findings

	Yes	No	Comments
Lesions	☐	☐	_____
Inflammation	☐	☐	_____
B. Vagina Lesions	☐	☐	_____
Discharge	☐	☐	_____
C. Cervix Lesions	☐	☐	_____
Inflammation	☐	☐	_____
Tenderness	☐	☐	_____

Draw on findings

		Yes	No	Comments
D. Uterus				
Position	Anteflexed	☐	☐	_____
	Anteverted	☐	☐	_____
	Retroflexed	☐	☐	_____
	Retroverted	☐	☐	_____
Masses		☐	☐	
If yes:	Location ____ Size ____			
	Tenderness _____			

		Yes	No
E. Adnexa	Masses	☐	☐
If yes:	Location ____ Size ____		
	Tenderness _____		

	Comments
F. Rectovaginal	_____
G. Stool	_____

Diagnoses

Atrophic vaginitis

Atrophy of the vaginal epithelium due to postmenopausal lack of estrogens. Symptoms and signs include watery discharge and macerated, irritated, erythematous mucosa. Dyspareunia and pruritus are not uncommon. The patient will have no odor; pH of the discharge is usually greater than 6.0. Evaluation with wet mount will reveal a decreased number of lactobacilli. Treatment includes estrogen cream to the vulvovaginal area and/or systemic hormone replacement.

Bacterial vaginosis

Overgrowth with *Gardnerella* bacteria. Symptoms and signs include a thin, homogeneous, whitish discharge and pink mucosa. The amine test is positive, and the pH is from 4.5 to 6.0. Evaluation with wet mount will reveal clue cells. Treatment is with antibiotics.

Bartholin's adenocarcinoma: See Bartholin's cyst/abscess.

Bartholin's cyst/abscess

Obstruction of the duct of Bartholin's gland due to primary infection with *Chlamydia trachomatis*, *N. gonorrhoeae*, or *Escherichia coli*, or secondary to a foreign body such as a grain of sand. Symptoms and signs include dyspareunia in the posterior vagina and fluctuant nodule in the posterior lateral labia minora. Erythema, warmth, and tenderness bespeak an abscess formation. Bilateral abscesses indicate *N. gonorrhoeae* as the agent. Evaluation in premenopausal women is with gonococcal and chlamydial cultures; in postmenopausal women an excisional biopsy is necessary to rule out **Bartholin's adenocarcinoma**. Treatment includes sitz baths and, if an abscess is suspected, systemic antibiotics. Refer the patient to a gynecologist.

Breast abscess

Abscess resulting from untreated bacterial infection **(mastitis)**. Puerperal abscess: *Staphylococcus aureus* infection associated with breast feeding. Symptoms and signs of puerperal abscess are a fluctuant mass in a wedge-shaped area of erythema (Plate 40) and warmth, starting at and involving the nipple. Nonpuerperal abscess: *S. aureus* and anaerobic infection. Symptoms and signs of nonpuerperal abscess are multiple fluctuant nodules in the sub-areolar tissue, with concurrent fever, purulent nipple discharge, or draining sinus tract. Evaluation and treatment include discontinuing breast feeding, systemic antibiotics, and referral to a general surgeon for incision and drainage.

Breast carcinoma

Malignant neoplasia of the ducts of the breast (intraductal to invasive carcinoma). Risk factors include HBCR gene in Ashkenazi Jews, long-term use of unopposed estrogens, early menarche, late menopause, history of a carcinoma in the contralateral breast, and first-degree relative with breast carcinoma. Symptoms and signs include a painless, unilateral, nontender, solitary lump of firm to rock-hard consistency in one breast. In advanced cases, there may be a mass, peau d'orange, nipple retraction, palpable axillary or supraclavicular lymph nodes, or even overlying marked edema, erythema, warmth, and ulceration—**inflammatory carcinoma**. A mammogram reveals a nodule or mass with clustered microcalcifications. Referral to a surgeon for excisional biopsy is mandated.

Candida vulvovaginitis

Candida infection. Risk factors include antibiotic therapy, systemic steroids, and diabetes mellitus. Symptoms and signs include a thick, white, chunky discharge that adheres to the mucosa, is moderately pruritic, and has little to no odor. Discharge pH is 4.0 to 5.0. Evaluation with a KOH preparation will reveal pseudohyphae. Treatment is with topical antifungals.

Cervical carcinoma

Epithelial-based neoplasia of the cervix, most commonly developing at the squamocolumnar junction. Risk factors include multiple sexual partners, early age of first intercourse, and cell-mediated immunosuppression [e.g., human immunodeficiency virus (HIV) and infection with human papillomavirus (HPV), especially types 16 and 18]. Patients are asymptomatic, with minimal findings until relatively late in the course. Advanced invasive lesions may have papules, nodules, and erosions on the os; the lesions are firm to hard and bleed easily, and the cervix may be fixed to the underlying fascia. Evaluation includes a Pap smear, using a cytobrush (Plate 45) and spatula to obtain a specimen. Treatment is immediate referral to a gynecologist for colposcopy and biopsy in all cases of suspicious or malignant smears.

Cervical polyp

Relatively common, invariably benign variant composed of endocervical columnar epithelium. The primary sign is a 2- to 3-mm pedunculated, red, soft, friable polyp in the cervical os. Treatment is simple removal, using a forceps to twist the polyp off; the specimen should be sent for histopathologic analysis.

Cystocele

Abnormal descent of the urinary bladder into the vaginal canal due to thinning and weakness of the pelvic fascial support. The risk factors include multiple vaginal deliveries, Valsalva maneuvers, and aging. Symptoms and signs include urinary stress incontinence and a soft, bulging mass in the wall of the anterior vagina; the mass may descend beyond the introitus. Concurrent conditions may be **urethrocele**, the abnormal descent of the urethra into the vagina, and **vaginal prolapse**, abnormal movement of the lateral vaginal walls inward and downward. Treatment includes Kegel's exercises, and, if symptomatic, referral to a gynecologist.

Detrusor dysfunction: See Incontinence.

Diethylstilbestrol exposure: See Ectropion/eversion and Vaginal adenosis/adenocarcinoma.

Ectopic pregnancy
Implantation of conceptus in the wall of the fallopian tube. Risk factors for ectopic pregnancy include antecedent PID. Symptoms include secondary amenorrhea, acute onset of lower quadrant abdominal pain (see Fig 6-2C,D, p. 117), and tender adnexal mass on bimanual examination (Plate 46) but no cervical discharge. Signs include a positive Chadwick sign, and, if ruptured, hypotension and Grey Turner's sign (see Fig 14-6). Evaluate the patient with a pregnancy test and ultrasound, seeking the cystic area in fallopian tube but no conceptus in the uterus. Treatment includes systemic antibiotics and immediate referral to a gynecologist.

Ectropion/eversion
Outward migration of the normal endocervical columnar epithelium to replace the squamous epithelium of the cervix itself. Risk factors include youth, oral contraceptives, estrogen replacement, and postpartum state. Patients are asymptomatic. Signs include a reddish area (columnar epithelium) around the os of the cervix that is clearly delineated from the pink (stratified squamous epithelium) on the remainder of the cervix. **DES exposure:** Exposure of the patient to DES in utero is associated with a marked ectropion; vaginal adenosis and a cervical hood (redundant fold of tissue at the superior surface of the cervix) are also common. Treatment is referral to a gynecologist for colposcopy.

Endometriosis
Endometrial glands and stroma in extrauterine sites, exclusively in women of reproductive age. Symptoms and signs include infertility, abdominal pain, dysmenorrhea, and dyspareunia. Signs are one or more reddish nodules in the mucosa of the posterior fornix and tender nodularity in the posterior cul-de-sac on rectovaginal examination. Evaluation and treatment include immediate referral to a gynecologist for laparoscopic imaging or magnetic resonance imaging (MRI) and surgical treatment.

Entropion/inversion
Inward migration of the endocervical columnar epithelium, which is replaced by the squamous epithelium of the cervix itself. Risk factors include increasing age and/or hormone deficiency. Patients are asymptomatic; on examination, there is no reddish area around the os of the cervix (i.e., the entire ectocervix is pink). No further evaluation is necessary.

Fibrocystic changes

Dilation of ducts and cystic changes, highly correlated with estrogen excess states (e.g., luteal phase defects). Symptoms and signs include multiple, bilateral lumps of various sizes that are larger and more tender before and during menstrual flow, but relatively quiescent at midcycle. Mammogram reveals multiple lesions of variable size, all noncalcified. Treatment is conservative: In the event of any dramatic changes or atypia on mammogram, refer the patient to a general surgeon for cyst aspiration and/or excisional biopsy.

Galactorrhea: See Nipple discharge.

Gartner's duct cyst

Failure of the embryonic mesonephric (wolffian) duct to degenerate appropriately, resulting in vestigial remnants that form mucus-containing cysts. Symptoms and signs include dyspareunia in large lesions and one or more nontender nodules in the anterolateral aspect of the upper half of the vaginal wall. Evaluation and treatment include referral to a gynecologist for resection of symptomatic lesions.

Incontinence

Acquired loss of urination control due to either stress incontinence (weakness of the pelvic floor caused by trauma or childbirth) or **detrusor dysfunction** [hyperactivity caused by urinary tract infection (UTI), spinal cord injury, or cerebrovascular accident (CVA)]. Symptoms and signs of stress incontinence include leakage of urine with Valsalva and cough or sneeze; concurrent rectal or cervical prolapse is common; symptoms and signs of detrusor dysfunction include spontaneous discharge of a large amount of urine and, in spinal cord defects, concurrent spastic paresis. Treatment for stress incontinence includes Kegel's exercises; treatment for detrusor dysfunction includes anticholinergic agents.

Inflammatory carcinoma (carcinoma erysipelatoid): See Breast carcinoma.

Intraductal papilloma

Intraductal papilloma can involve one duct or multiple ducts. Symptoms and signs include serous or bloody discharge, or both, from a specific duct in the nipple, with a concurrent, nontender, small subareolar nodule. Mammogram reveals a subareolar solitary or multiple nodule without calcifications. Treatment is by referral to a general surgeon.

Kraurosis vulvae: See Lichen sclerosis.

Leiomyomas (fibroids)

Very common, benign tumors of the uterine myometrium found in women of reproductive age. Symptoms and signs include menorrhagia or menometrorrhagia; one or more smooth, globular, irregular, rubbery masses in the substance of the uterus; and concurrent iron deficiency. Evaluation with ultrasound reveals multiple smooth nodules and masses in the uterus. Treatment is by referral to a gynecologist if symptomatic, consider myomectomy or vaginal hysterectomy.

Lichen sclerosis

Atrophy of epithelium with a sclerotic dermis due to autoimmune and/or local androgen imbalance in the vulva. Symptoms include severe vaginal pruritus in postmenopausal women. The signs include shiny, thin, atrophic skin, with symmetric white macules and patches and a paucity of skin appendages. Advanced cases manifest as stenosis of the introitus **(kraurosis vulva)**. **Squamous cell hyperplasia** and hyperkeratosis are closely related conditions. Signs in squamous cell hyperplasia include well-demarcated plaques on any site of the vulva. Evaluation includes a biopsy to rule out vulvar carcinoma. Treatment of lichen sclerosis is topical androgens and of squamous cell hyperplasia is topical steroids. The patient should thus be referred to a gynecologist.

Lipoma

A benign collection of adipose tissue. Asymptomatic, nontender, subcutaneous, soft, fleshy, mobile nodule, often present over the ribs and in the axilla. Evaluation and treatment include clinical recognition and reassurance.

Mastitis: See Breast abscess.

Nabothian cysts

Retention cysts lined with endocervical columnar cells and containing mucus; considered a normal result of the cervix's natural repair system. Patients are asymptomatic. Signs include one or more whitish to cream-colored papules or nodules, 5 to 25 mm in diameter, on the cervix. No further evaluation is necessary.

Nipple discharge

Due to milk production **(galactorrhea)** or infection (purulent material) or an intraductal papilloma or another breast neoplasm. The amount, color, and specific site of the discharge should be assessed, and examination of the breast for concurrent lumps is mandated. Evaluation and treatment include cytology on any bloody discharge, mammograms, and referral to a breast surgeon if indicated. If the discharge is purulent, culture and treat the underlying infection with antibiotics.

Ovarian neoplasia

Benign or malignant neoplasm of the ovarian epithelium that spreads via the peritoneum. Early signs include an asymptomatic unilateral adnexal mass. Advanced signs include ascites and the paraneoplastic dermatomyositis.

Evaluation with ultrasound may reveal a solid mass in or contiguous to the ovary. Treatment is immediate referral to a gynecologist.

Pelvic inflammatory disease

Infection of the uterus/fallopian tubes with one or more bacterial organisms, *N. gonorrhoeae, C. trachomatis,* and/or anaerobes. Symptoms and signs include dyspareunia, purulent vaginal discharge; on bimanual examination (Plate 46), tender uterus, unilateral tender adnexal mass, and **purulent cervicitis**. Evaluation includes a pregnancy test (negative) and ultrasound, which reveals edema and cyst with fluid in the fallopian tube. Treatment includes systemic antibiotics and immediate referral to a gynecologist.

Purulent cervicitis: See Pelvic inflammatory disease.

Retroflexion

The angle between the body of the uterus and the cervix tilts posteriorly toward the rectovaginal pouch of Douglas. Retroflexion is present in approximately 20% of women, and concurrent retroversion is not uncommon. Speculum and bimanual examinations are challenging. Evaluation consists of clinical recognition.

Retroversion

Entire axis of the uterus lies posterior. Retroversion is present in approximately 20% of women, and concurrent retroflexion is not uncommon. Demonstration of the cervix during a speculum examination may be more challenging, as the cervix is pointed more anteriorly. Likewise, the bimanual examination is also more challenging. Even in the hands of an expert, experienced examiner, the uterus may be difficult to outline in detail. Evaluation consists of clinical recognition.

Skene's adenitis

Abscess due to obstruction of one or more of the small glands located adjacent and slightly posterior to the urethra orifice due to *N. gonorrhoeae* infection. Symptoms and signs include acute onset of dysuria, urinary tenesmus, and tender swelling or fluctuant nodules adjacent to the urethra. Evaluation includes gonococcal and chlamydial cultures. Treatment includes systemic antibiotics and referral to a gynecologist for resection.

Squamous cell hyperplasia: See Lichen sclerosis.

Trichomonas vulvovaginitis

Sexually transmitted infection of *Trichomonas* protozoa. Symptoms and signs include thin, gray, frothy, profuse discharge and erythematous mucosa. The discharge is moderately malodorous and has a pH >6.0. Wet mount evaluation reveals motile protozoa. Treat the patient and her partner with metronidazole (unless in first trimester of pregnancy).

Urethral prolapse: See Uterine/cervical prolapse.

Urethrocele: See Cystocele.

Uterine/cervical prolapse

Abnormal descent of the cervix and even the corpus of the uterus into the vaginal canal because of thinning and weakness of the pelvic fascial support. Risk factors include multiple vaginal deliveries, Valsalva maneuvers, and aging. Symptoms include a feeling of fullness in the perineal area. Signs include cervix in the tunnel of vagina or even beyond introitus; if cervix is beyond introitus, ulceration of the cervix is common. Concurrent cystocele, or rectocele, or **urethral prolapse** (abnormal descent of urethra through its meatus) may manifest. Evaluation and treatment include referral to a gynecologist for pessary or vaginal hysterectomy.

Vaginal adenosis/adenocarcinoma

Abnormal development mucus-secreting glandular tissue in the normal stratified squamous vaginal epithelium. These areas of columnar epithelium are thought to be remnants of the embryonic müllerian epithelium. Women who were exposed to DES in utero have an increased risk of the development of vaginal adenosis, as well as dysplasia of the cervix and the vagina and of clear cell adenocarcinoma. Symptoms and signs include multiple, nontender, reddish, polypoid mucosal nodules in the vagina, with concurrent marked cervical ectropion and a cervical hood. Evaluation and treatment are by referral to a gynecologist.

Vaginal prolapse: See Cystocele.

Vulvar intraepithelial neoplasia: See Vulvar squamous cell carcinoma.

Vulvar squamous cell carcinoma

Malignant neoplasm of idiopathic origins. Risk factors include the precancerous associated lesion **VIN** and HPV infection. Early symptoms and signs include highly pruritic, white, well-circumscribed, hyperkeratotic papules and plaques. Advanced cases manifest nodules with edema and ulceration. Evaluation includes one or more biopsies, and treatment is immediate referral to a gynecologist.

CHAPTER 16
Male Genitalia

Palpate scrotum and groin

PROCEDURE: Use gloved hands to lift the scrotal sac gently. Palpate the structures within the sac by using the thumb and second digit. Note the size of the testes, the presence of tenderness in the testes, the location of the epididymis, and the location of any nodules or masses. Also palpate for masses deep to the inguinal ligament.

OUTCOME: If the left testis is lower than the right: ◆ **normal**

If a testis is 40 to 45 mm long (longitudinal axis) and 20 to 25 mL in volume: ◆ **normal**

If testis is smooth, firm, and rubbery in consistency: ◆ **normal**

If there is a convoluted cord-like structure on posterior side of each testis: ◆ **normal epididymitis**

If one testis is absent:
    ◆ **cryptorchidism**
    ◆ **surgical removal**

If both testes are small: ◆ **hypogonadism**

If there is a nontender nodule on the testis:
    ◆ **testicular carcinoma**

If the testes are large and tender: ◆ **orchitis**

If there is diffuse tenderness in the epididymis: ◆ **epididymitis**

If there is a nontender small nodule posterior to the head of the epididymis: ◆ **spermatocele**

If tender nodule in the head of the epididymis:
    ◆ **epididymal abscess (early epididymitis)**

If tender unilateral mass in the scrotal sac:
    ◆ **testicular torsion**
    ◆ **epididymal abscess**

If formless, nontender, unilateral fleshy mass, in the vas deferens, superior to the testis, feels like a bag of worms: ◆ **varicocele**

If nontender unilateral mass in the scrotal sac, anterior to the testis (opposite side from the epididymus):
    ◆ **inguinal hernia**
    ◆ **hydrocele (Fig 16-1)**

If there is tender, erythematous, edematous skin, with crepitus in the scrotum: ◆ **Fournier's gangrene**

If there is a mass beneath the inguinal ligament, into the proximal medial anterior thigh (see Fig 6-5, p. 119): ◆ **femoral hernia**

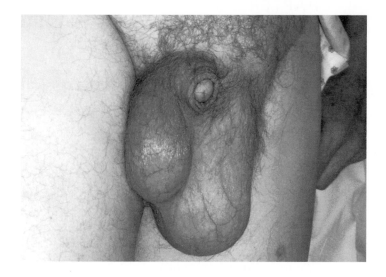

Figure 16-1 Left hydrocele. Transilluminable, nontender, fluctuant mass adjacent to left testis.

Advanced Examination

APPROACH TO A PATIENT WITH SCROTAL MASS OR TENDERNESS

Palpate scrotum and groin: See under Basic Examination.

Transilluminate mass in scrotum

PROCEDURE: With the patient supine, using gloved hands, localize the scrotal mass. Place a light source adjacent to the mass and shine the light source into the mass. Visually observe the transmission of light into the mass.

OUTCOME: If the mass is transilluminable (diffusely pink): ◆ **hydrocele**
If the nodule is transilluminable: ◆ **spermatocele**
If nontransilluminable: ◆ **another diagnosis**

Stroke medial thigh skin (cremasteric reflex)

PROCEDURE: Have the patient lie supine. Gently stroke the skin of the medial thigh with the handle of the plexor. Observe the activity of the ipsilateral testis within the scrotum. Repeat on the contralateral side.

OUTCOME: If there is involuntary cephalic migration of the testis (normal cremasteric reflex): ◆ **epididymitis/abscess**
If no cephalic migration of the testis on the painful side:
◆ **testicular torsion**

APPROACH TO A PATIENT WITH A PENILE COMPLAINT

Examine foreskin and glans

PROCEDURE: Visually inspect the foreskin and glans penis. Use gloved hands to palpate the foreskin, glans, and prepuce (foreskin opening) gently. Attempt to gently retract the foreskin to the base of the glans.

OUTCOME: If there is a tight prepuce in which the foreskin cannot be retracted (Fig 16-2): ◆ **phimosis**
If tight prepuce through which a tip of the glans penis is caught and protruding; there is an edematous ring of foreskin around the prepuce (Fig 16-3): ◆ **paraphimosis**
If there are redness, swelling, and irritation of the glans, with or without discharge (see Fig 14-7, p. 296): ◆ **balanitis**
If diffuse swelling and erythema of the glans penis and foreskin, may have concurrent phimosis: ◆ **balanoposthitis**

Figure 16-2 Balanoposthitis, phimosis. Significant erythema and swelling noted; a Foley catheter was placed to relieve the obstruction.

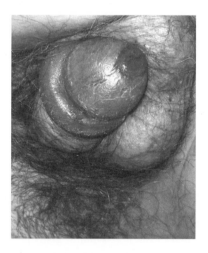

Figure 16-3 Paraphimosis. Severe edema of the glans as the result of retraction of a phimotic foreskin so that the glans is ischemic.

Inspect skin of penis and scrotum

PROCEDURE: Visually inspect the penis and scrotum. Use a gloved hand to palpate the skin in and adjacent to the scrotum and penis.

OUTCOME: If there is yellow purulent urethral discharge from the urethral meatus: ◆ **purulent urethritis/meatitis**

If a painless, nonerythematous, ulcerating plaque on the penis:
◆ **chancre (primary lues) (Plate 49)**

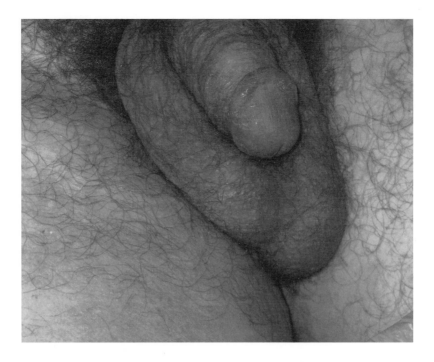

Figure 16-4 Herpes simplex, penis. Clusters of vesicles and erosions on the shaft, base, and glans of the penis.

If one or more clusters of painful vesicles are present on the skin:
♦ **herpes genitalis (Fig 16-4; see Chapter 14, p. 326)**
If there are several flesh-colored umbilicated papules, each with a creamy core:
♦ **molluscum contagiosum (see Chapter 14, p. 328, and Fig 14-12)**
If multiple soft, warty, cauliflower-like papules:
♦ **condylomata acuminata**
If swelling, pain, crepitus, and dark discoloration of the skin of the penis/scrotum: ♦ **Fournier's gangrene**
If there is a diffuse, erythematous, wet, macerated rash in inguinal areas: ♦ **tinea cruris (see Fig 14-7, p. 296 and p. 334)**
If painless ulcer with irregular borders, often with adjacent condyloma acuminatum: ♦ **carcinoma of the penis**

Keys to Recording Findings

MALE GU

"Unremarkable circumcised or uncircumcised penis; no penile discharge; testis present, nontender, no nodules or masses; prostate nonenlarged, nontender, without nodules or masses; stool sample obtained brown guaiac negative."

A. Note sites of any papules, vesicles or other skin lesions (see skin descriptors for specifics) on penis and/or scrotum

A. Note any penile discharge—color—white, clear, purulent

A. If uncircumcised, note the prepuce, note any discharge; note if phimosis—unable to retract or paraphimosis—incarcerated tip of glans

B. Note size and any tenderness, swelling, nodules or masses in the testes; transilluminate

C. Note prostate size, site of any tenderness, swelling, nodules or masses

D. Stool sample—describe color—brown, black, red and guaiac status

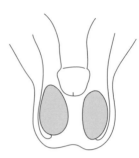

Penis		Yes	No	Comments
	Circumcized	❏	❏	_____
	Uncircumcized	❏	❏	_____
	Discharge	❏	❏	_____
	Lesions	❏	❏	_____
	Phimosis	❏	❏	_____
	Paraphimosis	❏	❏	_____

Testes	Left	Right	Comments
Location	❏	❏	_____
Nodules	❏	❏	_____
Transilluminable	❏	❏	_____

Prostate		Yes	No	Comments
	Tender	❏	❏	_____
	Enlarged	❏	❏	_____
	Nodules	❏	❏	_____

Stool	Yes	No	Comments
	❏	❏	_____
Guaiac ⊕	❏	❏	_____

Diagnoses

Acute prostatitis
Infection with gram-negative bacilli or *Chlamydia trachomatis*. Symptoms include dysuria, increased urinary frequency and hesitancy, and rectal pain. Signs include tender, diffusely enlarged, boggy prostate, with concurrent epididymal tenderness. Treatment includes systemic antibiotics (e.g., ciprofloxacin or doxycycline) and, if recurrent, referral to a urologist.

Balanitis
Diffuse inflammation of the glans penis due to *Candida* or an autoimmune process. Risk factors include uncontrolled diabetes mellitus and chronic steroid use. Symptoms and signs include redness and swelling of the glans penis (see Fig 14-7, p. 296). Evaluate the condition with the potassium hydroxide (KOH) test. Treatment is with topical antifungals and elective referral to a urologist.

Balanoposthitis
Chronic edema and inflammation of the glans and the foreskin, often due to moderate phimosis. Symptoms and signs include diffuse swelling and erythema of the glans penis (see Fig 14-7, p. 296) and the foreskin with a moderate phimosis. Purulent discharge from the prepuce may be present. Evaluation and treatment include obtaining a fasting plasma glucose, treatment with topical antifungal agents, and referral to a urologist for circumcision.

Benign prostatic hypertrophy
Slow idiopathic increase in size of gland, a very prevalent condition with increasing age. Symptoms include nocturia, urinary hesitancy, and increased frequency. On rectal examination, the prostate gland is diffusely enlarged, nontender, about the consistency of the biceps or thenar muscle in contraction, and without nodules. A distended bladder may be concurrent. Complications can include recurrent urinary tract infections and obstructive nephropathy. Evaluation includes urinalysis, and treatment is with prazosin or terazosin and referral to a urologist.

Carcinoma of the penis
Squamous cell carcinoma. Risk factors include human papillomavirus infection. Symptoms and signs include a painless, nonhealing ulcer; in advanced cases the ulcer is quite deep with enlargement of inguinal lymph nodes; concurrent condyloma acuminatum is usually present. Evaluation and treatment are by referral to a urologist for excisional biopsy.

Chancre (primary lues)

Sexually transmitted infection with the spirochete *Treponema pallidum*. Symptoms and signs include a single painless ulcer with raised edges and a necrotic center (Plate 49) located on the glans or shaft of the penis and appearing 10 to 14 days after exposure. Multiple ulcers are found in 20% to 30% of patients. Evaluation includes the VDRL (Venereal Disease Research Laboratory) and MHA-TP (microhemagglutinin *Treponema pallidum*) tests (nonreactive). The dark-field analysis will reveal spirochetes. Treatment is with benzathine penicillin, 2.4 million units intramuscularly (IM). The patient's sexual partners must also be treated.

Cryptorchidism: See Testicular carcinoma.

Epididymitis/orchitis

Infection with gram-negative bacilli or *C. trachomatis*. Symptoms and signs include a tender swollen epididymis. In severe cases or with abscesses, there is a tender nontransilluminable nodule or mass contiguous to the testis. Overlying scrotal edema, erythema, warmth, and, concurrently, a swollen boggy prostate may be present. Evaluation includes ultrasound with flow Doppler of any discernible scrotal mass present; treatment is with systemic antibiotics (e.g., ciprofloxacin or doxycycline) and referral to a urologist.

Femoral hernias

Anatomic defect in the fascia deep to the inguinal ligament, more common in females than males. The hernial sac passes out of the abdominal cavity and into the anterior thigh, that is, the femoral triangle (see Fig 11-3H, p. 239) via abnormal passage through the femoral canal, immediately posterior to the inguinal ligament. Because the defect size is usually small, it can easily incarcerate and strangulate. Signs include a soft mass in the anterior medial thigh deep to the inguinal ligament (see Fig 6-5, p. 119). The three discrete classes of hernias are reducible, incarcerated, and/or strangulated. Incarcerated hernias are nontender and nonreducible. Strangulated hernias are tender, nonreducible, and, if there is bowel obstruction, associated with concurrent abdominal distention with tympany. Evaluation and treatment include referral to a general surgeon for herniorrhaphy. For reducible hernias, surgery is elective; for incarcerated hernias, surgery is urgent; for strangulated hernias, surgery must be immediate.

Fournier's gangrene

Necrotizing cellulitis and fasciitis of scrotum and penis due to mixed anaerobes and gram-negative rods. Risk factors include uncontrolled diabetes mellitus and neutropenia. Symptoms include scrotal pain and swelling, with signs of scrotal/penile edema with crepitus, necrosis, and eschar formation. Evaluation and treatment include immediate referral to a urologist and broad-spectrum parenteral antibiotics.

Hydrocele

Congenital fluid-filled remnants of the processes tunica vaginalis. Symptoms and signs include a chronic, smooth, firm, nontender, and transilluminable mass in the scrotum (see Fig 16-1), with a concurrent inguinal hernia. Evaluation and treatment include referral to a general surgeon for elective repair.

Hypogonadism

Decrease in testicular function from congenital (Kleinfelter's) or acquired (cirrhosis or paramyxovirus infection) causes. Symptoms include breast enlargement, erectile dysfunction, and loss of libido. Signs include facial alopecia, gynecomastia, and a decrease in the size and firmness of the testes. Concurrent end-stage liver disease may be present. Evaluation for the acquired form includes obtaining serum testosterone and luteinizing hormone (LH)/follicle-stimulating hormone (FSH) levels; low testosterone levels and high FSH/LH levels indicate primary hypogonadism. For the congenital form, perform a karyotype for Kleinfelter's. Treatment is referral to an endocrinologist for potential testosterone replacement therapy.

Inguinal hernia

Defect in the connective tissue supporting the inguinal area, more common in men. Indirect: congenital form, with sac through internal and external rings into the scrotum or labium majus. Direct: acquired form, with sac through Hesselbach's triangle in the abdominal wall. Symptoms are minimal unless there is incarceration or strangulation. Signs include a nontransilluminable soft mass in the scrotum adjacent to the spermatic cord that may be easily reduced. Incarcerated hernia is nontender and nonreducible. Strangulated hernia is tender and nonreducible; a concurrent hydrocele or distention with tympany of bowel obstruction may be present. Evaluation and treatment include referral to a general surgeon for herniorrhaphy. For reducible hernias, referral is elective; for incarcerated hernia, referral is urgent; for strangulated hernias, referral is emergent.

Paraphimosis

Retraction of the foreskin behind the glans with resultant edema or ischemia of the glans. Risk factors include phimosis, balanoposthitis, and forced retraction of the foreskin. Symptoms and signs include pain at the tip of the penis; swollen, tender, edematous glans; and foreskin retracted and tightly apposed about the circumference of the penis (see Fig 16-3). Severe cases manifest with cyanosis or necrosis of the glans. Treatment includes referral to a urologist for immediate circumcision.

Phimosis

Constricted prepuce (foreskin opening) due to old trauma or balanitis. Symptoms and signs include dysuria, urinary dribbling, and inability to retract the foreskin (see Fig 16-2), with concurrent balanitis. Treatment includes referral to a urologist for circumcision.

Prostatic nodules/carcinoma

Prevalent disorder, usually an adenocarcinoma. The patient will be asymptomatic. Signs include a nontender, indurated nodule. Evaluation and treatment include a prostate-specific antigen (PSA) test and referral to a urologist for transrectal biopsy.

Purulent urethritis/meatitis

Sexually transmitted infection from the organisms *Neisseria gonorrhoeae* or *C. trachomatis*, or both. Symptoms include dysuria, hesitancy and urgency, and pyuria, a yellow crusty discharge on underpants/bed linen; the patient is usually sexually active. Signs include purulent discharge and swelling at the meatus. Evaluation includes culture of discharge for *N. gonorrhoeae* and *Chlamydia* species (spp). Treatment is with ceftriaxone, 250 mg IM, 10 days of oral doxycycline, and treatment of sexual partners.

Spermatocele

Benign inclusion cyst adjacent to the testis in the spermatic cord. The patient is asymptomatic. Signs include a nontender, transilluminable nodule in the superior epididymis. Evaluation is clinical recognition; no treatment is necessary.

Testicular carcinoma

Malignant neoplastic growth of germ cells. Risk factors include **cryptorchidism**, the abnormal retention of one or both of the testes within the abdomen. Symptoms and signs include a firm, nontender, nontransilluminable nodule or mass adjacent to a testis; if ischemia occurs, the mass may become acutely enlarged and tender. Evaluation includes serum alpha fetoprotein (AFP) and beta human chorionic gonadotropin (B-HCG) tests and referral to a urologist for resection.

Testicular torsion

Testis abnormally twisting on its spermatic cord with embarrassment of venous drainage from an arterial supply to the testis. Risk factors include trauma and testicular carcinoma. Symptoms and signs include an acute, painful, tender, nontransilluminable mass in the scrotum. Ultrasound with Doppler flow reveals a decreased flow of blood. Treatment is immediate referral to a urologist.

Varicocele

Varicosity in the spermatic vein. The left side more commonly affected because the left spermatic vein does not drain directly into the inferior vena cava. Symptoms and signs include a chronic, nontender, nontransilluminable mass with the consistency of a "bag of worms" in the area about the vas deferens that decreases in size with scrotal elevation. Treatment includes elective referral to a urologist with left-side cases and required referral with right-side cases.

References

1. Leach RM, McBrien DJ. Brachioradial delay: a new clinical indicator of the severity of aortic stenosis. Lancet 1990;335:1199–1201.
2. Lembo NJ, Dell'Italia LJ, Crawford MH, O'Rourke RA. Bedside diagnosis of systolic murmurs. N Engl J Med 1988;318:1572–1578.
3. Gooch AS, Cha SD, Maranhao V. The use of the hepatic pressure maneuver to identify the murmur of tricuspid regurgitation. Clin Cardiol 1983;6:277–280.
4. Grover SA, Barkun AN, Sackett DL. The rational clinical examination. Does this patient have splenomegaly? JAMA 1993;270:2218–2221.
5. Simel DL, Halvorsen RA Jr, Feussner JR. Quantitating bedside diagnosis: clinical evaluation of ascites. J Gen Inter Med 1988;3:423–428.
6. Katz JN, Larson MG, Sabra A, et al. The carpal tunnel syndrome: diagnostic utility of the history and physical examination findings. Ann Intern Med 1990;112:321–327.

Index

Note: Page numbers followed by *f* refer to figures; page numbers followed by *t* refer to tables; page numbers in **boldface** refer to principal discussion of diagnosis.